D1629609

ALSO BY KEN AULETTA

The Highwaymen: Warriors of the Information Superhighway
Three Blind Mice: How the TV Networks Lost Their Way
Greed and Glory on Wall Street: The Fall of the House of Lehman
The Art of Corporate Success: The Schlumberger Story
The Underclass
Hard Feelings
The Streets Were Paved with Gold

WORLD WAR 3.0

KEN AULETTA
WORLD WAR 3.0
Microsoft and Its Enemies

P

PROFILE BOOKS

First published in Great Britain in 2001 by
Profile Books Ltd
58A Hatton Garden
London EC1N 8LX
www.profilebooks.co.uk

First published in the United States in 2001 by
Random House, Inc.
www.atrandom.com

1 3 5 7 9 10 8 6 4 2

Printed and bound in Great Britain by
Clays, Bungay, Suffolk

The moral right of the author has been asserted.

A CIP catalogue record for this book is available from the British Library.

ISBN 1 86197 390 X

For Kate and Amanda
From here to the moon and . . .

Contents

x | CONTENTS

Chronology

1990   Windows 3.0 becomes an instant success.

The Federal Trade Commission launches an investigation of Microsoft's business practices.

Microsoft's revenues climb above one billion dollars.

1993   Judge dismisses Apple's suit against Microsoft, ruling that it did not infringe Apple's copyright.

After the FTC deadlocks over whether to bring an antitrust action, the Justice Department's Antitrust Division initiates probe.

JULY 1994   Justice and Microsoft sign a consent decree that will go into effect in 1995. The government agrees to drop its antitrust action, and Microsoft agrees to cease certain practices. The vaguely worded decree, however, allows Microsoft to develop "integrated products."

OCTOBER 1994   Microsoft announces a $1.5 billion acquisition of the dominant personal finance–software company, Intuit.

DECEMBER 1994   Netscape Communications, officially incorporated under this name in November, ships the first commercial Internet browser. Sales and Internet usage soar, with Netscape soon achieving an 80 percent market share, zooming from one million to fifteen million customers in a year.

FEBRUARY 1995   Federal District Court Judge Stanley Sporkin, after reviewing the consent decree, rules that it is an "ineffective remedy" to constrain Microsoft. The Justice Department and Microsoft join in urging a higher court to overturn Sporkin.

JUNE 1995   The U.S. Court of Appeals spanks Sporkin and reinstates the consent decree. Showing its fury, the appeals court removes Sporkin as the judge administering the consent decree and replaces him with Thomas Penfield Jackson.

In the face of Justice Department opposition, Microsoft drops its proposed purchase of Intuit.

At a secret meeting with Netscape at its California headquarters, Microsoft allegedly threatens to "cut off its air supply" if Netscape does not agree to cede its browser business.

AUGUST 1995   Microsoft introduces its own free browser included with each copy of Windows.

AUGUST 1995   Judge Jackson concurs with the Court of Appeals, upholding the terms of the consent decree.

DECEMBER 7, 1995   An alarmed Gates announces that the Internet compels Microsoft to alter its business model, and henceforth Microsoft will become Internet-centric.

AUGUST 1996   Netscape's attorney forwards to Assistant Attorney General Joel Klein a 222-page white paper sketching Microsoft's alleged strong-arm tactics. Klein orders the head of his San Francisco office, Phillip Malone, to investigate.

OCTOBER 1997   The Justice Department files a motion in Federal District Court charging Microsoft with violating the 1994 consent decree and asking the court to order the company to cease tying its "separate" browser to Windows and forcing PC makers to choose its browser. Microsoft insists the two products are "integrated."

DECEMBER 1997   The Justice Department hires renowned litigator David Boies to prosecute. Judge Jackson issues preliminary injunction, ordering Microsoft to decouple the browser from Windows 95, and appoints a "special master" to advise him on technology and the law. Microsoft files an appeal.

MAY 12, 1998   Court of Appeals unanimously supports Microsoft's request that it not be stopped from shipping Windows 98 in June.

MAY 18, 1998   After settlement negotiations collapse, the Justice Department and twenty state attorneys general file a lawsuit charging Microsoft with antitrust violations.

JUNE 23, 1998   A three-judge Court of Appeals panel overturns Judge Jackson and rules that Microsoft did not violate the consent decree by including a browser in with Windows. The court, however, did not exonerate Microsoft of possible antitrust violations.

SEPTEMBER 1998   On the eve of the biggest antitrust trial since the 1911 Standard Oil case, almost half of all American homes have a PC, and Microsoft's Windows serves as the operating system for 90 percent of these. Meanwhile, Internet usage has grown exponentially, with thirty-three million users now online.

Judge Jackson rejects Microsoft summary-judgment motion to terminate lawsuit.

OCTOBER 19, 1998	Federal antitrust trial begins in Judge Jackson's court and is expected to take six weeks.
NOVEMBER 24, 1998	America Online announces the purchase of Netscape, and Microsoft says this proves their contention that competition is alive and well.
DECEMBER 7, 1998	South Carolina withdraws from lawsuit, leaving nineteen states engaged.
DECEMBER 31, 1998	Microsoft's profits of nearly $4.5 billion are twice those of the world's largest corporation, General Motors.
FEBRUARY 26, 1999	The twenty-fourth witness concludes his testimony, and Microsoft rests its defense. Trial recesses for three months.
JUNE 1, 1999	The trial resumes for three weeks to hear six rebuttal witnesses.
NOVEMBER 5, 1999	Judge Thomas Penfield Jackson issues his Findings of Fact, concluding that Microsoft was guilty of holding monopoly power. He rejects most of Microsoft's proclaimed "facts."
NOVEMBER 19, 1999	Judge Jackson appoints Richard Posner, Chief Judge of the Seventh Circuit Court of Appeals, to serve as mediator, hoping to induce both sides to settle.
JANUARY 2000	Handheld and wireless devices are projected to soon outnumber PCs.
APRIL 3, 2000	After four months of effort, Judge Posner terminates the mediation. Judge Jackson issues his Conclusions of Law, finding that Microsoft violated the nation's antitrust laws. Microsoft appeals.
MAY 24, 2000	Judge Jackson holds a one-day remedy hearing.
JUNE 7, 2000	Judge Jackson issues his final judgment, ordering that Microsoft be broken up into two companies and imposing conduct restrictions on the company's behavior for several years.
JUNE 13, 2000	Microsoft appeals. The Court of Appeals announces a speeded-up schedule to consider Microsoft's claim, including its request to delay the remedies until a final ruling is made. The appeals court also announces that it will hear the case en banc, with all ten judges (save three who wished to be recused) participating. The government requests that the Supreme Court immediately hear the case, supplanting the Court of Appeals.

JUNE 20, 2000   Judge Jackson pleases Microsoft by staying all remedies until the appeals are exhausted and pleases the government by petitioning the U.S. Supreme Court to immediately hear the case.

SEPTEMBER 26, 2000   The Supreme Court, by an 8 to 1 vote, announces that it will not immediately hear the case, deferring to the Court of Appeals to first adjudicate.

FEBRUARY 26–27, 2001   The Court of Appeals, having received briefs, schedules two days to hear arguments from Microsoft and government.

Assuming that both the Court of Appeals and the Supreme Court review Judge Jackson's decision, and assuming that the parties don't settle and that a new president and all nineteen state attorneys general don't scuttle the case, a final legal ruling is unlikely before 2002.

Prologue:
Gilded Victim

Bill Gates was angry when he arrived at the annual meeting of the World Economic Forum in Davos, Switzerland, in January 1998. His anger was palpable, and it surprised many who did not know him but knew well the multiple reasons he had not to be angry: the planet's richest man was the co-founder of Microsoft, a company that for twenty-three years had outflanked and outthought its competitors, a company whose Windows software now served as the essential code in about 90 percent of all personal computers, a company whose stock price made it the world's most highly valued. Besides, unlike stock-market meteors such as Amazon.com and Broadcast.com that produced paper billionaires but globs of red ink, Microsoft enjoyed an astonishing profit margin of forty cents on each revenue dollar in this year, 1998; its profits, nearly $4.5 billion, were about twice as large as those of the world's largest company, General Motors; and its pockets then bulged with an even more astonishing $15 billion or so of excess cash.

What's more, Bill Gates had come to look forward to this annual summit of about two thousand CEOs and government, academic, and media leaders, who came to this tiny Alpine village for three to five days, dipping into seminars on topics from genetic engineering to Islam, listening to and giving speeches, maybe skiing, and, of course, scheduling one-on-one business meetings, all under the protective eye of the machine gun–toting Swiss Army. Of the many conferences Bill Gates attended, this one afforded the most unusual perspective, for entrepreneurs and tyrants, most in shirtsleeves, came together from all corners of the earth, each bringing their own definitions of capitalism, freedom, liberty, and community. Presidents, prime ministers, foreign ministers, the CEOs of the Fortune 500 as well as those of the newer dot-coms, such as Amazon.com and America Online, they all made the pilgrimage, and no one—not President Clinton or the presidents of China or Russia or the CEO of GE or Warren Beatty—was a bigger rock star here than Bill Gates. For the past several years, the coveted Sunday luncheon speech before the international press was reserved for Bill Gates. Heads of state lined up to hear what he had to say about the new economy and in private exchanges sought to encourage him to open a Microsoft facility in their country.

Gates enjoyed the attention, and he enjoyed the efficiency of Davos even more. At Microsoft, he carefully budgeted his time, allocating a set number of annual face-time hours to each senior executive and five speeches per year to software developers. For a busy executive, Davos was like one-stop shopping: in just a few days, Gates could assemble and speak with hundreds of his biggest customers, prearrange appointments to discuss deals, stack up private sessions with CEOs or government chiefs, and gather in one room editors and correspondents from the world's most prestigious publications.

Yet whatever reasons Bill Gates might have had to be ebullient going into Davos were overwhelmed by his burgeoning sense that he was a victim. He believed Microsoft was the engine of the new economy. So why, he wondered, was the U.S. government treating him like Al Capone? Software wasn't oil, he insisted, and he was no John D. Rockefeller, yet the Justice Department said that he, too, had violated antitrust laws.

As Gates moved about the conference center and hotel lobbies, his public-relations handlers surrounded him as if he were a heavyweight champion making his way to the ring. But they were not protecting Gates from his adoring fans; they were protecting him from himself. At the Sunday lunch for about one hundred reporters and editors, I was seated next to Gates at a table for ten that included his wife, Melinda, several editors, and the chairman and CEO of Coca-Cola, M. Douglas Ivester. Bill Gates has never been partial to small talk, and this occasion was no exception. Before the salad arrived, he had already berated me for a panel I'd moderated a few nights earlier called "Monopolies and

Technology." He complained that I had allowed enemies of Microsoft to pummel his chief technology officer, Nathan Myhrvold. Gates was not mollified to hear that Myhrvold more than held his own in the exchange, or that Nobel Prize–winning economist Gary Becker had vigorously defended Microsoft.

Gates sat huddled over, his arms folded across his chest, his brown hair unparted, unwashed, and combed straight down like a boy's. He rocked back and forth in his chair, his eyes fixed on the floor. His manner was gruff, and he was either unwilling or unable to hide his rage. Melinda Gates, a personable former Microsoft executive, tried discreetly to capture his attention, but he would not look up. The eight other guests at the table stared at him in wonder. Suddenly, his voice rising to a shrill pitch, Gates proclaimed, "Neither Nathan nor anyone from Microsoft will ever appear again on such a panel!" The lunch continued in silence.

Bill Gates did have ample reason to feel besieged. The federal government had placed his company in its crosshairs as early as 1990, beginning with what at first seemed to be a routine Federal Trade Commission investigation, which ballooned into a Justice Department probe, abated when both sides signed a consent decree in 1994, and then ballooned again in 1997 into one of the largest civil antitrust investigations in U.S. history. It was, Gates once told me, as if the government was announcing, "OK, we'll show that we can take some blood out of these boys!" But Bill Gates believed the threat would pass. He thrived on all-out competition, and the federal government, he thought, would retreat just as other foes had before the Microsoft juggernaut.

Gates took the government threat less seriously than he did his corporate foes, among which he felt particularly besieged by Netscape Communications, which in 1994 released its Navigator browser, providing an easy on-ramp to the World Wide Web and gaining a Microsoft-like 80 percent market share seemingly overnight. Perhaps more disturbing to Gates the seer was that he hadn't sensed it coming. Off in their own little world outside Seattle, where employees communicated with one another by an internal e-mail system and took most meals in the cafeteria and had relatively little contact with customers or rivals, Microsoft's visionaries did not hear the Internet buzz in Silicon Valley or on college campuses. Gates reacted to Internet enthusiasts much as he had to software pirates two decades previously: he thought they were a bunch of woolly-headed flower children with not a clue as to how to make money. Even in early 1995, Gates still believed that private corporate networks or intranets, as well as proprietary online services such as MSN, or interactive television, would dwarf the overhyped World Wide Web. In his first book, *The Road Ahead,* published in the fall of 1995 and which claimed to offer Gates's vision of the future, he downplayed the Internet, citing it less frequently than he did the television and the telephone combined.

In the spring of 1995, Gates got religion and suddenly shifted the company's direction. In May, he sent the now famous memorandum to his senior staff called "The Internet Tidal Wave," acknowledging that his view of the Internet had changed, that in fact "the Internet is the most important single development to come along since the IBM PC was introduced in 1981." And on Pearl Harbor Day, December 7, 1995, realizing that Microsoft's dominion was threatened by the development of the Internet and the twenty million consumers who surfed it daily, Gates announced that from then on Microsoft would be Internet-centric, that its every product would be redesigned with the Internet in mind. They would produce a browser, and it would be given away free, and it would be included as part of their current operating system, Windows 95. No longer would MSN be a proprietary network; it would be an Internet portal open to all. That Gates issued his proclamation on the anniversary of the 1941 Japanese surprise attack on the United States was typical, for Microsoft thought of business competition as war, and ramped up quickly for all-out combat.

In a conversion like those felt in offices across America in the late '90s, Gates "got" the Internet and the way it might diminish the importance of the Windows operating system. As long as Windows controlled about 90 percent of all PCs, software developers needed to write their new applications so they worked on Windows. And as a result, rival operating systems were impeded. Software developers needed from Microsoft the Windows application programming interfaces, or APIs. These secret codes are like the hooks on an aircraft carrier that grab descending jets, and independent software developers needed these secret codes to land their applications on Windows. Together, these technical and economic barriers were sometimes referred to as "the applications barrier to entry." But if a simple browser could sit atop Windows or any other operating system, employing a universal language code such as

Java, and if developers could hook onto the APIs of the browser, then the vital software on a PC might no longer be Windows but the browser. This browser software would be an alternative platform that software developers would have powerful incentives to write applications for: why write a program that ran only on Windows when you could write one that could run on *all* operating systems? This was the so-called middleware threat to which Bill Gates had awakened.

In its war with Netscape, Microsoft had two weapons Netscape could not match: the ubiquitous Windows and deep pockets. Microsoft would integrate its own browser with Windows, and give it away for free. Microsoft was aroused. The company held rallies on the grass of its corporate campus at which Executive Vice President of Sales and Service Steve Ballmer pumped up employees by leading them in a war whoop and screaming for the blood of competitors, screaming for victory. To Microsoft, such enthusiasm expressed its passion to excel. To others, it reeked of nineteenth-century robber barons. Eventually, the Justice Department agreed, holding that by tying its browser to Windows, Microsoft had violated a clause of the 1994 consent decree, hammered out in an earlier antitrust collision with the Justice Department, that forbade Microsoft to predicate the sale of a "covered product" (i.e., Windows 95) on the sale of another product.

Bill Gates believed the government was trying to dictate how he should run his company—to tell him how he could and could not market Microsoft, how he must construct contracts with computer manufacturers and Internet companies, even how he could design software. It enraged Gates to hear the Justice Department assert that Microsoft's inclusion of an Internet browser, Internet Explorer, with its dominant Windows operating system was both a violation of the consent decree and an illegal use of monopoly power. *Weren't the antitrust laws designed to protect consumers? Where was the consumer harm? Didn't the integration of the browser into the OS make computing simpler? Didn't consumers benefit because the extra features were free? How dare the government demand—as it did—that Microsoft either untie this package or include a rival browser, such as Netscape, with its own operating system? Would the government tell Coca-Cola to include a can of Pepsi in every six-pack? Would it tell Ford not to package a radio with each car?*

Within the company, a few brave souls gently urged Gates to calm down, to avoid a trial by acceding to at least some of the government's demands. But Gates and most of his senior staff were implacable. They invoked a term, "hard core," that described both their stance and their corporate culture. To be hard-core was to be a believer, a tough-minded warrior who preferred combat to compromise. They might look like "nerds," might use words such as *cool* and *neat*, might wear T-shirts and baggy shorts to work and play soccer on the grass of their 295-acre corporate campus in Redmond, Washington, but Microsoft executives were "tough." Rob Glaser, who joined Microsoft in 1983 and had been close to Gates before leaving a decade later to start RealNetworks, recalls warning Gates at an executive retreat that in light of the dominance of Windows 3.0, Microsoft had to restrain its competitive zeal. Microsoft was no longer David battling Goliaths such as IBM, he told Gates; Microsoft was now a Goliath. Gates demurred.

"Shouldn't we worry about the court of public opinion?" Glaser asked Gates.

"You're saying that Microsoft shouldn't compete hard!" Gates shot back, ending the conversation.

"I had a great job and a very candid relationship with Bill," said Glaser of Gates. "We could talk about anything. This was the sole exception."

Although Bill Gates barely noticed, Microsoft's hard-core approach was isolating it from many of the corporate leaders gathered in Davos. Six months earlier, for example, at the annual Sun Valley retreat put on by Allen & Company for communications-company CEOs, a group of tough-minded peers—News Corporation's Rupert Murdoch, NBC's Robert Wright, Sony's Nobuyuki Idei, TCI's John Malone, among others—were shocked during a Gates presentation, according to three participants, when he boasted, "I'm going to destroy three companies: Sun Microsystems, Oracle, and Netscape." Everyone in this audience wanted to beat the competition—but *destroy* them? Gates seemed so, well, *immature*, even if he didn't literally mean what he said. To these executives, business was business; it wasn't personal. They competed with one another in some arenas and cooperated in others. Murdoch's Fox Studios competed against Idei's Sony Pictures Entertainment, yet their companies were aligned in a satellite-TV effort in Japan; Malone's cable systems carried Disney cable networks, yet his cable networks also competed against Disney; Microsoft and America Online were bitter rivals, yet Windows featured easy access to AOL, and AOL chose Internet Explorer as its preferred browser. Sometimes these companies even competed against themselves, hedging their bets by investing in rival technologies, as Microsoft did by investing in cable and wireless modems that rivaled each other.

In Silicon Valley, it was not uncommon to hear new-media companies describe Microsoft as "the Great Satan." Increasingly, however, old-media companies were worried as well. Apple co-founder Steve Jobs spoke at a Disney executive retreat in 1997 at the invitation of Disney Chairman and CEO Michael Eisner, who hoped that Jobs would provoke them. Instead, Jobs scared them, warning that Disney would die if it continued to behave as if its primary competitors were the same familiar names: Time Warner, News Corporation, Sony, TCI, Viacom, Bertelsmann, General Electric's NBC, CBS. No, Microsoft was Disney's true nemesis, Jobs warned, for, just as it dominated PCs, it had a stealth plan to become the gatekeeper of the TV cable box, the Internet, and thus of entertainment, leisure-time activities, and e-commerce.

Although Eisner had been warned many times by his own executives about the looming Microsoft menace, when Jobs spoke the message sank in. Eisner became preoccupied with Microsoft and with building Disney's own websites and speeding its e-commerce efforts. In his memoir, *Work in Progress*, published the next year, he wrote, "Microsoft may be our most daunting competitor." The corporate chorus was growing louder: Microsoft was dangerous. Microsoft did not play by the rules. And the government was listening, even if Microsoft was not.

Gates was alarmed by something else: his conviction that technology and size were not Microsoft's friends. Since there was so much money to be made from information technology, the competitor Gates feared most was the anonymous inventor working out of a garage. Gates fretted about challengers surfacing everywhere. He worried about Apple's iMac, which was introduced in 1998 and quickly doubled sales of machines that used the Macintosh operating system. Gates worried about the free and open-source software movement made possible by the Internet, allowing users to customize and build their own applications, thus threatening Windows. He was particularly concerned about Linux, an operating system pioneered by a Finnish engineer, Linus Torvalds, that proclaimed itself open to all and was converting users and provoking considerable buzz.

Other threats to Microsoft's hegemony surfaced. The Internet was rewriting every company's playbook. Should Gates scrap his approach to expensive Windows-powered PCs and produce software for the cheaper "dumb" boxes touted by Sun Microsystem's Scott McNealy? Companies with huge investments in powerful servers—such as IBM, Sun, and Oracle—ballyhooed the cheaper network PC, which was loaded with no expensive software or sophisticated memory and pulled its software off servers. Should Microsoft sell services rather than products? Was Microsoft getting too big to be nimble? Should Microsoft take on more partners? Every day, it seemed, giant industries were converging, perhaps against Microsoft. The cable industry envisioned an operating system within powerful, new digital cable boxes and had dodged Microsoft's effort to become the sole provider of its software. The consumer-electronics industry promoted handheld devices such as the Palm Pilot, which did not use Windows CE and was one of the fastest-growing products in history. Sony's PlayStation, which was relatively cheap, might itself leap to become an operating system that steered all appliances in the home. Telephone companies such as AT&T were becoming cable goliaths, offering high-speed cable or telephone modems that promised instant, broadband Internet access, posing the possibility of a new tollbooth Microsoft would not control. Telephone companies envisioned wireless telephones that surfed the Internet using non-Windows operating systems. And while Gates worried about these elephants, he also belatedly worried about the mice—smaller upstarts that would nibble at Windows, scampering under and around lumbering Microsoft. And all the while he worried about the corporate battles ahead, the largest elephant of all—the government—was bearing down. As it did, Bill Gates's temperature rose.

Those of us sharing his luncheon table in Davos were stunned by the rawness of the emotion Bill Gates couldn't contain, but we assumed he would compose himself for his eagerly awaited speech to a room filled with a worldwide press corps. And, indeed, after he was introduced, Gates at first skillfully camouflaged his rage. He fastened on his best CEO mask and, displaying a half smile, spoke calmly for about twenty minutes, offering a compelling exegesis on the future of computing, the alarming velocity of change, and the necessity of finding business partners to co-navigate the treacherous terrain of cyberspace. He responded easily to questions from reporters about Microsoft's legal woes and about whom he saw as its potential business competitors. But then I rose and asked what could have been construed as an innocuous question:

"Unlike other companies, Microsoft is now stalked by an eight-hundred-pound gorilla, the government. And without passing judgment on the merits of the case, the government does have legitimate responsibilities: to seek to protect the public from monopolies, or from price gouging, or from invasions of privacy. What do you say to those who believe Microsoft has behaved arrogantly, as if the government had no right to ask questions?"

Perhaps it was the word *arrogant* that provoked an eruption, for Gates plunged into a five-minute rant memorable less for what he said than for the deep hurt he betrayed. Reporters were incredulous. After curtly taking several more questions, Gates returned to the table and, hovering behind me, bellowed, "What do you mean *arrogant?*" M. Douglas Ivester's CEO eyes widened, and the look on his face said, *This is not how Fortune 500 CEOs behave!* Melinda Gates looked stricken.

"Remember when you said neither Nathan nor anyone from Microsoft would appear on a panel again?" I said. "That was arrogant."

Just as suddenly as it had erupted, the storm subsided, and the belligerent Gates became a vulnerable adolescent. "What should I do?" he asked plaintively, in a subdued voice. Like everyone at the table, I froze in awkward silence until the luncheon mercifully concluded.

WORLD WAR 3.0

CHAPTER 1

The Prosecutors

BILL GATES'S NEMESIS, United States Assistant Attorney General Joel I. Klein, appeared an unlikely foe. Gates demonized the five foot seven, fifty-two-year-old chief of the Justice Department's Antitrust Division as a corporate-baiting populist, but in fact Klein was at first very much the voice of restraint in internal debates over whether to sue Microsoft. Klein was more Washington insider than maverick and proud of it. His was the classic second-generation immigrant-success story: he was a Bronx-born son of hardworking immigrant Jews from Hungary and Russia who pushed him to get the college education they lacked and who swelled with pride when he earned an academic scholarship to Columbia, where he majored in economics. After graduating magna cum laude from both Columbia and Harvard Law, where he was articles editor of the *Harvard Law Review*, Klein came to Washington in 1973 to clerk first for Chief Judge David Bazelon of the U.S. Court of Appeals for the D.C. Circuit, and then for Supreme Court Justice Lewis Powell, Jr., where Klein was a passionate advocate for social justice, seeking to nudge the more conservative Powell (a nudge Powell welcomed). In their book on the Supreme Court—*The Brethren*—Bob Woodward and Scott Armstrong offer a miniprofile of only one clerk: Joel Klein. "Powell had a profound impact on me," said Klein, who saw him as a philosopher-king. When Klein faces tough issues, he says he asks himself, "What would Justice Powell do?" What Powell usually did was move slowly, carefully.

After clerking for Justice Powell, Klein joined a public-interest law firm, the Mental Health Law Project, where he litigated on behalf of the mentally ill and retarded. Later, he and two colleagues started a law firm specializing in constitutional and health-care cases, and he remained active in mental-health issues, serving as treasurer of the World Federation for Mental Health and as chairman of the Green Door, a community-based mental health–treatment program in Washington.

Klein aspired to be inside the tent, and opportunities came at the annual Renaissance Weekends in Hilton Head, South Carolina, which were dominated by powerful Democrats and those who wanted to be, and which were co-organized by his Harvard classmate Philip Lader. Through this network, Klein came to the attention of Renaissance regulars such as Bill and Hillary Clinton, and when Clinton ran for president in 1992, Klein was aboard as a volunteer. When Clinton appointed Ruth Bader Ginsburg to the Supreme Court, Klein was asked to help prepare her for her Senate confirmation. In 1993, he was recruited by White House Counsel Bernard Nussbaum to succeed Vincent Foster as deputy White House counsel. He found himself quickly caught up in the internal debate over how much the Clintons should reveal about the failed Whitewater land deal and the proper handling of it. Klein pushed for full disclosure, and criticized Nussbaum's attendance at meetings with Treasury officials who were investigating the land deal. This position helped earn him the enmity of Nussbaum, who thought Klein too eager to please a braying press corps. "I don't talk about people I have nothing good to say about," snapped Nussbaum when asked about Klein. Klein proved correct in his assessment that if the White House didn't release all documents relating to Whitewater, they would see them drip out torturously, one at a time.

With White House support, Klein was chosen by Anne K. Bingaman, head of the Justice Department's Antitrust Division, to be her deputy in 1995. At the time Klein came aboard, he found that Microsoft was at the top of the division's agenda, as it had been since 1993, when the members of the Federal Trade Commission had deadlocked over whether Microsoft's business practices were unduly thuggish and Bingaman's department had launched a major investigation. A year later, Microsoft and Justice reached a settlement whereby Microsoft agreed to a consent decree that placed curbs both on its freedom to tie products together and on some of its contract restrictions, including one provision that had required PC manufacturers to pay a royalty to Microsoft for each machine sold regardless of whether it used Microsoft's operating system. But the consent decree also secured for Microsoft the right to "integrate" new features into its products, as long as these features or applications were truly integrated and not bolted on to kill competition. The provision was vaguely worded: Microsoft was allowed, for example, to *develop* new features but not to *sell* or *market* them, which might be a distinction without a difference and one over which the two sides might one day bicker.

Among Klein's first tasks on joining the division was to defend this agreement with Microsoft in a Tunney Act proceeding, a normal procedure whereby the courts certify that such decrees are in the public interest. Although a Tunney Act proceeding is meant as a check, usually consent agreements are rubber-stamped by a judge. In this case, Judge Stanley Sporkin of the U.S. District Court didn't cooperate, however. Sporkin took the unusual step of ordering two hearings, during which he made much of a book he had read on the beach that was critical of Microsoft, and he questioned each side about its content.*

James Clark, the chairman of Netscape, irate at what he felt were Microsoft's efforts to strong-arm its way to dominance in the browser business, asked Gary Reback, an attorney with the Silicon Valley law firm of Wilson, Sonsini, Goodrich & Rosati, to weigh in. Reback filed an exhaustive amicus brief on behalf of three anonymous clients, as is permitted under the Tunney Act, in which he asserted that the consent decree was toothless and therefore not in the public interest. At the end of the hearings, Sporkin concurred, ruling in February 1995 that the consent decree was an "ineffective remedy" to curb Microsoft's predations. Sporkin did not mince words:

> Microsoft has done extremely well in its business in a relatively short period of time, which is a tribute both to its talented personnel and to this nation's great ethic that affords every citizen the ability to rise to

---

*The book was *Hard Drive: Bill Gates and the Making of the Microsoft Empire*, by James Wallace and Jim Erickson.

the top. Microsoft, a rather new corporation, may not have matured to the position where it understands how it should act with respect to the public interest and the ethics of the market place. In this technological age, this nation's cutting edge companies must guard against being captured by their own technology and becoming robotized.

As a result, for the first, and perhaps the last, time, Joel Klein and Bill Gates were of one mind. The Justice Department and Microsoft swiftly joined to appeal this ruling, arguing that Sporkin had exceeded his authority. The Court of Appeals agreed, specifically removing Sporkin from the case and remanding the matter back to the district court, where Sporkin's colleague, Judge Thomas Penfield Jackson, was chosen at random from among fourteen colleagues to review the consent decree. Judge Sporkin, who shared an office-reception entrance with Jackson and is his friend, said of the two hundred or so cases each judge juggled, "We get a lot of junk." This case was not junk. In August 1995, Jackson upheld the decree, and in the process established himself as the judge who would adjudicate any future disputes between Justice and Microsoft. Many of Judge Jackson's colleagues were envious.

Klein was relieved, but not for long, since the truce between Justice and Microsoft was soon broken. Klein and his colleagues were annoyed that instead of appearing humble when Judge Jackson upheld the consent decree, Gates appeared on CNN's *Larry King Live* the same night and bellowed, "That whole thing really has no effect on Microsoft or how we work. . . . What it comes down to is that there is nothing significant that we needed to change, and that just confirms the way we've viewed it all along." Translated: we won, Justice lost.

Justice also challenged Microsoft's proposed $1.5 billion 1995 acquisition of Intuit, the dominant financial-software company. John Malone, who had his own battles with the government, remembers talking to Gates about Intuit. "He was saying they'd have no problem with the government over Intuit," Malone said. Malone questioned his judgment, but Gates ignored the advice. "I don't think his emotional side is in sync with his intellectual side," Malone said. Because Gates believed Microsoft "were good guys," Malone observed, Gates naïvely thought the government would think so, too.

Klein and the Justice Department would by the fall of 1995 become more convinced that Gates and Microsoft weren't "good guys." Nudging them toward this conclusion were Netscape and other Silicon Valley rivals. In the summer of 1996, James L. Barksdale, Netscape's CEO, was outraged to learn that Microsoft was sabotaging Netscape's business with Compaq Computer, then the world's number-one PC manufac- turer. If Compaq didn't terminate plans to feature the Netscape browser icon in its machines rather than Internet Explorer's, Microsoft said it would cancel Compaq's license to use Windows 95. Without the operat- ing system, a Compaq PC was a useless box. Compaq surrendered and switched to Microsoft's browser. Barksdale asked Gary Reback to prepare a white paper detailing Microsoft's anticompetitive behavior.* In August 1996, after he had read Reback's scorching 222-page brief, Barksdale dispatched a copy to Joel Klein, who in October 1996 became the acting head of the Antitrust Division.

Klein found Reback's brief compelling and instructed Phillip R. Ma- lone of his San Francisco office to investigate its allegations. Gates and Microsoft were not flustered; after all, Joel Klein had fought alongside them to reverse Judge Sporkin's decision, and in 1995 he had sided with them against America Online's complaint that Microsoft had violated the consent decree and antitrust law when it made its MSN online ser- vice part of Windows. Besides, Klein seemed too much the Washington insider to launch crusades.

But now Klein was struck by the rapacity of Microsoft's conduct and their utter lack of regret. When he hesitated, Klein was bolstered by Orrin Hatch and several zealous states attorneys general, giving him crucial political cover. Newly emboldened, powerful forces in Silicon Val- ley that believed Microsoft had to be stopped also weighed in. Some of Microsoft's most prominent enemies, including Sun's Scott McNealy, pressed Klein vigorously and spent considerable company resources to make the case. If Microsoft was not halted, each warned, it would lever- age Windows into every new platform and device: the cheap network computers that draw their software from the Internet, handheld devices, cellular phones, cable boxes, PlayStations, pagers, and the servers that process and store digital data. "If they are allowed to use that leverage before the world moves to a network computer," McNealy said, "they can squelch it." So consumed with stopping Microsoft did McNealy

---

*First reported by Joel Brinkley and Steve Lohr of *The New York Times*, June 9, 2000.

become that he put up three million dollars of Sun's money to fund "Project Sherman," a gathering of antitrust experts who met biweekly and were paid six hundred to seven hundred dollars per hour to help craft the legal reasons the government should sue Microsoft.*

In October 1997, Justice filed a petition in the civil case charging Microsoft with deliberately violating the 1994 consent decree when it bundled its Internet browser into Windows. Microsoft defended the move as a product enhancement and vehemently denied that it was attempting to harm Netscape. Gates could barely contain his rage. Two months later, his temperature rose still higher when Attorney General Janet Reno—who didn't even use a PC—accepted a request from Klein to reach outside the department to recruit one of America's foremost litigators, David Boies, 57—another computer illiterate—to sue Microsoft.

Members of Klein's staff badly wanted to take on Microsoft themselves, but Klein had other ideas. He knew he needed somebody special. When he was a partner at Cravath, Swaine & Moore, Boies had represented IBM in its thirteen-year antitrust battle. "He's been through the IBM wars," said Klein. "I didn't want to get stuck in some quagmire. You need someone who knows how to move a case." Klein knew Boies's usual hourly rate was just over six hundred dollars, and the most Klein could offer was the top pay scale for a GS-15 employee of $101,142 per year, which worked out to about fifty dollars an hour, somewhat less than the $113,000 Cravath paid its first-year associates. To help make the pitch, Klein reached into his network of friends. Klein had attended Columbia University with Boies's close friend and new law partner, Jonathan Schiller, then clerked with him on the same federal court, and later became his law associate. Klein phoned Schiller, and said, "I hear David Boies is the best trial lawyer in America."

"I agree with that," said Schiller.

"How would you like to share him with me for a while?"

Schiller and Boies had already spent eight hundred thousand dollars opening new law offices in Armonk (four miles from Boies's Westchester County home) and Washington, D.C., and Boies would not lightly leave his partner in the lurch. "You decide, Jonathan," Boies told Schiller. A

*This was reported by John Heilemann in the November 2000 *Wired*.

former star basketball player at Columbia, Schiller is a more openly passionate man than his partner, and he urged Boies to take the case as a righteous cause. Boies accepted. But he refused to treat the case as a crusade; he made no brave speeches expressing outrage or proclaiming that he was advancing the public interest by challenging the software giant. Boies compared himself to a doctor: "You don't expect a doctor to get outraged at cancer. It's something to deal with. It's your job. The thing I don't want to have misunderstood is that I'm not saying Microsoft is a cancer. We're professionals trying to reach a result." Had Microsoft asked first, Boies said, "I might have represented Microsoft. I certainly didn't think Microsoft was an evil empire. Nor do I think so now."

David Boies is sometimes mythologized in legal circles as the Clarence Darrow of his generation. If the hand of fate selected him for a special destiny, though, that was less than apparent to those who encountered him growing up in the tiny northern Illinois farm town of Marengo, where his father taught high-school history. The eldest of four, Boies did not read until the third grade. "They just thought I was slow," he said. Years later, he realized that he had suffered from dyslexia; even today, he reverses telephone numbers, has no facility for foreign languages, reads slowly, and despite his articulateness mispronounces words such as *superfluous* and *prodigy*. When an attractive teaching offer had come from a high school in Orange County, California, his father relocated the family when Boies was still a boy. Armed with a powerful memory, Boies grew into a star student in high school, but his interests tended more toward racing cars, cards, and girls. With his sharp features, verbal fluency, and pale blue eyes, Boies had girls flocking to his side. Instead of accepting a scholarship to Antioch College, he chose to stay home and marry his high-school sweetheart, Caryl Elwell. For almost a year, he worked on a construction crew and as a bookkeeper in a bank, earning extra money by playing in bridge tournaments, where his ability to remember cards served him well and gave him his first real taste of gambling, a lifelong passion. In the meantime, he and his wife had a son, David III. Prodded by her, he attended the University of Redlands. Elected to Phi Beta Kappa in just two years, Boies felt he had exhausted the college's resources by his junior year, and he applied and gained early admission to Northwestern Law School.

It was 1962, David was twenty-one, and for the next two years, while he worked nights as a motel clerk, he received perfect grades at Northwestern and became editor in chief of its law review. Along the way, his marriage collapsed. He courted Judith Daynard, the wife of one of his law professors, and she was to become his second wife. "David got kicked out of Northwestern Law School," said a close friend. "The dean called him in and said, 'You're our best student, but you have to leave.' The dean called and got him into Yale." Boies acknowledged that the dean asked, "Was there any other place I'd like to go?" Yearning to become a professor, he studied economics at Yale for a year, then switched direction again and finished his final year of law school, concentrating on antitrust law. He graduated with all As, ranking second in the class. Top law firms vied to recruit him, and he chose blue-chip Cravath, Swaine & Moore. His ascent there was meteoric; he quickly found himself in court on behalf of the firm's most important clients. His wife received a law degree from Columbia and not long after gave birth to twins. But his second marriage also failed, in part, he now thinks, because he was rarely home. "As you get older you learn how to balance things," he said.

In 1972, at thirty-one, Boies became Cravath's youngest partner and a key member of the litigating team representing IBM in its ultimately successful struggle to block not only the government's claim that it was an illegal monopoly but also the dozens of private lawsuits that emerged in the wake of that claim; he represented CBS in defeating General William Westmoreland's $120 million libel lawsuit; and he represented Westinghouse Electric in its victorious campaign to block the Philippine government from abrogating a $2.1 billion nuclear-power-plant contract because the company had allegedly bribed former president Ferdinand Marcos. Boies and his mentor, senior partner Thomas Barr, represented the Federal Deposit Insurance Corporation in its complaint against Michael Milken and his former Wall Street firm, Drexel Burnham Lambert, winning a $1.1 billion judgment. Except for a few years in the late seventies, when he left to become chief counsel to Edward Kennedy's Senate Judiciary Committee (where he met his third wife, Mary McInnis, a Carter White House domestic-policy assistant who had briefly dated Joel Klein), David Boies had been at Cravath his entire professional life.

Boies was seen as a star outside Cravath; inside, he could also be a source of controversy. He was a loner; his dress habits seemed strange to many of his sixty-odd fellow partners; his idea of a vacation, touring the country in a Jeep, did not jibe with theirs; his office was always littered with paper and cases of fine red wine that sometimes turned to vinegar in the sunlight because he didn't get around to moving them; he didn't use e-mail or voice mail or even a PC; and after pulling all-nighters to conclude a case, he would disappear from the office, sparking whispers that he was at the craps tables in Atlantic City or Las Vegas, which was often true. Boies liked litigating in courtrooms; he wasn't much interested in helping out his partners with the firm's many M&A clients or in returning partners' phone calls. "After Westmoreland, for the next ten years David didn't do a lot of mainstream Cravath work," said then presiding partner, Samuel Butler. "He worked mostly on his own clients." Butler estimates that from about 1992 to 1997, Boies was in the office only about a third of the time.

Butler both admires and resents Boies: "He's brilliant. He's hardworking when he has to be. He has absolutely spectacular courtroom skills, and a predisposition to look at things differently." Yet, Butler added, "He's extremely difficult to work with. Not in terms of his personality. He's pleasant. But you just don't know where he is. He disappears."

When Mary Boies's own law firm got involved in a civil suit against giant Cravath-represented pharmaceutical companies for conspiring to fix vitamin prices, Butler urged Boies to intercede. "She's suing one of our clients!" he told him. Boies refused to intervene.

Boies had represented George Steinbrenner and the New York Yankees since 1995, and when the Yankees' owner filed an antitrust suit in 1997 against Major League Baseball, claiming that they had illegally tried to block the Yankees' $95 million marketing agreement with Adidas, Cravath partners were upset. Cravath's foremost client was Time Warner, which owned the Atlanta Braves, one of the defendants in the suit. Time Warner CEO and chairman Gerald Levin telephoned Butler and said, "What are you doing? You're suing us!"

"We're not suing you!" exclaimed Butler, who had been completely in the dark about the Steinbrenner suit. Butler quickly summoned Boies, who said he was merely representing his client. "But you're suing the firm's largest client!" Butler replied and urged Boies to drop Steinbrenner. Instead, after thirty-one years, Boies resigned from Cravath. Said Butler, "I never tried to change his mind."

Boies's departure made the front page of *The New York Times*. At the time, he had been earning more than two million dollars a year. Within months, Boies established his boutique law firm in partnership with Jonathan Schiller, who had been a partner in the Washington office of Kaye, Scholer, Fierman, Hays & Handler. The new firm was just getting off the ground when Joel Klein called.

In choosing Boies, Klein knew he had to do some damage control with members of his own staff, who felt insulted. He was aware, too, of the irony of selecting Boies: after Boies was appointed, George Washington University law professor William E. Kovacic, a member of the Federal Trade Commission's Bureau of Competition during the Carter and Reagan administrations, observed, "One of the ironies of this case is that the very litigation successes that David Boies and his colleagues at Cravath had in the seventies and early eighties with IBM—assisted by the very able Dr. Franklin Fisher as their chief testifying expert—now become the obstacle to their prevailing in this matter. One of the big challenges for the government brief writers is to sidestep lots of the decisions from that period that embrace the idea that the dominant firms ought to be encouraged to compete and to compete hard."

Boies himself shrugged the matter off. Unlike Bill Gates, for whom business is personal, to Boies it's just business. He is not embarrassed to think of himself as a gun-for-hire, though he is more interested in the action than the money. And he said he still believed what he argued in the IBM case, that it was proper to compete hard, even ruthlessly; but Microsoft, he felt, was a monopoly, and IBM was not. After Klein's initial telephone call, Boies remembers thinking the Microsoft case would be "a great trial," one that might make new law, defining whether static antitrust laws should apply to fast-changing technology companies. "I had the view that antitrust laws applied to the software industry. I didn't have a view as to whether Microsoft violated antitrust laws. I did have the view that it was not entitled to a blanket pass."

In December 1997, days after Klein recruited Boies, Microsoft suffered another setback when Judge Thomas Penfield Jackson—yet another slave of pen and pencil—issued an order to stop Microsoft from "bundling" or "tying" its Internet Explorer browser with Windows 95 and its soon-to-be-released Windows 98 operating system. While Judge Jackson ruled that the "government has not clearly convinced the Court that Microsoft violated" the consent decree by including a browser with its operating system, he was sufficiently swayed to appoint Harvard law professor Lawrence Lessig as a special master, empowered to sift through the issues, to hold evidentiary hearings, and to report back by May 1998 whether he felt Microsoft had in fact violated the consent decree. To "maintain the status quo" while Lessig conducted his review, Judge Jackson required Microsoft to decouple the browser from Windows if computer manufacturers wanted a version of Windows 95 without a browser. And although the Justice Department had not urged this, Judge Jackson's ruling extended to Windows 98, which was scheduled to be introduced by the middle of the following year. Jackson seemed to accept the government's contention that Windows and the browser were separate products and were tied together not to help consumers but to harm Netscape.

Microsoft immediately appealed this decision, challenging the appointment of a special master and insisting that the browser and Windows were an "integrated" product permitted by the consent decree; removing the browser, Microsoft said, would cripple the operating system. "He just ordered it!" Bill Gates was heard to grouse. Microsoft's chief counsel, William Neukom, denounced Jackson for arbitrarily expanding the case "without giving Microsoft notice or an opportunity to defend itself." The Justice Department had simply asked that Microsoft be held in contempt, but Jackson had gone further, asserting the court's right to, in effect, review software design by ruling that Microsoft could not tie its browser to its Windows operating system. Despite Jackson's ruling, Microsoft announced defiantly that it would integrate a browser into Windows 98. Microsoft further "thumbed its nose at the judge," observed a company insider, when it said that it was "forced" to ship a "broken" operating system, since they claimed that decoupling the browser from Windows 95 would break the operating system. The Justice Department immediately asked the court to hold Microsoft in contempt.

At a January 1998 hearing in his courtroom, an incredulous Jackson asked Microsoft vice president David Cole, "It seemed absolutely clear to you that I entered an order that required that you distribute a product that would not work? Is that what you're telling me?"

"In plain English, yes," Cole replied. "We followed that order. It wasn't my place to consider the consequences of that."

Why would Microsoft flout Judge Jackson's order? "They were so convinced that Jackson was an idiot, and he's not," recalled Lessig. Looking back many months later, a Microsoft insider concurred: "It's the kid who thinks he's smarter than the rest of the class. That kind of shit comes back to you all the time."

This behavior helped shape Judge Jackson's impression that Microsoft was arrogant. Many months later, Judge Jackson told me, "Their response in purporting to comply with my order was a thumb in the eye. It was an obsolete version of their equipment. Or one that didn't work. And when the matter came on for a hearing, Microsoft brought in an executive and his testimony was that they assumed my order was for them to market a product that didn't work! That seemed to me to be a very sophomoric, arrogant reaction." Jackson concluded that Microsoft was disdainful, proud to operate outside business norms. "I thought they didn't think they were regarded as adult members of the community. I thought they would learn."*

More examples of Microsoft's alleged strong-arm tactics started to appear in the press. It was reported, for example, that at a June 1995 meeting at Netscape's Mountain View, California, headquarters, senior Microsoft executives offered an alliance with Netscape and an infusion of capital to the company—if it would abandon the principal browser market. If Netscape refused, a Microsoft executive reportedly threatened "to cut off its air supply." It was also reported that in August 1995 Gates exploded at his chip-making partner, Intel CEO Andrew S. Grove, warning him to stop investing in software that might one day compete with Microsoft. Gates allegedly threatened to support rival chip makers if Grove did not comply. Microsoft's insistence that Compaq Computer dump Netscape also attracted headlines.

Members of Congress were becoming restive, and in March 1998 Bill Gates was summoned to testify before the Senate Judiciary Committee. The day before, Gates's staff arranged a visit with editors and reporters of *The Washington Post*. It was to be a friendly reach-out session, a best-behavior sales pitch with an influential newspaper whose esteemed matriarch, Katharine Graham, is someone Gates adores and compares to his own mother in terms of her "warmth." But during the course of a question-and-answer session, he could not contain himself: Gates erupted. When the wealthiest man on earth loses his temper in a newsroom, he should not be surprised by the result. The March 3 *Post* ran its story on the front page:

---

*Judge Jackson would grant me a total of about ten hours of taped interviews.

Far from the usual cautious demeanor of business leaders visiting Washington, he was roaring with indignation and disdain for those who question his business practices. He dismissed one question as "unfair," another as "dishonest." "Come on!" he said impatiently to one questioner. "Give me a break!" he said a few moments later to another.

Before the Senate Judiciary Committee, Gates minded his manners, but he was considered less than helpful. Repeatedly, he was asked if Microsoft imposed contracts on Internet service or content providers that precluded them from promoting Netscape. Did Microsoft, in short, "restrain trade" or "attempt to monopolize," acts forbidden by antitrust laws? Gates bobbed and weaved and avoided many direct answers. When cornered, he admitted to restrictive contracts, but only reluctantly. Microsoft earned no congressional or Justice Department goodwill when, a month later, it waived many of these contract provisions.

Microsoft had won a minor victory in February 1998 when the Court of Appeals halted the work of Judge Jackson's special master until it could hear more evidence; but by spring it appeared certain the government would launch an antitrust suit. To try to head it off, a Microsoft team led by William Neukom flew to Washington to meet with the Justice Department. Gates himself had an audience with now Assistant Attorney General Joel Klein to explain Microsoft's position. They met in the late afternoon of May 5, in a corner conference room at the Washington office of Sullivan & Cromwell, the Wall Street law firm that has traditionally represented America's financial establishment—and a firm that has, for the past decade, done much of Microsoft's outside legal work. The White House, a block away, was visible from the window. "Gates was very passionate, very forceful," recalls a government official who was there. "He began with a presentation of his plans for Windows. . . . It was reasonably civil. When questions were raised, however, he grew angry, condescending, snide, and petulant."

Justice officials argued that Microsoft's power was impregnable because consumers were so dependent on Windows. His voice rising, Gates exclaimed, "You give me any seat at the table"—he mentioned Linux, the open-source operating system, and Java, a cross-platform

computer language created by Microsoft adversary Sun Microsystems—
"and I can blow away Microsoft!" If his competitors had half a brain, he
suggested, Microsoft would be weakened. Gates told me later that he was
also trying to say something else: "Where did this 'monopoly' come
from? Do I own all the diskettes in the country? . . . It's such a silly
proposition to think that in an intellectual-property area you don't have
massive competition. There is nothing that Microsoft has that guarantees its position."

Most government officials were surprised at what they interpreted as
Gates's arrogance. David Boies was less harsh in his assessment. "He
really said it with a twinkle in his eye," Boies recalled. To his mind, Gates
was just "being passionate, and maybe a little hyperbolic." Other Justice
officials, however, were surprised by something else. Normally, when a
target of a lawsuit asks for a meeting he is solicitous. Gates wasn't. "I
never had the feeling he was being unfriendly," said Boies. "I occasionally had the feeling he was saying, 'That's my position, and I'm not going
to change it.' " Neukom claimed that Gates was seeking common ground,
but that it was difficult because "Bill was frustrated that the government
seemed to have such a vague understanding of our technology." Government officials, Neukom recalled, kept asking why Microsoft needed
certain features included in the operating system, and Gates kept warning that government should not be in the software-design business.

This meeting was followed by a flurry of telephone calls among
Klein, Gates, Neukom, and various attorneys, all aimed at a possible settlement, and by a decisive weekend of negotiations. Microsoft's attorneys were talking to Gates "every step of the way," recalled Neukom's
deputy David Heiner. During this period, Gates remained in his offices
outside Seattle. He also remained hard-core, resistant to compromise.
State attorneys general, who had joined the case, and Boies, representing the Justice Department, were in Washington, D.C., expecting to file a
lawsuit against Microsoft in federal district court on Thursday, May 14.
The parties were racing a second clock, because Microsoft was ready to
ship Windows 98. After conversations with Gates and then Neukom,
Joel Klein thought he detected movement in Microsoft's position. "They
put on the table Thursday morning something that could have been, for
the first time, significant," Klein recalled. On the phone that week,
Microsoft indicated a willingness, according to Justice Department and
Microsoft officials, to address Klein's three conditions: that Microsoft

loosen its contract restrictions so that those who did business with Netscape would be free to promote a rival browser and would not be penalized if they did; that it loosen its restrictions on the Windows user interface, the first screen consumers see when they turn on their PC, thus allowing the PC maker the option of changing this screen; and that it give PC makers a choice of browsers, either by allowing them to insert a "ballot screen" so users could remove Microsoft's Internet Explorer icon and choose Netscape, or by incorporating a rival browser into Windows, or, Justice hoped, by agreeing to unbundle Microsoft's browser code from Windows.

Point three was the most contentious, for Microsoft was not about to follow the government's script and divorce its browser from its operating system. They said it couldn't be done; even if it could be done, they insisted, doing so would penalize consumers because the browser was free and consumers want their PCs to be simpler to use, not harder. Nor was Microsoft keen on the alternative, which would either promote a rival's browser or incorporate the rival browser into the Windows operating system. Klein and Neukom were searching for a way to fudge this third point, however. Microsoft had, after all, provided a choice on the opening Windows screen between AOL, which was located in an online-services folder, and its own MSN. "We said, 'OK, we'll at least sit and listen,'" recalled Gates. Klein thought he heard Microsoft signal a willingness to keep the Netscape icon on every Windows desktop but also, perhaps, either to insert Netscape's browser code into Windows itself or to delete the Microsoft browser icon. Both Klein and Neukom seemed to hope that the gap between them had narrowed.

On Thursday morning, the Justice Department and the states were scheduled to file their civil lawsuit. Searching for a compromise formula, Klein told Neukom over the telephone that morning that if Microsoft agreed to postpone the shipment of Windows 98 and was open to discuss various alternatives, he should fly to D.C. for face-to-face negotiations. Neukom got on the 1 P.M. flight to Washington.

Klein wanted to avoid a trial. As chief of the Antitrust Division, he had a lot on his plate. About half the division's time, he estimated, was expended reviewing proposed mergers to gauge whether they might threaten competition; a somewhat lesser amount of time was devoted to cartel enforcement, with thirty or so grand juries looking into cases such as the alleged price-fixing by vitamin manufacturers; and the remainder of the division's time was spent bringing antitrust cases against giant companies, as he would against American Airlines and Visa. A trial was an enormous drain of time and resources.

Klein had competing pressures to balance, starting with the law. He truly believed Microsoft had broken the law. But he knew all too well the vagaries of antitrust law, the history of which reaches back almost four centuries, to the first English common-law cases aimed at curbing monopolies. But antitrust in this country emerged as a force only after the Civil War, as the industrial revolution birthed corporations that rapidly consolidated and flaunted their wealth and power in the Gilded Age, which in turn spurred a backlash against corporate arrogance. The backlash manifested itself when state governments began to sue companies that rigged prices and choked competition. By 1888, public opinion was arrayed against corporate trusts, and the presidential platforms of both political parties thundered against wicked corporate "trusts" and vowed government retaliation.

Over the next several decades, two pieces of national legislation were enacted that remain the cornerstones of antitrust law. The first was the Sherman Antitrust Act of 1890, which is almost elegant in its economy:

> Every contract, combination in the form of trust or otherwise, or con-
> spiracy, in restraint of trade or commerce among the several States, or
> with foreign nations, is declared to be illegal. *(Section 1)*

> Every person who shall monopolize, or attempt to monopolize, or
> combine or conspire with any other person or persons, to monopolize
> any part of the trade or commerce among the several States, or with
> foreign nations, shall be deemed guilty of a felony. *(Section 2)*

The Clayton Antitrust Act of 1914 expanded the law's domain. It augmented the right of injured citizens or corporations to file lawsuits against antitrust violators. The Federal Trade Commission Act, in the same year, created the FTC, empowering the agency to determine unfair trade practices. A later amendment, the Robinson-Patman Act, banned price discrimination that lessens competition.

The words are spare and simple, but the interpretation has not been. Antitrust law is not a settled preserve, with clear boundaries of what is and is not permissible behavior. Throughout its history, the law has undergone as many twists and turns as an Albanian road. Legal scholars, like Thomas D. Morgan in his well-regarded law-school textbook, *Modern Antitrust Law and Its Origins,* describe the four epochs of antitrust law. The first epoch was its formative period from 1890 to 1914, which included the congressional and judicial debates leading to passage of the Sherman and Clayton acts. The second epoch, from 1915 to 1939, was marked by the efforts of courts to apply a phrase invoked by the Supreme Court in the 1911 *Standard Oil Co. v. U.S.:* the "rule of reason," providing enough flexibility so that the Sherman Act's blanket condemnation of "all combinations in restraint of trade" would come to mean all *unreasonable* combinations. The third epoch covered the next thirty years, from postwar to the mid-seventies, "a time of aggressive expansion of antitrust doctrine, much of it born of depression-era economics and premised on the idea that American business had become too powerful and American industries too concentrated," writes Morgan. The fourth epoch began roughly in the mid-seventies and extended well into the nineties and has been described variously as a period of "retreat" in antitrust law and as a return to a more flexible approach, asserting that legal nostroms that failed to focus on actual economic harm can unfairly retard companies and penalize success.

Joel Klein saw a Microsoft trial as a potential fifth epoch, for he believed it might determine whether antitrust laws could be applied fairly to the Information Age and the Internet, a realm in which classic monopoly characteristics—rising prices, financial or distribution barriers to entry, and choke-holds on innovation—are not as apparent, even if the coercive tactics are familiar. A characteristic of the new economy is that companies often engage in "winner take most" competition. Those who win huge market shares—Microsoft in software, Intel in chips, Cisco Systems in Internet plumbing, AOL in Internet access, Netscape in browsers—reap great rewards. Because the rewards from achieving near monopoly status are so great, it is argued, competitors lust to join the contest. Thus monopolies become temporary, not permanent, or so it is argued. Klein knew the Microsoft trial might help answer several other questions: should government or the marketplace set the rules for cyberspace? In a global economy in which size is often necessary to compete effectively, should government relax its domestic rules in order to promote home-grown industries overseas? How does one

square intellectual-property laws, which are meant to protect companies and provide incentives to innovate, with antitrust laws, which are
meant to protect the public? What if Microsoft is declared a predator but
has not harmed consumers? And in such a case, how can the courts
penalize a predator without penalizing the American economy? And
then there is the age-old question that applies to antitrust policy as well
as to democratic governance: how does one resolve the inevitable conflict between economic efficiency and egalitarianism? The trial, Klein
understood, might offer the Supreme Court an opportunity to update
and clarify what is and is not permissible corporate behavior.

Klein was also acutely aware that for every legal precedent cited by
the government, Microsoft could cite its own. The government could
invoke the 1912 *United States v. Terminal Railroad Association of St. Louis*
case, in which the Supreme Court ruled that a company that controlled
every rail route into and out of the city could not restrict access so as to
disadvantage its competitors. Microsoft Windows, the government
believed, exerted similar control over the PC. The government could
also cite the 1951 *Lorain Journal Co. v. United States* and the related
1985 *Aspen Ski Co. v. Aspen Highlands Skiing Corp.* In the *Lorain* case, the
Journal was the dominant source of advertising for this Ohio community, and the newspaper refused advertising from any business that also
advertised on a rival radio station. In the Aspen case, the Aspen Ski
Company, to harm its smaller ski-lift competitor, refused to renew a
joint lift-ticket agreement. In the *Lorain* case, the Supreme Court found
Lorain guilty of a predatory attempt to monopolize. In the *Aspen* case,
the court ruled that the guilty company illegally maintained a monopoly. The government could also cite the 1966 *United States v. Grinnell
Corporation*, in which the Supreme Court distinguished between benign
monopoly powers and a "willful" abuse of that monopoly power to suppress competition.

On the other hand, Klein knew that Microsoft could also invoke the
Grinnell case, explaining that the mere holding of a monopoly is not
unlawful unless it exists not because of superior products but because of
predatory acts. He knew Microsoft would cite a related case, the 1979
Berkey Photo, Inc. v. Eastman Kodak Co., in which an appeals court overruled a jury verdict concerning the illegal maintenance of a monopoly
and held that "any firm, even a monopolist, may generally bring its
products to market whenever and however it chooses" and must be

given freedom to innovate by bundling new features. Microsoft believed that when the Court of Appeals affirmed that Kodak could reap the rewards of its inventions and was not obliged to share its technology with competitors, it affirmed the principle of intellectual property and Microsoft's right to profit from its innovations. And Microsoft could, Klein knew, invoke *United States v. Aluminum Company of America*, in which Judge Learned Hand wrote the 1945 opinion for the Second Circuit Court of Appeals and concluded that Alcoa achieved its dominance through superior aluminum products.*

Of at least one thing Klein was certain: Microsoft had a choke-hold on the PC. The PC had by 1998 become a ubiquitous device in American homes and offices, with 48.7 million U.S. households having at least one desktop computer, up from 44.4 million the previous year, and 30 million desktop users were online, a number that had risen from 39.3 million the previous year and was expected to double in five years.** And the Windows operating system ran more than 90 percent of all PCs powered by Intel chips (as opposed to Macintosh machines, which used another chip). Klein had in his mind the American and United Airlines cases in the mid-eighties, when the Department of Transportation required the airlines to alter or change their dominant computer-reservation systems and stop steering customers to its own flights and away from the flights of competing airlines; he imagined forcing Microsoft to open its dominant operating system by at least assuring that they could no longer punish competitors by denying access to Windows.

Nevertheless, Klein was deeply conflicted. He did not want to step out ahead of President Clinton, who had appointed him and who had said nothing about Microsoft but had said much about how vital the booming high-tech industry was to America's economy. Nor was it the style of an aspiring Washington insider to press against the barricades; in Washington, people compromised. Yet with Microsoft, compromise had brought only ridicule upon the Antitrust Division. Anne Bingaman and the division had been portrayed as patsies for agreeing to a consent decree rather than taking Bill Gates and company to court. If Klein chose not to go to trial, the state attorneys general and others might tattoo him with the *soft* label. Already, he had been so accused by those who

*In the end, of course, the courts ordered the breakup of Alcoa.
**These numbers are from the January 1999 Forrester Report.

opposed one of his first acts as antitrust chief, what he refers to as "my toughest call," his blessing of the twenty-three-billion-dollar merger of two giant Baby Bells, Bell Atlantic and NYNEX. Even the conservative Republican attorney general of New York State was on the other side. "He was perceived as weak, not strong," observed an official in that office.

To win this case, Klein also knew he had to woo the companies of Silicon Valley to his side, which was no simple matter. He had to convince them he would truly take Microsoft to court. Only if they believed this might they agree to testify against "the great Satan." Then, if Justice won the case, these companies could help shape a remedy and provide political cover, buttressing the Clinton administration's claim that it was not antibusiness, just procompetition. This was important to Klein, who was no abstract theorist. He was a new Democrat, not a traditional New Deal liberal, and he believed this was a profoundly complicated case, in which the antidote to Microsoft's dominance might come not from government intervention but from rapid changes in technology. If true, then the marketplace rather than government would punish Microsoft.

Last, Klein wrestled with the complicated politics of this case. When it came to cyberspace, Congress did not fall into predictable left/right divisions. Democrats as well as Republicans clamored to prove their ardent devotion to the high-tech industry. If Klein sued Microsoft, would he be a general without an army to command? Klein's political antennae sensed that the Clinton administration—like his other vital constituency, Congress, which could reduce funding for his department—was deeply ambivalent, wanting government to be an honest referee yet not wanting it to be intrusive, wanting to curb abuses of power yet not wanting to slow America's most robust industry.

When Klein and Neukom and their teams gathered for the final round of negotiations in the cavernous conference room adjoining Klein's office at the Justice Department on Friday, May 15, 1998, Bill Gates was not present, but he remained a hawk, particularly concerning whether Microsoft could bundle new features such as a browser in with Windows. David Boies also did not attend this final weekend of meetings. "By that time, I had concluded the case should be brought," recalled Boies. Most of the state attorneys general were in agreement. They also thought Klein was playing his cards too close to the vest and worried he would decide not to sue, so they leaked information damaging to Microsoft to keep pressure on him. State officials, fresh from their ongoing battles with the tobacco companies, saw Microsoft as a slam-dunk proconsumer case, perhaps a rich source of revenues if government won, and an even richer source of headlines.

Throughout the sessions at Justice on Friday and at Sullivan & Cromwell on Saturday, where the parties moved because Justice offices were not air-conditioned on weekends, "bundling" was the most divisive issue. Bill Neukom was frustrated. He said Microsoft was asked to come up with ideas but that Justice was "just sitting there, telling us, 'Give us more.'" Neukom repeatedly told the Justice team, "I have to go back to Bill on this." Gates was off alone on one of the two "think weeks" he takes each year to read and ponder deeply, but this time his thinking centered on Washington and the law, not technology. Gates fretted that Justice was so vague, he told me later, so "open-ended" in its demands, that "anybody could be part of Windows"; it was as if Microsoft was to be the mule for the entire software industry. He was not about to agree to place Netscape's code in with Windows. And if Microsoft agreed to another vaguely worded consent decree, they would be right back where they were in 1994, with Justice as a backseat driver to every Microsoft software decision. Neukom also recalled what had happened to Sears after 1977, when it signed a consent order stipulating that it would encourage competition by not opening stores in malls, just before malls redefined shopping.

Neukom and Microsoft were upset that after opening the meeting on Friday morning, Joel Klein left, never to return. Klein entrusted the negotiations to Jeffrey H. Blattner, his special counsel for information technology, who had clerked for Supreme Court Justice Potter Stewart and, like David Boies, had served as chief counsel to Edward Kennedy's Senate Judiciary Committee. Blattner had just joined the Justice Department in March. In addition to Justice officials, the attorneys general of Iowa, New York, and Connecticut attended. Microsoft was upset when Justice likened Microsoft to the cable-TV industry or to telephone companies and proposed what it called "a must-carry solution," meaning that Windows must carry a competing browser such as Netscape not as a separate product but by incorporating its code into Windows. "We were trying to create parity in browsers," said Blattner. "The issue was how do we preserve browser competition in the short run." But the cable and phone companies were regulated local monopolies, and in return for opening their wires to carry broadcast signals or long-distance calls, they were paid something in return. Microsoft was not regulated and was offered no compensation. Microsoft was also upset that only they were expected to put their proposals in writing while Justice never did, giving Microsoft a sense that they were competing against themselves. At the end of Friday's session, Bill Neukom was gloomy.

They gathered again Saturday, with Blattner and Iowa attorney general Tom Miller chairing the meeting, but accounts of what happened diverge. According to Microsoft officials, Justice asked for concrete proposals and Microsoft caucused. When they returned, Bill Neukom slid copies of a single sheet of paper across the table to Blattner and the state attorneys general. Microsoft proposed three concessions:

- To "modify existing" contracts so that Internet-service or content providers or online services would no longer be restricted in "their ability to promote or distribute competing web browsing software." Microsoft further said it "will not enter into such agreements in the future." (However, a Microsoft official later admitted that it did not include its contracts with Internet-service provider AOL, which connected about 40 percent of all PCs to the Internet.)
- To allow PC manufacturers "to insert a screen or screens before the Windows desktop appears that they can use to promote their own or third-party products"; to permit them to "insert a ballot screen before the Windows desktop appears" giving consumers a choice of default browsers; and "if they select something other than Internet Explorer" then Windows will drop its "Get Connected" browser icon from the desktop screen; or the PC makers would be free to choose another default browser on their own and "may continue to use a majority of the space on the Windows 98 desktop." But Windows's browser would be neither disabled nor removed.
- "Not to condition" any Windows licensing agreement with PC manufacturers on whether they chose Microsoft's browser.

Blattner read the proposal, Microsoft officials claim, then slid it back across the table at Neukom and bellowed, "I don't negotiate off of lists," before rising and terminating the negotiations.

The government's account is that Neukom slid the paper across the table earlier. Blattner remembers sliding it back and saying, "I'm not going to bless a piece of paper that can leak." They continued talking, and around 11 A.M. Neukom and his team excused themselves to telephone Gates. The government team sat in an alcove and waited. After a one-hour delay, the meeting resumed. Since it was only noon and they had expected to negotiate through the afternoon, Blattner said he anticipated another round of talks. Instead, he said, Neukom politely announced, "It's clear we're at an impasse." The government blamed Gates for figuratively walking out in a huff. As they shook hands with Neukom, Jeff Blattner remembers standing beside Tom Miller and telling Microsoft's chief lawyer, "I know you gave your client your best judgment, but I have to tell you this can spin out of control for Microsoft. I thought you would have settled."

"Thank you," the tall, regal Neukom replied stiffly. To Blattner, "it was the kind of thank-you you get in a reception line when the host wants you to move on."

Both sides agree that the chasm between the two was too wide. The government's "key demands," Gates wrote in an open letter to customers, partners, and shareholders, "that Microsoft incorporate Netscape's competing Web-browsing software in every copy of Windows, or that we license PC makers to emasculate Windows by hiding its entire user interface and removing access to its Internet technology—appear to benefit a single competitor at the expense of consumers. . . . I want you to know that Microsoft will vigorously defend the fundamental principle at stake in this litigation. The freedom to innovate, improve, and integrate new features into products has been the mainstay of our industry. . . ."

The following Monday, May 18, Joel Klein, accompanied by Attorney General Janet Reno, held a press conference to announce on behalf of the United States government and attorneys general representing twenty states* and the District of Columbia that the Justice Department was bringing civil charges against Microsoft for breaking the law in two ways. First, it was a monopoly that tried to crush or coerce competitors and sometimes allies, thus harming consumers—a key test of antitrust law. And, second, Microsoft had attempted to preserve its Windows

*Subsequently, South Carolina abandoned the lawsuit, siding with Microsoft.

monopoly and to use this as leverage to enter and control new markets, thus harming competition. "What cannot be tolerated—and what the antitrust laws forbid—is the barrage of illegal, anticompetitive practices that Microsoft uses to destroy its rivals and to avoid competition," Klein said. Tom Miller, also the chairman of the Antitrust Task Force of the National Association of Attorneys General, said: "We are taking this action to give a fair shake to competitors and free choice to consumers in one of the most crucial industries in the nation."

Companies in Silicon Valley and elsewhere applauded the decision, which pleased Joel Klein and his staff. Observed a staff member, "One of the most fascinating parts of this case is how to behave cautiously yet convince those in the Valley that you are not dickless. We have to get these people to testify." More than a few high-tech notables were torn between a fear of Microsoft and a fear of government meddling. "I don't think there's much doubt as to the facts," said Eric Schmidt, the chairman and CEO of Novell, a software competitor. "There is a very large question about what to do about it. I don't think anyone's in favor of a Department of Microsoft Management." Esther Dyson, the Internet pioneer who chairs EDventure Holdings, was concerned about any sort of restrictions on Internet access: "You have to look at the browser not as an economic object to sell but as a means to control the vending machine and the newsstand that sits on everyone's desk. I don't know what you do about it because I don't want government controlling that space. But I don't want Microsoft or AOL to control that space either. The fact that I'm concerned about saying this is probably because in my industry people are really careful about what they say about Microsoft, and that's a bad sign."

Scott McNealy of Sun welcomed the government's lawsuit because he feared Microsoft would use Windows to "leverage into other businesses," such as Sun's powerful computer servers or handheld devices. Yet McNealy, like many Microsoft critics, often contradicts himself. On the one hand, he has said publicly that handheld wireless devices and a cheap network computer that retrieves its software off the Internet will turn Microsoft to "toast." On the other hand, he wants government to attack Microsoft as if it were a monster, not a dinosaur. He speaks of Gates as if he cannot be stopped because he will ruthlessly "squelch" all competitors, but then says that new technology has "the shelf life of a banana." Some, like Amazon.com founder and CEO Jeffrey Bezos, sided with Gates while recognizing his mistakes. "I don't know Bill Gates. I never met Bill Gates," he told me in January 1999. "I have no direct first-hand knowledge, but my opinion is that he is unfairly vilified by a high percentage of people that I run into in high-tech circles. . . . One of the mistakes Microsoft made was not to build relations in Silicon Valley. It's easy to hate someone you don't know."

CHAPTER 2

Hard Core

MICROSOFT RESPONDED to the lawsuit with the zeal of warriors. In a statement that foreshadowed its trial strategy of presenting itself as a pious and proper corporate citizen, not a practitioner of business hardball, it proclaimed: "Microsoft has focused on a single goal since it was formed in 1975: making the best possible products, and offering them at the most competitive prices, to benefit consumers." By refusing to allow the PC maker to control the opening screen, Microsoft insisted it was not trying to exert control but to assure "a consistent user experience" and to protect "the integrity of the Windows product." Gates invited the press to the Microsoft campus on May 18, the same day Microsoft was shipping Windows 98 to be sold in June. He declared, "federal and state regulators have taken the unprecedented step of intervening in America's most successful and growing industry by . . . [designing] software. . . . How ironic that in the United States, where freedom and innovation are core values, these regulators are trying to punish an American company that has worked hard and successfully to deliver on those values." While the government believed that Microsoft's Windows was so dominant that it ought be treated—like the Baby Bells' telephone wires—as an essential utility or "common carrier," required to carry (for a fee) the signals of telephone competitors, to Microsoft this analogy was absurd. It was never granted a monopoly, as the Baby Bells were, and was not being offered a fee.

The government's case was feeble, Bill Neukom privately assured Gates. Netscape's complaints were analogous to those made against Kodak. "Netscape knew we were going to provide Internet browsing in Windows 95," he said. "There was this reality sitting there, and they ignored it. That's our fault?" The antitrust laws were not meant to shackle competition, he told Gates. Besides, he said, Microsoft had the heavy guns of Sullivan & Cromwell on its side, and the government team was led by a man who didn't even use a PC. Neukom didn't know Boies, but, despite Boies's successful defense of IBM, Neukom was dubious that he could build a strong government case, given his ignorance of technology. A year earlier, Neukom had instructed the two computer-illiterate members of the Sullivan & Cromwell team—senior partners Richard Urowsky and John Warden—to master the PC and become conversant with the technology. No matter how smart Boies might be, Neukom didn't believe he could parachute into the courtroom and explain technological facts that were alien to him.

Neukom assured Gates that every company does what Microsoft did. He analogized Microsoft's behavior to that of Pepsi and Coca-Cola, each making exclusive marketing deals with vendors that exclude the other. A product given away for free (or below cost), as Microsoft's browser was, is commonly referred to as a loss leader. And, of course, every company invokes "shareholder responsibility" as a rationale to justify sometimes unpleasant corporate behavior, everything from ultimatums to massive layoffs. Along with *branding* and *synergy*, perhaps the most common corporate buzzword of the nineties was *leverage*. Neukom didn't have to tell Gates that most companies use leverage as a business weapon.

The day's headlines shouted as much. Independent television producers screamed that the broadcast-TV networks, which persuaded the government to relax restrictions on their right to own part or all of the shows they aired, now favor shows they own outright or lean on producers to grant them part ownership of shows—or else they don't get network airtime. The Hollywood studios, which are not supposed to limit where a movie can be exhibited or condition a theater chain's showing of a strong movie on the theater agreeing to "block book" the studio's weaker movies, sometimes do just that. The Baby Bell telephone companies are supposed to be common carriers, but competitors have long complained that the Baby Bells deliberately go slow in opening their monopoly wire. As Microsoft is accused of favoring certain business partners, so supermarkets employ leverage when they manufacture and promote their own brands, disadvantaging established brands. Consumers have reason to be pleased with how the costs of printers and fax machines have plunged, but printer and fax-machine manufacturers trap customers into paying exorbitant prices for replacement ink cartridges. The Federal Trade Commission would reach a settlement with five major music companies representing 85 percent of the music market—Time Warner, Sony, Universal Music, EMI, and Bertelsmann— which agreed to end the practice of paying for advertising in music stores only if the stores didn't advertise discounts, a price-fixing scheme the agency said cost consumers five hundred million dollars over four years. And, of course, Neukom didn't have to remind Gates that elected officials exert the leverage of "access" to extort campaign contributions from millionaires.

Bundling? Disney bundles its weaker soap-opera cable network with its popular ESPN, telling cable operators they must carry the weak if they want to display the strong. John Malone's Tele-Communications, Inc., owned pieces of more than forty cable networks partly because Malone was granted part ownership of these networks. As Microsoft induced customers to sample its browser by leveraging it with Windows, so Sun Microsystems tied its HotJava browser so thoroughly into its operating system that you couldn't install one without the other.

So not to worry, Bill Neukom told his client.

Gates was reassured, for when it came to legal matters, Neukom had had Gates's ear for two decades. After all, when Microsoft and Apple had been locked in a bitter patent dispute, with Apple claiming that Microsoft had stolen key features of its pioneering operating system, it had been Neukom who had told Gates and anxious colleagues to ignore the bad press and pay attention to the law. He instructed his lawyers to be careful not to talk to reporters, to stick to the facts. The Apple case did much to establish his legal prestige at Microsoft, for during this protracted battle the press was nearly as negative as it was to be during the antitrust trial. Microsoft was going to lose, it was said. And the stakes were at least as high then—Microsoft was betting its survival on the outcome. The patient patrician insisted that the law was on their side. He resisted advice to mount a public-relations offensive, saying the court, not the press, was the jury that mattered. And Neukom's old-school approach to the law was vindicated. Six years later, in 1993, the courts ruled as Neukom had calmly predicted. "We prevailed by doing it by the numbers: briefs, affidavits, evidence, arguments in court, all aimed at persuading the judge," Neukom said at the time in Microsoft's company newsletter. Neukom may not have had the notches on his belt that Boies did, might not possess either Boies's notoriety or his brilliance, but Microsoft people were comforted that Bill Neukom had rarely lost and always acted as if he'd win. He was an accomplished marathon runner, always patiently pacing himself and measuring when the time was right to employ his final push to try to win the race. "He's unflappable," observed Vivek Varma, who once worked as a Democratic legislative aide on Capitol Hill before becoming a Microsoft attorney and a Neukom confidant. "He sees the big picture. He's used to running marathons. That's the mentality he brings to his job."

Like David Boies, Neukom is fifty-seven and like Boies has been married three times; he has four rather than six children. But beyond that, the contrast between these two men could not be starker. Neukom is six foot four and has wavy silver hair that does not flutter in breezes. Sartorially resplendent, he never wears the same hand-tailored suit twice in one week. His shirts are crisply starched, their sleeves fastened each day by different gold or silver cuff links, and his vivid assortment of bow ties seems inexhaustible. While Boies craves the craps table, *Star Trek* reruns, Coca-Colas, and the open-top Jeep Wrangler cross-country summer vacations he takes annually with at least one of his kids, Neukom is partial to jogging and fly-fishing, as well as to fine art, jazz, and three-star restaurants. Neukom is an avid environmentalist, philanthropist, and patron of the arts, and he serves as a director of the Oregon Shakespeare Festival, the Seattle Art Museum, and the Corporate Council for the Arts.

Good manners came naturally to Bill Neukom. He is a man of elaborate courtesies, a trait he no doubt derived from his grandfather, who was an attorney for the Northern Pacific Railroad, and from his father, who established and ran the San Francisco office of McKinsey & Company. Bill shone from the start, graduating near the top of his class at San Mateo High School and again at Dartmouth, where he majored in philosophy. Only at Stanford Law School did he sink into the middle of his class. Though he wasn't marked for legal greatness, as Boies was, and wasn't a lawyer the best national firms exhausted every avenue to recruit, he was an attractive catch.

After graduating, Neukom accepted a clerkship with a Seattle superior-court judge. As a naturalist, he was smitten by the beauty of the Pacific Northwest, and after his apprenticeship he chose to stay in the area, joining a liberal, civil rights–oriented law firm, MacDonald, Hoague & Bayless. He immersed himself in the local bar group's legal-aid bureau and other pro bono work. One of his oldest friends, New York attorney Richard D. Emery, who met Neukom in 1971, says of him, "He has the demeanor of being an establishment guy. He's not. He's a romantic. He's emotional." Neukom was a man-about-town, someone women swooned over, and his friends were of the left. He exited his law firm after he fell in love with a young associate there.

Out of a job and divorced from his first wife, Neukom was at a personal and professional low point. Then, through another civic-minded lawyer he had met, William H. Gates, he was invited to join the small Seattle firm of Shidler, McBroom, Gates & Lucas (now Preston, Gates & Ellis, still Microsoft's primary outside counsel), where he toiled mostly in real-estate and business-contract law and on a few criminal cases. In his pro bono work, he represented the NAACP Legal Defense and Education Fund and filed briefs on behalf of prisoners. He even ran as a liberal Democrat on a good-government platform for Washington State attorney general in 1980, losing a primary convincingly in the year of Ronald Reagan's landslide.

One day in 1978, William H. Gates strolled into Neukom's office and said, "My kid's bringing his little business up here to Seattle, and would you take a shot looking out for him?" Neukom recalls. "To this day, I don't know why he stopped by my door." Bill Gates's father remembers why. "The company was becoming more and more important to the law firm," he explained. "We needed someone to work with it—someone with good judgment, with very good people skills." Among the issues Neukom dealt with was the amending of the lease on Microsoft's offices to accommodate Gates's nocturnal habits. "I remember having to convince the landlord that Microsoft had to have twenty-four-hour access to the offices," Neukom once told the *National Law Journal*. For the next half decade or so, Neukom represented Microsoft, until the company got so big that he advised them they needed a legal department. In 1985, a year before Microsoft first sold its stock to the public, the department consisted of Neukom and two other employees. Fourteen years later, it consisted of more than four hundred employees, of whom about 150 were lawyers.

Over the years, Neukom became an eminence: a leader and national officer in the American Bar Association; a Dartmouth College and University of Puget Sound trustee; a member of the executive committee of the Greater Seattle Chamber of Commerce; a board member of the YMCA of Greater Seattle; a tireless promoter of Microsoft's philanthropic endeavors; a founder of the Neukom Family Foundation, which invests in education and health-care projects for the poor. Among his gifts to the foundation was, in June 1998, 96,500 shares of Microsoft stock valued at nearly $5.5 million. Although Neukom won't discuss the worth of his Microsoft stock options, a colleague who knows him well pegged his 1999 net worth at about $600 million. Like other Microsoft millionaires, he has invested in a sports team—in his case, the San Francisco Giants baseball team. Neukom serves as secretary to Microsoft's board, which means he attends Microsoft's board of directors meetings. In addition to the legal department, all of Microsoft's relations with governments, including lobbying and political-action-committee contributions, are part of his domain, as is corporate philanthropy and community relations. Within the engineering culture of Microsoft, some dismiss Neukom as a legal nerd or a slick bureaucrat, but like most general counsels he has one client that matters. While not personally close to Gates—unlike some other senior Microsoft executives, he was not invited to attend Gates's 1994 wedding—by most accounts, he commands his attention.

In the early stages of this antitrust litigation, Bill Neukom's confidence seemed to be vindicated. In May 1998, the federal Court of Appeals granted Microsoft's request to stay Judge Jackson's injunction, allowing Microsoft to ship Windows 98. Another victory came in June, when the higher court overturned Jackson's December ruling that under the

1994 consent decree Microsoft must separate its browser from Windows. In overturning Jackson, the higher court found that by adding features to Windows Microsoft was not in violation of the consent decree. Jackson, the higher court ruled, had "erred procedurally" by issuing an injunction before Microsoft was allowed to challenge it and had erred "substantively" by acting as if judges should try to "oversee product design." And, it admonished, "any dampening of technological innovation would be at cross-purposes with antitrust law." Instead of being hurt, the court said, consumers benefited from a free, easy-to-use integrated browser. In affirming Microsoft's right to integrate or bundle products, the court declared: "We suggest here only that the limited competence of courts to evaluate high-tech product designs and the high cost of error should make them wary of second-guessing the claimed benefits of a particular design decision." The higher court asked the district court to use these benchmarks in evaluating the evidence.

Microsoft was euphoric, in fact overly so. The higher court had specifically limited itself to judging the terms of the consent decree; it had noted that there had been no trial and no presentation of evidence. The court had not addressed the larger question of whether Microsoft was a rapacious monopolist. By and large, the press also failed to stress this point and raise this cautionary flag.

Nevertheless, it was a huge victory for Microsoft. Now, however, came the long, hard march. Judge Jackson had limited antitrust experience. He had presided over only two antitrust cases, and a reading of his rulings offered no indication of how he would rule in this case. Bill Neukom had to be encouraged when he read Jackson's first antitrust ruling, a 1983 case* in which the Association for Intercollegiate Athletics for Women sued the National Collegiate Athletic Association. The AIAW charged that when the NCAA decided to include women's college sports in its membership, it had, in a predatory fashion, used its vast economic power to drive the smaller AIAW out of business, even insisting that the purchase of television rights to its popular men's-basketball championships must include the purchase of the women's championships. Citing the so-called good-monopoly precedents of both the 1966 *Grinnell* case and the 1979 *Berkey Photo* case, Judge Jackson rejected the lawsuit and ruled that the NCAA's actions "originated with its members" and

Association for Intercollegiate Athletics for Women v. NCAA.

were "the antithesis of the conspiratorial plotting of a would-be monop-olist to acquire surreptitious control of a market. . . ." Neukom also had to be pleased to read Judge Jackson's 1987 ruling in *U.S. v. General Motors Corp.* In this non-antitrust case, Jackson rejected highly techni-cal claims that the automobile giant should be held responsible for man-ufacturing a car with rear brakes that sometimes prematurely locked up the wheels and should recall and repair these and pay damages. School-ing himself in the arcana of automotive engineering, Jackson showed he did not harbor a reflexive hostility to corporate Goliaths, ruling that the evidence produced against GM was "anecdotal," not scientific, and that science revealed no such defect.

David Boies, on the other hand, could locate Jackson cases that offered encouragement to the government, most notably Jackson's 1983 decision against AT&T (*Jack Faucett Associates v. AT&T*), in which he ruled that the telephone giant attempted to monopolize trade by impos-ing an illegal charge to interconnect non-Bell equipment to AT&T's. Jackson found AT&T guilty of "predatory conduct," of acting in "bad faith," and of "intentionally delaying the provision and installation of interface devices." He found that AT&T's behavior had unfairly impeded competition, much as Microsoft would be accused of doing by failing to provide in a timely manner the Windows software code on which com-panies depended. (This decision was later reversed by the Court of Appeals, and AT&T reached a settlement with the plaintiffs.) Boies and the government also had to be pleased with a 1986 ruling (*FTC v. PPG Industries, Inc., and Swedlow, Inc.*) in which Jackson cautioned against the merger of two airplane-parts manufacturers that together had a 53 per-cent share of the market in aircraft windows. "Experience teaches," Jackson wrote, "that without worthy rivals ready to exploit lapses in competitive intensity, incentives to develop better products, to keep prices at a minimum, and to provide efficient service over the long term are all diminished to the detriment of consumers. . . . Among the dan-gers to competition is that the leading firm will engage in predatory pric-ing, the practice whereby it lowers prices until all competitors are driven from the market and then increases prices without fear of being under-sold." Although Jackson allowed the merger to proceed, he subjected it to a "hold separate" order that required the companies to remain inde-pendent until antitrust proceedings were completed.

Regardless of how Jackson's paper trail was parsed, Bill Gates remained distraught. He did not, he told me in an e-mail exchange, "expect competitors to try and use the government to help them get an advantage over us." He went on, "You are welcome to say I was naïve about this." He was shocked that his government had sued him and that it kept broadening the charges, shifting the thrust of its case from bundling to coercion. He was shocked to find the government hunched over his shoulder. And Gates, who always thought his work advanced a social good, was also shocked to find himself demonized. He began to feel sorry for himself, to think of himself as a martyr. Friends compared him to Joseph K. in Franz Kafka's novel *The Trial*—a man charged with vague crimes he does not comprehend. On the eve of his own trial, Gates moaned to friends, "This isn't justice!"

Several friends urged Gates to settle with the government. Over dinner, John F. Welch, the chairman and CEO of General Electric, pleaded with his business partner in MSNBC to seek a truce. A personal friend of Gates who also urged him to settle said the reason he didn't is composed of one part innocence and one part adolescence: "Bill is naïve. He should have seen the freight train coming down the track at him." Blinded by principle—for years he wouldn't buy influence in Washington with campaign donations, and he fervently believed government was wrong to bring this lawsuit, said the friend—Gates innocently betrayed his own hard-core principles. The adolescent in Gates exacerbated matters. The friend recalled a game of charades he once played with Gates. "Bill can be a bad sport at games," he reflected. On this occasion, Gates was losing badly, when suddenly, in the verbal equivalent of turning over the game board, he halted the game and accused his friends of cheating: " 'You're not allowed to do that! Wait a minute! This is an infraction!' If he couldn't win, he'd find an infraction. It was absurd. But when you think about it, it all fits: 'The government is wrong! They're just wrong!' "

With the benefit of hindsight, Gates and Microsoft don't seem hardcore at all; they seem naïve and impractical. Had Microsoft crafted a compromise that allowed PC manufacturers to offer, without restrictions, competitive browsers, or had it waived its restrictive contracts, as it did belatedly in the spring of 1998, Microsoft might have avoided a lawsuit. The government, David Boies told me, was willing to reach a much more modest settlement in May 1998 than after the lawsuit was filed. And as the case progressed, the government's proposed remedies were to become more severe.

And Microsoft knew that not to settle would have enormous negative repercussions. Microsoft would endure a loud, long, debilitating trial. Its good brand name would be tarnished. Valuable executive time would be diverted. The government would insert into the court record millions of pages of Microsoft documents and affidavits, potentially available as evidence to others who might sue. Had Microsoft settled, this evidence would have been sealed.

Microsoft confronted another risk: might its drive and passion subside as it was forced to perpetually keep the government in its rearview mirror, as happened to IBM for thirteen years and to AT&T for eight? By the time the Reagan administration abandoned the lawsuit, IBM was no longer dominant; exhausted by its legal struggle, AT&T decided in 1984 to end its ordeal and voluntarily break itself up. "The filing of a lawsuit traditionally does two things to the defendant and one thing to its competitor," William Kovacic of George Washington University Law School told me. It makes the defendant "somewhat more tentative and restrained in how it responds to business developments," and it diverts its attention, which becomes "a form of internal, silent bleeding that saps a company's strength. That's what happened to IBM. IBM triumphed over the government. It crushed its challenger in court. But, in a sense, it was a Pyrrhic victory. What it does to your competition is embolden them a bit."

On the eve of the trial, Bill Neukom disagreed. "The culture won't change," he told me. "Bill and Steve [Ballmer] won't let it change." Legal battles are nothing new for Gates and company. "Bill is never going to let the lawyers run this company. And the lawyers understand the magic of this passion for technology."

CHAPTER 3

The First Pitch

J UST BEFORE 10 A.M. on October 19, 1998, David Boies entered the blocklong, eight-story E. Barrett Prettyman United States Courthouse for the District of Columbia, rode the elevator to the second floor, strode past a line of reporters parked against a marble wall waiting to vie for the forty daily press seats and past an even longer line of potential spectators against the opposite wall, and entered Courtroom 2. Although Courtroom 20 was nearly twice as large, Judge Jackson wanted to conduct this trial in the same thirty-eight feet by fifty-eight feet courtroom in which Judge John J. Sirica had tried the Watergate defendants nearly twenty-five years previously.

The courtroom was dignified, if a bit dowdy. Five rows of walnut benches face the elevated platform from which the judge presides. The stately white marble walls rise two stories to an arched ceiling of white acoustic tiles, some loose or smudged with soot, crisscrossed with tubes of fluorescent lights and aluminum vents. There are no windows or street noises; cove lighting radiates through ten squares cut from slabs of stone that are as functional as the marble is grand. A short, swinging walnut gate separates the press and public from the participants, who cluster around two long tables. The government lawyers sat to the left, facing the judge, the Microsoft lawyers to the right. The jury box was occupied by sketch artists, who provided pictures of the trial as a substitute for the cameras that were not allowed in court. On a single bench behind Boies sat other government officials, including Joel Klein.

David Boies had stayed up late the night before, not to rehearse an opening statement but to watch the New York Yankees glide to victory in the second game of the 1998 World Series. Such behavior typified Boies's apparent effortlessness. As he entered the courtroom, Boies wore the same outfit he was to wear each day of the trial: a boxy navy suit with slightly overlong pants that draped over black sneakers, a nondescript blue and white pinstriped button-down shirt, a square-bottomed dark blue knit tie, which dangled above his beltless waist, and a thirty-five-dollar black Casio strapped over his left cuff, so he could read the time without suggesting to a judge or jury that he was bored or rushed. The suits, shirts, and ties were purchased in batches from Lands' End by his wife, Mary. Boies, like Gates, wasn't one to waste time deciding what to wear. Nor did he waste time worrying about the thinning brown hair that rested on his protruding ears, or about stocking the refrigerator in the modest apartment in the Landsburgh, a rental within walking distance of the courthouse for which the Justice Department pays (one of a dozen apartments it rents for lawyers and staff members from its San Francisco office). If she didn't plan to take off from her own legal practice one day a week to visit him and shop for food, Mary Boies fretted, her husband might forget to eat.

Despite his casual demeanor, however, Boies's intensity is such that he often walks past associates without noticing them. Like Bill Gates, he is a fierce competitor. Playing tennis, Ping-Pong, or pool, he plays to win, as he does in Las Vegas or Atlantic City. "When he plays craps," said Mary Boies, "he remembers every roll, every sequence. His whole thing is to try and reduce the house edge."

Another reason Boies commanded attention was that his reputation preceded him. In the 1985 *Westmoreland* case, each side was allotted one hundred hours to present its case. Boies slyly seduced the opposing counsel, Dan M. Burt, into keeping an effective CBS witness, producer George Crile, on the stand rather than summon more vulnerable network witnesses. At each break, Boies assured Burt of the brilliance of his cross-examination. *But couldn't you speed it up,* he beseeched Burt, so that CBS could call Mike Wallace and senior network brass to the stand?

By the time Burt was finished with Crile, he had consumed much of his allotted time, one reason Westmoreland subsequently dropped the suit. "He was a very skillful lawyer; I would use the word 'brilliant,'" General Westmoreland later told David Margolick of *Vanity Fair.** "I wished I'd had one like him." In the IBM monopoly case, Boies induced the government to withdraw its legal challenge. In his first antitrust defense of IBM, Boies did his best Columbo impersonation, seeming forgetful and disorganized. Initially, IBM executives worried about his eccentric work habits and that he was jetting off to Las Vegas on the weekends. Boies was pitted against one of California's savviest litigators, Maxwell Blecher, who represented California Computer Products. Blecher took a liking to the charming Boies and relaxed his guard. When Blecher rested his case, Boies stunned the courtroom by moving for dismissal, producing for the judge an exhaustive analysis of why the case was tissue thin. After lunch, the judge dismissed the case.

Boies settled in the seat at the end of the government table, facing Judge Jackson's empty leather chair. Klein was seated directly behind him, and Phillip Malone sat at the far end of the government table next to files of documents; other state and Justice lawyers were arrayed around the table. The three principals divided their task neatly: Klein served as chief strategist; Malone developed the facts; and Boies commanded the courtroom. Boies saw it as analogous to the U.S. Army in World War II: "Think of Klein as Eisenhower, Malone as Omar Bradley, and me as Patton."

To Boies's right, the corresponding seat at the Microsoft table was filled by William Neukom. Unlike Boies, however, Neukom was to remain silent throughout the trial, though he was present every day. He would not examine a single witness. He passed notes to his legal team, kept a record on yellow legal pads in his left-handed script, neatly folding back each page after he'd filled it. He attended all conferences with the judge, though Judge Jackson later recalled that he had been confused about Neukom's true role because Neukom rarely spoke a word. But it was Neukom whom Microsoft spokesman Mark Murray and his p.r. team consulted before going on the court steps to spin reporters.

Unlike the other Microsoft attorneys, who invariably wore somber charcoal or navy suits, Neukom often entered court wearing earth tones or plaids, though he sometimes wore expensive double-breasted char-

*David Margolick, "The Man Who Ate Microsoft," *Vanity Fair*, March 2000.

coals. This morning, as he always would, he politely held the gate for an opposing lawyer. Never did he appear rushed as he glided through the courtroom, rarely pausing to speak but always bestowing a gentle half smile. In sharp contrast to the accommodations of the government lawyers from out of town, Neukom boarded his entire legal and public-relations entourage at Georgetown's tony Four Seasons Hotel. And in sharp contrast to Boies and Jeff Blattner, Neukom and his team kept a respectful but frosty distance from the press.

Neukom relied on the blue-chip Wall Street law firm Sullivan & Cromwell. Neukom's designated "quarterback," as he liked to call him, was partner John Warden, an experienced appellate attorney with an affable manner who was the victorious counsel in *Berkey Photo v. Eastman Kodak*. His play caller, or "architect" was partner Richard J. Urowsky, a brilliant legal scholar with sparse black hair cut to an eighth of an inch, a tightly cropped beard, and a brusque, brittle manner. After graduating near the top of his class at Yale and attending Oxford for a degree in philosophy and then the Yale Law School, Urowsky clerked for retired Supreme Court Justice Stanley F. Reed, joined Sullivan & Cromwell, and became a partner in 1980, when he was thirty-four. Because of Urowsky's courtroom demeanor—he could barely conceal his contempt for both Judge Sporkin and Judge Jackson—Neukom substituted Warden, Urowsky's best friend, as lead counsel.

Neukom described his own role as that of a coach: "I've got to put the right team on the field." Sullivan & Cromwell partner Michael Lacovara, also a member of the defense team, put a different twist on Neukom's role: "A general manager is a better description. He was not arranging the outfielders. He was selecting, listening, and participating in major decisions, and otherwise letting the trial lawyers try the case." Either way, his role was uncommon, for usually a corporation's chief counsel maintains more distance from the playing field. In the IBM case, Sam Butler of Cravath said, General Counsel Nicholas Katzenbach did not sit at the defense table because he "wasn't a trial lawyer" and "had confidence in his team," and he wanted to be able to see over the treetops. As the trial unfolded, there was reason to question whether Neukom was too close to see the whole field.

At precisely 10 A.M. the door to the judge's corridor opened and Deputy Marshal R. Kirkland Bowden, who has worked in this court since 1962, called out, "All rise," as Judge Thomas Penfield Jackson entered and ascended his platform. When Jackson stopped behind the high-backed chair that was his throne, Bowden's rich baritone enveloped the courtroom: "All persons having business before the United States District Court Judge Thomas Penfield Jackson, now conducting civil trial, will draw a nigh and give their attention. God save the United States of America and this honored court. Please come to order."

Attention was paid to Judge Jackson's round, bulldog face, his thin gold-framed glasses, which glimmer, the friendly way he nodded with a welcoming smile to each table of attorneys. Jackson looked tanned and refreshed. A few inches shy of six feet tall, from the neck down Jackson looks like a barrel-chested high-school football coach, his belly pressing against his belt. From the neck up, he carries the distinguished mien of a jurist, his white hair highlighted by his black robe. While Jackson can display a deep, authoritative voice, spectators usually have to lean forward, straining to hear; what most spectators cannot see is that he has a small flesh-colored hearing aid in his right ear, which might account for his quiet voice. Jackson, 62, was the first judge appointed by President Reagan to this district court. *The Washington Post* once reported that Jackson was on Reagan's short list for the Court of Appeals but was passed over perhaps because he was a member of the then whites-only Chevy Chase Club. (Jackson admits race was decisive, but in a different way: "I was a white male. They were looking for people representative of the community. And I was not.") When appointed, Jackson was the president-elect of the District of Columbia Bar Association and a partner at Jackson & Campbell, a litigation firm founded by his father, Thomas S. Jackson, who also had headed the District of Columbia Bar Association.

Despite his conservative pedigree, Jackson was raised in a home where government was revered. His father's father came from upstate New York to the nation's capital to work for the Commerce Department; his mother's father moved to Washington from a town outside Pittsburgh when he joined the Bureau of Standards as a chemical engineer. FDR was a family hero. His parents met as students at George Washington University. "Pen," as he was called, was the first of two sons raised in a modest house in then rural Kensington, Maryland. While his father built a law firm and made a name for himself when appointed by the governor to serve as president of the Montgomery County School Board, his mother was the taskmaster, beseeching her sons to read, reciting poetry from memory, instructing them on proper table manners. In public school, Pen's sweet soprano voice earned him a choir scholarship to St. Albans. When his voice dropped an octave or two, he lost his scholarship and switched to public high school, where he played football and coedited the newspaper. "I was convinced I would be a journalist," he remembers. At Dartmouth College, where he received a Navy ROTC scholarship, he decided to study law.

After graduating with honors, Jackson served as a junior deck officer on a destroyer in the Atlantic. He exited the service a lieutenant and married a Mount Holyoke student he had met while in college; they would parent two daughters. He enrolled at Harvard Law School, in 1961, where he was forced to adjust in ways he never anticipated. "For the first time, at Harvard I encountered people who were indisputably more intelligent than I was," he recalled. He had always stood out academically, but not here, not with classmates such as Stephen Breyer, who was to rise to the Supreme Court, or Richard A. Posner, who was a senior and president of the *Law Review* when Jackson was a first-year student and who became chief judge of the Seventh Circuit Court of Appeals. Jackson wondered whether he should return to the Navy. "It was a very unique experience in my life," he said, revealing the serenity that became apparent as the Microsoft trial unfolded. "In an incoming class of four to five hundred students, everyone was an outstanding scholar at their college. I adjusted. I just acknowledged there were people smarter than I am. The fact that you're not on *Law Review* doesn't signal the end of the world."

He joined his father's firm in Washington, where, he said, he learned that "I was a much better trial lawyer than I was a Harvard law student." He also learned that his father was determined not to favor his son and was unrelentingly tough on him and cheap with compliments, keeping him at arm's length. As a trial lawyer, Jackson specialized in medical-malpractice suits, usually defending insurance companies and hospitals. "He was one of the premier trial lawyers," said Nick McConnell, his former partner and a friend with whom, until recently, he co-owned a thirty-five-foot sailboat. "A very elegant presence in the courtroom. He could explain complicated material without people feeling condescended to." Patricia Gurne, who joined the firm in 1971, remembered, "He didn't go in and act like a cowboy. Both he and his father deplored ad hominem attacks on other lawyers. They thought of

themselves as barristers; it was the clients' cause, not yours." To this
day, Jackson describes as "one of the big honors of my life" the day he
was welcomed into the American College of Trial Lawyers, a kind of
hall of fame now peopled by five thousand luminaries, including John
Warden.

Unlike his father, who did not switch party allegiances until later in
life, Pen Jackson aligned early with the Republican party. "My first political hero was Barry Goldwater," he explained. "I thought, What he's
saying made such eminent good sense. I remember liking the guy. He
gave straight answers. The guy he reminds me most of today is John
McCain." Inspired by Goldwater, Jackson became precinct chairman of
the minority party in Montgomery County. In 1972, a law partner at the
firm, Kenneth Parkinson, recruited him to defend the Committee to Re-
elect President Nixon against civil suits attempting to force CREEP, as the
committee was known, to disclose its campaign contributions. He was a
lean and dashing figure with dark, wavy hair and was enjoying his
moment in the sun. Then the Watergate case heated up and suddenly
friends were getting indicted. He believed the president and the attorney
general and the White House chief of staff wouldn't lie, and he was
wrong. He came away, he remembers, with "a highly personal dislike for
Richard Nixon. The man's conduct was reprehensible throughout."

This experience helped shape the way Judge Jackson viewed those
with power. The Nixon experience taught him "the importance of being
unwilling to be impressed by the stature of the litigant before me," he
explained. "So what if you're the secretary of state? I'm not so much in
awe of people and power. I think I'm a lot more cynical about motiva-
tion." Surprisingly, he is not as cynical about the government and makes
this sweeping statement: "I trust the lawyers from the Department of
Justice. I trust civil servants and the U.S. attorneys. I'm not hostile to
government." He continued, "In criminal cases, by and large, my experience is that when the government charges someone, they are probably
guilty. I give the benefit of presumptive innocence, but I know of no case
of a wrongful conviction."

Throughout the seventies, Jackson remained a staunch conservative.
In the 1980 primary battle between Ronald Reagan and George Bush,
he sided with Reagan. Jackson's name was subsequently on the list circulated for consideration for judicial appointment in Washington, D.C.,
by the new president. The list was short. "The D.C. Republican party

doesn't meet in Yankee Stadium each year!" joked Fred Fielding, Reagan's White House counsel from 1981 to 1986. "He was a good lawyer. He had a sense of humor. He was interested in many things." And Jackson was interested in getting the appointment. Former partner James Schaller, who joined the firm in 1968, remembers that Pen "was very interested in becoming a judge. He certainly loves being boss, and that aspect of being a judge appeals to him." A principal allure of serving as a district-court judge, Jackson told me, is the power entrusted in a single judge both to decide single-handedly whether a Microsoft was innocent or guilty of antitrust violations and to craft a remedy. "I think it's the best legal job there is, with the possible exception of being on the Supreme Court," Jackson said. "I don't know how this will sound, but I think it's largely because of the power that the office presented. And it isn't because I'm particularly enamored with the feeling of having the power, but it's the ability to produce consequences that seem to be eminently right. I have always viewed the offices of the U.S. District Court judge as the second most powerful office in the country."

When he left Jackson & Campbell, it employed twenty attorneys, and he was earning about two hundred thousand dollars a year. Jackson—like David Boies and Bill Neukom—has been thrice married. But unlike them, his salary as a district-court judge is a mere $141,003. "I'm a lot more mellow than I used to be," he said. "One factor that certainly changed me, certainly since 1991, is that for the first time I have a good marriage." His wife, Patricia, is director of development at Sidwell Friends School. They live in an apartment complex, with a Norwich terrier, and each weekend they drive to a home on the water in St. Mary's County, Maryland, where they sail, garden, and read, his taste tending to all things British, especially to the twenty sea novels of Patrick O'Brian.

On the surface, Jackson appears a safe conformist, an upright member of the Rotary Club, the vestry of All Saints' Episcopal Church, the Chevy Chase Club, and the Metropolitan Club. At the end of his workday, he often races to catch the train in order to walk his dog. Yet he is also a man of steely conviction, for whom defending President Nixon was just his first taste of notoriety. In 1986, he ruled that it was unconstitutional for his benefactor, President Reagan, to unilaterally defy the intent of Congress and impound more than two billion dollars of Housing and Urban Development Department expenditures approved by Congress.

Although Jackson privately believed a president should have line-item veto power, he said, "I held that it was unconstitutional because the Supreme Court was clear on the law." In 1988, he upheld the special-prosecutors law, rejecting former Reagan aide Michael Deaver's suit to block his indictment for perjury. In 1990, Jackson presided over the drug trial of former Washington mayor Marion Barry, provoking a storm of publicity—and a later rebuke from the Court of Appeals—when he ordered that Reverend George A. Stallings and Nation of Islam leader Louis Farrakhan not attend the trial for fear that they would sway the jury, as well as when he expressed disgust that the jury convicted Barry on only one of fourteen counts. For Barry's drug use and perjury, Jackson handed down the maximum sentence allowed. "Had I been able to give him more, I would have," he told me. (The Court of Appeals found that Jackson's sentence was too Draconian, and gently asked him to review it. He did, and reinstated his original sentence.) In 1993, Jackson ordered then Republican senator Robert Packwood of Oregon, who was accused of sexual harassment, to turn over his diaries, following a request by a Senate ethics committee.

Because he had generally kept a low profile and shunned the press, Jackson is a jurist about whom people say opposite things. He is said to be lazy, and he is said to be vigorous; a plodder and a quick study; a techno-logical caveman and a man unafraid of technology; a blustery bully and a fair-minded stickler for procedures. He is said to be tough on drug deal-ers and soft on white-collar miscreants. The fact is, Jackson was a mys-tery to most in his courtroom. An oft-repeated claim about him turns out to be untrue. Throughout the trial, reporters said that when he broke for lunch he dined most days with the swells at the Metropolitan Club. In fact, said his friend and colleague Judge Thomas Hogan, who was also appointed by Reagan in 1982, as a rule Jackson and Hogan and anywhere from four to ten judges brought bag lunches and chipped in to pay a part-time worker to fetch sodas or food and to clean up. They ate in a windowless sixth-floor room with a wall sign that read: ANYTHING SAID HERE IS NOT TAKEN OUT.

Privately, Microsoft feared that Judge Jackson was a foe. He had made a number of pretrial rulings deemed hostile to the company. They were especially unhappy that he modified an August 6, 1998, pretrial order that depositions "shall be submitted only in transcript form," issuing a new order on October 9 allowing videotaped depositions—notably Bill

Gates's pretrial deposition—to be played in court and the portions played thus be open to the press. Although there were precedents for this—videotaped depositions had been allowed in IBM's antitrust case—Microsoft suspected that Justice had somehow prevailed on Jackson to amend his earlier ruling. Jackson categorically denied this, but does not recall exactly why he issued the October 9 ruling. It also infuriated Microsoft that Jackson allowed Justice to expand its antitrust charges with new allegations unmentioned in the original lawsuit. (In fact, legal complaints are often amended and expanded.) They groused—only in the most unguarded private moments because they were terrified of offending him—that Jackson was biased and would rule in favor of the government.

Jackson ruled his courtroom with a tight fist. Before this trial began, Jackson announced his intention to speed it along by limiting to twelve the number of witnesses each side could call and by stipulating that all testimony be submitted in written form, so that all cross-examinations could occur without delay. He also skipped what would have been a prolonged effort to get both sides to agree to a set of court-stipulated facts, as is often done in antitrust trials.

While Jackson had a luxurious lifetime appointment, he was not liberated from pressure. He had the daily burden in this trial of learning a new language—terms such as *OS, browser, API, middleware, broadband, OEM, XML,* and so on. He had a knot of complicated facts to untangle: did Microsoft really gain on Netscape because Internet Explorer was technically superior to Netscape Navigator, as Microsoft claimed, or did Microsoft gain because they coerced companies, as Netscape claimed? This was no easy task for Jackson, who doesn't use e-mail or a browser or a PC. Privately, Microsoft was convinced Jackson was uncomfortable with technology, and therefore it worried that he couldn't comprehend the case. Jackson, however, insisted he was undaunted. He believed he was capable of learning on the job, just as he had done as a lawyer in complex medical-malpractice cases. In addition to learning a new language, Jackson knew that the Court of Appeals, which had already reversed him on the appointment of a special master and on the tying issue, would be looking over his shoulder. (On average, the Court of Appeals reversed about 11 percent of this district court's decisions.) Finally, Jackson had the weight of history to think about. Jackson knew that this was the case of a lifetime. Jackson had presided over cases that attracted media firestorms, but none that might be deemed truly historic. "Many people have referred to it as the biggest thing since the *Standard Oil* case," Jackson told me. "I don't know that. It is the biggest case I've ever had."

"This ranks with one of the great antitrust cases in the history of the Sherman Act," observed George L. Priest, the John M. Olin Professor of Law and Economics at Yale Law School. The questions the Microsoft trial would grapple with fell into four broad categories: technology; politics; economics; and the law. The crucial technology issue was this: in the Information Age, is the notion of a monopoly rendered antique because classic monopoly characteristics—rising prices, control of finite resources, distribution barriers to entry, availability of capital, and choke-holds on innovations—are not as apparent, even if the allegations of coercive tactics are familiar? With ideas, is it not possible for someone in a garage or a university computer lab to invent a new product—as Netscape's founders had—and get funding and instantly seize the market? Or can a giant such as Microsoft employ its power and its "applications barrier to entry" and sabotage the upstart? Bill Neukom said he does not believe that big companies can seriously impede great new ideas. Although he does not claim that antitrust laws can never apply to software, Neukom is dubious; even should a company forge a monopoly, he does not believe it would be durable. "Technology is a little like mercury," he said. "As I sit here thinking of the technology business, I can't imagine a monopoly because technology is so fluid."

And unlike, say, Standard Oil, which owned the oil as well as the refineries, the pipelines, and the railroads to distribute it, how can one claim a software monopoly when the world's most potent distribution system (the Internet) is open to all and capital to fund start-ups is plentiful? But is it open? What if the owners of the broadband wires jigger the architecture so that they control the tollbooth, as the cable companies did? If broadband competition is as scarce as cable or telephone competition once was, control will reside with a few giants. But if there are truly multiple broadband choices—the cable, telephone, fiber-optic, satellite, and wireless connections—then power resides with the customer who has choices, not the gatekeeper. Yet what happens if corporate elephants—AT&T, Microsoft, America Online, Disney, the Baby Bells, GE, etc.—have the wealth to buy the competition or to use their potent brand name to try to dominate Internet commerce? What if the brand matters more than the technology? What if Microsoft—with nearly twenty billion dollars in excess cash in late 1998, plus a stock valuation that permitted it to swallow most companies—or America Online, with an inflated stock value exceeding that of General Motors, decided to overpay to buy a potential competitor? What if the goal of mice is not to compete but to get bought by an elephant?

These questions spill over into the political realm. There are those who thought this court was a proper forum to argue—as the state attorneys general did in their briefs to the court—that government should intervene because Microsoft's profits and profit margins are "excessive" and thus betray their monopoly position. Two questions surface immediately: first, who determines what is excessive? And if government is going to police profits, who will aspire to enter such a business? It has long been a shibboleth of the political left that government must attack concentrations of corporate power. This was the view expressed in a famous 1948 Supreme Court dissent by New Dealer Justice William O. Douglas:*

> [Size] is the measure of the power of a handful of men over our economy. That power can be utilized with lightning speed. It can be benign or it can be dangerous. The philosophy of the Sherman Act is that it should not exist. For all power tends to develop into a government in itself. Power that controls the economy should be in the hands of elected representatives of the people, not in the hands of an industrial oligarchy.

For Douglas's view to prevail, the political climate in America would have to shift. Today, business leaders are often icons, celebrities, though there is some evidence this may be changing. Polls taken in the fall of 2000, for example, reveal a growing public antipathy toward Big insurance and pharmaceutical companies, Big tobacco, Big oil, Big tire companies like Firestone, Big HMOs. Nevertheless, the courts have moved farther away from the populism animating Douglas and preached by both Republicans and Democrats at the end of the nineteenth century. This is where a third issue—economics—intrudes. This political shift reflects more than a movement toward economic conservatism. It also reflects a change in the economics profession, away from

*United States v. Columbia Steel Co.

the sweeping theories of Adam Smith, Karl Marx, John Maynard Keynes, or Milton Friedman and toward what advocates say is a search for empirical evidence and critics say is just economic theory disguised as science. Today, fewer economists believe that a handful of oligarchs can control the American economy. They perceive a different economy, in which global competitors have emerged; in which size often poses its own limitations, including an inability to keep pace with smaller, more agile competitors; in which there can be "good" monopolies that enjoy less competition but deliver common benefits, such as the shared Internet plumbing of Cisco Systems, the common operating system of Microsoft Windows, or the telephone wires of the Baby Bells, which usually serve as a common carrier; and in which technological development can, in an instant, level the playing field. History shows that by the time creaky governments decide to address a problem, sometimes the passage of time has solved it. This happened with IBM, which was no longer a monopoly thirteen years after its antitrust battle began. Arguably, it happened with Standard Oil, as Ron Chernow observed in his biography of Rockefeller, *Titan*. By the time the court ordered the breakup, Standard Oil's market share of oil refining had slipped from 86 to 70 percent, and its share of crude oil had slumped from 32 to 14 percent.

The movement of economics toward empiricism dovetails with the movement of the law. The exemplar of economics as applied to antitrust law is probably Richard A. Posner. Long before joining the Seventh Circuit Court of Appeals in 1981, first as a professor of law at the University of Chicago and as an author, Posner had expressed unhappiness with the widening definitions of antitrust laws. There was an appetite, he believed, particularly in the sixties and seventies, to equate big with bad. He believed the antitrust laws were meant to address economic behavior and should not be burdened with the political or social whims of judges. In his influential 1976 book, *Antitrust Law: An Economic Perspective*, Posner dismissed the operative terms of antitrust law—*restraint of trade, substantially to lessen competition,* and *monopolize*—as too opaque. He wrote:

> the congressional debates and reports that preceded their enactment, and the other relevant historical materials, only dimly illuminate the intended meaning of the key terms. The courts have spent many years

interpreting, or perhaps more accurately supplying, their meaning, but the course of judicial interpretation has been so marked by contradiction and ambiguity as to leave the law in an exceedingly uncertain and fluid state.

Calling for a "thorough rethinking" of antitrust law, Posner stipulated that "the essential intellectual tool for this process of rethinking ... is the science of economics." The sole test of whether the antitrust laws have been traduced pivots on economics. Did the monopoly promote economic efficiency, or did it harm consumers by impeding competition? Even if the company monopolized an industry or controlled prices, if it produced superior products or promoted economic efficiency, then this was a good monopoly. Posner insisted that courts should not intervene unless real economic facts demonstrated consumer harm.

As companies merge and competition becomes global, courts have broadened their lens and now gauge the international as well as the domestic competition a company confronts. Increasingly, judges wonder whether monopolies don't die of their own weight. Business historian and theorist Peter Drucker argues that throughout history no monopoly has lived for more than fifteen years. Think back to the early days of the computer, when the dominant companies were Wang, DEC, IBM, Burroughs, Remington Rand, Unisys, and Kaypro—all since eclipsed. Increasingly, the courts—like many of us—worry that a government remedy for a corporate monopoly may be worse than the disease it's meant to cure. For Microsoft, these trends offered good news on the antitrust front and bad news on the competitive front.

From day one, the Microsoft trial highlighted the blurry nature of antitrust law. Courts don't speak with a single voice, and the rapid march of technology increases the blur, as judges are left to contemplate whether to impose penalties or to assume that the swift currents of technological change and a marketplace whose foundations float in quicksand will inevitably punish a monopolist. Increasingly, George Priest noted, the courts look at not just the size of a company but the nature of the competition, not just crude corporate behavior but whether consumer prices have dropped. One influential decision in shaping antitrust thinking was written in 1984 by a liberal Democrat, Stephen Breyer, now a Supreme Court justice who then served on the

First Circuit Court of Appeals. In *Kartell v. Blue Shield,* he wrote: "The Congress that enacted the Sherman Antitrust Act saw it as a way of protecting consumers against prices that were too *high*, not too low. . . . Courts at least should be cautious—reluctant to condemn too speedily—an arrangement that, on its face, appears to bring low price benefits to the consumers."

New technologies inevitably invite new questions about government's proper role, and the Microsoft trial promised to be the nation's laboratory for choosing between old law and new.

CHAPTER 4

Opening Salvos

ON THE FIRST DAY OF THE TRIAL, after a flurry of procedural maneuvers, David Boies stepped to the microphone and lectern in front of Judge Jackson to make the government's opening argument. Mary Boies looked on from the spectator section; Joel Klein, the bald top of his restless head bobbing, shifted in his aisle bench seat. Bill Neukom sat with his chin up, staring straight ahead, his tortoiseshell glasses on the tip of his nose, his Mont Blanc pen and legal pad poised.

For nearly three hours, glancing occasionally at a few subject headings he had jotted on a manila folder, Boies told a story, first in summary form and then in chronological order, of how he believed Microsoft had violated the antitrust laws. He focused on the Sherman Act, first section 1, which is concerned with "restraint of trade or commerce" by corporations who form trusts or use contracts to harm competitors and to protect a monopoly, and then section 2, which is aimed at individual companies that are monopolies or that use unfair means to preserve their power. Boies said he would show that Microsoft bundled its browser in with its dominating operating system in order to unreasonably restrain Netscape, which had been the dominant browser for navigating the Internet and was perceived as a broad threat to Microsoft, a violation of both sections. He said he would show that Microsoft used its control over operating systems to impose contracts on PC manufacturers and on ISPs (Internet-service providers, such as the telephone companies, America Online, or Prodigy) and on ICPs (Internet-content providers such as Intuit, the market leader in financial-services software) that hindered their freedom to do business with Netscape if they wanted continued access to Windows. Coercion, he claimed, was standard operating procedure at Bill Gates's Microsoft.

Since Netscape was the foremost victim, Boies called CEO James Barksdale as the government's first witness. He would then follow with other alleged victims: executives from America Online, Apple, Sun, Intel, IBM, and Intuit; and, after establishing how Microsoft had harmed competition and consumers, he would summon economists, who would show why Microsoft qualified as a monopoly. But Boies's most vital witness would be Bill Gates, who wasn't even listed as one. Boies did not assume, as did Bill Neukom, that only the facts mattered. He believed a complicated case such as this rested on credibility, and in Gates he believed he had a strikingly noncredible witness.

With a nod of his head, Boies signaled an aide, and Gates's image appeared on the large, flat screen to the judge's left, on a TV monitor at the judge's desk, and on two monitors facing the spectators. It was the first of many excerpts from Gates's three-day videotaped deposition that Boies would play—excerpts that gave a portrait of Gates utterly at odds with the decisive, fearless straight shooter of common lore. Slouched in a leather chair, compulsively sipping from a can of Diet Coke, Gates was taken by Boies through a June 21, 1995, meeting between Netscape and Microsoft executives at which Microsoft is alleged to have offered to divide the browser market. Gates professed ignorance: "My only knowledge of that" was when he read about it much later in *The Wall Street Journal*, he said.

BOIES: Are you aware of any instances in which representatives of Microsoft have met with competitors in an attempt to allocate markets?

GATES: I am not aware of any such thing, and I know it's very much against the way we operate. . . .

BOIES: Now have you ever read the complaint in this case?

GATES: No. . . .

BOIES: Do you know whether in the complaint there are allegations concerning a 1995 meeting between Netscape and Microsoft representatives relating to alleged market-division discussions?

GATES: I haven't read the complaint, so I don't know for sure. But I think somebody said that that's in there.

More than a few spectators guffawed at Gates's professed ignorance. Boies paced in front of the bench, pointer in hand, and asked an aide to roll the second video. The image of a surly Gates again filled the screen, and, in response to a question about his understanding of Netscape's strategy back in 1995, Gates told Boies, "I had no sense of what Netscape was doing." *I was barely aware of Netscape,* he seemed to say.

Dripping with sarcasm, Boies told the court: "They say they were going about their business developing Internet Explorer, designing their marketing and product plans, and they were doing that because that's the way they thought the best browser ought to be made, not because of what Netscape was doing!" Using his pointer to highlight, Boies introduced into the court record and displayed on the monitors various subpoenaed Gates missives,* including a May 26, 1995, memo titled "The Internet Tidal Wave," which showed that Gates explicitly spotted the Netscape menace. In it, Gates wrote to his managers, "A new competitor, born on the Internet, is Netscape. Their browser is dominant, with 70 percent usage share, allowing them to determine which network extensions will catch on." With control over how software worked online, Gates noted, Netscape could cheapen Windows and "commoditize the underlying operating system," by which he meant that software developers might move away from Windows by devising applications for this middleware. What Gates also worried about, said Boies, was that with Netscape in the way Microsoft could not extend its "choke-hold" to the Internet.

With a nod from Boies, e-mail written by Gates five days later and sent to his senior executives appeared on the screens. It said: "I think there is a very powerful deal of some kind we can do with Netscape"—a deal that would reduce competition. Gates then laid out what appeared to be a division of markets, with Microsoft's browser to be awarded the Windows consumer market and Netscape to be marginalized by being

---

*The government collected a total of three million documents from Microsoft and other companies.

allowed to sell its browser only to older versions of Windows and to non-Windows platforms. While Gates told Boies that he had told "someone" that the idea of investing Microsoft money in Netscape "didn't make sense to me," Gates told a different tale in the May 31, 1995, memo: "We could even pay them money as part of the deal, buying some piece of them or something." Then, just a few weeks before the meeting with Netscape—the meeting that Gates said he was not involved in—he wrote, "I would really like to see something like this happen."

Something like a market division was proposed at the June meeting, Boies argued as he produced e-mails from both Netscape and Microsoft. "What you have here is, in and of itself, an attempt at monopolization," he went on, a "restraint of trade" effort prohibited by law. Netscape would feel compelled to cooperate, Boies said, because Microsoft's leverage stemmed from Windows, which he said powered more than 95 percent of PCs. Microsoft threatened to crush Netscape if it did not comply, he said. There would be testimony, Boies promised, that one of Gates's "top lieutenants" threatened to "choke Netscape's air supply."

For three critical months, Boies charged, Microsoft withheld APIs that Netscape required for its browser to work with Windows 95. Unlike Netscape, which tried to sell its browser (earning nearly eighty million dollars from browsers in 1995), Microsoft adopted what Boies called "a predatory pricing campaign" and gave its browser away, bundling it with Windows. "Our business model works even if all Internet software is free," Gates told a reporter in an article cited by Boies. "We are still selling operating systems." Netscape, in contrast, said Boies, was "dependent on its Internet software for profits." Microsoft also imposed contracts on computer manufacturers and others, said Boies—on America Online and on software companies such as Intuit—restricting their ability to do business with Netscape. Microsoft was clearly cutting off Netscape's air supply, as promised.

In his narrative, Boies sometimes seemed to be speaking less about a software company than about the Mob. He produced Netscape co-founder Marc Andreessen's comment to *The Wall Street Journal* about the fateful June 1995 meeting: "It was like a visit by Don Corleone. I expected to find a bloody computer monitor in my bed the next day." Boies told of how Gates, seven months later, strong-armed America Online into dumping Netscape's browser and made AOL an offer it couldn't refuse: it would pay AOL to carry Microsoft's free browser. As evidence, he produced a January 21, 1996, e-mail from an AOL executive who described an encounter three days previously with Gates this way: "Gates delivered a characteristically blunt query: 'How much do we need to pay you to screw Netscape? This is your lucky day.' "

Boies went on to tell of Microsoft's desire to boost its browser share and its fury at learning that some OEMs (PC manufacturers such as Hewlett-Packard) and ISPs were reconfiguring the boot-up screen displaying the Windows 95 logo. He then produced e-mail from one Microsoft executive who asked, "Do you think we should look at making this harder?" "Difficult to do in Windows 95," came a reply, which contained this addendum: "We'll do something to make this hard" in Windows 98. In other words, Boies told the judge, "We're going to manipulate the technology not for innovation, not for consumer benefit, not for technological advances, but to hurt competitors." They would impose restrictions on OEMs, Boies continued, forcing them to choose between Windows, which they needed, and Netscape's browser, which they did not. PC makers were not happy. Boies produced a March 1997 memo from a Hewlett-Packard executive to Microsoft complaining about its refusal to allow Hewlett-Packard to customize the start-up sequence. "We were very disappointed," the memo began. "This will result in significant, and costly problems. . . . From a consumer perspective, we are hurting our industry. . . . If we had a choice of another supplier, based on your actions, I assure you that you would not be our supplier of choice." A Gateway 2000 document revealed the company's desire for a choice of browsers and their frustration that this would not be allowed under the Microsoft license. This plea went unheeded.

Microsoft, Boies continued, offered inducements to Intuit to spurn Netscape (Intuit declined), and it also threatened to terminate the vital software applications it had been providing for the Macintosh if Apple didn't restrict its ties to Netscape. Boies described how, when Apple's senior vice president of software engineering, Avadis Tevanian, Jr., wrote to Gates complaining that an important Apple product, Quick-Time, wasn't working on Windows, Gates e-mailed a senior Microsoft executive this twist-their-arm guidance: "I want to get as much mileage as possible out of our browser and Java relationship here. In other words, a real advantage against Sun and Netscape. Who should Avi be working with? Do we have a clear path on what we want Apple to do to undermine Sun?" Boies looked at the judge and declared, "This is not a situation of competition on the merits. This is a situation, I respectfully suggest, Your Honor, of clear restraint of trade."

Even Microsoft's close allies, Boies said, were bullied. He told of how irate Gates had been in the summer of 1995 when he met with Intel, which supplied 80 percent of all microprocessor chips, about their software research on native-signal processing (NSP), which would allow the Intel microprocessor to perform such multimedia tasks as audio processing and imaging very quickly. If this software worked—and Microsoft insisted it would not work with Windows 95—it might strengthen the middleware threat to Microsoft. The threat was that this software, like Netscape's browser, would sit atop Windows and could become a middleman, communicating directly with Intel's microprocessors and permitting software applications to be written to this middleware software. Gates told a group of Intel executives, including Chairman Andrew S. Grove, that he wanted them to abandon this quest. In one e-mail to Grove, Gates wrote: "I don't understand why Intel funds a group that is against Windows 95." Not by coincidence, Boies suggested, that same day Gates also announced that Microsoft would help fund an Intel competitor, Digital Equipment Corporation (DEC), in its development of a rival microprocessor.

NSP remained a contentious issue between Intel and Microsoft in 1995. After a three-hour dinner with Grove, Gates sent an internal e-mail on July 7 in which he reported to his team, "We are trying to convince them to basically not ship NSP." Slowly pacing the courtroom but keeping his eyes fixed on Judge Jackson, Boies declared, "Again, what you have is Microsoft trying to tell another company what products it can and cannot ship. Now, ultimately, Intel agreed, and part of the pressure was that—and the evidence will show that—Microsoft went around to all the OEMs." Boies continued, "Microsoft went to the OEMs and said, 'We don't want you to have anything to do with Intel and NSP,' and the OEMs fell into line, and Intel backed off." Indeed, in a July 8, 1996, *Fortune* interview with both Gates and Grove, the Intel chief admitted, "We basically caved."

Boies continued: "And you have a Gates memorandum—again, this is a memorandum from Mr. Gates personally—October 18, 1995, and he says, 'Paul,' directing this to [Group Vice President] Paul Maritz, 'Intel feels we have all the OEMs on hold with our NSP chill. For example, they feel Hewlett-Packard is unwilling to do anything relative to MMX [upgrading the Intel Pentium chip to permit improved audio, video, and 3-D rendering on the PC] exploitation or the new audio software Intel is doing using Windows 95 unless we say it's okay.' What Microsoft has done is it has gotten the OEMs, and it has told them they're not supposed to do anything in connection with software and Intel unless Microsoft approves.

"Mr. Gates goes on. He doesn't say, 'Well, this is against company policy.' He doesn't say, 'That's a bad thing to do. It would be wrong, that's for sure.' What he says is, 'This is good news because it means OEMs are listening to us.'" By mid-1998, Netscape's share of the browser market had dropped from nearly 80 percent to about 50 percent, while Microsoft's browser share climbed from 20 percent at the beginning of 1997 to 50 percent. By one estimate, Microsoft was now capturing 76 percent of new browser users, Boies said.

The courtroom's own air supply was spent, and as Boies went through these statistics and displayed a series of charts, the heat seemed to make Judge Jackson and more than a few spectators and reporters drowsy; Jackson rubbed his eyes and sometimes closed them, then suddenly jolted upright. He strained to stay awake by chewing on ice cubes and by leaning forward while rubbing his left cheek with two fingers, hard. Boies took this cue and deftly applied the brakes, quickly summing up. Without "some kind of intervention," he said, Microsoft would soon succeed in murdering Netscape. Boies promised to prove his case by using the very technology Microsoft relied upon for communication: e-mail. The more than three million pages of e-mail and other documents that the government had collected from Microsoft were the equivalent, Boies implied, of the kinds of wiretaps the government used to snare criminals. "We would ask the court," Boies concluded, "as the evidence comes in both from our side and from the other side, to do what I know the court will, which is to look at that evidence in context; and when somebody attacks the evidence, to ask yourself. . . . 'Is what I'm being told something that can be squared from the written record that people left behind at the time that they were actually doing these things?'"

Had the audience been permitted to clap, Boies would have received thunderous applause. Despite the one statistic-laden patch, he had succeeded in offering an easy-to-follow narrative and a motive for Microsoft's behavior. He had dragged Bill Gates into the courtroom and presented him as the chief villain. He had laid the groundwork for an assault on Microsoft's credibility and thus on its facts. He had shown that the actions in question were not the work of one or two executives but the product of a warped corporate culture.

But Boies's presentation was not without vulnerabilities. Boies and the government insisted that Microsoft controlled about 95 percent of all desktop PCs, but the math was suspect. It counted only PCs that used Intel chips because they were the dominant chip maker. It did not include Apple computers, since they didn't use Intel chips. It did not include Sun workstations—computers linked to Sun servers which used its Solaris operating system—or the burgeoning market for handheld devices, in which Microsoft trailed badly. Furthermore, Boies posited that this Microsoft monopoly, as was true of John D. Rockefeller's a century earlier, controlled the distribution of its product through various channels: manufacturers, ISPs, and ICPs. However, as opposed to the *Standard Oil* case, in which the company was found guilty of "unreasonable" restraint of trade, the government was here pushing a new interpretation of the antitrust laws, asserting that Microsoft both controlled distribution and constrained innovation. This assertion is vulnerable on two counts. First, the Internet is a distribution system unlike any the world has seen before, holding out the promise of free distribution. Consumers can download Netscape over the Internet. Second, a software company does not produce tangible assets, like oil. It produces intellectual property. A company with a better idea could, presumably, distribute it over the Internet—or by mailing disks—and best the market leader. Perhaps it couldn't, but it remained for Boies to prove this.

Nor had Boies yet proved consumer harm, which is one crucial test for antitrust law, and with computer prices plunging and Microsoft giving away its browser and making access to the Internet easier, this would not be a simple case to make. The government could argue that Microsoft's prices had not fallen speedily enough, or that its software now consumed a larger slice of the cost of each PC. Or, more forcefully, the government could claim that innovation was retarded because software developers would not design applications for competing systems because there was little economic incentive to do so, and sometime in the future consumers would pay on account of this "applications barrier." But assertions about the future depend upon a crystal ball. Easier to demonstrate would be the claim that Microsoft used its dominant position to mug other companies, which might qualify as restraint of trade. But here is one of many gray areas of the law: how to distinguish between common business hardball and illegal coercion? Microsoft did leverage its strength (Windows) to swell its share of the browser market. But using leverage is not uncommon. Why is it considered legitimate "leverage" when cable operators such as John Malone extracted part ownership of cable networks in return for distributing that network but illegal "coercion" when Microsoft awarded AOL space on its desktop in exchange for AOL essentially dumping Netscape? No question, Microsoft had contracts limiting the commerce AOL (and others) could do with Netscape. But restrictive contracts are commonplace in business. Despite Microsoft's piety, it did give its browser away free to harm Netscape. However, companies frequently offer products below cost in order to build market share. Pricing is always a business weapon. It isn't at all unusual for companies to strive to defeat competitors by underpricing them, or by offering inducements to Wal-Mart for better shelf display space.

Finally, a predicate of the government's case was the economic "network effects" theory. Once Microsoft had achieved market dominance, it would automatically maintain it because in this Information Age market share becomes contagious and the first to dominate a market gains an insuperable advantage, or so the argument goes. But the graveyard is littered with products for whom this economic "law" did not apply—in a moment, the Hayes modem company went from market leader to bankruptcy, even though the modem standard it popularized endures; word-processing market leaders such as WordPerfect and Manuscript (by Lotus) were overtaken by Microsoft Word; Prodigy was supplanted by AOL; DEC supplanted IBM's mainframes with minicomputers, which were then displaced by powerful PCs that DEC and others dismissed as "toys"; the Xerox Star operating system was eclipsed by the Mac OS and then by Windows; and the Wang computer was shoved aside by the IBM PC, which was then cloned and routed by upstarts named Compaq and Dell. A much read and discussed business book around the time of the trial—*The Innovator's Dilemma: When New Technologies Cause Great Firms to Fail*, by Harvard Business School professor Clayton M. Christensen—claimed that size was a hindrance, not an asset, in an economy in which innovation was usually the enemy of corporate giants. Had Microsoft wanted to concede that Windows was a monopoly, it could have argued that the new economy is distinguished by fleeting monopolies that push down prices in order to dominate a market and then succumb to new entrants, new technologies, that seek the same rewards.

At the end of the trial's first day, for example, Scott McNealy of Sun appeared on CNN's *Moneyline News Hour* and said he supported the government's case because the government has to protect consumers. Yet he also said he hoped that one day he'd be so successful that the government might be all over Sun. That's how he'd know he was successful.

These arguments were for another day. Boies had finished by two-thirty, an hour and twenty-five minutes earlier than the time Judge Jackson had announced they needed to adjourn so he could attend the investiture of a new colleague. Jackson was impressed. He kept by his side a bright green, oversized, lined hardcover notebook with RECORD stamped on it. Throughout the trial, he neatly numbered and jotted in blue ink the major points each lawyer or witness made. He reduced Boies's presentation to ten points and later said of it, "It was excellent. Lucid. Grammatical. Systematic. Direct. And devoid of histrionics."

Jackson looked down from the bench and asked John Warden, "Do you want to start now, or would you prefer to defer until tomorrow morning?"

"Tomorrow morning would be fine, Your Honor," said Warden.

Boies couldn't believe it. He was delighted. He remembered what he had done on behalf of Westinghouse in 1992 when the government of the Philippines was suing. After the plaintiff's lawyer had finished a brilliant opening statement, the judge looked at his watch and said the court would adjourn for the day. From the defense table, Boies had bolted from his seat and insisted that he was so outraged by the falsehoods his opponent had uttered that he couldn't bear the thought of jurors spending the night burdened by them and pleaded with the judge to allow him fifteen or twenty minutes to commence his opening statement. The judge relented, and Boies reversed the momentum. "If I had let the jury walk out of there without challenging the integrity of what they had heard, it would have been an uphill battle," Boies recalled. Faced with a similar choice, John Warden chose not to confront Boies. "If it had been left to me," Boies later told me, "I would have jumped to speak and declare, 'I cannot let a moment go by without rising to protest.'" By doing so, Microsoft failed to even partially mute Boies's opening thrusts in the first day's news cycle.

Privately, Judge Jackson faulted Microsoft's media strategy but not its legal strategy. He later told me he agreed with Warden's decision to defer his opening statement until the next day: "It's common learning among trial lawyers that you don't want to interrupt your presentation, you want to maintain the continuity of your presentation. In terms of news media, that may have been a mistake. In terms of the court, it was of no consequence."

Before adjourning, Boies rose to tell Jackson that members of the press had asked whether the government could make available all the documents used in court today, including (in fact, especially) Gates's full video deposition. He said that though these had already been cited in court, several of them had not yet been introduced as evidence. Microsoft immediately objected, and Jackson sided with Microsoft: the press must wait to get the full twenty hours of videotape.

While Microsoft had won this point, Boies was content. The ruling made Microsoft appear defensive, as if it were trying to hide something, Boies said. It also meant that Gates's deposition would not become stale news. Gates would become an easier target. Each time Boies dribbled out a segment of the eight hours of Gates's deposition he would use in this trial, reporters hungry for fresh meat would feature it. Boies also had to be pleased with reviews of his initial performance. "David Boies is the single best antitrust lawyer in America," raved former Federal Trade Commission member Christine Varney, who was in court on behalf of Netscape.

The spectators began to clear, and, in what was to become a daily ritual, reporters clustered just outside the courtroom, checking quotes, since no recording equipment was allowed in court, and, more subtly, checking what one another planned to say. Then the reporters raced down a flight of stairs and out onto the granite courthouse steps facing Constitution Avenue, where cameras waited—twelve the first week— with the Capitol Dome behind them. Meanwhile, upstairs, in a fourth-floor courtroom, no press and only eight spectators attended the trial of former Agriculture Secretary Mike Espy, accused of accepting illegal gratuities from businesses seeking his favor. Outside, David Boies stood on a step and spun his version of what happened in court, answered questions, then ceded his space to the Microsoft team, which spun its version.

Resplendent in a dark suit, white shirt, and red bow tie, Bill Neukom squinted into the warm sun and accused the government of using "snippets taken out of context" and material "based entirely on loose and unreliable rhetoric." E-mail, he said, is written in haste, is often full of bluster, and is not necessarily an accurate reflection of what people think and do. "None of these snippets, none of this rhetoric, even approaches proof of anticompetitive conduct." Of course, when given an opportunity to allow the press to look at the whole context of Gates's deposition, Microsoft had declined. Microsoft spokesman Mark Murray, who had served as press secretary to the mayor of Seattle and was usually Microsoft's sole spinner on the courthouse steps for the first several months of the trial, cracked to reporters that Boies's opening statement was so long it nearly put the judge to sleep.

The disparity between Microsoft's public stance and its private angst was vast. Late that night, after he had monitored the TV, radio, Web, and print news as well as the talking-head accounts, Greg Shaw, a former newspaperman who was the number-two executive in Microsoft's eighteen-person corporate public-relations department, wrote a two-page memorandum and e-mailed it to the company's senior executives, including Bill Gates. The first sentence minced no words: "Opening day of the trial today was as tough for Microsoft's image as we all expected. It was very bad." The p.r. team was obviously upset that John Warden had not chosen to begin Microsoft's opening statement, for the internal e-mail included this lament: "the day was dominated by the government."

The next day, there were still no reporters covering the Espy trial, and Courtroom 2 was packed with reporters and spectators eager to hear Microsoft's opening arguments. Neukom took his place, silently watching as John Warden stepped forward. By contrast with the thin, slightly disheveled Boies, who takes small, quiet steps in his black sneakers and lugs a battered briefcase, Warden, who is portly, fairly announces himself. He wears dark-framed circular glasses, has a round face, carries a thick, expensive leather case in one hand and often a bowler in the other, and marches down the court corridor in dark, three-piece, pinstriped suits and colorful ties, arms pumping, wing-tip shoes pointing out and slapping the floor. Like Boies, whom he has known for years and who is a neighbor in Westchester County, Warden, 58, also owns some trophies. He has represented some of the world's elite companies, including British Airways, the Bank of New York, Gulf Oil, Goldman Sachs, and British Petroleum. Perhaps his biggest prize came when he persuaded an appellate court to reverse a jury verdict against his client, Eastman Kodak, in the landmark 1979 monopoly case, *Berkey Photo, Inc. v. East-*

man Kodak Co. Kodak was accused by Berkey, a mini-Kodak, of trying to protect its film monopoly by inventing new film that worked only with a Kodak Instamatic camera. Berkey claimed it was caught by surprise and needed time to prepare for this new market. The appellate court declared, however, that companies should be free to bring their products to market as they choose. Warden's success in this case was among the reasons Neukom chose him to be the courtroom quarterback. Another was that Warden is a true team player, who welcomed input from the other lawyers and was respected as a good sounding board for them as well. He was also less abrasive than Richard Urowsky, who treated people who said hello as if they were about to mug him. While Neukom dubbed Urowsky "brilliant" and the "architect" of their legal strategy, he chose Warden to lead them because, he told associates, "he has more of a common touch."

Warden is a devout Republican, a member of the Knickerbocker Club in Manhattan, a trustee of the American Ballet Theatre, a wearer of Hermès neckties and hand-tailored English shirts, a confirmed Anglophile with a degree in English history from Harvard and a wife, Phyllis, who is famous in Bedford, New York, for the quality of the English flower, vegetable, water, and rock gardens she tends, each set off by formal squares and paths. Yet Warden is also a meat-eating, backslapping, unabashedly profane man who unapologetically seeks the richest, fattiest dish on a menu and slathers his bread with butter. On the surface, he is a man of contradictions. Despite the good-old-boy demeanor, at the University of Virginia Law School he stood out because he rarely was without a shirt and tie, sometimes wore bowlers, was prone to dropping references from English history, served as the editor of the *Law Review*, and "had the reputation of being the smartest guy in the class," recalls classmate Barry E. Hawk, a partner at the law firm of Skadden, Arps, Slate, Meagher & Flom and a noted antitrust scholar at Fordham Law School. "John is about as at-home as Eustace Tilley." While Warden is ferociously critical of Bill Clinton's ethical lapses, he is nevertheless a fierce proponent of former Republican senator Alfonse D'Amato, whose own ethical lapses attracted headlines when the Senate Ethics Committee investigated whether as ranking Republican member of the banking committee D'Amato violated that body's rules when he accepted inside information from a brokerage firm on a pending public offering, resulting in, among other things, a one-day profit of $37,125. While the committee found that the senator received special favors, they tortuously concluded that no law was broken, and therefore he committed "no improper conduct."

Warden's voice commands attention because it is both piercingly loud and because its accent is so unexpected. He elongates vowels, as many Southerners do. At first it sounds as if the Harvard-educated Warden contrives to appear to be a good old boy or is slightly inebriated and is slurring words. In fact, born in Indiana, he was raised in Cairo, Illinois, one of the towns on the Mississippi River made famous by *The Adventures of Huckleberry Finn*, a town with magnolia trees that in more ways than not was quite Southern. Sam Butler of Cravath has great respect for Warden's work in various merger deals but thinks he is "a little too folksy" to be a good trial lawyer. "If you're going to do that, you should dress like David Boies or Joe Jamail. John always comes off as a little bit of a fop with a Southern accent."

Hands clasped firmly on the sides of the lectern, Warden was surprisingly formal in court, in stark contrast to Boies. He introduced himself, Neukom, and each of the seven other members of the legal team. He would not make the "good" monopoly argument he did in the *Kodak* case. The Microsoft strategy was to deny misbehavior and to bombard the court with hundreds of facts. E-mail missives were full of bluster and were thus not a material fact. Bill Gates not remembering was not a material fact. Neither was Windows's market share. The nature of competition in the new Internet economy eviscerated old monopoly notions. The only fact that mattered, Microsoft believed, was whether Microsoft had actually harmed consumers and killed competition. They would not concede a single misstep, aside from occasional bad manners. Unlike David Boies's, John Warden's legal game plan relied much less on credibility.

Warden read from prepared remarks:

As an initial matter, let me say that the government's case is long on rhetoric and short on substance. The effort to demonize Bill Gates in the opening statements is emblematic of this approach, which wrongly characterizes evidence of tough competition as proof of anticompetitive conduct.

The antitrust laws are not a code of civility in business, and a personal attack on a man whose vision and innovation have been at the core of the vast benefits that people are reaping from the Information

Age is no substitute for proof of anticompetitive conduct and anti-competitive effects. The evidence will show that companies such as Microsoft and Intel that develop complementary products must talk to each other on a routine basis to prevent the creation of technical incompatibilities that adversely affect the operations of their products and, thus, consumers.

Disagreements between Microsoft and Intel, he said, should surprise no one. And "the fact that such disagreements occur is hardly evidence of an antitrust violation. Nor is it a violation that disagreements are resolved by adopting a common plan to develop new technologies jointly."

A weakness of the government case, he continued, is that it "relies heavily on snippets of Microsoft e-mail messages that are taken out of context." He would not today answer each distortion, but he did cite a few examples. Though Boies had quoted Microsoft executives as wanting to design Windows 98 in such a way that computer makers or ISPs could not reconfigure the boot-up screen and display Netscape's browser in a more prominent position—"We'll do something to make this hard," one Microsoft executive wrote—Warden asserted that there was no evidence that Microsoft had actually done that. Similarly, the government had quoted e-mail from Bill Gates to Andrew Grove pressing Intel to abandon NSP software. But what the government failed to read, said Warden, were the other paragraphs in the e-mail that made it clear that Gates's technical people warned Intel that this software "would cause problems for both Microsoft and the OEMs because it did not work with and hadn't been tested with Windows 95. And if it were preinstalled and then something went wrong, the OEMs and Microsoft would take the heat." In other words, Gates was worried about the customer.

The government had also sought to "demonize" Bill Gates, Warden said, by chopping up his videotaped deposition so that his statements were taken out of context, particularly where Gates said "that he had first learned by reading *The Wall Street Journal* that an allegation had been made that Microsoft had proposed or discussed with Netscape, in the summer of 1995, division of markets. There is nothing that will come into evidence that will impeach that. There is no report within Microsoft of proposals to divide markets." And it was a fact that markets were never divided. Of course, Warden continued, Bill Gates did not deny knowing "that there were discussions between the two parties." He only denied knowing of proposals to divide markets. Warden was being literal here, specifying that Gates and Microsoft did not use those red-flag antitrust words, even though the spirit of what Microsoft proposed to Netscape amounted to exactly that.

Warden turned to the government's bundling claim—"the allegation that was at the core of the government's case back in May and was the purported source of the fictitious urgency that led to the highly expedited schedule we have had." (Microsoft was not happy that Judge Jackson had decided to move quickly to trial and had limited the number of witnesses and streamlined the court processes.) The government's assertion that Microsoft had artificially bolted a browser onto Windows was fallacious, Warden continued, for "the evidence will confirm what Microsoft has been saying all along, namely that Internet Explorer technologies are an integral part of the operating system and cannot be removed from Windows 98 without seriously degrading it. The government's ward, Netscape, agrees with Microsoft on this fundamental point. Unlike Mr. Boies, I am happy to have the court focus on the letter that proves this point." He quoted from a March 6, 1998, letter from Netscape's counsel to Joel Klein, certifying that "it is simply not possible to delete any portion of IE or of the browser functionality from Windows 98, as presently configured, without severely interfering with the operating system." The two are integrated, dependent on each other to perform, said Warden, like "the shutter in a camera." Of course, while the "integrated" version of the two may be hard to disassemble, this still begs a question: did Microsoft not offer them as separate products because it intended to harm Netscape? Warden contended that point was inconsequential and tried to undermine the government's attack on Microsoft's intent: "The government has tried to inject motive into the discussion of integration. In our view, motive is irrelevant," since what matters is whether the browser is truly integrated and whether there are real "consumer benefits . . . flowing from that integration."

Somewhat disjointedly, Warden strayed to talk about the benefits to consumers of combining the browser with Windows, before coming back to make an essential claim: Microsoft did not suddenly slap its browser onto Windows 98 but instead worked on it "at the initial design stage." This was done prior to October 1994, when Netscape released its first (beta) test version of its Navigator browser. (This is only technically true, since at this time Microsoft began to discuss but had not geared up to develop its own browser.) The reason Microsoft ultimately offered an integrated product, he said, was "to provide consumers with seamless access. . . . The fact that Microsoft may have been spurred into accelerating its efforts to build support for Internet standards into Windows by the rapid commercial success undoubtedly achieved by Netscape is precisely how the competitive process is supposed to work."

The consumer benefits of this integrated product are readily apparent, Warden said. The browser is free, though he did not dwell on this as he might have. And: "As John Rose from Compaq will explain, ordinary consumers who buy computers at Wal-Mart have no interest in piecing together an operating system from a grab bag of separately marketed components. . . . They want their new machine to come out of the box— consumers do—and just work." Because the first two versions Microsoft offered consumers of Internet Explorer did not work as well as Netscape's Navigator, despite the fact that Microsoft had merged them with Windows, "the vast majority of consumers continued to use Netscape" until Microsoft produced a better browser. Consumers now chose Microsoft's browser because it was technically superior. Besides, Warden asked, if Microsoft were truly a comfortable monopoly, why does it spend three billion dollars a year on research and development?

Hands still firmly gripping the lectern, rarely gesturing, Warden read on as if he were reciting a term paper, turning now to the coercion charges. The government contends, he said, that Microsoft's contracts with PC makers and others were examples of "exclusive dealing agreements" prohibited by the antitrust laws. Not so: "These contracts were entered into when . . . Microsoft's Web-browsing software was used by less than 10 percent of those browsing the Web. These contracts were, therefore, actually not only competitively unobjectionable but procompetitive because they helped to reduce Netscape's overwhelming dominance and gave consumers a choice." Besides, these contracts "are cross-promotional agreements, common in all consumer businesses, and all are short-term. None is truly exclusive." Microsoft had contracts with only thirty-one of the thousands of ICPs, none of them "a major distributor of Web-browsing software. As a result, the notion that they foreclosed anything is ridiculous."

Foreclosure, of course, would be achieved more effectively by ISPs, to whom customers usually pay a monthly fee to access the Internet. He said Microsoft had contracts with only eleven out of more than three thousand, and these contracts did not prohibit ISPs from doing business with Netscape. Although he conceded that Microsoft's contracts did specify a minimum number of Microsoft browsers for the ISPs to distribute, he said they didn't punish anyone "for failing to achieve the target level of Internet Explorer distribution specified." Besides, since these contracts "became a lightning rod for criticism of Microsoft," he went on, the company had already suspended many of these provisions. Nor would Microsoft enter into any more contracts of this kind, "so this issue is truly moot."

Well, not quite, since the intent of the contracts was to limit Netscape's business and since one such contract was with AOL, the largest ISP, which provided access to nearly half of all Internet users. But AOL was "a special situation," Warden said. It was a "short-term" contract because AOL had the option of canceling within the next ten weeks, on or before January 1, 1999. Microsoft and Netscape did compete head-to-head to become the browser AOL would feature, he said, and Microsoft triumphed because it produced a better product. "Now, the government has and will focus on only one aspect of Microsoft's victory, the supposedly huge importance to AOL of placement on the Windows desktop." But because AOL was so popular, the evidence would show that leading computer manufacturers already placed AOL on the opening desktop screen, he said. And the so-called advantage to AOL of being placed prominently in the online-services folder of Windows accounted for a very "modest" number of AOL subscribers, he said.

The contracts Microsoft had with computer manufacturers, Warden claimed, would show that "Microsoft does not even purport to limit the ability of computer manufacturers to preinstall whatever software they like on top of Windows 98. If they think it adds value, that is their business." Nor, he asserted, dancing around complaints that Microsoft had put the manufacturers in contractual straitjackets, did these contracts prevent PC makers from choosing Netscape's browser over Microsoft's; nor had Microsoft denied Windows 98 to any manufacturer. "The evidence will show the opposite, that Microsoft makes huge quantities of information about its operating systems available to software developers because it is in Microsoft's business interest to have as many products as possible compatible with its operating systems. Netscape is a significant beneficiary of that policy." Nor did Microsoft prevent manufacturers from promoting their brands on the computer screen. Microsoft will, he continued, offer a testimonial from Compaq, the world's largest manufacturer of PCs, as to what a superb business partner Microsoft is, while "the government will present no witness from a computer manufacturer who licenses Windows 98 from Microsoft." Instead, the government would "devote five of its twelve witness slots to experts, many of whom repeat the same testimony."

For a consumer, the most crucial distribution vehicle for a browser is the PC itself, on which it arrives already loaded. Computer manufacturers are also affected by the critical functions performed by the browser's source code. Since computer makers benefited, held Warden, consumers were not harmed. Yet Warden did not dwell on this, perhaps because the government did produce correspondence from Compaq, Hewlett-Packard, and others that made it clear that Microsoft had foreclosed their business choices. Instead, Warden tried to show that other channels of distribution were open to Netscape. Citing Netscape's own figures, Warden said they would "distribute between 150 and 175 million copies of Netscape's Web-browsing software this year alone. That's half as many copies as there are users of the Internet in the world." Nor have customers been hindered in their ability to download Netscape on their PCs: sixteen million copies were downloaded in June, July, and August 1998 alone. Nor have customers been denied access to Netscape from such "major" PC manufacturers "as Fujitsu, Gateway 2000, IBM, Packard Bell/NEC, and Sony." (He omitted no fewer than four of the largest manufacturers: Compaq, Dell, Hewlett-Packard, and Toshiba.) Nor was Netscape impeded in its sales to Fortune 1000 companies, where it was strongest, since 90 percent used Netscape's browser, a figure that was actually rising, Warden reported.

Now Warden turned to the charges that Microsoft had sought to choke off the Java programming language and to divide markets with Netscape. Rather than subvert Java, he said, Microsoft is actually its "largest distributor," packaging it in most of its products, including Windows 98 and Windows NT. Rather than "pollute" Java, as the government asserted and as Sun Microsystems, its creator, proclaimed in a California lawsuit, Microsoft, Warden said, has designed Windows to not only run any program written in Java but also "[to run] those programs faster and better" than any other operating system "including Sun's." And although Microsoft has "created additional tools so that people can write programs in Java and also call Windows directly, Microsoft has not sought to require anyone to take advantage of that option."

The claims made about the June 1995 Netscape meeting and the alleged "air supply" threat were equally bogus, he said. Evidence would show Netscape's account of this meeting was "fantastical," a concoction that either sprang from "the naïveté of its author, Marc Andreessen," or was a device to enlist "the government as Netscape's protector in the competitive battle with Microsoft." The discussions with Netscape, as with Apple and Intel, were normal in a software industry in which companies compete and cooperate, always "urging your prospective partner not to ally with your principal competitor. You want him to support your technology, not theirs."

An hour into Warden's opening remarks, Judge Jackson's eyes were shut and his large head, like a mighty oak tree, about to fall. Desperate to shake off his fatigue, Jackson rubbed his eyes, poured a glass of ice water, and chewed intently on the cubes. Oblivious to Jackson's state, Warden continued: "This talk of market division and threats purportedly evidencing monopoly power leads me to market definition—"

Bolting upright, Jackson interrupted him: "Before you get into market definition, would this be an appropriate time for the morning recess?"

After a ten-minute recess, Warden resumed reading. A crucial concept for the court to comprehend, he said, is that "the drawing of hard-and-fast lines between separately identifiable product markets in the software business is not just difficult, but is impossible. As the court is well aware, software is comprised of lines of code that tell a computer what to do. There is an infinite variety of ways in which instructions can be arranged." Judge Jackson sharpened his gaze. After staring intently at Warden, he lifted his pen and wrote something in his green notebook that was to become significant: "Software code is infinitely malleable."

Microsoft was not a monopoly under any legal definition, Warden continued, because in the software business competitors faced "no structural barriers to entry. No factories to build, no mineral deposits to locate, and no distribution infrastructure to develop." There were also no constraints on how many copies could be produced—just brains, and the capital to support them, were required, and both were plentiful. He noted, "Any competitive position can be lost overnight if someone else creates a technically superior or more user-friendly product."

There is a theory advanced by some economists and embraced by the government, he continued, that superior products will not always win. This theory—called "increasing returns" or "network effects"—posits that in certain industries, high-tech among them, products with a large market share will tend to lock in customers. A firm such as Microsoft, which greatly influences the standards of the computer industry, is thus said to ensnare still more customers because consumers care less about how an operating system functions than about whether it works with most printers, games, word processors, spreadsheets, and other devices. Why invest in the allegedly superior Betamax videocassette technology, the argument goes, when most movies available for rental are on VHS cassettes? Warden attacked this theory as "ephemeral—if such lock-in effects existed, it would have been impossible for Microsoft to make a dent in Netscape's commanding lead in Web-browsing software, a point the government's economic experts ignore." PC makers have alternatives, Warden insisted, but "they install Windows because that's what their customers want."

Concluding his presentation, Warden said he hoped the court will decide "that this is not really an antitrust case but a return of the Luddites, the nineteenth-century reactionaries who, fearful of competition, went around smashing machines with sledgehammers to arrest the march of progress driven by science and technology. . . . The government's case is a fundamentally misconceived attack on the creation of innovative new products by operation of the free market." Warden then thanked the judge and stepped back. His presentation was an hour shorter than Boies's, but it seemed longer, because it meandered and was animated by neither chronological storytelling nor a dramatic videotape.

And Warden's opening argument had more vulnerabilities than Boies's did. For Gates to pretend Microsoft was not consumed by its competition with Netscape was preposterous. Any reporter who covered Microsoft between 1995 and 1997 knew that the company believed it was in a death struggle with Netscape and invoked Netscape as a spur, a way to keep Microsoft hard-core. As in any war, the company fought hard—gave its browser away, delayed software upgrades, threatened retaliation, and wrote restrictive contracts—to figuratively cut off Netscape's air supply. Bundling the browser with Windows was a weapon to beat Netscape, not just a means to better serve consumers, as

Microsoft sanctimoniously proclaimed. The only plausible rationale for Gates to say "I had no sense of what Netscape was doing" is that he was offering a narrow legal answer, saying that he was not privy to their inner deliberations. It was somewhat like Bill Clinton at first telling reporters there "*is*" no—as opposed to "*was*" no—improper relationship with Monica Lewinsky, or later adopting the dodge used by teenagers when he said in a deposition he had not had sex with her, meaning he had not had vaginal intercourse.

The new economy may have different rules of business competition, but under the antitrust laws one thing doesn't change: neither a high-tech nor an old-industry giant may use coercive tactics to protect or extend its monopoly, though prevarication, excess piety, or uncivil behavior do not necessarily qualify as violations of the antitrust laws. Other companies may exert leverage, may brazenly use muscle to get their way, but when a monopoly does so we graduate from hardball to restraint of trade. Coca-Cola muscles McDonald's, but Coca-Cola doesn't dominate the soft-drink market the way Microsoft dominates PC operating systems. Consumers still have an effective choice of sodas. Did PC manufacturers have an effective choice of operating systems?

When he talked about the future, Warden often sounded like a woolly professor, insisting that other platforms had equal access to the market. They did not, in large measure, because Microsoft stood in their way. And even though Warden dismissed the government's embrace of "network effects" or "increasing returns," a similar theory had been advanced eloquently by none other than Bill Gates. In a keynote speech to the Conference on Internet and Society at Harvard University in May 1996, Gates said, "The world of operating systems becomes more and more homogeneous over time. Today something like 85 percent of the computers on the planet run the same operating system [Microsoft's]. There's sort of a positive feedback cycle here—if you get more applications, it gets more popular, if it gets more popular, it gets more applications." Despite the trial, Gates again made the "positive feedback loop" claim in his 1999 book, *Business @ the Speed of Thought*.

Finally, Warden had dwelled on potential violations of section 1 of the Sherman Act. But even if Microsoft was judged innocent of restraining trade or foreclosing competition, there were other legal obstacles before it. Few areas of antitrust law are more ambiguous than a section 2 charge of coercive behavior, observed George Washington University professor Kovacic. "The icebergs that Microsoft has to navigate are cases that don't rigorously insist on proving actual harm." There are cases Microsoft doesn't like to advertise, ones in which the courts have suggested that even if a company did not foreclose markets or restrain trade, if its conduct was "pernicious" it was deemed guilty. And there remains the question of business ethics. For while the antitrust laws, as Warden cautioned, are not a "code of civility in business," to accept this premise doesn't automatically exculpate Microsoft's behavior. Even in context, to read many of Microsoft's internal e-mails is to be struck by their arrogance. They might not be illegal, but who would hold it up as a model of behavior?

With Warden finished, Judge Jackson recessed for lunch. Privately, he complimented Warden's presentation as "cogent," but the line he wrote in his notebook—"Software code is infinitely malleable"—was to prove fateful. "The significance of that didn't emerge in my consciousness until much later on in the case," Jackson subsequently told me, "because they were making so much of the contention that once [the browser was] integrated it could not be disintegrated." Was this a smoking gun? Observed Jackson, "It was harmful to the central thesis of their defense for the tying plan."

Or was it? To Microsoft, the idea that code was malleable was self-evident and hardly incriminating. Because software code can be created and arranged in various ways, intellectual-property laws apply to it. This is why Microsoft and Lotus and Sun and Oracle have patents. Code is like language; words can be arranged in a variety of ways, as the words of William Faulkner or Danielle Steel can. Cut chunks of Faulkner and mix in Steel, Microsoft could argue, and it would no longer be Faulkner, and the same is true for browsers. Microsoft could have chosen to make a browser separate from Windows, but they chose to create an integrated product. Had Microsoft's lawyers been aware that Judge Jackson thought it revelatory that software code was malleable, they would have seen it as another ominous sign that he was a technological dolt.

But if parsing Microsoft's intent were only a matter of understanding the technology, the questions before Judge Jackson would have been simpler—more "fact"-based. But throughout the trial, Jackson's dilemma was that it seemed as if two different companies were being described.

Each government witness painted a dark picture of Bill Gates, Microsoft, and its preying culture, and each Microsoft witness offered a glowing portrait of a model entrepreneurial company. Did Microsoft combine the browser with Windows to help consumers, as they asserted, or to punish Netscape and any company that chose the Netscape browser? To address this core question, David Boies would turn to the story of Netscape.

CHAPTER 5

The Government's Story

A T THE HEART of the government's foreclosure-and-coercion case was Netscape, and for this reason the government called as the first of its twelve witnesses James Barksdale, the CEO.

The history of Netscape archetypally demonstrates the blinding speed of change in the Internet economy. It was originally known as Mosaic Communications when it was formed in 1994 by Marc Andreessen and other young computer programmers at the University of Illinois. The company introduced a browser program that promised to allow PC users to navigate the Internet simply. James H. Clark, a former Stanford associate professor who had founded Silicon Graphics, bet that Mosaic would help carry the Internet revolution on its back, and in April 1994 he bought Andreessen's company and later rechristened the firm Netscape Communications. By late 1994, the beta version of Netscape's first browser was on the Web. With the browser allowing simple access to the Internet, new websites blossomed. When Netscape's stock went public on August 9, 1995, its opening price jumped from 28 to 58 on day one, which became the unofficial launch date for the bull market in high-tech stocks. Andreessen, like others, often immaturely boasted of how Netscape would slay "the beast from Redmond." A grown-up, James

Barksdale, was hired as CEO. His mission: to transform Netscape into a business as well as a cause. Netscape would spurn Microsoft on each of its increasingly anxious efforts either to acquire or at least to invest in Netscape.

Microsoft became alarmed that the browser could become a de facto operating system for PCs. So it embarked on a crash effort to develop a competitive browser, using this threat to galvanize the company. Shortly after Gates's "Pearl Harbor" announcement, Barksdale, asked to assess the Microsoft threat, responded glibly, "God is on our side." God may have been, but as the World War II–era song had it, "Praise the Lord and Pass the Ammunition." Netscape was seriously outgunned and quickly found itself reeling from the Windows/Internet Explorer onslaught.

Barksdale's written direct testimony, which like all the testimony was distributed to reporters in advance, ran to 126 double-spaced pages. In it, he said that Microsoft had crossed a legal line by using the "bullying and tough tactics" of a "monopolist" to "squelch competition in the browser market" by coercing key distributors, by tapping their own cash reserves, by subsidizing and offering a Web browser for free to consumers who were asked to pay $39 to $49 for a Netscape browser, and by inserting "unnecessary technical incompatibilities" into Windows to disrupt the way Netscape functioned with it. He described the June 1995 meeting between Netscape and Microsoft, the one in which Microsoft allegedly proposed to divide the browser market, as "something I had not ever seen happen in my more than thirty years of experience with major U.S. corporations." He disputed Microsoft's assertion that as early as April 1994 it intended to build a browser into Windows, since throughout 1994 Microsoft usually disparaged the Internet and even as late as January 1995, Microsoft "had only 4 people working on developing a browser." It wasn't until May 1995, he said, that Gates reversed engines and told his executive team they should "assign the Internet the highest level of importance." While Barksdale acknowledged that Microsoft was alive to the potential of browsers in December 1994 when it licensed the original technology on which Netscape was based "and expected to use this code as the basis for its own commercial browser product," he portrayed the June 21, 1995, meeting as part of a Gates panic attack, a frantic effort to catch up to Netscape and the booming Internet.

That key executives from the two companies would convene is hardly surprising. Such meetings are commonplace. At this one, however, the

Microsoft team, led by the general manager of new technology, Daniel Rosen, "proposed a division of the browser market between our companies," Barksdale said, explaining that Microsoft told Netscape to give up its roughly 80 percent market share and accept about a 10 percent share. "If Netscape would agree not to produce a Windows 95 browser that would compete with Internet Explorer," Barksdale testified, "Microsoft would 'allow' Netscape to continue to produce cross-platform versions of its browser for the relatively small market of non-Windows 95 platforms." And if Netscape said no? Microsoft said it "would crush Netscape," Barksdale testified, "using its operating-system monopoly." As a further inducement, Microsoft raised the possibility, he said, of taking "an equity position in Netscape," which Barksdale rejected. Near the end of the meeting, Barksdale said he asked Rosen why Netscape had not been able to get from Microsoft its Windows "technical specifications" (its APIs) so that its browser could run on Windows 95. Was it, he asked, "conditioned on agreeing to Microsoft's proposal to divide the market and take an equity position in Netscape?"

"It certainly isn't independent," Rosen responded curtly. This was really a veiled "unilateral disarmament" proposal, noted Boies. In other words, it was either a "restraint of trade" violation prohibited by section 1 or, more likely since Barksdale blocked it, an "attempt to monopolize" prohibited by section 2 of the Sherman Act.

Barksdale appeared in person to testify on the second day of the trial, but before he was sworn in John Warden rose and moved that parts of Barksdale's written testimony be stricken because it contained "multiple layers of hearsay," which in some cases was "fourth-hand hearsay." In all, Barksdale's testimony contained sixty-nine paragraphs brimming with "inadmissible hearsay," he maintained. Barksdale and the government were submitting, as evidence, newspaper and magazine articles and notes from people who attended meetings at which Bill Gates was reported to have said something to someone else. (Of course, Microsoft would also submit as evidence similar press accounts.) Judge Jackson immediately ruled that if this was a jury trial "it might be dealt with somewhat differently" but that he would "admit the testimony in toto," and he would recognize hearsay evidence as such. In response to Microsoft concerns that the government was introducing new allegations beyond the scope of the charges, Jackson said he "would not be making any findings" and "would not predicate any relief" on these assertions, certainly not without giving Warden every extra opportunity to rebut it. Hiding his disappointment that Jackson had relaxed the rules of evidence, as judges often do, Warden politely thanked the judge; Bill Neukom registered no emotion as he impassively scribbled notes at the head of the Microsoft table. But this ruling infuriated Microsoft, reinforcing their sense that Jackson was racing along too fast, was too impatient, too much of a shoot-from-the-hip jurist and not a careful sifter of facts.

Weeks later, at a small cocktail party to which I was invited and Gates hosted before proceeding to a dinner in New York in his honor, Gates was still furious about this, cursing and sputtering about what an outrage it was that the judge had permitted hearsay to masquerade as fact at the trial. More temperately, Bill Neukom told me, "It appears to us that a significant amount of testimony is hearsay. But when the court issues its findings, it will have to be based on admissible evidence, not hearsay."

Barksdale was a formidable-looking witness—a handsome man with wavy gray hair, a conservative charcoal suit, white shirt, and gray tie, with courtly manners and a slow drawl left over from a youth spent in Jackson, Mississippi. He had an unusual résumé for Silicon Valley. He was neither a young inventor with more hubris than experience nor a passionate entrepreneur who disdained management. Nor was he a bigmouth. Barksdale, 55, wore more management ribbons than most executives in the Valley, starting with his first eight years—from 1965 to 1972—spent at IBM, where he began as a salesman; followed by a stint running data processing for Cook Industries and serving as president of its insurance subsidiary; followed by time at Federal Express, where he rose to chief operating officer, and revenues climbed from one billion dollars to nearly eight billion by the time he left in 1991; followed by his most recent role, as president and chief operating officer of McCaw Cellular Communications, the cellular giant that had been acquired by AT&T in 1994. In January 1995, he became the president and CEO of Netscape. There were two million users of its pioneering Web browser when Barksdale joined the company; a year later, there were fifteen million.

In contrast with the procedure followed with most of the government's witnesses, Boies briefly led Barksdale through his biography and the highlights of his written testimony, then turned him over to the other side, a process that would be reversed when Microsoft called its witnesses. From the moment he introduced himself to the witness and

Barksdale responded, "Nice to meet you, Mr. Ward," John Warden set out to undermine Barksdale's credibility, like a prizefighter pounding away at the body of an opponent. He opened by pummeling Barksdale with questions: when did Netscape first meet with the federal government? Was the first contact initiated by Netscape? How many meetings did Netscape have with the Justice Department? How many times did Barksdale personally meet with Joel Klein? How many hours had Barksdale spent with Justice since this lawsuit was initiated? All were meant to show that Netscape—and Barksdale in the six meetings he remembered holding with Justice prior to the filing of the May 1998 lawsuit—really hoped to get the government to do for it what it could not do for itself: defeat Microsoft.

Instead of exhausting a single topic or telling a story by following a clear time line, Warden chose to literally follow, page by page, Barksdale's written testimony. From the beginning, Neukom and his legal team believed their mission was to refute nearly every assertion submitted by a government witness. While attacking Barksdale's credibility, they saw it as much more important to attack his facts. The problem was that Warden seemed to confuse the trees with the forest. In his cross-examination, Warden stuck so scrupulously to Barksdale's written testimony that he asked him a stupefying number of questions, including a request that he explain "the improvements" Netscape had made to its software, which is not the best request to make of a former salesman. Barksdale obligingly enumerated its many new features, ending with "I could get you a long list?"

"That will do, thanks," Warden stammered.

"I hope you buy the product," said Barksdale, a sly smile parting his lips.

Theatrically, Barksdale won, but Warden had also driven home a point: ever since the advent of the PC, when customers were required to pay extra for options such as spreadsheet programs and disk drives, computer companies have tried to combine features—spell checkers, a thesaurus, graphics, bookmarks—to enhance their customer appeal, just as Microsoft had done. But instead of staying with this subject, or any subject, Warden kept jumping around, asking obtuse questions; once, when Warden asked about Netscape's revenues and profits, he paused to ask, "By the way, did you change—this year change—your fiscal year to the end of October?" At times, Warden's approach seemed to perplex the judge. When Warden tried to get Barksdale to define what he meant by *monopoly product*, which Barksdale said was "a product that has a clear dominance in the market to the extent that the market no longer has a free choice," Warden pressed the witness to distinguish between a diamond monopoly and a soup monopoly.

"What's your question?" asked the judge.

"My question is he's used the term *monopoly power*, and I want to know what it means."

"I thought he defined it once."

After a while, Warden brought up the "air supply" quote and asked when Barksdale had first heard it. Barksdale pleasantly surprised Warden by saying he had heard that Larry Ellison, the chairman and CEO of Oracle, used it to mean to "disadvantage a competitor." The idea was thus planted that it wasn't only Microsoft executives who talked like cowboys. Warden burrowed in, asking whether Barksdale had actually heard it from Paul Maritz, the senior Microsoft executive who was said to have uttered that phrase. Barksdale admitted that he had not. Nor did he remember when it was said, though he knew it had been reported in the press. Although Warden had scored a point, as quickly as he raised the subject he moved on, dancing over a series of mostly pointless questions on a variety of topics, before delving into whether Netscape's ambitions were to sabotage Microsoft by using its browser as a middleware substitute for Windows.

Barksdale maintained that he had never said this was his intent but admitted that the inventor of his browser, chief technologist Marc Andreessen, 26, had made such a claim; in fact, Andreessen had once blustered that Netscape would "reduce Windows to a set of poorly debugged device drivers." This was the joke of "a young man," Barksdale said, and not for a minute did he believe Netscape could fully replace Microsoft's Windows platform as the jumping-off point for other applications. He did concede, however, that Netscape believed it could "substitute for some of the characteristics" of Microsoft's platform. In other words, maybe Bill Gates had reason to fret about the middleware threat from Netscape.

By the end of the witness's first day, Warden had covered only the first thirteen pages of Barksdale's written testimony. And in Barksdale he confronted a careful man who paused deliberately before answering questions and came off as appealingly honest, especially by contrast with the sometimes plodding questions. Of course, tedious factual questions are features of most antitrust cases, but Warden, at least this first day, seemed to wander. The sense that Microsoft floundered a bit and that the government had a clear direction was reinforced when the judge adjourned for the day and Boies, his baggy Lands' End suit jacket open, appeared before the throng of reporters and cameras on the court steps, easily answering questions and bantering with reporters, spinning about what "a compelling witness" Barksdale was, while no member of the Microsoft legal or public-relations team appeared to shape the way the press interpreted the story.

Reporters always search for narratives, for story lines, and in many ways the first few days established a story line for this trial: David— Boies, that is—slays a bumbling Goliath. Boies had at his disposal a full arsenal of weapons, including a quick wit. While questioning Barksdale, the non-PC user asked the CEO about his "log in" to an Internet-service provider.

"No, it's 'log on,'" corrected Barksdale.

Boies smiled. "I knew that! I was just testing to see whether you were paying attention." The judge and the spectators laughed, and a small intangible negative was turned into a small intangible positive.

By contrast, Warden, who had more courtroom experience arguing briefs before appellate judges than he had grilling witnesses, continued his drip-drip-drip cross-examination, meandering in and out of subjects, sometimes prompting the judge to ask that he speed things along, at other times casting a spell of sleep over the courtroom, as the large head of the judge—as well as those of more than a few scribes—readied to drop. At the end of Barksdale's second day on the stand, as Warden, trailed by Neukom, marched out of the courtroom, I asked Warden if he was having fun. "I can't comment on anything!" he said, stern-faced, slapping his wing tips on the burgundy carpet as he continued out the door. He quickly passed Boies, who was standing just outside the courtroom surrounded by reporters. The reporters thought Microsoft's legal team was rigid; Microsoft's lawyers thought they were obeying court rules, which said that journalists were not supposed to interview lawyers in the courthouse. This was a rule that bent as the trial went on. But each day in the beginning, Mark Murray first consulted with Neukom and then walked outside to face the cameras and a battalion of reporters. He told reporters how thrilled Microsoft was. For example:

"This obviously was a very important week of testimony and we feel we changed the dynamic of the case. We built in a browser to help consumers, not hurt Netscape." Murray reflected Neukom's instructions, which were, essentially, to humor reporters with an upbeat spin and get back to courtroom business. Often, it sounded like a prerecorded announcement. Microsoft's aloof behavior in the courtroom and on the steps reinforced an impression, a budding narrative, that Microsoft was being guided by legal pedants who focused only on the courtroom trial, ignoring the larger public trial in which Microsoft and Bill Gates were getting clobbered.

This helped obscure some good Microsoft news: Warden had scored at least a few points over Barksdale and the government in the courtroom. Seeking to demonstrate that Netscape had first proposed that Microsoft become an investor, Warden submitted as evidence a December 29, 1994, e-mail sent at 3 A.M. by James Clark to Brad Silverberg, a senior Microsoft executive. The e-mail was sent at a moment when Netscape had yet to soar, when its revenues were slim and its capital was shrinking. Barksdale, like everyone in court, leaned forward and read Clark's abject missive: "We want to make this company a success, but not at Microsoft's expense. We'd like to work with you. Working together could be in your self-interest as well as ours. Depending on the interest level, you might take an equity position in Netscape. No one . . . knows about this message. . . ."

Barksdale appeared disconcerted and told Warden that this was the first time he had seen this e-mail. Then Warden, in perhaps the most dramatic moment of his cross-examination, asked Barksdale if he considered Clark "a truthful man." Barksdale did not respond immediately, and when he did he hardly gave Clark a ringing endorsement: "I regard him as a salesman." Barksdale went on to say that he thought Clark was freelancing at the time. Warden, however, had introduced an element of doubt: maybe the June 21, 1995, meeting was Netscape's idea? Maybe Netscape was the aggressor, not Microsoft? Maybe Netscape, not Microsoft, proposed to "divide the market"? Maybe Microsoft, not Netscape, was on the side of consumers?

"And are consumers better off with the browsers they get free today than they would have been with the browsers that they would have to pay for in your hypothetical world?" Warden asked Barksdale. Barksdale replied that in the long run a free browser would hurt consumers because it eliminated incentives for other software companies to improve their own browsers. This, of course, was conjecture on Barksdale's part; what was concrete was that the browser was free. And that Netscape, though its market share had fallen, nevertheless had not had its oxygen supply cut off. Warden observed that Barksdale's own Netscape shares were then worth about two hundred million dollars. And if customers wanted to download Netscape's browser, they could do so from one of two hundred thousand websites. Warden repeatedly asked the questions posed by the Sherman and Clayton antitrust acts: where's the consumer harm? Where's the harm to competition? Where's Microsoft's choke-hold on the market? Besides, he wondered, what about Netscape's complicity in its own decline? Netscape's January 1995 IPO prospectus had warned that Microsoft was going to bundle its own browser with Windows, yet Barksdale and Netscape allowed Microsoft, by its fourth-generation browser version, to surpass Netscape's browser in quality and to win better technical reviews; in addition, as Microsoft snatched market share, Netscape did not galvanize around a single business strategy to compensate for the lost income, never quite making up its mind whether it was a browser or a server or an intranet or an e-commerce or an Internet-portal company.*

After Warden cross-examined Barksdale for four days, Boies came forward on the fifth day to again question his witness. Each side is allowed to interrogate its own witnesses after the opposing lawyer chews on their legs, a process that's called a redirect examination. Boies used his time not just to italicize points Barksdale had made or to contradict Warden but to introduce as evidence a small mountain of e-mail and other correspondence, which he deployed as an X ray of Microsoft's warrior corporate culture and thus of its behavior.

Boies produced an e-mail from Microsoft's Daniel Rosen to Bill Gates and other executives the day after the June 21, 1995, meeting in which Rosen said their priority was to "establish Microsoft ownership of the Internet client platform for Win 95"—meaning that starting with Windows 95, Netscape was expected to surrender most of its browser business to Microsoft. Boies produced e-mails Netscape executives had sent after the June 21 meeting complaining that Microsoft had not given

*A critique that faults Netscape's business execution as well as Microsoft's ruthless behavior is contained in Michael Cusumano and David Yoffie's book, *Competing on Internet Time.*

them components of the API codes for Windows 95, which was to be released that August. Microsoft executives e-mailed back that they were working on it, but according to a Netscape e-mail Boies read into the record, "Microsoft did not provide these APIs until October 1995, which caused us to miss most of the holiday selling season." Thus, those who wanted to use Windows 95 at first did not have the choice to use Netscape's browser.

Although Microsoft denied that its executives deliberately stalled to hurt Netscape, Barksdale—and the seeming weight of evidence—suggested that it did. "Our product cannot operate without the operating system on which it resides," Barksdale said. And since Microsoft "controlled the plumbing" for most PCs, "that makes all independent software vendors dependent on them. And here we were a competitor, and they were treating us one way, and the other guys who weren't competitors, they got to get this thing." Boies produced handwritten notes Fred Anderson, Apple's chief financial officer, had made to prepare for a telephone conversation with Barksdale. Apple computers have their own operating system, but Apple is dependent on Microsoft software developers to produce many of its applications—two hundred developers worked on the Macintosh Office suite of programs alone. And later, in the summer of 1997, when Apple badly needed an infusion of cash, Microsoft offered to support Apple—if it dumped Netscape Navigator as the default browser and substituted Internet Explorer. Anderson's shorthand description of why Apple surrendered to Microsoft's demand: "Apple needed to ensure that Microsoft would continue to provide MS Office for MAC or we were dead. They were threatening to abandon MAC. Trading card was making Internet Explorer Default browser."

Barksdale proved to be the government's strongest witness. Still, one witness did not a case make. Microsoft's lawyers knew Barksdale had been potent, but they thought he had failed to demonstrate how Microsoft had "foreclosed" Netscape. Justice, by contrast, thought he had demonstrated that Microsoft conspired to restrain competition and preserve its software monopoly. Judge Jackson later told me he was impressed with Barksdale. "The characteristic I would ascribe to his testimony was courageous. Here was a lifelong, hard-charging, highly competitive businessman who was appearing in a role that, in other contexts, would cause him to be characterized as a snitch. It was a man who had a long and successful career in business, and had undoubtedly played hardball himself, but was willing to come forward and say, 'I know illegality when I see it. This I think is illegal.'" Jackson thought that Barksdale testified "convincingly about what he comprehended . . . as a blatant demand, if you will, that there be a division of the market."

David Boies, not surprisingly, thought Barksdale's testimony and the documents the government placed on the court record had helped reveal Microsoft's cold Conradian heart, its arrogance: "They thought they could do whatever they wanted to do to win. . . . The rules didn't apply to them." The chief culprit, Boies said, was the man he thought of as a king, Bill Gates: "Part of what happened is he has been so successful, yet has so little grounding in the sort of normal business norms of behavior. Everything is a new choice for him, a new decision. That can be a real strength—not to be tied down to the old ways. But it's also a risk. . . . He's someone who's never been forced to conform."

Bill Gates was one reason Warden took four long days to interrogate Barksdale and then all of Tuesday afternoon to conduct his recross-examination. Boies had made a mistake by announcing late in the first week of the trial that he hoped to spend a chunk of the second week playing excerpts of Gates's video deposition. Microsoft thus avoided ending the first week with Gates, which would mean that the deposition would be repeated on television newscasts over the entire weekend; and when the trial resumed on Monday, Microsoft just wanted to avoid it altogether, hoping to gain more time to devise a legal and public-relations counteroffensive. By playing the videotape, Boies intended to frontally attack Microsoft's credibility, knowing that the "facts" introduced by Microsoft's lawyers in court were undermined by an obstinate, absentminded Gates. Since only the parts of the Gates deposition actually played in court could be released to the public, this rationing aroused the kind of carnal news interest usually reserved for celebrity videos or pornography. The courtroom, which had already begun to thin, was again packed with people hoping to glimpse the second installment of the Gates soap opera, including former Supreme Court nominee Robert Bork, who was working for Netscape as a consultant/lawyer. But Warden's stall backfired, for Judge Jackson became increasingly irritated by the delaying tactics, as the early part of the second week was consumed by Barksdale.

Finally, on Wednesday and Thursday the government called the next scheduled witness, America Online Senior Vice President of Business Affairs David M. Colburn. The government could have subpoenaed any witness and risked a lot of "I don't recall"s. They needed cooperative witnesses to best make their case. And in America Online Boies was summoning to the stand a vital witness for the government—an Internet powerhouse that by 1998 steered 40 percent of all online users onto the Internet. The government was calling to the stand a company they believed had been bludgeoned by Microsoft and a company with a history of battling Bill Gates.

When it was launched in the mid-1980s, America Online was widely expected to soon perish, the victim of better-positioned foes such as Prodigy, CompuServe, and, eventually, MSN, with their deep-pocketed backing from companies such as H&R Block, CBS, IBM, Sears, and Microsoft. Over the years, AOL has had more death notices than a frail pope. It was said that Steve Case would soon exhaust AOL's limited money supply. It was said that Microsoft co-founder Paul Allen would buy them.

Bill Gates and the smart money—including TCI's John Malone, who passed on investing in AOL—put their bets on Microsoft's MSN. But while Gates and Case had had their clashes over the years (most memorably in 1993 when Gates was trying to acquire AOL and, according to Kara Swisher, had blustered to a flabbergasted and subsequently rage-filled Case, "I can buy 20 percent of you or I can buy all of you. Or I can go into this business myself and bury you"), Gates had never been a member of the AOL-is-doomed chorus, even when the chorus was ear-splittingly loud. And though few would admit to being a member of that chorus today, at its peak it was *very* loud. For years, whenever anyone cited AOL as a cyberpower, people smirked. It was too clunky, too *uncool*—"the JC Penney of cyberspace," haughty critics called it, critics who wouldn't be caught dead with a *you've-got-mail* e-mail account. AOL was a private online service that would be derailed by the Internet, they said. AOL was a classic middleman, they said, deemed superfluous by customers who didn't want to pay monthly access fees and by a distribution system (the Internet) that empowered users to bypass middlemen. Or, they said, AOL would be pulverized by online competitors—like then mighty CompuServe, which nearly acquired AOL (then known as

Quantum) in 1991, or several years later by MSN, which enjoyed the advantage of being bundled into each new version of Windows 95. Or, they said, AOL would self-destruct, as it almost did in the mid-nineties when Case's crusade to build market share collided with the service's frail infrastructure, overwhelming it with telephone calls, hang-ups, credit-card fraud, and customer turnover approaching 50 percent. This crisis sent AOL's stock price plummeting below 2. And yet, by 1996, Bill Gates was so eager to make Internet Explorer AOL's default browser that he sacrificed MSN by awarding AOL a prominent place on the Windows desktop. And by early 1998, AOL had eleven million subscribers and on any given night had a bigger audience—625,000—than MTV.

By the time Steve Case had reached age forty, America Online had given him quite a ride. From 181,000 AOL members in 1992, the size of his subscriber base had vaulted to more than fourteen million. The year of AOL's greatest travails (1996) was also the year it moved onto a thirty-eight-acre campus not far from Dulles Airport in suburban northern Virginia, forty-five minutes west of Washington, D.C. Unlike Silicon Valley, where fast-food restaurants are everywhere, or Redmond, Washington, where the Microsoft campus is surrounded by one-family suburban homes, AOL's campus was once a British Aerospace hangar that now contains two glass office buildings—known as CC1 and CC2—and lots of space to accommodate expansion. From Case's spacious fifth-floor office he sees nothing but highway and farmland; the only nearby store is a Wal-Mart. Case works at a large slate semicircular desk, with a Hewlett-Packard PC on it and a Macintosh on the credenza behind it. Plants flower in the sunlit office, and the walls are largely bare, save for a few mementos, including a guitar given to him and signed by the rock group Aerosmith that rests on the carpet. Case's typical workday attire is a blue knit AOL shirt, chinos, tan sneakers, and white socks.

Case has a knack for survival. "In terms of the Internet, I'm ancient. I should be in a museum, stuffed," he told me one day in his office. "I've been in the business seventeen years and in this company for fifteen years. We were laughed at when John Malone promised there would be five hundred cable channels and when Time Warner said that television, not the Internet, would be the true interactive medium. Then Time Warner's Pathfinder and Rupert Murdoch's Delphi were supposed to drive AOL out of business. Then a rash of Internet-service providers. Then push technology. Then broadband."

The computer was not Steve Case's first love, as it had been Bill Gates's. The second of four children, he was serene, shy, and somewhat preppy, unlike Dan, his older brother. His father was a corporate lawyer, his mother a schoolteacher, and they ran a strict household, with set mealtimes, regular chores, and limited television. Growing up in a large house in an upscale neighborhood of Honolulu, Case's mild form of teenage rebellion was to proclaim that he wanted to become part of the music business, maybe managing a rock band, maybe playing in one. He thrived on gadgets, whether it was making a toy rocket or wiring a radio, and he disappeared for hours into his upstairs bedroom, often flooding it with the sounds of the Rolling Stones and Aerosmith. When he played basketball with Dan, they were each no less competitive than Bill Gates; the Case brothers treated basketball as if it were a war. "We figured as long as we were out there playing, we might as well win," Steve Case told Mark Leibovich for a June 4, 2000, *Washington Post* profile. He dreamed of becoming an entrepreneur, and before he was a teenager he set up his own businesses, first selling lemonade, then going door-to-door to sell greeting cards. A music critic for his high-school newspaper, he thought of becoming a music impresario. He attended his father's alma mater, Williams College, where he had a disappointing B-minus average but did wonders for the college's music scene, as he lured well-known rock bands to his small, out-of-the-way Massachusetts campus.

Case soured on a music career, and he searched for other fields of endeavor. "His least favorite course was computer programming," writes Kara Swisher in her compelling book, *AOL.com: How Steve Case Beat Bill Gates, Nailed the Netheads, and Made Millions in the War for the Web.* "Case hated the punch cards and the confusing tech-speak. Only one feature intrigued him: the ability of the college's computers to talk to others located elsewhere. 'The faraway connections seemed magical,' Case remembers. 'It struck me as the most completely obvious use for them, and the rest was just for computer wonks.'" He had read, noted Leibovich, Alvin Toffler's *The Third Wave*, which envisioned machines talking to each other, and Case did not think this science fiction. But first he needed to better understand consumers, sensing that marketing was his true calling. After graduation, he opted, just as Steve Ballmer did, to learn about the marketplace at one of America's foremost consumer-products companies, Procter & Gamble. The first product he marketed, a towelette with hair conditioner that was rubbed into the scalp, was an utter flop: consumers weren't interested.

Two years later, he hopped over to Pizza Hut, headquartered in Wichita, Kansas, where he used a rented car to visit the chain's various branches, testing new pizza toppings. He quickly learned that consumers didn't like exotic or cluttered toppings. At both companies, he learned the business value of a brand name and of keeping things simple.

Dan Case, a Rhodes scholar at Oxford and a rising star at the Hambrecht & Christ investment firm, knew of his brother's interest in technology and periodically sent him the marketing plans of emerging high-tech companies. In the late seventies, Steve Case had become enthralled with the Atari video-game machine and the promise of interactive TV and the first PCs. "It was clear that something was emerging," he told me; as an entrepreneur, he wanted to ride this wave by creating an interactive consumer service. He got a Kaypro computer and, while he was furious at how user-unfriendly it was, he was enraptured by logging onto an embryonic online service, the Source, and suddenly connecting to people around the country via a database that supplied news, weather, and even e-mail.

At a Las Vegas trade show in 1983, Dan Case introduced Steve to Bill Von Meister, the mercurial founder of Control Video, whose aim was to create an online company whose chief product was a video game connected to cable boxes. Soon, the company became Quantum, and Steve Case's mission was to sell Apple a private online service and manage it. He sold similar services to Commodore and Tandy. By 1989, Quantum was renamed America Online, and two years later Steve Case was named its president.

Ask Case to describe his special skills, and the first things he says are: "Passion. Really believing in the medium and its possibilities and ability to change the world. A consumer-centricity. Understanding that what happens on the screen is ultimately all that matters—it had to be more useful, more fun, more engaging." The next skill he mentions is that "I take pride in what I am not doing as opposed to what I am doing. The art of delegating. A lot of people measure their effectiveness by how many memos they get, how many meetings they attend, how many decisions they make. I measure my effectiveness by how few."

Case had proved to be a brilliant marketer and strategist, but by the mid-nineties his company was chaotically managed and required a hands-on executive. His initial hire as number two, Bill Razzouk, 48, the former executive vice president of Federal Express, did not work out.

With customer-service problems multiplying—the incessant busy signals and disconnects earned AOL the appellation America On Hold—in 1996 Case turned to a new member of his board, Robert Pittman, 42. The son of a Mississippi Methodist minister, Pittman had lost his right eye in a farm accident when he was six, but this did not make him reticent; he was as outgoing as Case was shy. Few were aware that Pittman, who has a full head of thick black hair, round, unrimmed eyeglasses, and radio announcer's voice and delivery, had not graduated from college. Pittman had started out as a disc jockey, first in Mississippi and then in a succession of other places, before making a name for himself as a radio programmer in New York City. From radio he segued to WNBC, a broadcast TV station in New York, then to cable television, where as an employee of Steve Ross's Warner Amex Satellite Entertainment Company in 1981, he helped launch MTV. When Ross decided to sell MTV, Pittman could not acquire it himself, so he started a successful media-investment company that produced, among other dubious offerings, the trash TV of Morton Downey, Jr. In the late eighties, Ross recruited Pittman to come back to work for him in business development at Warner Communications, which soon merged with Time, Inc. Pittman became something of a businessman celebrity, aided by his marriage to Sandy Hill, a longhaired beauty who climbed mountains while he piloted airplanes and Harleys. Together, they became an *it* couple, spotted at notable parties, posing for pictures in *New York* magazine.

Pittman was more wedded to making money than he was to the media business. For Ross, Pittman helped acquire and then ran the Six Flags Theme Parks in 1990. He succeeded in marketing the theme parks and fetching an attractive price for their resale. When Six Flags was eventually sold, Pittman became rich as well as famous. But with Ross now dead, Pittman left Time Warner to run Century 21 Real Estate. Case invited Pittman to become an America Online director in 1995, to become CEO of AOL Networks in 1996, and president and COO of the company in 1998. After they helped steady AOL, Case and Pittman took aim at Microsoft, which they viewed as a colossus that could crush them but that had to be attacked, though quietly at first.

Each man understood the enormity of this task. At the end of 1998, Microsoft was ranked by *Fortune* as only the world's 287th-largest corporation, with revenues of $15.2 billion, but this was a deceiving statistic. Microsoft's profits of just under $4.5 billion ranked fifteenth among all corporations, ahead of the world's largest, General Motors, and Microsoft's profit margin of over 30 percent topped the Fortune 500. Nor was Microsoft complacent in the way that IBM had become by the eighties when PCs subverted their mainframe business, or the way that American auto companies had been oblivious in the seventies to the advent of smaller, more fuel-efficient cars. In that respect, Case and Gates were alike. "My job is to delegate paranoia," Case told me. A similar dictum was expressed by Gates in his most recent book: "Sometimes I think my most important job as a CEO is to listen for bad news." Case admired the speed and effectiveness with which Gates, after being late to recognize the impact of the Internet, suddenly turned his large and unwieldy company around in 1995, even if Case came to be enraged at the way Microsoft behaved. But unlike Gates, who seemed to drive his company using only one gear—maximum speed—Case used several, and his even temper provided ballast. "I view myself as a sort of a shock absorber for the company, evening out the highs and the lows," Case said.

While he admired Microsoft as a competitor, he hardly thought it was invulnerable. Microsoft's profits still grew at a robust 30 percent in 1998, but this was a drop from 57 percent in 1997 and 51 percent in 1996. And Microsoft had had its share of failures. In an attempt to overtake Lotus 1-2-3, it wasted a lot of money on its Multiplan spreadsheet but failed so miserably that it abandoned the product in 1990. Its personal-finance software, Microsoft Money, flopped, thus encouraging the company to try to buy Intuit, its dominant competitor. Microsoft abandoned "Bob," its effort to make the PC more user-friendly, and its Omega database, and its interactive-television software, code-named Tiger. Despite several new launches and an investment of tens of millions of dollars, MSN still had not caught on. But Windows's dominion over the operating-system sector forgave a multitude of sins.

So as America Online's David Colburn prepared to take the witness stand, everyone in the courtroom knew Steve Case was rooting for the government. Case later told me, "We decided that even though we had a point of view regarding the trial and thought the government case had merit, we did not have a lot of interest in engaging in a public brawl with Microsoft. There were strong government attempts to get me to testify and even to subpoena me to testify." The compromise was to offer Colburn, a man with a stubbly beard who wore cowboy boots and a perpetual smirk. Colburn made the same hubristic mistake many Microsoft witnesses would of wanting to prove he could outwit and outsneer the opposing lawyer. *Get out of the way, I'll show 'em!*

But as James Barksdale had, Colburn offered still more evidence of what Microsoft considered normal hardball tactics and the government considered illegal coercion. Concerned that Microsoft had too much power, AOL had signed an agreement with Netscape on March 11, 1996, to license its browser. Unwilling to cede the portion of the browser market held by AOL's then five million subscribers (thirteen million by the day of Colburn's testimony), Microsoft offered to downplay its MSN online service by featuring AOL on Windows 95—if AOL agreed to an exclusive contract, limiting the distribution and promotion of Netscape's browser. If AOL insisted on using Netscape's browser, its customers would have to endure the somewhat laborious process of downloading it; Microsoft's Internet Explorer browser, by contrast, would be integrated into AOL. On March 12, 1996, AOL acceded to Microsoft's terms, abandoning the deal it had made a day earlier with Netscape.

In his cross-examination of Colburn, Warden produced a 1997 Netscape/AOL contract and noted that Netscape prohibited AOL from promoting rival software; he also produced internal AOL documents showing that by 1996 the company viewed Microsoft's browser as technically superior—in other words, AOL had chosen Microsoft on the merits. He also produced a January 1996 memo in which Steve Case reported on a conversation with James Barksdale that seemed to suggest that AOL sought to divvy up markets and muscle Netscape, just as Microsoft was accused of doing. AOL made money primarily by charging a monthly fee for Internet access, and Netscape's primary source of income had been supplying software for servers to people with Internet connections. Case was concerned that Netscape might expand and become an online competitor, and he wrote that he and Barksdale discussed two options to allay this fear. One was for America Online to get a seat on Netscape's board. The other, Case wrote, was for AOL to "completely run their [World Wide Web] site so there is no risk of contention there. . . . I think getting the entire web site under our management control and keeping them completely out of the web service business would be better for us." Reading a draft of another memo from

Case, Warden noted that Case agreed with Andreessen's description of Microsoft as "the Beast from Redmond" and called for a "grand alliance" among AOL, Netscape, and other companies to defeat this corporate monster.

Warden asked, "In your various dealings with the Department of Justice, stirring them up against the 'Beast from Redmond,' did you disclose that you made a market-division proposal to Netscape?"

No, Colburn said. Also, it wasn't a market division, it was a common search "for a strategic relationship."

Nonetheless, Microsoft was establishing a theme: every company does what Microsoft was accused of doing. Warden showed that AOL bundled new software advances into its basic online service. He showed that had they divvied up the online-services market as proposed, AOL not only would have received a royalty-free license to Netscape's browser in return for spending ten million dollars on promotion, marketing payments, and software, but would have kept Netscape out of AOL's core business.

America Online, like Microsoft, played with sharp elbows. In 1997, for example, it made Barnes and Noble its exclusive online bookstore. However, AOL had earlier sold to Amazon.com exclusive rights to sell books on AOL.com, the website its members use to reach the Internet. Initially, AOL had a contract with ABC to provide written, video, and audio news. But when CBS came along in early January 1999 with a richer offer, AOL did not hesitate to dump ABC for CBS, just as it had dumped Netscape's browser for Microsoft's.

Warden might have recounted what it's like for AOL customers who sign on and then click the Internet icon at the top of the screen. Up pops a small screen containing seven choices, six of them steering the customer to AOL sites. If the user clicks "Go to the Web," he or she goes to a choice of AOL channels, bumping into advertisements while scanning each choice. And if the user clicks on "Internet Connection," even then he or she is not allowed out of AOL but is instead trapped in a confusing screen that tries to guide him or her to other AOL channels; among the blizzard of choices, there is one that allows escape—but only if the user knows the correct Web address. The intent is to corral the user in AOL's proprietary world.

The weakness of this argument, as Boies replied, is this: not every company is a monopoly, and the law prohibits a monopoly from doing what nonmonopolies may do. What the testimony by Colburn revealed about Microsoft's behavior was that it compelled the dominant online service to shun a competitor, Netscape. If Judge Jackson concluded that Microsoft was a monopoly, this behavior was probably illegal. If Microsoft wasn't a monopoly, it was good business.

To address this monopoly theme during week three of the trial, the government called Dr. Avadis Tevanian, Jr., the senior vice president of software engineering for Apple Computer. Like America Online, Apple was an ostensible ally of Microsoft. And like AOL's witness, Apple's would not have agreed to testify for the government without at least a wink from his interim CEO, Steve Jobs. According to Joel Klein, who invested countless hours seeking to persuade key figures in the computer industry to testify against a bully, "Steve [Jobs] has every reason to be very concerned. If Microsoft pulls its support of Mac Office, he'll get hurt. He's being helped by them now, but he's completely at their mercy." Microsoft's Office claimed 90 percent of the market for business software, and Apple needed Microsoft's cooperation to offer a version of Office for its corporate customers.

This co-dependency was a bone in Apple's throat. Jobs and Gates, who are contemporaries, had long been billed as rival oracles. Jobs was the cool one, who wore black turtlenecks and jeans and gave mesmerizing presentations without notes; Gates was the geek with the shrill voice who often read his remarks and acted like someone you wouldn't invite to your dinner table. To purchase a Macintosh wasn't just a commercial decision, it was a statement of personal aesthetics. Steve Jobs and Apple portrayed themselves in ads and at confabs as rebels, first against giants like IBM, then against Microsoft. And while Microsoft's ads were effective, they had as much romance as those for Tide detergent. Yet the cool guys lost. Apple felt they had the better operating system and resented that Microsoft's won. Apple commercially introduced the mouse and graphical user interface, yet Microsoft succeeded in popularizing them, prompting a six-year Apple lawsuit, which Microsoft won. By the early nineties, Apple's market share had slipped, and Jobs had been ousted. Then Apple's market share slipped even more as its management made a succession of dumb choices, prompting a succession of CEO changes, finally leading to Jobs's triumphant return in 1997. But throughout the nineties, one fact didn't change: Apple was now a vulnerable company, dependent on Microsoft. But with Jobs back, and aided by old associates such as Dr. Tevanian, Apple believed it could re-create the old magic. Of course, if Apple's Macintosh was resurgent, Microsoft's grip on the market would loosen.

On Monday morning, November 2, David Boies was wearing the same baggy blue suit, too short blue tie, button-down shirt, and black sneakers he wore every day; in fact, his only physical change since the trial began was that his hair was longer because he hadn't bothered to get a haircut. Before Dr. Tevanian took the stand, Boies approached the bench to announce a treat: he wanted to begin the day by playing and thus releasing more of the Gates video deposition. Microsoft immediately cried foul, charging that Boies was slyly using Gates as a thirteenth witness and objecting to the public release of the tape. This just stoked Microsoft's paranoia. Among the Microsoft team there was a palpable sense that they were operating behind enemy lines, their sullen faces suggesting that they felt surrounded by a hostile government in a hostile city with hostile reporters eager to write hostile accounts of the trial. When Senior Vice President Paul Maritz materialized at the trial one day and was asked how long he planned to be on hand, he snarled, "I don't plan to stay at this circus!"

Looking up at Jackson, Boies told him it was the government's understanding that once the excerpt of Gates's video deposition was played in court both the transcript and the tape of the exchange could be released. With Bill Neukom stoically erect behind him, John Warden approached the bench and said he had no objection to releasing the transcript but did object to releasing copies of the tape, which could then be broadcast on television. Since court rules prohibit cameras in the courtroom, said Warden, making the video available for "use outside court, it seems to me, both violates the rule and it provides differential treatment . . . of videotaped depositions as opposed to live testimony in the courtroom." It was also unfair, he claimed—a "kind of selective disclosure of visually recorded evidence"—because unlike in a courtroom, those who watched it saw only the witness on the screen, not the counsel or "the surrounding circumstances." Warden's was a compellingly logical argument.

"If it were open to me, Mr. Warden, I probably would adopt your position in toto," Judge Jackson responded. But more than strict logic was involved. The rule he had followed all along, he explained, was "that anything which is presented in open court is available to the press, and to erect artificial impediments to the press . . . is not only unworkable, but it is probably likely to incur more criticism for us and for the process than it would be if we were to enforce the rule as if this were an extension of cameras in the courtroom."

Accepting that he had lost the ruling, Warden declared, "I must say that I do take personal exception to the comment apparently made to the press by someone on the government's side that I was somehow filibustering last week to prevent the playing of the Gates deposition." Boies interjected, offering a homily that was totally at variance with his whispered asides to me. "I do not believe Mr. Warden was filibustering, and I do not intend to second-guess any trial lawyer's decisions," Boies told the court.

Warden thanked him, and Jackson, a bemused look on his round face, cautioned, "Let's not get in a war with the press, gentlemen."

"Oh, no. I have no desire to do that—" began Warden.

"Because," Jackson interrupted, "it's one we're going to lose, all of us."

Reporters were surprised by Jackson's ruling, for they had been convinced he would be hostile to them. After the Marion Barry trial, Jackson had made remarks at Harvard that he thought were off-the-record about what a disgrace Barry was. *The Washington Post* reported every last injudicious word, and Jackson was livid. Jackson, reporters guessed, was also livid when *Washingtonian* magazine, in a June 1996 article about judges, implied he was lazy and pronounced that he was "one of the least-respected judges on the federal bench." Jackson gave a speech about the press at a 1997 judicial conference that was reprinted in *Federal Trial Lawyer,* and many who covered this trial winced when they read:

> As a general proposition, the orderly working of society is of little interest to the press. Disorder and acrimony offer richer ore to mine for "news." If a case presents the opportunity to disturb public complacency about something, the press will seize it. . . . I have a visceral sense that the relationship between a potentially newsworthy case and the press is roughly comparable to the relationship between a healthy organism and an infectious disease. Like any infectious agent, the press will infiltrate any orifice and search for the most vulnerable part of the host organism.

Lost amid Jackson's colorfully cynical remarks was his coldly practical advice for judges: first, ignore what the press reports. Second, don't befriend reporters, but take care not to "deliberately antagonize" them. Third, don't comment about a case, even off-the-record, because the press will use it. Fourth, "open as much of the proceedings to media scrutiny as possible," because an "innately suspicious" press will treat anything "it cannot observe" as "sinister." It was Jackson's cynicism about the press, not an idealism about openness, that prompted him to open Gates's deposition to the public. It was a fateful decision, for Gates's testimony helped frame the press's David-versus-Goliath trial narrative.

The crowded courtroom was filled with a sense of anticipation. For the next two hours, Gates's was the only image that appeared on the courtroom's various screens. The videotaped deposition had been taken in a conference room at Microsoft's headquarters over three days in late August and early September 1998, and on this day Gates had worn a hunter-green suit and brown-striped tie. He had combed his mop of hair straight down into bangs that hung unevenly across his pale forehead. Sipping from a can of Diet Coke, he rarely looked up at his off-camera interlocutor and alternately rocked slowly back and forth or slouched forward, looking either bored or lost in thought. The three attorneys who had flanked him—Neukom, his deputy David Heiner, and Richard Urowsky—were invisible to the camera. Gates was quizzed by Boies and a New York State assistant attorney general named Stephen Houck, the affable fifty-one-year-old head of the state's antitrust division.

The first sentence of the page-one story by Steve Lohr and Joel Brinkley that appeared in *The New York Times* the next day captured the shock experienced in the courtroom by those who had now seen Gates on tape several times: "The William H. Gates on the courtroom screen this afternoon was evasive and uninformed, pedantic and taciturn—a world apart from his reputation as a brilliant business strategist, guiding every step in the Microsoft Corporation's rise to dominance in computing." It was similar to the shock people felt earlier this century during the Standard Oil antitrust trial as they watched a dour, formidable John D. Rockefeller transformed into a sweet, senile old man on the witness stand.

When Gates was asked by Houck whether he ever had internal discussions about trying "to undermine Sun" and its Java software language, Gates hemmed and hawed and said he didn't remember or didn't know. Well, did he have discussions with Apple "to help you undermine Sun?"

"I don't think I was involved in any discussions, myself, with Apple about that," said Gates.

Houck then handed Gates an August 8, 1997, e-mail he had written to Paul Maritz, the last line of which reads: "Do we have a clear plan on what we want Apple to do to undermine SUN?"

What did he mean by that question?

"I don't remember," said Gates.

Houck wanted to show Microsoft blackmailing Apple and mentioned an upgrade of Mac Office that Apple was eager to receive. Did Apple, he asked, think this was "very important to them?"

"I really have a hard time testifying about the belief of a corporation," said Gates. "I really don't know what that means."

In deciding "what you would ask of Apple," said Houck, did you consider exchanging Mac Office for something you wanted?

"I have no idea what you're talking about when you say *ask*," responded Gates.

Houck handed Gates a copy of a February 13, 1998, e-mail from Microsoft executive Don Bradford to Ben Waldman, Microsoft's liaison to Apple, with copies sent to Gates, Maritz, and others. The e-mail reported that Apple wanted to offer both the Microsoft and Netscape browsers and said Microsoft wanted to find a way to induce Apple to turn against Netscape. Bradford wrote: "Getting Apple to do anything that significantly materially disadvantages Netscape will be tough. Do you agree that Apple should be meeting the spirit of our cross license agreement and that Mac Office is the perfect club to use on them." Gates told Houck he didn't understand what Bradford meant, nor why he had sent a copy to him.

Trying to demonstrate that Microsoft had committed a breach of section 2 of the Sherman Act by an "attempt to monopolize," Houck asked Gates if he ever told Bradford that it was wrong to attempt to induce Apple "to do things that would significantly or materially disadvantage Netscape."

"No."

The remainder and longer portion of the deposition consisted of questions from Boies, who asked if Gates had ever threatened to cancel Mac Office. After Gates said no, Boies stopped the tape and told the court that he would like to introduce four new exhibits. The first of these was a June 27, 1997, e-mail from Ben Waldman to Gates asking him to agree to complete the upgrade of Mac Office and "detach this issue from the current Apple discussions." Waldman continued: "The threat to cancel Mac Office 97 is certainly the strongest bargaining point we have, as doing so will do a great deal of harm to Apple immediately. I also believe that Apple is taking this threat pretty seriously, and at least someone there seems to want to move forward." Attached was Gates's e-mail response the same morning, in which he asked when Microsoft might be ready to ship the updated version of Mac Office, and then asked: "2, can we avoid Apple knowing how far along we are for the next 30 days?"

The next exhibit was an e-mail sent on the same day from chief financial officer and chief deal maker Greg Maffei to Gates and Waldman: "Great mail, but need a way to push these guys and this is the only one that seems to make them move." Later that evening, Waldman proved he was hard-core when he replied to Maffei, sending a copy to Gates. Waldman wrote that although he was arguing that they go forward with Mac Office, he didn't tell this to Apple: "When I spoke with Gable [an Apple executive] yesterday, I told him that we had almost given up on any hope of progress, and that you would be recommending to Bill that we cancel Mac Office 97." Without the upgraded version, Mac Office would be less attractive to business customers.

On tape, Gates said he didn't recall receiving these, and, besides, it concerned nothing more than an "internal debate" about a single upgrade.

Boies then handed Gates a June 23, 1996, e-mail he had sent to Maritz and several senior executives about an earlier meeting with Apple. "I have 2 key goals in investing in the Apple relationship," Gates wrote. "Maintain our applications share on the platform; and two, see if we can get them to embrace Internet Explorer in some way." Gates did not deny that the e-mail was his, but he insisted that "our top goal in thinking about Apple for many, many years" was the patent dispute between the two companies, not the two issues cited here.

"Do you have any explanation for why you would have written . . . that those were your two key goals in the Apple relationship?"

"No," said Gates, "they weren't involved in the patent issue at all, so when I write to them, I'm focused on the issues that relate to them."

Boies was incredulous, wondering how Gates could cite his "two key goals" and insist that even though the patent dispute with Apple was barely mentioned it was really "our top goal" with Apple. The reason

Boies was confused, suggested Gates, was that he discussed the patent dispute when he talked about doing a "deal" with Apple but not when he talked about the "relationship" with Apple. "The word *deal* and the word *relationship* are not the same word," Gates admonished Boies. Although Boies reminded Gates twice that he was under oath, Microsoft's chairman insisted he didn't mention the patent dispute as a top goal to Maritz because Maritz knew he was addressing the Apple "relationship," not the Apple "deal." On the face of it, Gates was weaseling.

In August 1997, Apple and Microsoft finally made a "deal" about their "relationship," and Apple endorsed Microsoft's browser. Now Boies asked, "Does the deal prohibit them from shipping Netscape's browser without also shipping Internet Explorer?"

Gates said he wasn't sure.

"It's your testimony, sitting here today under oath, that you simply don't know, one way or the other, whether Apple is today free to ship Netscape's browser without also shipping Internet Explorer?"

"That's right."

Boies produced an August 21, 1997, e-mail from John Ludwig, a senior Microsoft executive, which discussed one of the executive staff meetings Gates conducted four times each year, this one held the night before. "Bill's top priority," he wrote, is to get Microsoft's browser included in Macintosh's October 1997 operating-system upgrade. Gates said he did not remember pressing this point.

Boies read from a second paragraph of Ludwig's e-mail concerning Microsoft's desire to keep Apple from aligning with its sworn enemy, Sun Microsystems: "Bill was clear that his whole goal here is to keep Apple and Sun split. He doesn't care that much about being aligned with Apple. He just wants them split from other potential allies." Boies then asked Gates, "And that relates to Java, does it not, sir?"

"I don't have a direct recollection, but if you read the sentence in front of it, that paragraph seems to relate to Java runtime."

In a moment, Boies handed Gates an April 14, 1997, e-mail sent to him by Dan Slivka, who was responsible for assuring that Microsoft's software and Java could mesh. Slivka listed six "pointed questions" he understood Gates had about Java, including "How do we wrest control of Java away from Sun?"

"I don't think that I would have put it that way," said Gates.

Like a dog who won't let go of a bone, Boies wouldn't leave a question until he got the answer he wanted. Even if he looked as if he was asking a dumb question, he kept coming back, asking it in slightly different forms. After going in circles for a few minutes, Boies asked if Microsoft proposed to divide the market: "Did Microsoft offer to have Apple continue to offer a multimedia player for the Mac platform and to assist Apple . . . if Apple would agree not to distribute that multimedia player for [and thus compete with] the Windows platform?"

"As I said, I don't think there was any discussions about not distributing some old thing but, rather, a question was could something new be created which would be better for both companies."

Boies asked if Gates was aware of "assertions by Apple representatives that Microsoft representatives tried to get them to agree to divide the market?"

"No."

And if they had, that would be contrary to Microsoft policy and "would be appropriately dealt with?"

"Yes."

Boies then cited a July 23, 1998, article in *The Wall Street Journal* reporting that the Justice Department was investigating allegations that Microsoft had tried to convince Apple to "stay out of the multimedia software market." Wasn't Microsoft trying to "divide markets"? asked Boies.

Gates said he did not recall seeing this article, and with that stunningly implausible statement Boies abruptly halted the tape and said he was done with the Gates deposition for this day. Later, outside the courtroom, Bill Neukom—who had sat as stoically silent through the three days of Gates's deposition as he did throughout the trial—told reporters that Boies distorted Gates by resorting to an edited videotape instead of actually calling him as a witness: "This is little more than a gimmick to get snippets in the headlines rather than get at the facts pertinent to this lawsuit." The flap over Gates's deposition was a sideshow, John Warden told me: "If Bill Gates doesn't remember, misremembers, or remembers something correctly, that's irrelevant. The issue is: what happened?" Even if Gates skirted the truth, Microsoft suggested, this didn't mean he was guilty of creating a monopoly. Disagreeable behavior is not always criminal.

Whatever the company's spin, the Gates deposition and the testimony of Dr. Tevanian badly wounded Microsoft. In his written deposition,

Tevanian, who is tall and thin with dark curly hair, swarthy good looks, and the intensity of a scientist in a laboratory, described Apple's Macintosh operating system with its then 5 percent market share as "the only real alternative to Microsoft's Windows." He told of how Apple offered customers both Microsoft's and Netscape's browsers bundled with their operating system. In the late 1990s, Apple and Microsoft fell into a dispute over whether Apple would use Netscape's browser and over whether Microsoft had infringed Apple's patents. Apple threatened to file a $1.2 billion lawsuit, charging Microsoft with the theft of several Apple technologies.

The dispute got nasty. In May 1997, Tevanian recounted, Microsoft negotiators threatened that if Apple did not bend on the two main issues in their dispute, Microsoft would withdraw its team of software engineers that was assigned to devise applications to run on the Mac operating system, particularly the team working on Mac Office. Microsoft's withdrawal might, he said, compel "independent software vendors to reassess" their work for Apple, thus creating a so-called applications barrier to entry for Apple. Microsoft was also making noises about Apple's relations with Sun Microsystems.

With a gun to its head, Dr. Tevanian said, on August 5, 1997, Apple surrendered and agreed to bundle the Microsoft browser as the default browser on all its operating systems for five years. Other browsers might be included, but only Microsoft's could be promoted and only Microsoft's could appear on the opening desktop screen. Apple also agreed to settle the patent dispute. Apple was hardly a victim, however. At a time when Apple was reeling from business losses and its stock price had plunged, in return for these concessions, Steve Jobs induced Bill Gates to become a part owner of Apple by investing $150 million in it. In addition, Microsoft would supply its browser for free and provide software support for Mac Office and other Apple applications.

However, Dr. Tevanian said a new dispute arose late in 1997. It concerned Apple's QuickTime technology, which enables the playing of audio files and video images. Since QuickTime competed with Microsoft's Media Player, Dr. Tevanian said, "Microsoft has written steps into its operating system to ensure that a QuickTime file will not operate reliably on Windows. Microsoft has also caused misleading error messages to appear that trick the user into believing that QuickTime technology is part of the problem actually caused by the Windows operating system." Microsoft, he said, not only considered multimedia-playback software as competitive with its own efforts but also saw it as potential middleware that could undermine Windows because it featured its own API hooks for which software developers could write applications. Microsoft, he testified, was determined to subvert this threat. To resolve this dispute, he said, citing the sworn deposition of two other Apple executives, Microsoft proposed that Apple abandon QuickTime and concentrate—much as they had allegedly asked Netscape to—on a "much smaller portion of the market," in this case the one "for software tools used to create multimedia content." Apple declined, he said, and Microsoft declared war, pressuring computer manufacturers—as they had pressured, say, Compaq to forgo Netscape's browser—not to include QuickTime on their machines.

Microsoft was ready with its written rebuttal before Dr. Tevanian took the stand, and it denied each and every one of his assertions. It might have gained more credibility with Judge Jackson—and the media—had it acknowledged its middleware concern or conceded its legitimate interest in keeping Apple away from Sun. Instead, the Microsoft statement held that for seventeen years the two companies have competed to offer the best operating system and cooperated to "ensure that our respective tools and applications interoperate for the benefit of consumers. . . . Microsoft has worked with Apple to ensure that QuickTime for Windows works great on Windows." Microsoft quoted Steve Jobs's public declaration that Internet Explorer was "the best browser out there." Microsoft insisted that Apple chose their browser—as it said AOL had—because it was technically superior to Netscape's. Coercion was foreign to Microsoft. Nor had Microsoft leaned on Apple to abandon QuickTime. Rather, "Microsoft was interested in combining the great work that both companies had done on multimedia playback and streaming media technologies to provide better solutions for customers." Nor had Microsoft pressured computer makers to avoid QuickTime, since they "have always been free to offer any third-party software they choose to their customers." Nor had Microsoft sabotaged Apple. QuickTime's bugs were caused by Apple's engineers, not Microsoft's. Why would Microsoft harm the ten million Mac customers who used Microsoft's Office software? Rather than damaging Apple, Microsoft had stood by it when Apple was on its heels, beset by unstable management, declining market share, and mounting losses of $800 million in 1996 and more than $1 billion in 1997. Demonstrating its commitment to Apple, Microsoft's brief noted that its two hundred employees developing software for Mac Office was the largest Mac software group outside Apple.

But Microsoft's cross-examination of Tevanian did not shake him. Tevanian had turned to the left to look directly at Judge Jackson as he answered each of Warden's questions, and Jackson looked back, nodding at certain points. In open court, Tevanian tutored the judge on how difficult it really was for most consumers to make Netscape their default browser on the Macintosh, which Microsoft had said every consumer could do easily. When Microsoft's counsel continued to press the point, Judge Jackson exclaimed, "It certainly doesn't tell me how to do it!" Tevanian also expounded on the applications barrier to entry, explaining that few software developers could profit from working for Microsoft competitors, and thus few did.

Although Bill Neukom did not think Tevanian a particularly effective witness, other members of his trial team did. Tod Nielsen, 31, a technical whiz with the ebullient personality of a salesman who was belatedly dispatched to the trial to help brief lawyers and reporters and who sometimes talked directly to Paul Maritz, Bill Gates, or Steve Ballmer from the courthouse on his cell phone, worried. "The lawyers talk of 'the record,'" he said. "All I know is the impression people make. The first day of Tevanian I called back and said, 'It's not going well. It was a rough morning.' Dave Heiner said, 'It was a great day. For the record we got our points across.'" Members of the public-relations team back in Redmond worried as well. They had wanted to attack Tevanian, to aggressively inform the press, even before he got on the witness stand, that QuickTime for Windows was sabotaged not by Microsoft but by Apple's own bugs. They also wanted to make public documents suggesting that Apple sometimes behaved like a thug. The company had always had a love/hate relationship with Microsoft, and because it was in perilous financial shape it had tried to extort $1.2 billion to settle its patent dispute. They beseeched Neukom: *Let's tell this story! You appear on the court steps at the end of each day and tell Microsoft's story!* Neukom responded, *No, we want to surprise Tevanian on the stand. We want to argue the case in court, not in the press. We don't want to risk offending Judge Jackson.* In the end, Tevanian's charges received more attention than Microsoft's defense.

More ominously, Judge Jackson was offended by Microsoft's stone-walling defense, by what he described as their constant "spin," their effort to explain away everything and admit nothing. "The sense I got was that Apple was genuinely apprehensive that Microsoft was going to pull the plug on them, and I believed them," Jackson later told me. A shadow was lengthening over Microsoft's courtroom fortunes.

CHAPTER 6

Microsoft's Hole Gets Deeper

T HE MICROSOFT LEGAL TEAM settled into its daily routine: gather at
Sullivan & Cromwell's offices in the morning, head over to court,
huddle for lunch in a back room at the Mark, just a few blocks away,
then return to S&C at the end of the day. At about 6:00 each evening, the
legal team conducted a conference call they dubbed the Heiner report,
after David Heiner, who was thought of as the team's defensive coach.
On the phone were the lawyers, usually all twelve of Microsoft's scheduled witnesses, and any other Microsoft executives who chose to partici-
pate. Bill Gates, who told the world that he and his employees were
focused on building great software, not dwelling on events in a distant
courtroom, participated in some of these calls. Heiner briefed everyone
on what had occurred each day and on what to expect. Neukom also dispatched e-mail updates to Gates. The public-relations team, under the
direction of Mark Murray, also hosted a conference call with the various
managers of Microsoft's media efforts, including representatives from
their two outside public-relations advisers, Waggener Edstrom and Edel-
man Public Relations Worldwide. Late each night, the lawyers often
came together for a nightcap at the Four Seasons bar. Even later at night,
Greg Shaw usually composed an e-mail missive recounting for everyone,

including Bill Gates, how they had fared in media coverage of the trial that day.

The trial lawyers did not sleep on bare mattresses, but they were on combat footing. Most weekends, the team stayed together to prep for the next week. It was Bill Neukom's mission to create a sense of esprit. Although he was silent in court, Neukom made a point of thanking every lawyer at the completion of a witness examination, and he thanked everyone in the office when they worked late. As partial compensation for rarely allowing them to get home to their families in Seattle or New York, Neukom sometimes treated the members of the group to "morale dinners," usually on Saturdays; sometimes he'd reserve several pool tables and dispense cigars.

Going into November 1998, Neukom's own morale still seemed unwavering. Despite the setbacks Microsoft had endured, he was no less optimistic than he had been on the first day of the trial. He insisted over breakfast one morning that the government's case evaded the central conclusion of the Court of Appeals decision permitting Microsoft to tie a browser into its operating system. "The Court of Appeals ruled, simply, that we could bundle so long as there's a plausible benefit to consumers," he told me. "The law is designed to encourage companies to innovate and enhance services for consumers. . . . The Sherman Act says vigorous competition is good." As he did throughout the trial, Neukom returned repeatedly to the Court of Appeals ruling. Neukom was especially dismissive of Washington's political culture for ignoring that ruling and for demonizing Gates: "You have a strange disconnect in that the government lost a lawsuit hands down, but their approach to this case and their stature in this city doesn't seem to reflect that fact." Without question, the Court of Appeals ruling was a tremendous victory for Microsoft, but what Neukom didn't acknowledge was that it was a narrow ruling that merely said that Microsoft's integration did not violate the consent decree. The higher court did not decide whether Microsoft was a monopoly, did not decide that tying products was permitted under the Sherman Act, and did not exonerate Microsoft's behavior based on a comprehensive review of evidence.

The disconnect between what Microsoft and what the government considered normal corporate behavior only widened with the government's fourth witness, Intel Vice President Steven D. McGeady. So did the gap between the Gates of legend and the Gates on video display.

The fact that an Intel executive testified against Microsoft was unusual. Intel had long been Microsoft's foremost ally. Since 1984, the two had worked side by side to assure that Intel's processors could power PCs running each new version of Windows, sharing chip-architecture specs and software code long before their products came to market. Joined, Intel chips were the motor and Windows the central nervous system of each PC. This "Wintel" axis dominated the industry, animating more than 80 percent of all PCs. Yes, there had been strains, particularly since Intel's chairman, Andrew Grove, was a generation older than Gates and often found him immature; none had proved crippling. Nonetheless, while Intel insisted that McGeady was testifying only because he was asked by the government and that it was "neutral in this dispute," one sensed that McGeady would not have testified as enthusiastically as he did without at least a nod from his boss.

This was true only up to a point. That point came when McGeady warned Intel he would hold nothing back if the government, his government, insisted on his testimony. As John Heilemann would report in *Wired* (November 2000), McGeady was so fervent a believer that "Microsoft is a fucking evil corporation" that even when his Intel superiors tried to intervene and threatened to fire him if he testified against their ostensible corporate ally, McGeady told them to stuff it. The day McGeady was set to give his deposition, Intel induced Joel Klein to withdraw his government attorneys, threatening that if Klein deposed McGeady they would drop their neutrality and side with Microsoft. By the fall of 1998, when Justice said it wanted him to testify, McGeady defied his superiors and consented. So convinced was David Boies and Justice that McGeady had a powerful tale to tell that he was the sole government witness to testify without first being deposed.

The tale McGeady told in his testimony was familiar: Microsoft was a bully, to allies as well as adversaries. The morning before McGeady was summoned to the stand and before Microsoft's lawyers got a shot at the witness, David Boies played another installment of the Gates deposition. It was excruciating, for Microsoft's omniscient chairman suddenly became senescent. Asked whether his company ever made an effort to convince Intel not to do business with Sun, Gates slouched in his chair and for an interminable thirty seconds rocked back and forth, his eyes on the floor, saying nothing. "Not that I know," he finally whispered. Did he try to persuade Intel not to dabble in the software business? Again, a long silence, followed by, "No."

When McGeady began his testimony later that afternoon, he flatly contradicted Gates. He described an August 1995 meeting at which Gates warned that if Intel didn't cease work on certain software projects and curb its 750 software engineers "who were, in his view, competing with Microsoft," then Microsoft would withdraw its support for Intel's next generation of microprocessors. Boies also introduced Microsoft and Intel e-mail, including a damning one from Gates to senior executives describing a July 1995 meeting with Andrew Grove: "One point [I] keep pushing to Andy is that we are the software company here and we will not have any kind of equal relationship with Intel on software." At the time, McGeady described the meeting this way: "Bill Gates told Intel CEO Andy Grove to shut down the Intel Architecture Labs. Gates didn't want IAL's 750 engineers interfering with his plans for domination of the PC industry. Gates made vague threats." Microsoft was particularly unhappy about Intel's effort to improve the multimedia performance of PCs by building native signal processing (NSP) into its chips. NSP, like Netscape's browser or Apple's QuickTime, was theoretically middleware: software developers could circumvent Microsoft's operating system and write programs for NSP. According to documents Boies introduced as court exhibits, Gates was determined to force Intel to kill it, and Microsoft sent word to computer manufacturers (OEMs) to stay clear of it.

Boies produced notes McGeady had made describing a Gates speech to Intel executives on July 11, 1995, one year after Microsoft and the government had signed the consent decree. Gates was quoted as predicting that "this antitrust thing will blow over" and boasting, "We haven't changed our business practices at all." What we may change, said Gates, was our "e-mail retention policies." Boies suggested in court that he was shocked that Gates would say such things to a business partner. To the government, this was a stark demonstration of Microsoft's unrepentant arrogance. To Microsoft spokesman Mark Murray, it was an irrelevant "sideshow." In some ways, Murray was right. Microsoft's actions were on trial, not its words. And there is a perfectly benign interpretation of Gates's remarks: he was just attempting to reassure a partner. What was he supposed to say: *We're in a hell of a bind. Perhaps Intel should find another partner?* A CEO has a responsibility to be truthful, to be sure, but also to lead, to inspire allies, shareholders, and employees.

Even if Gates was literally correct, however, Boies seemed to better grasp that when intent is at issue, words matter. For example, in his videotaped deposition, when Gates was asked about an e-mail in which a Microsoft executive called the browser battle with Netscape a "jihad," Boies asked Gates, What did the executive mean? "I think he is referring to our vigorous efforts to make a superior product and to market that product," replied Gates.

Microsoft might have attacked Intel for behaving much as the government accused Microsoft of acting. They might have noted that the Federal Trade Commission was investigating Intel, pursuing charges that the chip-making monopoly withheld vital information about its next generation of chips from three PC manufacturers that required it to design their machines, punishing the companies for refusing to settle patent disputes on Intel's terms. But Intel was too crucial an ally. Microsoft certainly went after McGeady, attacking him as a disgruntled executive who had missed out on promotions, whose memory of events was disputed by other Intel executives, and who didn't understand that NSP would not work properly with Windows 95 and would thus slow PC sales. But they struck no telling blows. Privately, Judge Jackson found McGeady convincing. It was significant to Jackson that McGeady came from an equally dominant corporate entity. "He had nothing to lose, or gain, by testifying," Jackson later told me. "They're still going to do business together." In his oversized green notebook, Jackson wrote: "Gates complained that their software competed with Microsoft" and "Gates wanted advance notice of what Intel was working on."

The fifth week of the trial, starting November 16, 1998, brought the fifth government witness, Glenn E. Weadock. A computer consultant and independent software executive, he was summoned to challenge Microsoft's assertion that its integrated browser better served customers. Not so, Weadock's written testimony read. In fact, many of the nation's largest companies resented the bundled product because it was a costly inconvenience. If a company didn't want the browser—and many companies didn't, either not wanting their employees distracted by Internet access or already using Netscape—they had to pay to remove Internet Explorer. And if they kept two browsers, they wasted computer space. "Organizations typically consider browser software as applications software, like E-mail or word processing. . . . No corporate PC manager, in fact no one outside of the Microsoft organization," Weadock declared, "has *ever* described a Web browser to me as operating system software." Weadock echoed the government's central assertion: Microsoft integrated two separate products because it intended to maim Netscape.

In challenging Weadock, Microsoft made the valid point that the distinction between an application and an operating system was becoming more muddled, as customer expectations rose and what was once an option became an essential. In turn, this went to the heart of the dispute between Redmond, Washington, and Washington, D.C. Microsoft believed the government was trying to impose software definitions on an industry; the government, with its own allies in Silicon Valley, believed it was trying to induce Microsoft to obey the law.

Again, however, questions of intent intruded. To attack Microsoft's claim that it merged a browser with Windows to benefit consumers, Boies offered another taste of Gates's videotaped deposition. It started with Boies showing Gates an e-mail Gates had written on January 5, 1996, in which he told Paul Maritz that boosting Microsoft's browser market share was a "very, very important goal for us."

BOIES: Are you aware of documents within Microsoft that describe browser share as the company's number-one goal?

GATES: No. I'm aware of documents within Paul Maritz's group that may have stated that.

BOIES: Is Paul Maritz's group within Microsoft?

GATES: Yes, but his—he doesn't set the companywide goals. . . .

BOIES: Now, let's say that you meant browser usage because that's what your testimony is. What browser usage were you talking about in terms of what your share of browser usage was? What browsers?

GATES: I'm not getting your question. Are you trying to ask what I was thinking when I wrote this sentence?

BOIES: . . . You don't have an answer to that question, let me put a different question.

GATES: I have an answer. The answer is I don't remember.

BOIES: OK. You don't remember what you meant. Now let me try to ask you—

GATES: I don't remember what I was thinking.

BOIES: Is there a difference between remembering what you were thinking and remembering what you meant?

GATES: If the question is what I meant when I wrote it, no.

BOIES: OK. So you don't remember what you were thinking when you wrote it and you don't remember what you meant when you wrote it; is that fair?

GATES: As well as not remember writing it. . . .

BOIES: What non-Microsoft browsers were you concerned about in January of 1996?

GATES: I don't know what you mean, "concerned"?

BOIES: What is it about the word *concerned* that you don't understand?

GATES: I'm not sure what you mean by it. . . .

BOIES: Is the term *concerned* a term that you're familiar with in the English language?

GATES: Yes.

BOIES: Does it have a meaning you're familiar with?

GATES: Yes.

BOIES: Using the term *concerned* consistent with the normal meaning that it has in the English language, what Microsoft—or what non-Microsoft—browsers were you concerned about in January of 1996?

GATES: Well, I think I would have been concerned about Internet Explorer.

The government's sixth witness was John Soyring, who joined IBM in 1976 and was its director of network computing–software services. Soyring had witnessed IBM's transformation in the latter half of the nineties under CEO Louis Gerstner from an atrophying giant into a muscular one. By 1999, its revenues were more than four times those of Microsoft, and its e-commerce efforts—selling goods and services and engineering over the Internet—now accounted for $20 billion of its $87.5 billion in revenues. IBM had its more mature, slow-growth divisions, such as those selling PCs and mainframe computers and storage systems, as well as a fast-growing global-services unit of 130,000 consultants to help companies establish state-of-the-art computer systems. In addition, under Gerstner IBM was striving not to repeat the mistake it made in the early eighties when it failed to retain exclusive rights to Microsoft's DOS operating system and later declined a stake in Microsoft; instead, IBM went out and acquired Lotus, a software company whose products often competed with Microsoft's. By calling Soyring, the government hoped to show how Microsoft could even bully such a powerhouse, how the applications barrier to the operating-systems market blocked IBM's efforts to launch OS/2 as a rival to Windows, and how Microsoft saw Sun's Java programming language as a threat that might eliminate this barrier.

In his written deposition, released the morning before he appeared to testify, Soyring recounted how IBM had introduced OS/2 in 1987, invested "hundreds of millions of dollars" in it, saw it heaped with praise, but watched in dismay as its market share stalled. Nearly ten years after its launch, OS/2 accounted for a mere 6 percent of world-wide PC operating systems, compared to Windows's 92 percent. Soyring left no doubt as to the reason: Microsoft and its applications barrier.

> Customers purchase PCs in order to run application programs, which are particular software products that allow users to do the things they want to do such as write letters or handle their personal finances. Many important applications designed to run on Windows have not been made available in versions designed to run on OS/2 or have only been made available with limited function or significantly later than the Windows version of the same application. Examples include popular games, leading desktop publishing applications, and office productivity products. This unavailability of applications has been an important reason for OS/2's relatively limited acceptance.

The roadblock IBM encountered, Soyring continued, was that for a software application to work on an operating system it must attach itself to the system through the system's applications programming interface (APIs). Since these codes are not standardized and are usually proprietary, companies that develop software applications (commonly referred to as independent software vendors or ISVs) usually do so for "the most widely used operating system. This gives them the greatest opportunity to make sales, recover their cost and make the most efficient use of their limited development resources. . . . This, in part, explains why there are not more applications for OS/2." No market, no software; no software, no market; a brutally simple cycle.

The other part of the explanation, Soyring said, was Microsoft's restrictive contracts, which limit a software maker's ability to sell its product to a Windows competitor. OS/2 started with a small market share, which provided little financial incentive for software developers to devise OS/2 applications, and the vise was tightened by Microsoft, which restricted developers from working with OS/2. Thus, members of the entire PC industry, from software developers to PC makers to manufacturers of such products as printers and graphics cards, "tend to focus their resources on ensuring their products work with Windows." This network of coercive relationships was a reason Microsoft was sometimes described by its rivals as an "evil empire."

Soyring went on to describe Microsoft's heavy-handed response to the emergence of Sun's Java, the software language that threatened Microsoft's hegemony because it was intended to run on any operating system. Microsoft reacted, Soyring suggested, by licensing Java from Sun and then releasing its own version of Java for Windows. Microsoft connived, Soyring said, to use its version of Java to block software developers from writing universal applications that ran on alternate systems. And by insisting that its own version of Java be part of its own browser, Microsoft negated the potential of Netscape's browser, which had been "the prime distribution vehicle for Sun's Java technology, to undermine Windows advantage." To demonstrate Microsoft's paranoia about Java, David Boies introduced e-mail written by Bill Gates to his executives in October 1997: "The Java religion coming out of the software group [at IBM] is a big problem. . . . They continue to use their PCs to distribute things against us."

In court, Microsoft countered by producing IBM documents justifying at least some of Microsoft's paranoia. IBM clearly had allied with Sun and Netscape, as an August 1997 e-mail from John M. Thompson, chief of IBM's software division, revealed. To Scott McNealy of Sun and James Barksdale of Netscape, Thompson wrote: "We must work together using all of our collective contacts to establish Java as the standard. We must move quickly to pre-empt Microsoft." Microsoft argued that IBM conspired to collude with Sun and Netscape to recruit Apple, Oracle, and Novell for a joint campaign to, in Thompson's words, "put Microsoft on the defensive." IBM's OS/2 failed, Microsoft said, because it was harder to use than Windows, because it was suitable for only the most powerful machines on the market since it ate up too much memory, and because Microsoft courted software developers and IBM did not. IBM, not Microsoft, was responsible for these strategic mistakes. Nor was it Microsoft's responsibility, the company argued, to guarantee that software applications using Windows APIs could run on other operating systems. As long as Microsoft did not restrict developers' freedom to work elsewhere, they could not be held responsible for a so-called applications barrier. And as for Java, the reason Microsoft devised its own version was not to raise the barrier but to improve Java, since Microsoft's Java allowed applications to run better and faster.

But on November 17, 1998, while John Soyring was still on the witness stand, a district-court judge in California ordered Microsoft to stop shipping Windows 98 until it removed its version of Java. Sun Microsystems claimed that Microsoft, which signed a licensing agreement in 1995 to ship Java with Windows 98 and with its browser, had decided to "pollute" Java so that its non-Windows version would not work as well on Microsoft operating systems, while the Java for Windows version would not work on non-Microsoft operating systems. The judge sided with Sun, at least in this first round. (In the second round, in January 2000, a federal court ordered Microsoft to follow Sun standards when selling products that use Java.)

More bad news struck Microsoft during the appearance of the seventh witness, Frederick R. Warren-Boulton, an economist who had served in the Reagan administration. His appearance lingers less for his proclamation that Microsoft was a monopoly or for his vague assertion that Microsoft's prices were "significantly" higher than they would be if they faced real competition than for a dramatic moment that came during a private meeting in Judge Jackson's chambers, recorded by the court stenographer. To illuminate some of Warren-Boulton's statements, Boies had been forging ahead in playing excerpts from Gates's deposition, and Microsoft was desperate now to shut down this drawn-out embarrassment. "There is no legitimate purpose vis-à-vis the trial in playing this deposition in bits and pieces," John Warden complained to Judge Jackson. Just play it all at once, he urged.

Judge Jackson quickly dismissed this request, saying, "If anything, I think your problem is with your witness, not with the way in which his testimony is being presented."

Startled, Warden said, "Your Honor doesn't expect me to address that last comment at this time, I take it."

"I think it's evident to every spectator that, for whatever reasons, in many respects Mr. Gates has not been particularly responsive to his deposition interrogation." If there was any doubt in the Microsoft camp about how they were doing, Jackson's words should have dispelled it.

Warren-Boulton's testimony was further overshadowed by an event that occurred outside the courtroom: on November 24, 1998, America Online announced that in exchange for $4.2 billion of its stock, it was acquiring Netscape, and it was also joining with Sun Microsystems to build an Internet-service company that could rival Microsoft and IBM. Gleefully, Microsoft's attorneys transformed this "bad" news into "good." On the witness stand, an economist testified that Microsoft was a monopoly, but in the real world America Online had just acquired a browser with a declining but still hefty 40 to 50 percent market share; nine million registered visitors to its portal site, Netcenter; a full-service website favored by its many corporate customers who used it as a jumping-off point to the Web; a pool of talented programmers, led by Marc Andreessen; and a business-sales support staff of seven hundred. The partnerships brought together three Microsoft rivals into a single potential colossus with real potential to hurt Microsoft. If AOL now decided to replace Microsoft's browser with Netscape's, Netscape would overnight become the dominant browser again.

Usually, Bill Neukom did not appear on the front steps of the courthouse after court recessed, but on the day the merger was announced he was eager to. "From a legal standpoint, this proposed deal pulls the rug out from under the government," he told the assembled reporters. "It proves indisputably that no company can control the supply of technology. We are part of an industry that is remarkably dynamic and ever changing." Days after the merger was announced, Microsoft took out full-page newspaper ads to say essentially the same thing.

"I think they're delighted that we announced the Netscape deal," Steve Case told me, a smile creasing his intense face. "It gave them an excuse to change the subject."

David Boies did not try to camouflage the damage. On the courthouse steps, he conceded that even if Microsoft lost the trial it could win remedy relief: "All of the elements of the way the industry looks are going to be relevant when it comes to the issue of remedy." If Judge Jackson concluded that Microsoft confronted genuine competition, he would presumably veer from breaking up Microsoft.

With the next government witness, Dr. James A. Gosling, the Sun Microsystems executive who led the small team that created Java, Boies focused on the Java threat. While Boies delighted in showering the courtroom with Microsoft e-mail describing their "jihad" against Netscape or Sun, it was undeniably true that there was also an anti-Microsoft jihad, and the mullah leading it was Scott McNealy, the CEO of Sun. Utter the name *Gates* or *Microsoft* in front of McNealy and he gets agitated, rarely missing a chance to assail them as "evil." Unlike many colleagues—Steve Case, Louis Gerstner, Steve Jobs—who were

Microsoft adversaries but maintained discreet silences about the trial, McNealy flat-out supported the Justice Department's lawsuit. And because he believed Bill Gates and Microsoft were incapable of altering their own behavior, he said Microsoft should be split into many parts. The deep personal animosity between McNealy and Gates was also reflected in their business competition. Although Sun had only about half Microsoft's revenues, it was also a darling of Wall Street stock pickers. As a hardware company that built high-end servers, disk-storage systems, and workstations, Sun did not bump into Microsoft. But in programming powerful computer servers with software for corporations, they fiercely collided, for Microsoft Office was upgrading to pursue this market. And they collided in software: with Java, which was meant to be an alternate platform; with Solaris, an operating system for servers; with Java and Jini technology incorporated in operating systems for wireless devices, a market Microsoft chased with Windows CE; and with professional services, where Sun had a team of more than two thousand corporate consultants, a business Microsoft coveted. And Sun evangelized incessantly for a cheap network PC that drew its software off the Internet, claiming that this would destroy Microsoft's monopoly and serve consumers.

Before Gosling uttered a word, Boies played a thirty-minute installment of the Gates videotape, in which Gates denied that he was concerned about Java, and Boies introduced a Gates e-mail composed around this time that said, "[Java] scares the hell out of me." Gates denied he was ever concerned about the Netscape browser because it carried and spread Java, and Boies submitted as evidence an e-mail from Paul Maritz to Gates in which Maritz wrote: "If we looked further at Java being our major threat, then Netscape is the major distribution vehicle." In another exchange, Gates became petulant when Boies asked about an internal e-mail stating that Microsoft was "just proactively trying to put obstacles in Sun's path." "I don't know what that means," he huffed.

In his cross-examination, Microsoft attorney Thomas Burt took the sheen off Sun and its bearded, longhaired witness. Burt produced documents showing that Sun developed Java in part as a means of "attacking the Microsoft franchise" and becoming a new platform standard for the industry. He read e-mail messages Gosling had written to McNealy stating that Sun should give Microsoft "the illusion of working with them" while conspiring with others to "beat them." He introduced another e-mail in which a Sun manager described meetings with Netscape at which the two companies agreed not to compete in Internet software. "Unify browser efforts; stop competing," read one memo. He produced Sun e-mail that was every bit as juvenile as Microsoft's could be. He produced independent technical support for Microsoft's assertion that Java was flawed. His probing prompted Judge Jackson to intervene with his own questions, and at one point Jackson asked the witness how he would respond to Sun and Microsoft documents that suggested Microsoft "produced in a relatively short time a better version of what you were working on and simply couldn't wait for you to catch up." But no Microsoft barrister could erase the glaring credibility gap between Bill Gates's videotaped deposition and his contemporaneous e-mail.

By the trial's seventh and eighth weeks, in December 1998, the government's case was winding down. Its ninth and tenth witnesses were David J. Farber, a computer-science professor at the University of Pennsylvania, and Edward W. Felten, a Princeton University computer scientist. Each in his own way tried to address the government's bundling claim. Each tried to demonstrate that Microsoft's browser was artificially bolted to Windows, strengthening the argument that Microsoft pretended these separate products were one as an excuse to savage Netscape. Felten testified that combining the browser with Windows was a marketing decision and offered consumers no technological benefit they couldn't have if the products were separate. Felten testified that he had fashioned a computer program that did what Microsoft said was impossible: remove the Microsoft browser without disabling Windows. He conducted an eye-glazing demonstration to prove this.

Microsoft rigorously challenged both men. Sullivan & Cromwell attorney Steven L. Holley portrayed Farber as a troglodyte who would deny consumers the convenience of easy computing and Internet access. He compared Farber's argument to the business model of the company that made Heathkits in the sixties, a product that gave technically competent people the choice of building their own electronic machines. "Most people don't have any interest in buying Heathkits," Holley said. "They wanted to go to the store and buy a radio that was already assembled." As for Felten's computer program, Microsoft attorney David Heiner went through a technically elaborate demonstration to show that Felten had not deleted the four files that activate the browser in Windows 98 but rather deleted a stub loader file that activates the Web browser. Felten had hidden the browser, Heiner said, not removed it. Of course, Microsoft's arguments may have been technically correct, but they did not address the issue of intent. If the browser couldn't be unbundled, was this not because Microsoft deliberately designed it that way? Even if most consumers wanted a browser, what was the harm in offering a browserless version of Windows? Because Microsoft had backed itself into a corner where it couldn't acknowledge that *any* of its business practices were intended to strike at Netscape's market share, it was left to quibble with every little point, elongating the trial and irritating Judge Jackson.

Watching from the gallery, Microsoft's Tod Nielsen seemed increasingly skeptical of the company's courtroom posture, even if he couldn't quite say so. Once, as he watched Judge Jackson labor to follow Microsoft's technical arguments, he shook his head and winked to a reporter in a way that signaled concern. Outside the courtroom he explained, "I don't have expectations for this judge that it will be a positive outcome. This is a technical topic. I don't think he understands it." But he also feared that neither Microsoft's attorneys nor the company understood that their pedantic approach was losing the theatrical war, if not the legal one as well. "Because our culture demands that we must respond to every false piece of mud thrown at us, it means that we clutter things up."

When the trial resumed, on January 4, 1999, after a holiday break, Microsoft's p.r. efforts were more visible. Bill Neukom seemed to have undergone a modest personality makeover, for he was noticeably less aloof. Instead of passing reporters in the hallway with a polite nod, as he usually did, this day he stopped and mingled, inquired about vacations, informally answered questions. He seemed more of a salesman; from this time on, he appeared almost daily at the end of the day to field questions. Standing beside Neukom in the corridor outside the courtroom was a notably more jovial John Warden, who made a point of walking across the hall to greet the government's eleventh witness, William Harris, then the president and CEO of Intuit.

A short man with round, wire-framed eyeglasses and a Kennedyesque shock of dark hair streaked with gray, Harris was perceived by Microsoft as part of the anti-Microsoft Silicon Valley cabal, and not without reason. Intuit had thus far trumped Microsoft's Money software package with its own, Quicken, a product as dominant in the personal financial-software marketplace as Microsoft was in operating systems. Intuit's chairman, William V. Campbell, was on Netscape's board of directors. Why else would Harris have agreed to testify? Intuit was a key player in the browser wars because copies of its Quicken software were distributed on a CD-ROM which also contained software to download a browser. Thus, in the battle between Microsoft and Netscape, Intuit could be a potent distributor of browsers. But Harris declared in his written deposition that the important distribution network was provided by computer manufacturers, and here Microsoft was the gatekeeper, since every PC maker needed Windows. And, Harris noted, any software applications Intuit introduced had to work on Windows, and therefore Microsoft held the upper hand since Intuit depended on its goodwill. Besides, Intuit needed access to a browser, since a larger and larger share of its future revenues would come from its website, on which it would sell ads, charge transaction fees from third parties that sell services through it, and garnish user fees. Because Intuit's business was increasingly predicated on access to a browser, Harris said Microsoft used its market power to force Intuit to promote Internet Explorer "and to forgo business relationships with Microsoft's browser competitor, Netscape, including our then-existing arrangement to distribute and promote Navigator." To seal the deal, Microsoft ceded Intuit a prime spot on the Microsoft desktop screen for its Internet-based offerings.

Harris was there to show that Microsoft had used its monopoly power to coerce Intuit and others to shut out Netscape and thus to foreclose competition and illegally preserve its monopoly, in violation of section 2 of the Sherman Act. The government also planned to use his testimony to introduce the subject of remedies, as he was eager to prevent Microsoft from further abusing its enormous power. In his written testimony, Harris warned that because Windows was so prevalent, Microsoft was poised to capture a "choke point" over the Internet, and he proposed that Judge Jackson declare Windows "an essential service" and order that it should be "neutral"—to be neither denied to any customer nor used to bundle or unfairly promote other Microsoft applications and products. If conduct remedies fell short, Harris suggested, the judge should preside over Microsoft's breakup.

Again, before David Boies conducted his redirect examination of the witness, he first played a segment of Gates's video deposition. The tape showed an obviously irate Gates staring down at the floor while Boies asked, Did Microsoft, in its 1997 negotiations, urge Intuit not to support Netscape?

Gates said he did not know.

Did Microsoft ask Intuit to forgo promotional agreements with Netscape?

Again, Gates said he did not recall.

Boies handed him a Microsoft e-mail that Senior Vice President Brad Chase had forwarded to Gates on April 17, 1997. It contained "the highlights" of the agreement between Intuit and Microsoft. Under "Intuit obligations," it listed seven, including the proviso that Intuit would "not enter into marketing/promo agreements with Other Browser manufacturers," even if the other browser would be promoting Intuit.

Did Gates remember this e-mail?

No, Gates answered.

Did he remember being told the terms?

No.

Any reason to doubt he was told?

No.

Boies was intent on showing that Gates had shaped this agreement and would later introduce a July 24, 1996, e-mail Gates wrote to several of his senior executives in which he recapped discussions he had had with Intuit cofounder Scott Cook. In the e-mail, Gates had recounted his talk with Cook: "I was quite frank with him that if he had a favor we could do for him that would cost us something like $1M to do that in return for switching browsers in the next few months I would be open to doing that." In the courtroom, Boies referred to this offer as "a bribe, an inducement."

When John Warden cross-examined Harris, he managed to cloud Harris's claim that Intuit was blackmailed into dumping Netscape. Warden reminded the court that Harris, in his written testimony, admitted that Intuit's technical team found, in 1997, that Microsoft had added features (componentized) their browser so that it would launch silently, quickly, and without interrupting the sequence with its own opening screen. Netscape had failed to produce a browser that included features that Intuit had demanded. Warden also effectively raised the specter of ham-handed government regulation if the court followed Harris's proposed remedy: a "national operating-system commission" that would have to decide what software products and revisions Microsoft could introduce. Microsoft explained its insistence on exclusivity by maintaining that it was engaged in "strategic barter." More than with any other government witness, Warden used Harris to raise an issue that is at the heart of this case: are Microsoft's tactics normal or aberrant in corporate America? And even if normal, if Microsoft was deemed a monopoly would the tactics be permissible?

In defending itself against Harris and other witnesses, Microsoft sought to show that its corporate behavior was not only ethical but commonplace. Warden did trap Harris into conceding that Intuit and others have, in some respects, behaved as Microsoft had. Harris admitted that his Quicken software had a market share of between 65 and 80 percent but insisted that it wasn't a monopoly because "all of these products are subject to effective competition." Harris admitted that Intuit offered financial inducements, much as Microsoft had, to computer manufacturers to load Quicken onto PCs. Harris admitted that Intuit had agreed to pay a bounty of thirty million dollars to AOL to display Quicken as its "primary" personal-finance Web channel. And Harris admitted that Intuit negotiated a deal with the Excite portal site to become its "exclusive provider and aggregator of financial content," just as Microsoft negotiated exclusive deals.

It is the natural order of things for a business—any business—to extol capitalism's risks while striving to eliminate them. "Every businessman wants one hundred percent of his market," observed investment banker Herbert Allen. "Just as every writer wants to hog the bestseller list." Ray Kroc, the founder of McDonald's, once said of competition in the fast-food industry: "This is rat eat rat, dog eat dog. I'll kill 'em, and I'm going to kill 'em before they kill me." Chalk this zeal up to human nature, said former Federal Communications Commission chairman Reed Hundt, a onetime antitrust lawyer: "It's not immoral. It's business." When it becomes onerous, he continued, "that's where government has to step in." One mission of government is to police "factions," to check the excesses of a free market, and, however imperfectly, to strive to protect the public interest. But the law treats monopolies differently from other businesses, and Microsoft was betting the company that this court, and higher courts, would not judge Microsoft a monopoly. One night at the Capital Grill, not far from the courthouse, David Boies said it's true that "everyone does it. But everyone is not a monopoly." Microsoft's operating system is the essential plumbing on which applications like Intuit's Quicken relies, which is why Microsoft is a monopoly and Intuit is not. Besides, added Boies, "some of the actions they've taken are more brazen, maybe more heavy-handed, than you typically see." Perhaps this is because antitrust laws have become more relaxed in recent years, he said.

Did Boies think of Microsoft as more cynical or more childish than most? "Maybe the answer is both. What leads them to go to Intel and say, 'You can't engage in software that you want to.' That is not normal corporate behavior." Did he think of them as children? "There may be something to that," he said. "I don't know who's socializing them. If you looked at a lot of things they've done a fair question to be asked is, Do they really think they're doing anything wrong or do they think that's the way the game is played?" In interpreting antitrust law, the courts obviously seek to make a distinction between corporate hardball and coercion, between competition and foreclosure, between "good" and "bad" monopolies, between playing by the rules or bending and breaking them. Under the law, the crucial first question is whether the company is a monopoly.

To advance the claim that Microsoft met the definition of a monopoly, the government called as its final witness Dr. Franklin M. Fisher, an economics professor at MIT. A white-haired professor with a wrinkled gray suit, Fisher was known as David Boies's favorite economist, since Boies first relied on him to testify in the IBM case in 1970, in which he argued that the computer giant was not a monopoly, and has since used him as an expert witness in other antitrust cases.

Dr. Fisher was paid five hundred dollars an hour to prepare and testify, and he tried to address the core issue that would help determine Microsoft's guilt or innocence: was Microsoft a monopoly? "Computer manufacturers," he testified, "do not believe they have any alternative to the acquisition and installation" of Windows. He quoted the depositions of various PC makers, who said that even if Microsoft hiked the price of Windows by 10 percent, they would feel obliged to purchase it. Fisher went further, claiming that Microsoft's price was already excessive. He cited as proof the fact that Windows 98 was more expensive than Windows 95 (ignoring that Windows 98 offered more features), and that, even though the price of PCs had declined, Microsoft's software now hogged a larger percentage of the cost of each PC. By bundling and giving away its browser, Fisher said, Microsoft was guilty of classic "predatory" behavior. By inducing AOL and other ISPs to enter into exclusionary agreements and by imposing restrictive contracts on PC makers, he said, Microsoft had effectively blocked Netscape's channels of distribution. And because of its market dominance, Fisher believed future competitors would succumb to the law of "network effects" or "increasing returns." He said it was "a joke" to think that Microsoft was seriously challenged by competing operating systems such as Macintosh, Linux, Be, or OS/2. There was no money to be made by software developers if they wrote applications for these, he said, because riches were only to be made working for the market leader, Windows.

Then, after speculating that future consumers would be harmed by the way Microsoft hobbled Netscape and that Microsoft would thus be free to raise prices, Fisher was asked if current consumers were being victimized by Microsoft. After at first hesitating and mumbling, he declared, "On balance, I would think the answer was no, up to this point." A small smile creased Bill Neukom's normally expressionless face. David Boies had a blank, stoic look, as did Joel Klein, for each knew they had some damage control to do. William Kovacic, who had been reading the daily transcripts of the trial and occasionally attending, later told me that Fisher's admission was "the single greatest testimonial blunder for the government" in the entire trial, ranking with the harm done Microsoft by Bill Gates's videotape. The real harm to consumers, Fisher hurried to assert, would appear in the future, when Microsoft raised prices and it became clearer that Microsoft impeded innovation.

Of course, this fell into the realm of speculation, not evidence, and Sullivan & Cromwell attorney Michael Lacovara did his skillful best to sabotage Fisher. Wasn't it true, Lacovara asserted, that devices other than the PC could access the Web? Wasn't it true that there might be a shift away from the PC as the sole computing platform? Perhaps people would access the Internet using a handheld personal digital assistant, such as a Palm Pilot? Perhaps a cellular phone? Perhaps a cheap device pushed by Sun and Oracle could use a browser to connect to massive servers or to the Internet? Perhaps a rival technology was being invented in a garage at this very moment? Didn't Netscape burst forth in just one year? The handheld Palm Pilot instantly rocketed to sales of more than two million. Wasn't it true that other software—Be or Macintosh or Linux or OS/2—could become a rival operating system? Perhaps a browser or RealNetworks middleware would, as Microsoft feared, supplant Windows? Wasn't it true that AOL's merger with Netscape and their joint alliance with Sun was a setback for Microsoft?

Lacovara proceeded to read to Fisher excerpts from a November 24, 1998, press conference at which the CEOs of America Online, Netscape, and Sun appeared. Steve Case boasted of a "new era" that would be based on Sun's "operating system" and alternative platforms to those of Microsoft. Wasn't this a competitive threat? Fisher responded by stating his belief, one that Microsoft halfheartedly challenged, that for "the fore-seeable future" Microsoft would remain paramount. The real debate is not over the next few years but three to ten years out, and here Fisher reiterated his faith that Microsoft would manage to squelch competition, and Lacovara expressed his faith—citing the facts of the market share of the Palm Pilot and other devices—that competition would flower. This debate about how the future will unfold was pivotal, for if the market-place will punish Microsoft there might be no need for a drastic govern-ment-imposed remedy.

Judge Jackson leaned forward throughout, intently following the exchange. At one point, he read aloud from an op-ed column in that morning's *Washington Post*, written by David Ignatius, in which Steve Case was quoted as contradicting what was said at the November 24 press conference. Case told Ignatius: "AOL's merger with Netscape has no bearing on the Microsoft case, as nothing we're doing is competitive with Windows. We have no flight of fancy that we can dent in any way, shape or form what is a [Microsoft] monopoly in the operating system business." The judge introduced the column as "Court Exhibit No. 1" and asked Fisher if he agreed with Case. To no one's great astonishment, he did. Microsoft's legal team quietly seethed, aghast that the judge would choose a press interview with a Microsoft adversary as the first piece of evidence the court itself introduced. They registered this as another indication of Judge Jackson's hostility to Microsoft.

Judge Jackson later turned to the lawyers and asked whether they planned to summon Case as a witness to end the confusion. Perhaps as a rebuttal witness, Warden answered, noncommittally.

When Fisher completed his testimony just prior to lunch break on January 13, 1999, the trial was at the theoretical halfway point. Bill Neukom, not surprisingly, said that he was pleased. "From a lawyer's standpoint, it's going well. We haven't seen a critical mass of permissible evidence presented by the government. I still think our motion for a summary judgment"—rejected by Judge Jackson—"is a motion that should have been granted. They can't prove foreclosure—that Microsoft did something that foreclosed the marketplace." Neukom could recite from memory Judge Learned Hand's famous dictum in the 1945 *Alcoa* case: "The successful competitor, having been urged to compete, must not be turned upon when he wins." David Boies also expressed pleasure. The government's witnesses, he believed, demonstrated that Microsoft enjoyed monopoly power, that they had "shut off channels of distribution" and strong-armed other companies, and that they relied on the applications barrier to entry to effectively foreclose competition and to assure their continued monopoly. Boies, for his part, could recite from memory parts of the 1912 Supreme Court ruling in the *Terminal Railroad Association* case, in which the Court found that the railroad station was what is now called an "essential facility" and said the association that owned it was guilty of restricting access to every rail route in and out of Saint Louis. Boies was convinced that the weight of evidence revealed that Microsoft's operating system was also an "essential facility" and that the company had illegally abused this power. So strong was the government's case, Boies told me, that he expected Microsoft to seek a settlement before the judge issued his ruling. Nevertheless, Microsoft had yet to present its first witness.

On the courthouse steps, fifteen cameras awaited the spin. Off to one side with the government team was Assistant Attorney General Joel Klein; in another cluster with the Microsoft team was Bill Neukom. While Klein scrupulously avoided regular press conferences and interviews with the daily reporters, he was not oblivious to the star power generated by this showcase trial. A recent bachelor, he wore Hermès ties and kept in the social mix of Washington with rotating tennis doubles matches and with coveted invitations to Georgetown dinner parties. He kept in touch with a parade of prominent Clinton supporters on trips to New York and California, and, along with more than a few captains of the industries he monitors, he attended a forty-sixth birthday party for Bertelsmann AG's CEO, Thomas Middelhoff. On the courthouse steps this day, Klein told the assembled reporters how well the government had done in proving that Microsoft had sought to "crush competition," to "coerce" friend and foe, to "restrict consumer choice," and to impose "high prices."

A moment later, Neukom stood ramrod straight before the same cameras and declared, "The curtain is coming down on a feeble case presented by the government." He accused the government of relying on e-mails that represented "isolated examples of language." He spotlighted the weakest part of the government's case—the claim that consumers were harmed—by reminding the reporters of what they had heard in court: the government's chief economic witness acknowledged "under oath that he has not detected any harm to consumers." In the flurry of press questions, I asked him: "Why would Microsoft spend hundreds of millions of dollars to develop a browser and then give it away for free?" Just trying to help consumers, he said. "We invest in technology to meet the needs and demands of our consumers."

"Why not just say: we were trying to kill Netscape, which was trying to kill us?"

"Microsoft is relentless in trying to improve our system to help consumers," Neukom responded placidly, chin tilted up.

CHAPTER 7

Spin

NOT LONG AFTER the government rested its case, Bill Gates again traveled to the World Economic Forum, in Davos, Switzerland. Before he made the annual luncheon speech on Sunday, his handlers instructed the conference emcee to announce, "Mr. Gates is not prepared to comment on the Department of Justice trial." Before the press could groan, Gates stepped forward and declared, "I'll take one or two questions on it, but at some point I'll get tired of it." He didn't tire of it. One of his close friends had told me that morning that Gates was terribly depressed and angry about the antitrust suit, but Gates himself told a different tale onstage. Did the trial make him upset at the Justice Department?

"No, I don't think bringing an emotional response to an issue like that is very constructive."

How was the case going?

"I have not been in the courtroom, but any e-mail I get from my lawyer tells me not to use the press as a lens in the courtroom." To personal questions, he was equally opaque. I rose and noted that last year when he was asked whether Microsoft was guilty of arrogance, he became angry. How did he respond as a human being, I wondered, when much of the world thinks Microsoft has done good yet the government says he and Microsoft had done bad? "I have a great deal of faith in the U.S. Constitution," he answered, going on to speak of the competition Microsoft faced but not about how he *felt*. Asked by *Washington Post* columnist Richard Cohen to express whether he worried that Microsoft might win the legal case yet lose its reputation, Gates invoked polls that showed his company was popular and went on to praise "the exemplary behavior" of Microsoft. He sounded as if he was reciting a press release.

Gates also sounded like the robotic panelists who joined him onstage the next day in the Congress Centre, before an overflow crowd of close to two thousand government and business leaders: the CEOs of Toshiba, Hewlett-Packard, Du Pont, Microsoft, and ABB Asea Brown Boveri of Switzerland. Their assignment was to talk about doing business in the global economy. The format was stilted: the moderator read a prepared text, followed by rote speeches by the panelists. As Gates waited his turn, he alternated between slumping low in his chair and tilting forward with his shoulders hunched, his lips pulled tight in a cross between a smile and a smirk. One sensed the restless boy in him. Like the others, he was wearing a suit and tie, but their outfits were dark and sober while his navy suit was set off by a bright-green polka-dot tie and a light purple shirt. He seemed ready to shout: *This is boring!* Jacques Manardo, the European chairman of Deloitte Touche Tohmatsu, who served as moderator and seemed to be hustling business, given the way he lacquered panelists with praise, said, about fifteen minutes into his remarks, "I could go on." Gates's eyebrows extended, and he let loose a tiny, muted squeal. But the little boy never did pop out. Gates politely waited his turn and then spoke extemporaneously. And at the end, the audience of world potentates still treated him like a rock star, directing their questions to him as if he were alone on the stage.

Around this time, Gates's charitable activities became significantly more visible. At a December 1998 black-tie benefit dinner in New York hosted by Rosie O'Donnell, Bill and Melinda Gates were honored—along with Michael Eisner of Disney and Jane Eisner—by the For All Kids Foundation. The next day, the Gateses held a press conference to announce that the William H. Gates Foundation was making a one-hundred-million-dollar gift to speed the distribution of vaccines throughout the third world, where more than two million children die each year from preventable diseases. This was the first part of what Melinda and Bill Gates expected to be a gift of $950 million. The Gates Foundation and the Gates Learning Foundation had made many generous gifts in the past, but what was unusual about this gift was that it was made in such a public way. The Gates Foundation, which was administered by Gates's father and focused on world health and population issues, and the Gates Learning Foundation, which was run by Patty Stonesifer and targeted education and bringing PCs to schools and libraries, in February 1999 received a total of $3.3 billion in new assets from Bill and Melinda Gates, bringing the total the Gateses had bequeathed to their foundations to nearly $5.5 billion. Bill Gates became America's most generous living philanthropist.

It is usually the Microsoft way to seize the initiative, to be proactive, and this approach extends from software development to public relations. Late in 1998, Microsoft retained Mark Penn, President Clinton's and Vice President Al Gore's pollster, to explore how to increase the public's perception of Gates and Microsoft as good corporate citizens. Penn adopted the same strategy that had worked in his last great war, just as Neukom did when he applied his anti-Apple legal strategy to this antitrust litigation. Penn's advice to Gates was the same as it was to Clinton during his impeachment imbroglio: since polls revealed he was popular with the public, while Microsoft might do better in making its case to opinion leaders, it need not panic and rip up its playbook. Shift the blame to opponents, Penn said; talk constantly about the plot by competitors to induce the government to sue Microsoft. Don't stop talking about Microsoft's primary concern, which is innovation and providing better software. Don't bow to the press ayatollahs. Don't show weakness. Penn reserved a prominent space on his Pennsylvania Avenue office wall for a framed front page of *The Washington Post* from the day the Senate voted not to remove Clinton from office. Written over the headline is the inscription, "Mark, thanks. Bill Clinton." For the Microsoft strategists who stared at it, and for all prospective clients, it was a reminder that they would survive if they listened to Mark Penn.

In some ways, however, Microsoft had already altered its playbook. After a mild internal debate over the Christmas holidays that pitted Mich Mathews's public-relations department (including Greg Shaw and Mark Murray) against Neukom, Bill Gates decided that Neukom should be more aggressive with the press. And the company that had once shunned the Washington political game had by 1999 doubled its spending on lobbying, recruiting as lobbyists former Republican National Committee chairman Haley Barbour, former Christian Coalition executive director Ralph Reed, House Majority Leader Richard K. Armey's former chief of staff Kerry Knott, former Clinton White House Special Counsel Mark Fabiani, as well as former Democratic House member and chairman of the Democratic Congressional Campaign Committee, Vic Fazio. These were in addition to those put on the payroll earlier, including Ronald Reagan's former media guru Michael Deaver, former Republican congressman Vin Weber, and two close friends of Vice President Al Gore, media adviser Carter Eskew and former Democratic congressman Thomas J. Downey. Microsoft's campaign contributions jumped as well.

An internal Microsoft e-mail exchange illustrates the company's altered approach. On February 22, 1999, David Kaefer, the marketing-research manager, sent an e-mail to Barbara J. Dingfield, the director of community affairs, who reported to Bill Neukom, and to nine other staffers, including public-relations chief Mich Mathews. "This mail is intended to recommend and spur discussion concerning which five or six image attributes we should use to access the effectiveness of our branded philanthropic communication efforts," Kaefer wrote. He then listed "image attributes we have used in past research": approachable, arrogant, caring, greedy, good corporate citizen, only looking out for itself, and others. Kaefer said that a senior executive, Ann Redmond, had asked him to consult experts to "help us arrive at a preferred set of attributes" and reported that Mark Penn had advised them to concentrate on "helping the community, being a good corporate citizen." Pollster Peter Hart advised: "The CEO—Bill Gates—is generous, Microsoft is providing access to computers for people who can't afford them." After reviewing what other "experts" told him, Kaefer narrowed the list of contenders to push to "six attributes":

- Microsoft cares about making a difference in my community
- Microsoft is a leader in good corporate citizenship
- Microsoft's charitable giving improves the lives of many people
- Microsoft is honest
- Microsoft is a company I trust
- Microsoft is a generous and supportive corporate citizen

But spin has its limitations. To be believed in a courtroom and not just in the court of public opinion, Microsoft still had to explain away the

Gates question that bedeviled courtroom regulars: how could such a smart man give such a dumb deposition? Who was to blame for his dismal deposition, Gates or his lawyers? Netscape's Christine Varney blamed Gates: "He's got really good lawyers. I suspect he didn't listen to them. . . . Microsoft's lawyers are treated like gardeners." Gates gets heated, it is presumed, and his advisers cower and back off.

Many attribute Gates's misbehavior to character defects. Bill Joy, the chief scientist at Sun Microsystems, has a simple explanation: Gates is forever stained as a liar. "It's like *The Scarlet Letter.* How can anyone ever believe he's a straight person after viewing that videotape?" A Gates friend put it more gently: "I see it as argumentative, as failing to concede the obvious. . . . It sets him up to be untruthful because he contradicts things he need not have contradicted. It stems from a belief that he can out-debate, out-microlanguage Boies. I get that impression because I know the guy. If I didn't, I'd be stunned. It's like in a gangland trial where the gangster says, 'No, I'm in the olive-oil business!' It seems disingenuous."

David Boies blamed Gates's lawyers. "He couldn't have been briefed." His proof? "Watch the deposition. This is a very intelligent man." He noted that Gates's lawyers sat beside him. If their client was veering off on tangents or was unresponsive, Boies continued, it was the lawyers' task to rein in their client or to interrupt and request a brief recess. This is what President Clinton's attorney did when Special Prosecutor Ken Starr's office took Clinton's videotaped deposition at the White House, also in August 1998. "If I were his attorney and in the room, I would have stopped the deposition," said Boies. They didn't interrupt, Boies believed, because they feared their client's wrath. "He's created problems he need not have."

This was Judge Jackson's private view. "What is astounding to me . . . [is] that the Microsoft lawyers let Gates go on as long as he did, exhibiting the demeanor that he did in the deposition." As a former trial lawyer, he, too, would have called for a recess. "I suspect Neukom is afraid of him. He's his meal ticket." Jackson didn't understand how John Warden—who he (wrongly) believed was in the room throughout the deposition and whom he admired and thought of as guiding Microsoft's legal strategy—could have acquiesced. Gates "may be such an intimidating personality that even John Warden is buffaloed by him," Jackson said. "But at some point an experienced trial lawyer has to take his client aside and, in addition to telling them to answer truthfully, has to say, 'You're not doing yourself a service by not answering.' "

A Microsoft insider who was intimately involved in mapping the trial strategy said that Gates was better prepared in at least one respect: he did review the e-mail traffic. "There were no surprise documents he was shown. Bill took a lot of time to be prepared." But, this insider continued, "a larger share of the blame lies with the lawyers. He's not just a big client. He's the richest man in the world engaged in the largest antitrust case of the era. He's a major public figure. The appropriate counsel to have given was to depart from the usual advice." Instead of being combative, he said they should have advised, "Don't fight over the meaning of words. You tell your story." Although Gates had performed miserably during the first two days he was deposed, and there was then a five-day break before his third day of deposition, neither the lawyers nor Gates altered their truculent stances.

That Gates didn't do this suggests still a third explanation for his odd behavior: that Boies is to blame. On other occasions where Gates has testified, he has been considerably more disciplined. In this case, observed one of Microsoft's twelve witnesses, Gates was so incensed at the government, so emotionally wrought up, that he was ready to blow. And Boies seemed to get under Gates's skin, goading him to compete. For example, contrast the combative, forgetful deposition Gates gave with the informed, polite deposition he gave less than a year later to lawyers for Bristol Technology, a small software firm in Danbury, Connecticut, which sued Microsoft for violating antitrust law. It could plausibly be said that by the time of the Bristol deposition Gates understood the penalty he had paid for his prior obstinacy and was on his best behavior. However, it could also be said that Boies brought out the worst in Gates. Since Boies is quite smart and unafraid to repeat a question fifteen different ways—and since he controlled the questions and thus the agenda— Gates was doomed to fail.

There is another explanation for Gates's deposition, which Boies tended to downplay: his lawyers programmed him too much, leading Gates to reflexively deny everything. This is the view propounded by Bernard Vergnes, the chairman of Microsoft Europe, who is based in Paris: "He was asked by the lawyers to not be himself." Novell chairman and CEO Eric Schmidt agreed, "He got bad advice. I do depositions, and I'm told to smile a lot." Another senior Microsoft executive blames both the lawyers and Gates's combative personality: "Bill was given the world's worst instructions for his deposition. He was told: 'Chew up lots of time. Make them be specific because they're going to try and trap you.'" This fed into a Gates weakness, he continued: "If you try and weasel-word with Bill, he gets his back up."

Gates himself seemed to blame Boies and Jackson. At a December 7, 1998, press briefing in Washington, D.C., Gates appeared from Redmond on a screen and, regarding his deposition, told reporters he was surprised that a video deposition that was meant to be for written trial use only was somehow in wide release. (Gates did know when he was deposed that he was being videotaped and that a written transcript would become public, but it's true that at the time Judge Jackson had signed an order that the depositions would be admitted only in transcript form in court.) Gates also told reporters he was surprised that Boies didn't ask substantive questions, such as, Why did Microsoft integrate the browser? What is the nature of competition among technology companies? Instead, "He'd present a piece of mail to me, and since I get over ten thousand pieces of mail every year, I don't remember receiving a specific piece of mail, so I answer 'no.'"

Hampton Pearson of CNBC asked, If you're so "dissatisfied with how the government has used your deposition during the trial, why not come and testify in court?" Gates responded, "My coming to testify would not stop them from using the video deposition." (He was technically correct but wrong. Had Gates agreed to be one of Microsoft's twelve witnesses, it is unlikely that the government would have extensively played his deposition in court. The same is true if the government had selected Gates as one of its original twelve witnesses, as Gates noted they could have. The government didn't because once Boies saw the truculent Gates captured on tape, he had no interest in placing on the stand another version of Gates.)

To another question, from Joseph Nocera of *Fortune*—"If you had to do the deposition over, would you have done it in a different way?"— Gates insisted he had "answered truthfully every single question that was put forward to me." He talked, as Neukom had, about "snippets." Though his demeanor remained tranquil, his fury shone through: "And, you have to understand, Mr. Boies has made it clear in the negotiations leading up to the case, he's really out to destroy Microsoft. He's really out to take all the good work we've done and make us look very bad."

In the end, blame is an imponderable; what matters is that Gates might have been more credible with the media and the public had we not witnessed the extent of Gates's evasiveness. Microsoft had announced to the world in the mid-nineties that it was fixated on Netscape, for example, so why not admit it in court? One reason not to admit this was that Gates had difficulty being less than noble and admitting publicly that his aim was to beat the hell out of the competition. There are at least two other interpretations of Gates's performance. Maybe the adolescent in Gates got the better of him. Or maybe, like many self-proclaimed nerds, Gates didn't care how he looked. Bill Neukom, for one, dismissed each of these theories as hokum. "He was advised to be precise," Neukom told me, defending both Gates and himself. Neukom assumed that Gates was a victim of a powerful government: "Someone comes to your office with a camera. Puts you under oath. Has had virtually unlimited access to your handwritten notes, to e-mail that has been sent to you, whether you received it or not." Anyone would be cautious, would hedge, he said.

Why didn't Gates admit he played rough, that he was concerned with Netscape's browser market share or with companies aligning with foes such as Sun? "Because when people volunteer information in depositions or in courtroom testimony they create a bigger target for a trial lawyer," Neukom answered. "And when you don't, as I don't, believe there is merit to their case, and people are looking to cobble together a case by a snippet here and a piece of rhetoric there . . . you shouldn't trust them. You're entitled to wonder if they are searching for the truth." This argument parallels the one made by lawyers for the other Bill—President Clinton—during his impeachment hearings and could explain, for example, why his answers to the eighty-one questions submitted by the House Judiciary Committee seemed to be so maddeningly obtuse. David Heiner, who sat off camera but beside Gates during the deposition, said they took breaks every ninety minutes, so there was ample time for briefing. The problem was not with Gates or his lawyers, he insisted. "Bill is very logical, as programmers tend to be. He is very careful. He's listening to their questions, so he knows they are designed to trip him up. In the public viewing, that can come off as looking bad."

It was worse than that. While Microsoft thought Boies played to the galleries by offering Gates's videotaped deposition, the opinion that really counted was not those of the lawyers or the press but that of Judge Jackson. Microsoft would not have been pleased to learn what Jackson thought of Boies's tactic and of the answers Boies elicited from Microsoft's chairman. "It was a masterstroke," Jackson told me. "Look at the witness's testimony. I've seen enough witnesses in nineteen years on the bench and eighteen in practice to know when witnesses are evasive, dissembling, defiant, arrogant. All of those qualities were evinced in that deposition."

On a visit to Redmond, I asked Gates to explain the gap between the take-charge CEO described by employees and the phlegmatic man seen on the videotape. He stopped rocking on the edge of an armchair in his modest office. There were no framed photographs from presidents or celebrities on the walls. Dressed in khakis and a blue shirt buttoned at the sleeves, Gates pleasantly, almost sweetly, answered: "I'd love to have you pick any part of the deposition and let me answer."

What about the part, I said, where you refused to say you were "concerned" about Netscape?

Gates replied, "[Boies] was trying to make it [look] as though we only had one competitor, which was Netscape. Look at that sequence of questions. . . . Take market share. There are so many ways of measuring browser market share. . . . Whose job is it to ask precise questions? That's the lawyer's job." As he continued, his temperature seemed to rise: "Are you saying that you wish that when he asked, 'Are you concerned?' I had just said, 'Yes, that's the only thing I was concerned about,' and under any definition of the word *concerned* the answer absolutely has to be 'yes'? That is, totally, a misportrayal of those years. . . . I don't know what it means for a company to be 'concerned.' Honestly, I don't. I mean, am I concerned about Squiggle Corporation right now? I've never heard of Squiggle Corporation. Is it possible that some guy is writing e-mail that says, 'Oh, Squiggle is going to put us out of business.' Are you saying I shouldn't have tried to give precise answers? Is that what you're thinking? The issue is to give truthful answers. I gave totally, absolutely truthful answers. You're saying that 'Oh, it didn't look good.' OK, fine. That's not what a deposition is about." What really bugged him, he continued, was "some notion that somebody says I don't have a good memory about things, that I showed a poor memory about things. That is an unbelievable lie! There is no part of that deposition where in any way, in any time, I show anything but the most excellent memory."

Although Gates is being disingenuous, he bridles, in part, because he feels demonized by David Boies. Boies is "a showman" intent on using emotion to move the court, said Gates's friend Nathan Myhrvold, who participated in the daily conference call with the lawyers. (In the summer of 1999, Myhrvold took a leave of absence from his job as chief technology officer of Microsoft and ultimately decided not to return.) "This is the Johnnie Cochran school of law, swaying people with emotion!" That Boies was theatrical did not surprise Myhrvold, who had long pressed internally for Gates to be more conscious of the public dimensions of this battle.

David Boies does not dispute that he stereotyped Bill Gates. In one of many candid admissions that tend to boost his credibility with reporters or judges, Boies told me: "It's easy to fall into the trap of thinking of Bill Gates as the image on the deposition screen and in the e-mail. It's easy to do because that's what we're all doing. It's a trap. What goes on in the courtroom is only a slice of what is relevant about him. This is not a trial about Bill Gates. It is only in a limited way a trial about Microsoft. This is a trial about certain aspects of Microsoft's conduct. And it may not be the most important aspects of Microsoft. To get a sense of Gates as a person, you have to look far beyond what we're talking about in this trial."

CHAPTER 8

The Real
Bill Gates

B ILL GATES wouldn't be picked out of a lineup as a leader of men. Crowds do not part when he enters a room. His voice has a high-pitched trill. There is no poetry in his speeches, no elegance to his gait. His appearances are usually bereft of jokes, and there is little social fore-play in his conversations. He is partial to words such as *cool, neat,* and *super.* He sits slumped when on a stage, looking less like a mogul than a boy ordered to wear a suit. "In no other epoch in history would Gates have risen to prominence, much less become the world's richest man," Michael Lewis once wrote. "In ancient Greece, he'd have been a clever slave; in the British empire, a scrupulous bookkeeper."*

Yet in his own way, Gates is a leader. Rick Rashid, Vice President of Research at Microsoft, was among America's foremost computer scientists when he left Carnegie Mellon University eight years ago to join Microsoft. He describes the "awe" he and other scientists at Microsoft feel

---

*This is a view Gates seems to share, for in *Business @ the Speed of Thought* he wrote, "I'd much rather be alive today than at any time in history—and not just because in an earlier age my skill set wouldn't have been as valuable and I'd have been a prime candidate for some beast's dinner."

when they meet with Gates after he has read their technical briefing papers. One moment Gates is jotting equations on a whiteboard or arguing passionately with the mathematicians about incipient infinite clusters, and the next he is arguing with economic specialists about monetary trading. Gates's breadth of knowledge continually astonishes Rashid. Gates's curiosity, he said, generates "the extremely good feeling that the guy who runs the company is passionate about what they're working on. Most company or university people tend to have a cynical attitude about the people they work for. They complain that their company doesn't understand them. That just doesn't happen here." This leadership—not speeches, or jokes, or likability, he said—"inspires them to work harder," to please Bill.

At his birth on October 28, 1955, Bill—William Henry Gates III—was given the same name as his father and grandfather, and he was nicknamed Trey. His parents were powerful: his mother, Mary, the daughter of a banker, was a former schoolteacher who devoted her considerable energies to a myriad of charitable and civic activities, most notably serving as chair of United Way International and president of the University of Washington's board of regents. His father, an imposing physical presence at six feet six inches and a dominant partner in his law firm, was himself the son of an entrepreneur who had established a well-known furniture store in the Seattle suburbs. The couple lived comfortably if unostentatiously in a contemporary house sandwiched between neighbors on a one-acre plot of land on Lake Washington in Seattle's upscale but unpretentious Laurelhurst section. When Gates was a child, the family had a box at University of Washington football games and counted the governor and members of Congress as friends.

Mary and Bill Gates possessed the easy charm and manners of aristocrats. "My mom was naturally social in a way that was incredibly great," Gates told me, adding that she "immediately made a stranger feel her warmth." Barbara J. Dingfield, Microsoft's director of community affairs, served with Mary Gates on the International Women's Forum. "She was smart as a whip. Very well spoken," she recalled. "Although she never had a career as one might call it today—being a lawyer, a doctor—she really made her career in philanthropy. She had a warmth I always admired." Yet she exuded a no-nonsense quality, an utter lack of artifice. Bill Gates describes his parents as a wonderfully harmonious team. What he remembers from his childhood most about his father was that he was always rigorously analyzing issues and asking probing questions. Their son, whose birth came between those of two daughters, did not display much charm. He wasn't social, preferring to read. His idea of amusement was to ingest the *World Book Encyclopedia*, A to Z, or to memorize the Sermon on the Mount.

Over lobster salad in the dining room of that same unremarkable suburban house (a nearby road is now called Mary Gates Memorial Drive), his father, who is seventy-five, told me, "We knew he was a smart kid. That was pretty evident. More than smart, he was so curious about everything. He did not possess the innate social skills that a lot of other kids come up with. He was shy and didn't have a lot of self-confidence." He was, in short, a classic nerd. He was full of restless energy, always swaying in his crib, a motion he transferred to a rocking horse and then to any chair. He loved to jump over just about anything and would startle people by suddenly leaping over a chair without warning, a habit he retained through adulthood.

Bill had friends as a boy, but he preferred individual sports to team ones, ice-skating and waterskiing to football and basketball, being a Boy Scout to the school choir. As a teenager, he had a slight frame and big feet, wore pants hiked high over his waist, buttoned the top button on his shirt, forgot to comb his hair and sometimes to bathe, and never put things away unless his mother intervened. His parents moved easily in social and political circles; their son buried himself in books and later computers.

The Gates family was extraordinarily competitive. Television was banned on weeknights, unless Bill and his sisters got straight As, in which case they were also awarded twenty-five cents for each one. Trivia and bridge contests followed Sunday dinners. During the Gateses' summer vacations at rental cabins on the Hood Canal, his parents organized competitive microgames. "Winning mattered," Bill's dad told Walter Isaacson of *Time* in January 1997. Among Bill's favorite games was Risk, the board game in which armies are pitted against each other and players attempt to occupy territories and control entire continents. The victor rules the world.

To mask his shyness and social awkwardness, Bill often played the class clown at the public school he attended, though sometimes he displayed a hair-trigger temper. Thinking their son immature and an underachiever, his parents sent him at age eleven to a psychiatrist. Gates spoke of the psychiatrist in a July 1994 *Playboy* interview: "He said some profound things that got me thinking a little differently. He was a cool guy." Bill went for a year and a half, became fascinated by Sigmund Freud's writings, and learned that he needn't battle his parents; it was "a fake battle" not worthy of his energy because, the psychiatrist advised, " 'They love you and you're their child. You win.' "

At twelve, Bill was transferred to the more demanding and private Lakeside School, a leafy campus with about three hundred boys enrolled in grades seven through twelve and where students wore jackets and ties. In his seventh-grade class picture, Bill Gates's hair is the color of wheat and combed neatly, his plaid shirt buttoned at the neck and sleeves. He is smiling but not showing his teeth. He kneels, white socks showing, without his glasses, and sweetly looks straight at the camera.

At Lakeside, he and schoolmate Paul Allen discovered computers. Not long after, Gates was briefly thrown out of the computer students' club for being too immature. Then, as now, his behavior—the rocking, the volatile outbursts, the jumping, the engaging brilliance, and the sometimes painful shyness—set him apart, as did his formidable intellect and just as formidable self-confidence.

His parents were desperate for him to be more well-rounded, more social. They wanted him to go to a fine college like Harvard. But Gates had a rebellious streak; he identified with the outsiders in his two favorite novels—Holden Caulfield in *The Catcher in the Rye* and Jay Gatsby in *The Great Gatsby*. That streak had found an agreeable outlet in the Lakeside School's computer club, where he fell in love with an ASR-33 Teletype. The machine had a keyboard, a printer, and a modem that shared a phone line with the school's business office and could connect to a GE Mark II computer. At night, unbeknownst to his parents, Gates crawled out his basement bedroom window to sneak back to the computer lab.

The computer gave him a sense of both liberation and power. He issued orders to the machine, he once said, "and it would always obey." Gates and Paul Allen became addicted, staying late to write code; before the term was widely known, they became "hackers" who stole time on the school's computer. They dreamed up ways to pay for computer access: they wrote a program for class scheduling that told the school which students were taking what classes. The software programs they wrote, Gates recalled in a 1995 speech he made at Lakeside High School, were meant "to play monopoly, play tic-tac-toe and do neat things. And Paul and I were deeply engaged. In fact, we ended up doing a lot of teaching of computer programming and really started to wonder— where was this thing going? What could it really become?" Gates displayed traces of the arrogance that was to be on written and taped display in a federal courtroom three decades later. He was impatient with those who were less smart. Regularly he barked, "That's the stupidest thing I've ever heard of!"

Gates's early talent for computers was matched by an early talent for business. He once got his older sister, Kristi, to sign a contract allowing him to use her baseball glove in return for five dollars. By tenth grade, he was borrowing his dad's copy of *Fortune* and reading it late at night by flashlight. When they were writing the scheduling program at Lakeside, Gates and Allen snared a master key to the school and hired a few classmates. They won a contract from a major corporation to analyze the electrical-power needs of the northwest and Canada. To Gates, a computer was a mathematically perfect business tool: neither age nor personality mattered. "No one knew then we were just in ninth and 10th grades," Bill Gates told *People* in 1983. The Lakesiders were also hired by a company to write a payroll program in exchange for computer time. Here Gates displayed a competitive streak that was to be glimpsed on a much larger future stage. When he wanted more flexibility in using the computer, he got the computer contract amended so that it ran an extra six months and permitted two additional programmers to use the machine for free. These changes "provided young Bill Gates his earliest lesson in how the world could turn on a minor contractual phrase," Stephen Manes and Paul Andrews wrote in their balanced biography, *Gates: How Microsoft's Mogul Reinvented an Industry—and Made Himself the Richest Man in America.*

Since young Bill also loved politics—he listened attentively as his parents brought home tales of the political candidates they worked for, and he had been thrilled to get a summer job in 1972 as a U.S. Senate page, as part of which he personally retrieved the signatures of every member of the Senate—it's a mystery why, years later, his own government relations were so inept. (Perhaps the answer is found in something he later told me: "You don't have to have a lot of political protection to innovate." Translation: Politics may be fun, but it's not rational.)

Soon after young Bill Gates transferred to Lakeside School, his attitude toward academics changed markedly. "I remember when they sent me to Lakeside I thought, 'Should I do well or not?' " he recalls. By the time of his first quiz in geography, a favorite subject, he had decided to shine. He graduated in 1973 as a National Merit Scholar and with a perfect 800 score on the math SAT. A letter of recommendation to Harvard from Vernon Harrington read, "Gates is one of those who does everything well. If he is not the most able student in the State, he is very close to being so. . . . In every way he is a stimulating, resourceful and ambitious student, one who is determined to succeed."

Along the way, his mother became his most trusted confidante, a relationship that continued into his adulthood. Nobuyuki Idei, who was a general manager of a Sony division in the early eighties, vividly recalled the two things that struck him when he first met Gates: first, the young man's feet, for Gates had taken off his shoes and had a gaping hole in one sock; second, Gates told him that his mother had urged him to ask Sony officials when they thought he should take Microsoft public. "His mentor was his mother," Idei reflected. To a Japanese executive, it was incomprehensible that Gates and his mother usually talked daily about business and that Mary Gates sometimes accompanied her son on business trips.

At Harvard, Bill Gates's math skills were advanced; his social skills were not. He was not engaged in his classes, signed up for almost no campus activities, pulled all-nighters to play poker rather than to study, slept in a sheetless bed, and rarely ventured out—except when dorm mate and fellow math whiz Steve Ballmer, the garrulous Detroit-raised manager of the football team who was active on *The Harvard Crimson* and the literary magazine, persuaded him to attend parties. Gates spent much of his time in Harvard's computer lab, where Professor Thomas Cheatham, who ran it, noticed that Gates was an outstanding programmer and a thoroughly disagreeable young man. "In terms of being a pain in the ass, he was second in my whole career here," Cheatham told Stephen Manes and Paul Andrews. "He's an obnoxious human being. . . . He'd put people down when it was not necessary." By his own admission, Gates was depressed while in Cambridge, wondering what he would do with his life, until Paul Allen, who had left college to work at Honeywell, outside of Boston, visited him one weekend and showed him a copy of *Popular Electronics*. It contained a cover story on the MITS Altair 8800, one of the first PCs, which was being sold with a kit for just $360 by a New Mexico company. In early 1975, Gates and Allen wrote to the president of MITS, telling him that he needed their software. That they didn't actually have any software was a minor impediment.

At the time, the major computer companies, such as IBM, DEC, and Hewlett-Packard, concentrated on mainframes and big machines for corporations. If the Altair had a basic software program, Allen and Gates envisioned that it could reach not just businesses but consumers. In their letter, which they also sent to many other computer time–sharing companies, Gates and Allen promised to deliver a number of software programs. The president of MITS expressed interest, and that winter the two programmers holed up in Gates's dormitory and madly wrote code. Allen then flew to Albuquerque to demonstrate how their software would animate the machine. Altair went for it. For three thousand dollars and a slice of royalties, Gates and Allen, 19 and 21 respectively, had decided what to do with their lives.

In the spring of 1975, Allen signed up as MITS's software director, and in June Gates took a leave from Harvard to join him. By July 1, they were shipping their BASIC 2.0, as it was called. That November, the Gates-Allen partnership was christened Micro-soft, and they sought other clients. The partners were infused with fervor; they were going to change the world. The desktop computer was, from day one, central to their business vision, and their corporate motto became *A computer on every desk and in every home running Microsoft software.* They believed, rightly, that the most vital part of the computer would be its software, not its hardware. The more articulate of the two partners, Gates at twenty had become a guru, invited to give keynote speeches at computer conventions. By mid-1976, Gates and Allen were selling software to other corporate customers.

BASIC 2.0 was already being pirated by hobbyists, however, which enraged Gates. This was business. In February 1976, the man who had stolen time on the Lakeside lab computers and who twenty years later offered a Microsoft browser for free, penned an "Open Letter to Hobbyists," claiming they were stealing his intellectual property: "As the majority of hobbyists must be aware, most of you steal your software. Hardware must be paid for, but software is something to share. Who cares if the people who worked on it get paid? Is this fair? . . . One thing you do do is prevent good software from being written. Who can afford to do professional work for nothing?"

In appearance, Gates and Allen were not to be confused with capitalists. To look at early pictures of Gates, Allen, and their Albuquerque band of two female and seven male employees is to see what looks like a group picture from Woodstock. Gates was a skinny, baby-faced young man with doelike eyes, a mop of unkempt brown hair swept across his forehead and nearly touching his oversized, octangular, clear-framed eyeglasses; Allen wore identical glasses and a dark Karl Marx–style beard. But these were not flower children. By the end of its first full year of operation, Microsoft, now hyphenless, had twenty-two thousand dollars in revenue. Gates and Allen shared offices in downtown Albuquerque. At first they stayed in motels, then in rented apartments, where pizza boxes piled up. Gates averaged "only a few hours" of sleep each night, he once recalled. Unmindful of speed limits, he collected a pile of tickets, most of which he neglected to pay. Once he got thrown into jail for speeding and driving without a license and then challenging the officer by repeatedly asking, "Why do you need my license?" Gates was for a while too young to meet local customers in a bar or to rent a car, so he took taxis to meetings. While Gates inspired co-workers with his brains, his passion, his hard work, and his endless curiosity, he was also a shouter. He sometimes screamed so loudly that the milder-mannered Allen would flee the office in disgust. Tensions between them grew. They were partners, but Gates was more equal, claiming 64 percent of the stock to Allen's 36 percent; Gates was anoited chairman, Allen executive vice president. "I dropped out of school to run Microsoft without being paid while Paul had his MITS job," Gates told me. "We adjusted the number twice after that I think."

In 1979, Microsoft moved to the Seattle area. While driving up from New Mexico, Gates—finding it difficult to follow the rules of others—collected three speeding tickets. By this point, his and Allen's gifts were becoming ever more apparent. Microsoft had twenty-eight employees and nearly $2.5 million in revenue, and its BASIC software was fast becoming the lingua franca for a new computer industry. An early spotter of Gates and Microsoft was H. Ross Perot, the billionaire founder of the Texas-based technology-consulting company EDS. After failing to induce Steve Jobs to sell Apple, Perot made a run at Gates, but his bid was also spurned. This was the first of several fateful decisions Gates and Microsoft made or had the good luck to have made for them. A second was IBM's decision to license software from it. IBM had contracted with Intel to produce computer-processing chips for the first sixteen-bit personal computers, which could process and retrieve data much faster than the existing eight-bit machines; now it needed an operating system.

Mary Gates played a role in the marriage of Microsoft and IBM. At a United Way board meeting, she approached fellow board member John Opel, the chairman of IBM, mentioned that her son's company was doing some work with IBM, and encouraged Opel to get to know him. Weeks later, IBM engineers who were developing their first PC made a presentation to IBM's management committee and in talking about software they referred to Microsoft. "That wouldn't be Mary Gates's boy, Bill, would it?" Opel reportedly asked. Failing to understand that software, not hardware, was to be the oil of the Information Age, IBM chose in 1980 to license MS-DOS (Microsoft Disk Operating System) and other software programs from Microsoft. It was a fateful decision, for Microsoft became as dominant in software as OPEC is in the production of oil.

A third decision of considerable importance that occurred around this time was the hiring in 1980 of Gates's Harvard friend Steve Ballmer, who had become a Procter & Gamble marketing executive and then attended business school at Stanford. Ballmer helped professionalize the sales, marketing, and management at Microsoft; he freed Gates from many administrative chores; he focused attention on recruiting talent to manage a business that had outgrown its baby stage; and he was a cheerleader—a loud, profane, unabashed enthusiast for Team Microsoft. "I love this company! I love this company! I love this company!" he shouted at the start of sales meetings. Sometimes his immaturity served to reinforce, rather than check, Gates's. When U.S. Attorney General Janet Reno announced that the government was going to sue Microsoft, Ballmer yelled out during a speech to computer dealers, "To heck with Janet Reno!" He has been more General Patton than Eisenhower, Paul Maritz told *Business Week* in 1998. With a large, nearly bald head and the frame of a linebacker, Ballmer is an exponent of business as warfare. He once made a call to David Dorman, then the CEO of Pacific Bell, a major corporate customer with thirty-four thousand desktop PCs that used Windows. Ballmer was agitated because Dorman had chosen Netscape's browser for the Baby Bell's new Internet service, and he screamed at Dorman, the telephone-company executive told *The Wall Street Journal* in a front-page story that appeared on October 27, 1997: "You're either a friend or foe, and you're an enemy now." (Ballmer pointedly declined to dispute Dorman's account.) Ballmer owns 5 percent of Microsoft's stock and is today among the world's richest men.

Three years after Ballmer arrived, Paul Allen left. He'd been diagnosed with Hodgkin's disease, but that was not the sole reason for his departure. Relations between Gates and Allen had become tempestuous, with the more subdued, research-oriented Allen fatigued by his boyhood friend's propensity to yell, to be so damn competitive, to cavalierly ignore Allen when making decisions. Allen recovered from his illness but chose not to rejoin Microsoft. His relationship with Gates endured a long frost—one that did not thaw until the mid-nineties. Today, they are again friends, and Allen sits on the board and remains the company's second-largest shareholder.*

In 1983, Microsoft introduced its version of the mouse, which permitted users to point and click rather than type in commands. That same year, it birthed the Windows operating system and introduced its word-processing program, Microsoft Word, which soon supplanted WordPerfect, the market leader. Over the next several years, many in the industry snickered that Windows was a dud, a crude and blatant imitation of the Macintosh system—so blatant that Apple sued Microsoft for copyright infringement. The real winner in the competition, it was said, would be the IBM-backed software, OS/2. But when OS/2 finally appeared, it had bugs and hogged too much memory. After trying and failing three times, the fourth version of Windows Microsoft produced, Windows 3.0, was crowned king of the operating-system market. Bolstered by the results of several other crucial decisions—Microsoft's 1984 decision to continue working closely with Intel on its ever more powerful software and microprocessor chips; IBM's decision to cede software to Microsoft; and Apple's long-held decision not to license its innovative operating system but rather to insist that it be used only on Apple machines—Microsoft and Intel came to supplant IBM and Apple and to dominate the PC industry. In 1984, Microsoft's sales almost doubled from the previous year, to just under one hundred million dollars.

It was a propitious time to take Microsoft public, and after Bill Neukom signed off on the legal documents, on March 13, 1986, Microsoft stock went on sale for $21 per share. Before taking the company public, Gates had offered IBM the opportunity to own 10 percent of it. IBM

---

*In November 2000, Allen again left the Microsoft board.

foolishly declined. Microsoft's stock has since split eight times. A ten-thousand-dollar investment in 1986 would by 1999 be worth more than five million.

By 1988, Bill Gates's company had 2,793 employees and nearly $591 million in revenues and had surpassed Lotus as the world's foremost software vendor. In 1990, a new version of Microsoft Windows was ready to be launched, decoupled from IBM, which had chosen to go with OS/2. Gates bet the company on a new Intel chip and his fourth version of Windows, with a new graphical user interface. "Windows! Windows! Windows!" Steve Ballmer chanted so loudly at a sales meeting that he damaged his vocal cords.

Microsoft's software business model was predicated on inducing customers to constantly upgrade Windows. In a fifteen-page, September 8, 1992, memo to Gates and senior colleagues, Nathan Myhrvold explained:

> Regular upgrades are important for both revenue and loyalty. A feeling of progress and improvement is necessary to keep users loyal to a product because it helps balance any desire to avoid the hassle of a competitive upgrade. This is also an important way to produce revenue. . . . Upgrades represent the closest thing we have to an annual fee or subscription. This is a powerful way to draw revenue from the installed base, and to keep them loyal to our product. The more regular the frequency, the more we can get people in the upgrade habit, and have a sense they can depend on continual improvement.

Microsoft got "people in the upgrade habit." By 1993, there were twenty-five million licensed users of Windows. With corporate revenues of just over $3.7 billion, Microsoft was out from under the shadow of its sometimes contentious relationship with IBM. Bill Gates now saw only two dark clouds looming on the horizon: complacency and the Apple lawsuit. Regularly, he recited to members of his management team a memo by John Walker, founder of Autodesk, who after leaving that software company wrote of how his child had grown complacent and had sweetened profits at the expense of long-term investments. And of the Apple lawsuit claiming copyright infringement Gates warned in a May 1991 "Challenges and Strategy" memorandum to his executives, "This is a very serious lawsuit. If the judge rules against us, without making it clear what we have to change or asks me to eliminate something fundamental to all windowing systems (like overlapping windows) it would be disastrous." Bill Neukom assured Gates they would prevail, and on June 1, 1993, the U.S. District Court of Northern California ruled in Microsoft's favor. Bill Gates might have worried as much about the FTC and the Justice Department, but he did not. He referred to government internally as a "visible" problem, which suggested that it was not a real one. He said in the early nineties, "I take the FTC inquiry seriously"; however, he was certain Microsoft was right and declared, "I hope we can quickly educate the FTC on our business."

Now Gates began to look for new worlds to conquer. Ignoring the still faint chatter about the World Wide Web, he began to think of expanding into the content business. He launched MSN as an online source for news. It was a proprietary service, open only to subscribers. He explored buying CNN from Ted Turner, before Turner sold his company to Time Warner. He turned his attention to Hollywood, where he spent many hours locked in conversations with Michael Ovitz and his team at the Creative Artists Agency, exploring ways to invest in the movie industry. "Bill Gates was the first person to call me—the very first—when I left Disney," recalls Jeffrey Katzenberg of his separation from Michael Eisner in 1994. Gates beseeched him, "Please come up to Seattle and sit down with me before you do anything. I'd love to talk to you about what's next." Gates and Myhrvold and others began to explore relationships with media companies such as MCI, AT&T, TCI, and the company Katzenberg eventually forged with Steven Spielberg and David Geffen, DreamWorks SKG; they lunched with Hollywood stars, such as Robert De Niro and Steve Martin. They eagerly awaited Myhrvold's report after he visited Los Angeles and spent a week in Katzenberg's office studying the movie business. "Content," Gates wrote in his January 3, 1996, syndicated newspaper column, "is where I expect much of the real money will be made on the Internet, just as it was in broadcasting." Of course, he defined content liberally to include Microsoft's software.

Gates engineered a series of investments to extend Microsoft's reach: into Hollywood, with a 1995 joint venture with the DreamWorks studio to develop interactive games and entertainment products; into cable, with a billion-dollar 1997 investment in Comcast; into news, with a joint investment with NBC in a twenty-four-hour news cable channel and website, MSNBC; into WebTV, to access the Internet via TV sets; into software to produce interactive television; and into online city guides and magazines.

Gates understood earlier than most that to compete in a world where the distinctions among various industries were eroding—where computers and cable and broadcast and Hollywood studios and consumer electronics and telephones and publishing were converging and the sharp demarcation between software and content was blurring—Microsoft must invest aggressively. So Microsoft reached into its deep pockets and invested five billion dollars in AT&T, which was now the nation's largest cable as well as long distance–telephone company. With its seat at the cable table, Gates hoped to extend Microsoft's operating-system dominance from the PC to the cable box. To assure a seat at the high-speed, broadband Internet-access table, Microsoft invested $212 million in Time Warner's Roadrunner cable modem, in addition to the stake it claimed in the @Home cable modem through its AT&T investment. Gates did not just invest; like a female spider after mating, sometimes he devoured his partner. Between June 28, 1994, and December 29, 1999, Microsoft acquired part or all of 130 companies.

The rationale for these moves was laid out in a March 7, 1994, memo sent to Gates by Myhrvold, his principal internal gadfly. Entitled "External Investments," the memo asserted: "The emergence of the information highway and the convergence of various media in information will create some new opportunities for us to leverage our cash which were not available in the PC market." Microsoft, he continued, had to act as both bank and venture capitalist, buying various positions in "the food chain of the new digital world." Myhrvold continued: "Financial plays—in joint ventures, co-production deals, minority investments, acquisitions and start ups of capital intensive businesses are going to be extremely important in getting ourselves into position for this new world. . . . The winning software on the information highway is going to be the one which has the most support from other parts of the food chain." The challenge was to construct a web of communications companies to partner with and gain leverage over. The traditional objective did not change: vertically integrating all aspects of communications—from owning the ideas, to owning the factories that turn the ideas into products, to owning the means of distributing these products. But corporate America was changing in that companies now strove to weave a parallel, horizontal web of joint partnerships. They would compete *and* collaborate. The Japanese have a name for this kind of horizontal web: *keiretsu.* For Microsoft, the problem with partnering was that it was better at control than cooperation. As Microsoft bought and occupied seats at various tables, it sought to make decisions, not just have input.

Inevitably, Microsoft, which had prided itself on being a David to industry Goliaths such as IBM, had become the Goliath. Gates remained afraid that Microsoft was one minute away from extinction; he kept citing IBM as the exemplar of a company that lost its edge and became self-satisfied, smug, lazy. By always insisting that Microsoft see itself as the underdog, Gates created a corporate mentality that saw business competition as a battle for survival, a battle in which there could be only one winner and one loser, not two winners. "We still think of ourselves as a small, scrappy start-up," Microsoft executive Tod Nielsen told me after one long day in court. Paul L. Saffo, Director of the Institute for the Future, a business consultant in Silicon Valley, put it another way: "Bill has the instincts of a monopolist. It's not enough to be number one. You want to crush the competition. . . . Microsoft is like a hundred-and-twenty-pound German shepherd. Microsoft still thinks small, which is its strength. But it's big, and it doesn't realize it."

To retain its lead, Microsoft did what many companies do: it identified a threat, then leveraged strength to shore up weakness. It incorporated new software applications into Windows, including such features as simple word processing, a calculator, a calendar, new graphics, games. It enticed customers to buy regular upgrades to enjoy new features, and to keep them from straying to a competing product. It imposed restrictive contracts on companies, prohibiting them from distributing competing software. Microsoft trumpeted that all software vendors were free to write programs for Windows, but for years those who competed with it have complained that Windows rejected their software applications while accepting those produced by Microsoft or its allies. Also, the "beast from Redmond" would hear of a new multitasking software product from, say, Vision or GEM, and then, in an attempt to preempt the market, announce that it was about to bring out a comparable product, which it did not always do. These "products" became known as vaporware.

This relentless competitiveness is a reflection of the company's co-founder. Gates and his wife, Melinda, have been known to purchase identical jigsaw puzzles and to compete to see who finishes first. When Microsoft employees came for outings to Bill's house on Lake Washington or to the family compound, leisure activities were transformed into Olympian contests. They would have, recalled his father, as many as 110 guests, and they were divided into teams and given T-shirts and instructions from Mary and Bill Gates, Sr., with Gates family members serving as game masters and referees. Patty Stonesifer, who joined Microsoft in 1988 and had risen to the upper rank of executives by the time she left in 1997 and who now presides with Gates Senior over the Gates Foundation, remembers how purposeful the games were. Often, they were themed, sometimes historically, and at times participants had to create their own form of binary code, which they communicated through smoke signals or some other tool used in the century they were mimicking. Unremarked upon by those who extol the contests is that they were also focused on Who's smartest? Who could swim fastest? Who wrote the funniest song? Who won the pickle-ball tournament? "Most people had a good time," recalled Rob Glaser, "but it was a very competitive social discourse." Even at casual dinners at their home today, between courses Bill and Melinda will joyously ask everyone to turn over their place mats and draw maps of the United States. Senior Microsoft executive Jeff Raikes loved the contest, but not as much as did Steve Ballmer. "Oh great," he remembers Ballmer saying when the Gateses once announced the game. "I just did this last week on an airplane." Naturally, Ballmer won.

"Like many bright people, he's aggressive," observed John Malone, who went on to say of Gates, "It's like the old joke of the wasp and the frog." Assured that he would not be stung, a frog agrees to carry an injured wasp across a pond. As soon as they get to shore, the wasp stings the frog. Why? " 'I couldn't help it,' said the wasp. 'It's my nature.' That's Bill's nature. To win."

He conducts much of his communication through e-mail. He prefers to drill down, focusing a couple of hours on a single meeting. Before he appointed Steve Ballmer president in 1998, Gates sometimes spent ten hours on a single midyear review of one department. Palms would sweat as executives waited for "face time" with Bill. No matter how relaxed the venue, employees are nervous. "I know I'm up against a mind that's better than mine," explained Deborah Willingham, Vice President of Human Resources.

Whatever trepidation Gates inspires, he usually goes out of his way not to shield himself from harsh news. While Gates won't stand on ceremony and freely sends e-mail to junior employees, his time is jealously guarded. Regularly, he and Ballmer get together and review Gates's schedule, then draw up a Gates time budget, allocating the number of hours of face time (as opposed to e-mail time) he will spend annually with each of his executives, with customers, with the sales force, at conventions, and in travel. Communications chief Mich Mathews, for example, was allotted sixteen hours of face time in 1999, and so as not to exhaust these she did much of her communication with Gates through e-mail. Tod Nielsen was given five events a year for Gates to, says Nielsen, "speak to the geeks" at software-developer gatherings. Most years, Gates spent about one quarter of his time on the road, packing his schedule so tight with meetings, wrote Brent Schlender in the May 26, 1997, *Fortune,* after taking a trip with him, that he "left no time for serendipity, much less any sightseeing other than what he could observe out the window of the white Mercedes-Benzes that shuttled him between airports, hotels, and government offices."

Many associates think Gates honest rather than rude. Yusuf Mehdi, who is thirty-two and directs marketing for Windows, describes a Gates grilling by noting that his questions are so unadorned, so rigorous, that just as a student wants to impress a respected scholar, "you want to be able to go in and answer all his questions." Ann Winblad, a cofounder of Hummer Winblad Venture Partners, who dated Gates in the mid-eighties and has since been a close friend, said Gates is so inquisitive, so innocent, that if a visitor from Mars wanted to understand him, she would send the visitor to Gates's office. Although the visitor would want to ask questions, Gates would barrage him with his own. "Bill would be extremely curious about what's going on on Mars. He would say, 'Cool. What's it like there?'"

As a manager, Gates does not leave his office and poke his head into cubicles to chat. His style is to forgo small talk, to be, in his words, "acutely conscious of the value of time." It is business sex, without the foreplay. Gates can't bear small talk for the sake of lubricating relationships. An intimate remembers once being in the office when Gates was on the phone with the CEO of a major auto company, rolling his eyes, impatient to hang up. After he finally did, Gates sputtered: "That guy wanted to talk to me about cars!" At social functions, Melinda Gates often tugs at his sleeve when he offers a limp handshake and a perfunctory hello. Gates's friend Patty Stonesifer, who now co-heads the Gates Foundation, admitted, "Bill by his own admission doesn't spend a lot of time on niceties. You don't go into a meeting with him asking 'How are your kids?' He's very targeted."

Friends are offended, however, when he is described as an unfeeling automaton. Stonesifer said of Gates, "He's a wonderful friend." When Suzie and Warren Buffett and the Gateses traveled by train and bicycle through China in 1995, Gates made sure there was an ample supply available of Buffett's favorite foods: hamburgers and French fries. "He just had it arranged so that I didn't have a bite of Chinese food in seventeen days!" said Buffett appreciatively. In 1993, when Russell Siegelman was a senior executive at Microsoft and bogged down trying, as others have since, to jump-start MSN, he blacked out one day and required emergency brain surgery. Siegelman, who is now a venture capitalist, remembers the note he received from Gates: "It was so Bill-ish. It said, 'We're with you. Don't rush. It's your job when you come back.' He's not this guy who just thinks of business. If you believed the Bill you read about, you'd think he would have said, 'Sorry, but we gave your job to someone else.'"

Ann Winblad describes him as passionate about more than just Microsoft. "He sends hand-done birthday cards to friends. He adores his daughter. He adores his wife." And at parties he loves "to lead sing-alongs," she added. "There are not a lot of opportunities for him to do that now. Bill knows the complete words to Broadway shows, the whole libretto." Bill Gates bursting into song is not an image that springs to mind while watching his video deposition in court. Nor is the unusual friendship he has with Winblad. Each spring, these two technology intellectuals spend a long weekend alone, usually at her North Carolina beach cottage, where they golf, take walks on the beach, read, and ponder big, and small, questions. "Bill has a small set of friends who he has trust with," said Winblad. To those who cock an eyebrow at a married man vacationing alone with a female friend, Winblad answers, "People wouldn't ask if Bill went with a male friend."

Gates has mellowed some since marrying the Texas-born Melinda French on New Year's Day 1994. French joined Microsoft in 1987 with an engineering degree and an M.B.A. from Duke. She became a product manager working for Patty Stonesifer, and wound up dating the boss. At their engagement party, Gates dressed as Jay Gatsby and Melinda came as Daisy Buchanan. In an e-mail exchange with John Seabrook published on January 10, 1994, in *The New Yorker*, Gates described why Gatsby is such a romantic figure to him: "Gatsby had a dream and he pursued it not even really thinking he might fail or worse that what he dreamed of wasn't real." For their wedding day, they rented every helicopter on the Hawaiian island of Lanai so reporters could not snoop on the wedding party, which included such friends as Warren Buffett, Katharine Graham, Paul Allen, Jeff Raikes, Nathan Myhrvold, and best man Steve Ballmer. Melinda, said Raikes, has become "a rudder" for his friend. Patty Stonesifer, who was Melinda's supervisor at Microsoft and works with her daily at the Gates Foundation, was asked to describe her impact on Gates and said, "It's hard to separate her influence from the stage of his life he's in. Melinda shares his interests. He has a partner who loves foreign films, as he does. And who shares an interest in an extended family, as he does. He's more joyful than ever. He's always been a guy who enjoyed having a good time. But you see them together shoulder to shoulder, and they delight in sharing it." Of his daughter-in-law William Gates said, "She has developed their lives so that his involvement with the company is not so dominant in his life." In a 1999 interview with Charlie Rose for CBS's *60 Minutes II,* Gates was asked to describe the most important person in his life. Gates, lower lip quivering, fought back tears before offering his wife's name. Asked to cite the biggest misconception people had about him, he replied that people said he had forced Melinda to sign a prenuptial agreement, which he hadn't.

Melinda and Bill Gates's home certainly overshadowed anything F. Scott Fitzgerald imagined for Jay Gatsby out in West Egg, Long Island: a seventy-five-million-dollar, forty-thousand-square-foot compound on Lake Washington that was built by an architect selected in an international competition. It features five pavilions and underground passages and includes a dining room that can seat one hundred guests, parking for thirty cars, an indoor pool, and a huge indoor trampoline. Many movies, songs, television shows, and works of art can be instantly summoned and displayed. Why someone who is seemingly unconcerned with money should choose to live so ostentatiously is a mystery. "That surprised us a bit, too," admitted Gates's father. "He loves that place. He really enjoys it." In an e-mail, Bill Gates explained his thinking: "I had a couple of things in mind when I planned it. One was to make it a showcase for technology. The other was that I wanted to make it big enough so I could have up to a hundred people over for charity events or to celebrate company successes. Having a great library or the incredible screens has been a lot of fun but I still can't enjoy these things without feeling a little guilty about it." Not too guilty, however. Around the base of a library dome is this inscription from *The Great Gatsby:* "He had come a long way to this blue lawn and his dream must have seemed so close he could hardly fail to grasp it."

How did a computer nerd become such an adept businessman? How can Bill Gates be so volatile yet so strategically canny? How is it that such a generally caustic man is such an effective leader? There are no simple answers. Even allowing that his own family was competitive and steeped in business, it is a mystery from whom or where Gates derived the business zeal and skill that stand out as unusual even among his peers. "That's something that surprised us all," acknowledged his father. Bill Gates himself traces whatever business acumen he possesses to several factors: to being exposed to business by his father at the dinner table, where he discussed his extensive corporate legal work; to his own innate and insatiable curiosity; and to the incessant questions he asked and the retentive memory he is blessed with. "We were students of these things," Gates told me. The microprocessing power of Gates's brain is surely a major factor in his business success. "Bill is sort of like a machine where you keep pouring random facts in the top and you get back orderly facts," observed Craig Mundie, who reports to Gates and is a member of the select Business Leadership Team, a group of about a dozen executives who gather almost weekly to strategize with Gates and Ballmer. It's more than IQ. "If you're making a computer analogy, . . . Bill's ability to file thoughts away, retrieve them, and integrate them is just greater than anyone I've ever known."

But a brain alone does not supply focus or passion, which are Gates qualities that are harder to measure. Gates possesses, said former deputy Rob Glaser, "a unique combination of impatience and persistence." What he is, said Ann Winblad, "is a fabulous student, and most people stop being a student, and they become a pontificator." The humility to ask questions, the brains to process the information he retrieves, and an insatiable appetite for more data are the key ingredients, thinks Bill Neukom. Imagine, he said, that you had the most horrific workweek in memory and it was late Saturday night and you were exhausted and finally escaping the office. However, you bump into Gates on the way out of the building. You mention still another question to be pondered in the coming week. Gates would immediately seize on the question right then and there, Neukom said, and insist on answers. "He would have the resilience to work through that problem."

Warren Buffett has a simpler explanation for people like Gates, who, Buffett says, ranks among the finest businessmen he's ever met: "They're wired in such a way that when they see business questions or problems or activities they tend to get the picture very quickly—my partner Charlie Munger is this way. They don't get tangled up in prejudices or biases they may have. They just tend to get the right answers. It's sort of like 'Why was Ted Williams a great hitter?' There's just some coordination that goes on that made him a little bit better at meeting the ball than other people. And that's what happens with business. It certainly isn't a function of IQ to any huge degree. It's just some wiring that takes place. It's not a function of education in my view. It's about seventy-five percent DNA."

Unlike Thomas Edison, who claimed an astounding 1,093 patents but was a hapless business executive, Gates's true genius may be as a businessman more than as a seer. Microsoft is less famous for innovation than for popularizing the innovations of others. "Gates is the Bing Crosby of American technology, borrowing a tune here and a tune there and turning them all into great boffo hits—by dint of heroic feats of repackaging and sheer Herculean blandness," wrote Yale computer-science professor David Gelernter in *Time*. Gates has acknowledged that Microsoft's great successes—DOS, the graphical user interface, Windows—have been clones. Over the years, Microsoft has successfully reinvented itself because it has always thought of itself as more than a technology or software company. "Steve Jobs got in trouble at Apple because he's a passionate technologist," observed industry consultant Paul Saffo. "Others treat technology as a religion. Bill treats it as a business. That's his advantage."

CHAPTER 9

Children at Play

I F BILL GATES the businessman is mature beyond his years, a corporate executive who knows him well concedes that in "emotional areas he's younger than his age." Gates has, after all, never had a boss, never been reprimanded or fired, never been forced to conform to the norms of superiors or to temper what he says, never been poor, never served in the military, and never really endured business adversity. An elder whom Gates much admires said that while Gates is an admirable businessman and friend, he is not fully developed as a person and is too "monomaniacal, too hot-tempered," too much of a boy, really.

At times, this boyishness can be endearing. For example, in August 1998, Melinda and Bill Gates organized a two-week vacation for themselves and four couples: Suzie and Warren Buffett; Margaret and William R. Hearst III, a partner in Silicon Valley's Kleiner, Perkins, Caufield & Byers, and a grandson of William Randolph Hearst; Tricia and Jeff Raikes, a senior Microsoft executive; and Emmy and John Nielson, another senior company executive. The Gateses considered the Nielsons "our closest friends," said Gates, and John was just recovering from a first round of chemotherapy. On the trip, they celebrated the treatment's apparent success.* The excursion began on a boat in Alaska, where they inspected glaciers under the tutelage of a Gates-arranged glaciologist; then they flew to Livingston, Montana, to meet a bus and tour Yellowstone Park with an expert on the history of the West; then they boarded a train and traveled through the Pacific Northwest for a week; and then concluded in northern California. On the next-to-last night of the trip, Gates made a reservation in a small bed-and-breakfast in Carmel that is noted for its fine restaurant. Buffett remembered it vividly: "We get there, and the proprietor pulls Bill aside and says, 'We've got this terrible problem. I'm embarrassed to tell you, but there was this couple married here twenty years ago, and they said they were going to come back to observe their twentieth anniversary, and we forgot all about it. And they're here!'"

The couple said they were from Colorado, and Gates invited them to join his group. "This woman sits down next to me, and the guy is right across," continued Buffett. "The woman is obnoxious to start with, pulling out all these pictures of her kids and telling me how wonderful they are and just going on and on and on. Very much kind of in my face. And the guy had had too much to drink and then football comes up and he says, 'Where are you guys from?' And there's a fella there, Jeff Raikes, . . . who's from Nebraska and who's a much bigger Nebraska football nut than even I am, and we said, 'We're from Nebraska.'"

"Oh, that's where they have the convicts playing football!" the man shot back. He began disparaging the Nebraska football coach, Tom Osborn, whom Raikes revered and who had been a surprise guest at his fortieth birthday party the year before. Raikes, who looks a little like Gates but is less volatile, got beet red and was ready to explode.

"We started getting very agitated," said Buffett. "It got to the point where we were ready to punch him." Suddenly, the couple smiled and identified themselves as actors hired by Gates. It was quintessential Gates, thought Raikes. It was, said Buffett, just another indication that Gates "is a very thoughtful guy," who takes time to think "about what would make his guests have a terrific time."

Gates's boyish qualities manifest themselves in less attractive ways. In a 1994 interview with Connie Chung of CBS, when he didn't like what he called a "childish" comment, Gates announced, "Well, I'm done,"

*The cancer flared up again, and John Nielson died the following year.

removed his microphone, and stalked off. A fellow communications mogul who has both tangled with and worked with Gates (and who does not wish to be named) described him as a nine-year-old: "To Bill Gates, everything is emotional. He is enraged at being wronged. Most businessmen, it won't come up further. With Gates, all you hear is a nine-year-old's wail. All conversation winds up being emotional." When they differed in one particular negotiation, he recalled, Gates pointed his finger at his chest and said, "I know every one of your contracts. I will buy every one. I will put you out of business!" When Gates and John Malone were banging heads several years ago over the Gemstar International Group, a direct-broadcast satellite service that Malone partly owned—Gates wanting Gemstar to use only the Windows operating system for its digital cable box, and Malone and Gemstar not wanting to be totally dependent on Microsoft—Gates confronted Malone at the annual Allen & Company retreat for communications-company moguls. Oblivious to the many peers witnessing the exchange, Gates yelled, "Why are you trying to screw me?" Malone shrugged him off.

Square-jawed, tough, and laconic, Malone, 58, has an engineering Ph.D. but thinks of himself as a cowboy and is partial to checked open-necked shirts. He was a cable pioneer who conquered the West and built the country's largest cable system, telling governments—and sometimes customers—to go to hell. Malone makes his home in the mountains of Colorado, and he is a rugged negotiator who seemed to drive Gates to distraction in their dealings; Gates often screamed into the phone at him, "How could you do this to me? I thought we were friends!" Malone contrasted Gates with Rupert Murdoch, saying that while he respected Gates's honesty, he thought he tended to make differences personal, while Murdoch never did. "If Rupert is going to cut your throat, he'll tell you," said Malone. (Malone is the second-largest shareholder in Murdoch's News Corporation.)

Did Malone think of Gates as a child? "That's for the psychiatrists," Malone said. "Is he a child? No. Psychologically, he needs to win. [It's a] 'you're with me or you're against me' kind of thing. I think he sees things a little more black-and-white than I do. I'm more of a gray tone. Emotionally, does he still have some childlike attributes? Sure. We all do in certain ways. I think that Bill very badly needs to win. And the huge wins he's had up to now obviously haven't done it for him. At the end of the world, if there's only one dollar left, there will be two hands on it. One will be Gates's, the other with be [Viacom's Sumner] Redstone's."

Malone has negotiated with every major media-company CEO. Asked if he could think of one who has the propensity for emotional tantrums that Gates has, Malone said: "I've known guys who have done that, but I always regarded it as manipulation. They do it to change the mood. . . . Barry [Diller] will cry, he'll rip your heart out—how poor Barry 'never' gets enough money . . . how Barry didn't get a big enough piece of this deal. . . . how he's getting 'knifed in the back'. . . . how 'You promised me. Now you're reneging.' Barry uses emotion. But I always figured that with Barry it was crocodile tears. He's a master manipulator. . . . With Bill, it tends to be more real, more human. He's really showing you how he feels." Throughout his antitrust trial, Gates would whine to aides, "Why are they doing this to me?"

But Bill Gates is not, simply, an adolescent, as even David Boies concedes. Though Boies can and does recite many of Gates's childlike lapses, on balance he does not view him as immature. "For me, adolescence usually means lack of discipline. I think Gates is extraordinarily disciplined. I think adolescence implies someone who doesn't stick to something when the going gets tough. I think Bill Gates sticks to things in an amazing way. Adolescence implies emotional thinking. I don't think that applies to Bill Gates." By 1999, Microsoft had a research-and-development budget that is the envy of most of the corporate world, a model of clear-eyed, strategic corporate behavior. Gates also strove to keep Microsoft employees focused on their tasks as he and Neukom and Ballmer "put a fence around" the trial, observed Patty Stonesifer. And while Gates may have a temper, Microsoft's culture prizes talking back to the boss—what Gates calls "push backs." Observed John Malone admiringly, "Bill plays the whole field."

Listening to descriptions of Microsoft's conduct in a Washington courtroom, one had the impression that Gates and his adjutants had seen too many *Godfather* movies. But the more court documents one read, the more the impression solidified that Microsoft's behavior was more childlike than Mob-like. That the Microsoft culture has Bill Gates's fingerprints all over it is evident to anyone who spends real time in Microsoft's headquarters. In Redmond, far removed from regulators in Washington, D.C., and competitors in Silicon Valley, employees refer to where they work as a campus, not an office. The campus consists of forty-five buildings and is a self-contained realm where phones rarely ring, where most waking hours are spent in front of a PC screen and e-mail communication is said to total three and a half million exchanges per day, and where the cafeteria is cheap, open for dinner, offers international cuisines, and sets out that anthem of youth—Tabasco sauce—on tables. Jogging paths and organized sports also help keep employees on campus. Shorts and jeans are ubiquitous.

In 1999, the average age of the more than thirty-one thousand Microsoft employees was only thirty-four, and raw intelligence matters more than judgment or experience in determining who gets hired. Craig Mundie, Senior Vice President for Consumer Strategy, described Microsoft "as a company full of a lot of high IQ people who have relatively no experience." In obvious ways, the Microsoft culture is egalitarian; almost all employees have the same modest one- or two-module office, the same standard computer equipment, the same gray industrial carpet, the same whiteboard; they receive the same free coffee and sodas, eat in the same cafeteria (there are no executive dining rooms), drop their waste in the same environmentally correct receptacles for cans, paper, and general garbage, and receive the same relatively modest salaries (Gates's base salary, in 1999, was, for a CEO, a puny $369,000; programmers were paid about $80,000, directors about $100,000, and general managers between $110,000 and $150,000; vice presidents start at about $200,000). The real money is made from every employee's access to Microsoft's generous stock-option grants, as a result of which there are probably more employees who are millionaires at Microsoft than at any other company. Although Tod Nielsen, for example, was only thirty-one, he had been an employee for about a dozen years, and his stock, said a close friend, was worth about one hundred million dollars.

Microsoft is an overtly competitive meritocracy, where people are pitted head-to-head against each other as a matter of course. To come up with new software, Gates establishes competing teams and lets them race to win. Rob Glaser said of Microsoft employees, "They think of the world as a very Darwinian place." Glaser described the peer pressure as creating an environment in which one is always pushing, always priding oneself on being paranoid, because once you lose that edge you become like IBM was: swollen with pride, cautious. A Gates negotiation is more a head-on competition than an opportunity for both sides to win. Glaser continued:

I do think the Microsoft culture was one where being hard-core and not being seen as less than hard-core was very important and very highly valued. The Microsoft culture is one where people are not chastised for being paranoid or overly competitive. . . . When you're in the lead, you can play a statesmanlike role of not winning every concession. While still maintaining leadership, you don't have to leverage every advantage that you have. Gates thought it was a vague, inarticulate idea. There was no middle ground. And he thought it would be a huge distraction to try and find it. The belief is: concessions lead to a slippery slope or undermine the formula that made the company so successful. That's a belief you can't prove false. Yet it's one I never found a willingness there to discuss it analytically.

The culture of Microsoft has been stamped by Bill Gates: it is a tough, competitive, passionate place. It was part of the company's culture "to take extreme positions sometimes to push ourselves," Microsoft executive Brad Chase later testified in court. That culture succeeds in part because it empowers people to make decisions, to act, but "there is a double-edged sword to that empowerment," concedes Ann Winblad. It can relax internal checks and balances, encourage adolescent behavior, and offer no guidance to employees who are not far removed from their own adolescent years and who may have spent too many hours in front of a PC rather than interacting with people and learning the art of compromise. This isolation was compounded because Microsoft—unlike companies such as America Online or AT&T, which assiduously courted government regulators—kept a disdainful distance. To be hard-core is a prized value, and Bill Gates sets the example.

It was a short step from pushing his own people to pushing around other companies, from yelling "Why are you trying to screw me?" at John Malone to vowing "to destroy" Sun, Oracle, and Netscape. In mid-1998, after a group of wireless-telephone manufacturers—including Nokia and Ericsson—backed Symbian and Psion's EPOC operating system rather than Windows CE to provide software support for "smart phones," Gates stormed. Symbian was creating a proprietary system, which meant Microsoft's software could not link to it. The phones were, however, designed to support Java software, which anyone was free to adapt to. Despite the fact that the Justice Department and the states had filed their antitrust lawsuit against Microsoft the previous month, Gates e-mailed his senior managers soon after he had a private meeting with the CEO of Nokia, Jorma Ollila, on Sunday, June 28, 1998. Gates urged them to be "hard core" and to lean on these companies by leveraging Microsoft's many assets:

> Their protocol is proprietary on the server side which is clever (a cleverness we need to consider for a lot of things). We have to be able to build phones that can receive the pages and objects that will be sent to other phones. If they are going to try and block this then they are sort of declaring war on our ever doing an intelligent phone and we will have to try and make them pay for working with the PC or other Microsoft driven devices. . . . The Nokia CEO seemed to appreciate how hard core I was on this. If . . . these guys are really at way [war] with us . . . we should do the most extreme things we can.

Nobuyuki Idei still shudders with disbelief when recalling an encounter he had with Gates the following year, after the antitrust trial had commenced. Sony had just invested in a start-up Silicon Valley company, TiVo, whose software stores television programs on a PC hard drive rather than a videocassette. Sony could use the TiVo platform to promote TV shows and movies from its own Hollywood studio. One of TiVo's prime competitors would be Microsoft's WebTV digital-storage scheme. Gates erupted, "That's our business!" as if competition was off-limits. A Microsoft spokesman explained that Microsoft and Sony were engaged in discussions about becoming strategic partners and complained that Sony refused to first look at Microsoft's solution. "Bill's complaint was that this was not how you should treat a partner." But Idei was to have similar conversations with Gates when Microsoft wanted Sony to adopt Windows CE for handheld devices and Sony refused, and again later in 1999 when Gates raged to Idei that the Sony PlayStation shouldn't compete with Windows as an operating system for the home. "With Microsoft, open architecture means Microsoft architecture," Idei told me.

As part of Microsoft's ongoing attempt to extend its operating-system hegemony from the computer box to the cable box, Microsoft raced to make Windows CE software the standard system for set-top digital boxes. Soon after Gates purchased an 11.5 percent stake in Comcast, then the nation's fourth (now third) largest cable-television operator, he held a series of meetings with leaders of the cable industry. The proposal Gates pitched them was for Microsoft software to transform their cable boxes to provide interactive TV and Internet access and to do this at a cut-rate price of just three hundred dollars per box. After several false starts, the cable industry was excited. At a climactic July 7, 1997, summit meeting at Time Warner's headquarters, Gates revealed the rub: that he sought, in the words of John Malone, to be "the conductor of the symphony." Microsoft wanted Windows to be the sole operating system for the cable box, as it is, in effect, for the PC. Gates asked for not just a per-box fee for the software but a per-transaction fee—what Myhrvold in one memo to Gates called "a vig." What Gates asked for, said Malone, was 50 percent of all cable advertising revenues. Not so, insists Microsoft: what it asked for was 50 percent of all new interactive-advertising revenues, and in return they would share 50 percent of the costs. Either way, after Gates made his presentation at this cable summit, he was greeted by stunned silence.

But only for a moment. His business ally, Comcast chief Brian Roberts, broke the silence: "Bill, let me be the first to express our reaction: No fucking way!" They saw that Gates wanted Microsoft to be a gatekeeper, claiming part-ownership of cable's pipes. Of that fateful meeting, Malone observed: "That day, if Bill had not overplayed his hand, the whole industry would have signed up for his box." Instead, Malone made a deal with General Instruments, and the others dispersed.

Why the insistence on total control? Immaturity is one answer. Another is that Microsoft always sees itself at war. "Microsoft always works best when it's on a jihad," Jeff Raikes would tell *Fortune*. But, of course, jihads and wars lead to excesses. This stance requires fervor and perceived enemies, which can warp judgment. After working at Microsoft for six months in 1999 to help design the next update of Microsoft Word, writer James Fallows penned a thoughtful piece for the *Atlantic Monthly* describing Microsoft's culture. There were surprises, he said: "The people are nice" and funny, and they slave fewer hours than is commonly assumed, and they conduct more meetings than he anticipated. But he discovered that "Microsoft is like the military," a self-contained company that "thinks of itself as separate from the rest of the industry," a mighty army that pulls together and focuses all its energy on beating the enemy and building *cool* software. Assistant Attorney General Joel Klein offered a less charitable view: "They grew up in a culture where they didn't learn the responsibility of being corporate citizens. They were not a bunch of kids doing a prank. This is people saying, 'We don't care. This is what you do to win. Let the lawyers worry about technicalities.'"

Such behavior is not peculiar to Microsoft, of course. The first time James Barksdale heard the expression "cut off their air supply," he admitted in court, was from the lips of Oracle CEO Larry Ellison. Microsoft was galvanized to target Netscape as a competitor because young executives such as Marc Andreessen missed no opportunity to swagger that they were going to "kick the shit out of the beast from Redmond." Sun's Scott McNealy has regularly called Gates "butt-head" and referred to his competitor as "the evil empire." Because he had convinced himself that Microsoft was evil, Ellison would embarrassingly concede in the summer of 2000 that Oracle had paid a private detective agency to snoop through the trash of a Microsoft-funded software group; when caught, Ellison's defense was that his investigation of Gates was his "civic duty." Lest we forget, this is an industry that popularized "flaming," where disagreements are treated as opportunities to drop verbal nuclear bombs. Andrew Grove of Intel wrote a book entitled *Only the Paranoid Survive: How to Exploit the Crisis Points That Challenge Every Company*, which implicitly communicates that to survive companies must remain on a warlike footing.

The frequency of the attacks and the looseness of the language may set dot-com companies apart. "What I mostly see is not childish, it's childlike enthusiasm," said Jeffrey Bezos, the founder of Amazon.com. "I cannot think of any industry I know where people are more passionate about what they do." Chimed in Bill Neukom, "This is a very exuberant industry. It's a very youthful industry. Everyone has an opinion. It's very open. And it's very disputatious. Companies act towards each other in ways companies don't act in more mature industries." Remember, Ann Winblad cautions, "most of these people scored high on their math SAT"—and lower on the verbal part of the test. They work long hours, become obsessed with making money, which is their measurement to gauge success, and lose the balance that comes with play, relationships, kids.

But while bombast and belligerence may not be peculiar to Microsoft, under the law a company that is deemed a monopoly may not behave like everyone else. And Microsoft's jury of one, Judge Thomas Penfield Jackson, was not to prove particularly sympathetic to the larger context of Microsoft's behavior. Jackson conceded that as the trial progressed he became increasingly troubled by what he learned about Bill Gates and the Microsoft culture. Throughout the trial, Jackson later told me, he couldn't get out of his mind the group picture he had seen of Bill Gates and Paul Allen and their shaggy-haired first employees at Microsoft. What Jackson saw there was not a portrait of a CEO and lieutenants who would create one of the world's most profitable corporations. Rather, Jackson said, what he saw was "a smart-mouthed young kid who has extraordinary ability and needs a little discipline. I've often said to colleagues that Gates would be better off if he had finished Harvard."

CHAPTER 10

Elephants and Mice

A NTITRUST TRIALS are not like Perry Mason courtroom dramas. There are few jaw-dropping legal thrusts and climactic moments at which witnesses suddenly shrivel or crack. It is drip-drip-drip, the slow accretion of irrelevant fact piled on relevant fact, often without indication of how to distinguish between the two. In late January 1999, Microsoft began to present its witnesses. As they had from the start, Bill Neukom and his team said they fervently believed that the facts would be decisive and would show Microsoft had not violated the law.

They were not alone. After reading trial transcripts of the government's twelve witnesses, Yale law professor George Priest said a crucial fact the government had yet to overcome, one that threatened to topple their entire case, was that there was no clear demonstration of consumer harm. Sure, Microsoft had a monopoly and could have behaved with "greater delicacy," he said. "But I don't know where the consumer was harmed. I use the Netscape browser. I have no trouble getting it." Priest did not believe hard-to-pin-down impressions such as ones of credibility or intent would play significant roles in the outcome, particularly not with the Court of Appeals or the Supreme Court. At the appeals level, "the credibility of the witnesses, the e-mails, that's not important in terms of the law. That's fluff."

Or is it? To adjudicate "facts," Judge Jackson and the appeals courts would need to adjudicate "intent." And if they found that Microsoft intended to hurt competition and to foreclose markets—if this led Judge Jackson to believe the government's facts, not Microsoft's—then it wouldn't be "fluff." Certainly Microsoft didn't seem to think it was. While most Microsoft decision makers subscribed to Bill Neukom's belief that they would win this case, if not in Judge Jackson's court then on appeal, increasingly they were vexed that they were losing the other trial, the public-perception trial. Indeed, the internal e-mails Greg Shaw sent Bill Gates and senior executives on the media coverage of the trial constantly reminded them of this. An at-first mild internal debate over this issue had begun in late 1998, one side led by Neukom and the lawyers, the other by Mich Mathews and her public-relations team, joined by Tod Nielsen and a handful of other executives. Neukom and most of his lawyers believed that as officers of the court they had pledged to follow the rules, and no matter what theatrics or leaks the government engineered, they would not follow suit. It was contemptible, beneath them. And it was impractical. Leak information about a witness's vulnerability and you take away the ability to surprise him with questions in court. Leak information and risk offending Judge Jackson. Relax, Neukom reassured them. This was a marathon, not a sprint, and the law was on Microsoft's side, just as it had been in the Apple patent lawsuit, in which Neukom had totally straight-armed the press.

While Neukom complained about a "disconnect" between what happened in court and what the press reported, members of the public-relations team and a few senior allies—Chief Technology Officer Nathan Myhrvold, Chief Financial Officer Greg Maffei, and Vice President of Technology Development Dick Brass—were beginning to complain more insistently that it was the lawyers who were out of touch. Those in public relations recognized that legal considerations had to take precedence, said a Microsoft insider, and yet at the same time they believed "we needed to be nimbler. We haven't done as good a job as the government has." They wanted the lawyers to be more accessible to reporters. They wanted Neukom to untie their hands and allow more leaks. They worried that even though polls showed Gates and Microsoft were admired by the public, in the long run the company would be tarnished because editors and other opinion molders could one day turn the public against them.

Neither side wished to acknowledge the elephant in the room: the person who probably harmed Microsoft's credibility most with his testimony was Bill Gates. Neukom might honestly believe Gates was credible. The public might believe him—a November 1998 *Business Week*/Harris Poll revealed that only 8 percent of the public had an unfavorable view of Gates, a number that had not changed since June. But those on the other side of Neukom in this internal debate believed this would change. Besides, the audience that counted in this trial was not Microsoft, polls, or the press. Judge Thomas Penfield Jackson, alone, adjudicated credibility and facts. And from Judge Jackson's pretrial rulings and comments in court, Bill Neukom was not as confident as he pretended to be that Microsoft's "facts" would reign in Jackson's mind.

As the Microsoft witnesses prepared to testify, those at Microsoft who believed they were losing the public-relations trial became more vocal. For the first time, cracks appeared in the legal team's facade, as Michael Lacovara and some younger members of Sullivan & Cromwell started to plead for a less rigid approach.

Lacovara and the Young Turks were overruled by their senior partners, Richard Urowsky, John Warden, and Steven Holley. During one gentlemanly debate, Holley cried out, *We will not conduct this trial as if it were* The Oprah Winfrey Show! When the public-relations team argued that Microsoft had to steer the debate and admit mistakes, since it was obvious mistakes had been made, Neukom and the senior members of the legal team quickly shut them down. Recalls a participant in this debate, "The lawyers were saying, 'No, we cannot admit to any bit of aggressiveness because that would be seized upon by the government as evidence that we crossed the line.'" On the face of it, Microsoft's legal team was sabotaging its own credibility.

Finally, Gates tipped the balance. During the Christmas break, he leaned on Neukom: Microsoft should be more proactive, more sensitive to public relations. Gates became convinced, he told me, that the government had turned the case "into a show trial with the primary goal of embarrassing us every day, rather than focusing on the facts of their damaged case. In some ways, when we started this trial, we were a little old-fashioned—we believed the real trial was in the courtroom."

This explains the legal team's altered behavior when the trial resumed in January. And it was probably no coincidence that around this time Gates began to show a warmer side. In December, he appeared, wearing a gray sweater, on *The Rosie O'Donnell Show* and made it clear that he was there to talk not about the trial or about competitors but about his two-and-one-half-year-old daughter—what she liked to have read to her and how she liked to play. He allowed O'Donnell to break the news that Melinda Gates was again pregnant. He talked about his new home. And he showed off Arthur, a Microsoft talking toy. In January, he appeared on Martha Stewart's TV program, where he talked about his daughter again and also about Stewart's mother, who, Stewart said, was now on e-mail. "That's fantastic," Gates purred.

Microsoft was milking a relatively new fact of business life: a CEO could be a celebrity. We had traveled a fair distance from the fifties, when William H. Whyte's *The Organization Man* characterized leaders as faceless conformists and reported that the real corporate star was the system. This was before television infected the culture with a hunger for illustrated storytelling, for finding a picture or face to accompany the story; before CEOs—Iacocca, Trump, Eisner, Gates—were regularly induced to write and tell their stories and before Jack Welch of GE was paid a record $7.1 million advance to cowrite an autobiography; before CEOs were commonly featured on the covers of magazines; before the stock market became a casino for the middle as well as upper class and before a high-profile CEO could help boost a stock's price. Gates is such a magnet for attention that there is even a website on the Internet known as the Bill Gates Personal Wealth Clock (www.webho.com/wealthclock)—that regularly calculates his wealth.

None of Microsoft's p.r. and other efforts in the courtroom, however, assailed the government's case as effectively as did events outside the courtroom. The competitive landscape was shifting swiftly, buttressing Microsoft's claim that monopolies were fleeting, whether Microsoft was one or not. Judge Jackson had this very much on his mind: after the America Online/Netscape/Sun alliance was announced, he declared from the bench that this "might be a very significant change in the playing field" and "could very well have some immediate effect on the market or on the definition of the market." Since the Justice Department routinely collected internal documents as part of its review of such a proposed merger, Jackson said he was inclined to honor Microsoft's request for additional evidence about this new business alliance by sharing such documents with Microsoft. Bill Neukom understood that the merger would not obviate any of the allegations about Microsoft's brutal behavior, but it could invite Jackson to conclude that real competition was on the way; thus, even if he found the company guilty, he might tame any proposed remedy.

The tectonic plates—the "playing field," as Judge Jackson referred to them—seemed to shift daily, as companies scrambled to function on "Internet time" and companies and ideas flashed across the sky. Pointcast and push technology, the rage in 1997—meriting a March 1997 *Wired* cover story proclaiming that the browser was "about to croak" and would be replaced by technology that would "push" to users whatever they preselected—had by 1998 become yesterday's news. In 1996, AOL read its own death notices; by early 1999, it had become a global power. The Internet itself had exploded faster than any medium in history. It took telegraph companies more than thirty years to lay the wire and cable in order to achieve speedy if primitive communications in the mid-nineteenth century. It took twenty-five years after its invention in 1876 for the telephone to eclipse the telegraph, and in 1901 there was a telephone in one out of ten American homes. By contrast, according to Forrester Research, the World Wide Web, which was officially christened by Tim Berners-Lee in 1991, seven years later was accessible in nearly 40 percent of American households, and by 2003 was expected to be reachable in almost two thirds of U.S. homes. Online retail commerce, which generated sales of $8 billion in 1998, were in three years expected to mushroom more than twelvefold to $101 billion. It took television nearly three decades to achieve comparable penetration.

Contrasting historical periods can be an intellectual parlor game, but an argument can be made that any number of other inventions—the wheel, the printing press, railroads, and electricity, for example—have had a more profound impact on society than the computer and the Web. Step back and think about the products and advances made possible by electricity: lightbulbs, telegraphs, telephones, power to run machines, trolleys and trains, television and radio, refrigerators, toasters, air conditioners, elevators, X-ray machines, and computers, among others. These are not easily surpassed. But what is different today is the lightninglike speed of change.

Inevitably, this velocity of change produces paranoia among Information Age competitors. From the moment he awakens each morning, America Online's Robert Pittman frets that his company will be struck by a sudden tsunami. He described the sense of panic that grips him when he lifts the morning newspaper: "What you worry about most is what you don't know. The marketplace is changing very quickly. What we see on the horizon we think we have a strategy to deal with. What you don't know is what suddenly appears tomorrow. No one really saw Amazon.com coming. You can argue that people didn't really see AOL coming. I wake up in the morning and I almost dread reading the newspapers and turning on the TV because it could turn my whole world upside down. There could be one piece of news and 'Oh my God! I got to deal with that.'"

Pittman's boss, Steve Case, in a 1998 speech likened the gut-wrenching daily contest to a car race: "I sometimes feel like I'm behind the wheel of a race car. I need to keep my eyes on the horizon, but I also need to keep my attention on the rearview mirror to see who's gaining on me. From the passenger seat, consumers are telling me where and when they want to be dropped off, and behind me my shareholders and business partners are engaged in loud backseat driving. One of the biggest challenges is that there are no road signs to help navigate. . . . And the finish line is a long, long way away."

Perhaps the biggest challenge of the race Case is in is to know when to pull in for a pit stop to overhaul and upgrade your car. In no sector of the economy is deal making more frenzied than in the communications industry. The Netscape–America Online merger was Case's grittiest pit stop, a $4.2 billion stock transaction whose value multiplied to $10 billion as Netscape's share price soared before the deal closed. The deal cemented a three-way axis with the leader of the anti-Microsoft jihad, Sun Microsystems. AOL's extensive subscriber base was pooled with Netscape's software and the nine million registered users of its Netcenter portal to the World Wide Web. The deal was costly: AOL agreed to purchase five hundred million dollars' worth of computer systems and services from Sun over the next four years and to make "reasonable efforts to maintain the existing Netscape browser" as an alternative to Microsoft's browser; to pay thirty-two million dollars annually for technical support and to license Sun's Java products; to promote Java technology platforms for handheld devices such as cellular phones or personal digital assistants and for inexpensive network PCs that retrieve software from servers or the Internet. For its part, Sun agreed to commit about $1.3 billion to assist in the purchase of Netscape; to spend money to license software and to market AOL; and to instruct Sun's seven-thousand-strong sales force to sell Netscape software.

On the surface, America Online's goal was simple. As Case told *Newsweek:* "We want AOL to be as ubiquitous as the telephone." And as lucrative, he hoped. One of the few Web companies to actually turn a profit, AOL was pioneering a different Web-revenue model. While it was to rely on monthly subscribers and on selling advertising aimed at those subscribers, it would also sell Netscape software and technical assistance to corporate customers and speed into e-commerce, using the world's foremost online service as a giant shopping mall, on which it would charge rent. Bob Pittman, whose career began in broadcasting, where the sole source of revenue was advertising, and then moved to cable, where revenues came from subscriptions as well as advertising, now envisioned AOL's business model containing no less than six sources of revenue: advertising; monthly subscriptions; the rental of space on its Internet mall; software sales; sales of services; and sales of goods or fees charged to enable others to engage in e-commerce. As in broadcasting, AOL essentially sells access to eyeballs. "We rent a relationship to our members to people," said Pittman. By late 1998, AOL's annual nonsubscriber revenue had risen to $181 million. By the end of 1998, the price of AOL's stock, which sold for $21 a share prior to the November 24 merger, had nearly doubled to $38.78.

Bill Gates did not need road signs or a rearview mirror to see that AOL and others were on Microsoft's tail. In the fall of 1998, in his Chairman Mao mode, Gates wrote a ten-thousand-word memorandum, "The Era Ahead." Its first sentence proclaimed, "Our position today within the computer industry is stronger than it has ever been," but Gates went on to warn of looming dangers. He invoked the middleware threat from software developers who might decide that it would be easier to write applications for the Netscape browser. He portrayed Java as a threat to Windows, cautioning that "our largest competitors, including Sun and IBM," were rallying around Java. Although Gates believed in a PC-centric universe because of the advantages provided by the horsepower of the desktop computer, he worried about competition from network PCs and handheld devices, about hard-to-use, unreliable PCs that suddenly crash, about the new race against competitors such as AOL to locate "must have" services that people demand as part of their new "Web Lifestyle," about powerful servers from Sun, IBM, and Oracle that might offer corporate customers more than Windows could.

While Steve Case and the government portrayed Microsoft as a comfortable monopoly, by early 1999, on the eve of calling its first witnesses,

Gates and company painted a starkly different portrait. They said they were terrified of AOL. They feared that AOL might switch to Netscape's browser; that AOL, using Netscape's browser and Sun technology, could forge an alternative platform to Windows, creating an experience whereby customers enter an AOL realm from the moment they turn on their PC to when they navigate the Web to when they sign off; that AOL would use its marketing muscle to encourage customers to adopt hand-held and other devices that connected to Sun servers. Microsoft was ter-rified because AOL already counted as customers about 40 percent of all online users and further terrified that AOL's reach might provoke another "inflection point," a paradigmatic shift to non-PC devices. And Microsoft was terrified that America Online could use its lofty stock price to acquire more new companies and competitive technologies.

Microsoft shared one advantage with America Online and other new-media companies. Old-media companies such as AT&T, Disney, News Cor-poration, CBS, or Viacom, no matter how aggressive, were freighted with a common malady: they weren't growth stocks. They were "value" stocks, and often with not terribly compelling value at that if their price-to-earnings ratios were any indication. They lacked what John Malone called "invasion currency" to do deals. When Malone looked at the business landscape in late 1998, he thought America Online's stock market value made it a potential rival to Microsoft. "If anybody can eclipse Microsoft, it will be them," he said. He noted that the market cap or total stock-market value of Rupert Murdoch's News Corporation empire was, at the time, maybe $35 billion; by contrast, the infant new-media company @Home, which provided high-speed cable-modem access to the Internet and had yet to earn a profit, was worth about $40 billion. Even though AT&T had a cash flow of about $10 billion compared to America Online's then pid-dling $135 million, America Online's stock-market cap was nearing $200 billion, exceeding the value of AT&T's. The "game right now in this space is market cap," Malone said, "because if you've got a big enough market cap then you can acquire the things that you need to complete your port-folio. If you don't, you can't play in that game. AT&T can't play with its stock in that game because it's too dilutive for them. Rupert can't play in that game because the values have run past him and it's too dilutive for him. You need invasion currency to play in that game. So who has inva-sion currency? AOL, Amazon, have invasion currency." As does Microsoft.

Despite its deep pockets, Microsoft knew that technology was no longer its friend. Since there was so much money to be made from information technology, the best minds had headed for the veritable garage, hoping to invent the next big idea. New challengers were surfacing everywhere, including the free and open-source software movement made possible by the Internet, over which can be distributed software and source code that users can use to customize and build their own applications. Of particular concern was Linux, an operating system that by proclaiming itself open to all and concerned with quality was generating new users and considerable buzz. Companies such as IBM, Sun, and Oracle were also ballyhooing the cheaper network PC.

Outside the computer industry, too, Bill Gates saw giant industries converging, seemingly against Microsoft. The cable industry envisioned an operating system in the home with powerful new digital cable boxes. The consumer-electronics industry promoted handheld devices like the mushrooming Palm Pilot, which did not use Windows CE, and the Sony PlayStation, which might be able to control all appliances in a home. *Business Week* predicted in January 1999 that this "will be the year that home networks start to make sense." Telephone companies such as AT&T were now cable giants and offered a high-speed cable or telephone modem that promised instant broadband Internet access and also held out the possibility of a new tollbooth that Microsoft would not control. Telephone companies envisioned wireless telephones that surfed the Internet using non-Windows operating systems.

At the same time, government added to the uncertainty. Would the federal government be a passive spectator or an involved referee? Would government, for example, assert that the Internet—its software code, its broadband, high-speed access, its core technology—was an essential facility with certain "public trust" obligations, as it has for the broadcast, cable, and telephone industries? Already, champions of the Internet—such as Lawrence Lessig, who in 1999 published a thoughtful book on the subject, *Code and Other Laws of Cyberspace*—fretted that without government to referee, the democratic premise of the Internet will be subverted by corporate elephants. In a sense, the battle today is between elephants and mice, between AOL Time Warner or AT&T and a myriad of upstarts. According to Lessig, "The mice win in the first round and the elephants take some time to figure out how to regroup. What troubles me most about this is that with the original architecture of the Internet the elephants wouldn't have been able to regroup. They wouldn't have been able to effect any control over this innovation." The original architecture of the Internet was "end to end," which meant clear passage for everyone from sender to destination. The Internet did not discriminate among those who communicated on it.

But under the new broadband architecture, the owners of the cable or telephone pipe, said Lessig, claim there is not enough bandwidth to accommodate everyone, especially competitors; they "control the experience of the customer and make some horizons look sunnier and other horizons look darker," or they feature content they own, or they try to steer users to their own content sites, by featuring these or by making it easier for visitors to use them, or they invoke copyright laws to control the space and pressure authors or artists so that they own a work's electronic rights in all media. To say government shouldn't do anything about this, said Lessig, "is to allow commerce to restructure the net in a certain way," a way that may be inimical to the public interest.

By early 1999, the elephants were on the move. AT&T, for example, acquired John Malone's cable company, in the process becoming the largest shareholder of @Home, a cable-modem service that promises the kind of high-speed access to the Internet that allows moving pictures to appear on a PC as they do on the TV. What this would also permit, Malone candidly told me in late 1998, was for AT&T to become the gatekeeper for the Internet. AOL might have more Internet subscribers than any other Internet-service provider, but without high-speed access AOL might remain a classic middleman, offering only a service without the means to distribute it to customers. "AOL provides content and transport," Malone said. "They need to subscribe to our network to get to their customers at high speed. They have to go through us."

Other companies' maneuvers also posed threats to Microsoft. IBM's nearly eighty-two billion dollars in 1998 annual revenues were more than five times those of Microsoft and dwarfed the combined revenues of America Online, Netscape, and Sun. There is no way Microsoft—or AOL—can win at e-commerce without tackling the world's leader in it. As *U.S. News and World Report* noted in December 1998, IBM's electronic business totaled twenty-seven billion dollars worldwide, or about equal the combined electronic revenues of Microsoft, AOL, Netscape, and Sun.

Gates also had Sony on his mind. Every time Sony designed a new product, be it a powerful new PlayStation game platform or software for set-top boxes for cable or satellite transmission, said Sony's chief executive, Nobuyuki Idei, Gates berated him. Idei saw himself involved in what he called a few "regional wars" with Microsoft—games, an operating system for the TV box, a PlayStation 2 that might rival the PC to control all home appliances—while cooperating with or not bumping up against Microsoft in most of their businesses. But Gates reacted as if they were engaged in a world war, prompting Idei to tell me, "I don't want to be controlled by Microsoft, and they want to control us."

When he wasn't thinking about these elephants, Gates thought about the mice. Microsoft was eager to find new revenue streams and had edged into the lucrative travel market. Yet Priceline.com had built a significant market share by creating a reverse-auction system, letting consumers name the prices they would be willing to pay for hotel rooms, airplane tickets, or home mortgages and then waiting to see if the sellers would match the prices or to assess what price they did offer. Microsoft had invested in building its own online Expedia travel service and was readying to do battle with Priceline.com. Preemptively, Priceline.com founder Jay Walker secured patents for his reverse-auction technology. Walker's company, like others—including Amazon.com—now use the leverage of the patent protection they have received from the government not only to shelter inventions but to protect what are essentially business practices, assuring that competitors may not employ them. Thus, Priceline.com has a patent for its auction method and is suing Microsoft's Expedia for using a similar technique. Nathan Myhrvold believes patent laws properly protect intellectual property, but he scoffed at the arrogance of Priceline.com in thinking they could use them to protect a familiar business model: "The notion that naming your own price is unique and something they invented? Come on! I was in a Casbah in Marrekech and I was invited to name my own price!"

Another mouse irritating Gates was his former assistant, Rob Glaser of RealNetworks. By 1998, four years after its birth, Glaser's company had attracted more than twenty-seven million computer users, who could use RealNetworks software to listen to and watch radio and television programs over the Internet from more than ten thousand stations; RealPlayer was downloaded one hundred thousand times daily by users who wanted free audio from the Internet, and its "Jukebox" had lured a total of twenty million different users. This represented a market share of more than 80 percent, and Microsoft wanted a piece of it. Microsoft paid thirty million dollars to license the product and purchased 10 percent of RealNetworks in 1997. Then, worried that this streaming software was another middleware threat, it spent seventy-five million dollars to acquire a rival streaming-software company. Later, using the same playbook it used against Netscape, Microsoft announced that it was integrating the competitive Media Player into Windows and its browser. Unlike Netscape, Glaser anticipated this move. He testified before Congress in 1998 that his old employer "is taking actions that simply stop our company's products from working" on PCs, the same charge Netscape and Sun had lodged. The government did not intervene. They didn't have to. By the end of 1998, Glaser's RealNetworks remained far ahead of Microsoft.

Thus, there was a growing divide. Inside Judge Jackson's courtroom, an impression grew that Microsoft's credibility was wanting. Outside the courtroom, an impression grew that maybe the trial was dealing with yesterday, while the industry it was concerned with was being transformed tomorrow. Maybe Microsoft was as vulnerable outside court as inside? Maybe Microsoft's paranoia was justified.

CHAPTER 11

Microsoft's Witnesses Speak

A S THEIR FIRST WITNESS readied to take the stand in mid-January 1999, Microsoft's legal team professed unbridled optimism. Michael Lacovara declared: "We haven't started getting our licks in yet. I'm confident we have great witnesses," who would show that Microsoft neither foreclosed markets nor harmed consumers or competitors and thus violated no antitrust laws.

But the first order of business for the Microsoft legal team was to attack the government's assertion that Microsoft possessed monopoly power. To do so, they called as their initial witness Dr. Richard L. Schmalensee, the dean of MIT's Sloan School of Management. His written testimony ran to a mind-numbing 364 pages, much of it contradicting his former mentor, Dr. Franklin Fisher, who stayed in court to watch. Guiding Schmalensee through the highlights of his written testimony was Richard Urowsky, who was making his maiden appearance at the lectern.

Pay no heed to the "small mountains of e-mails," to the "speculation" over who might be harmed, said Schmalensee, for what counted was whether consumers were actually harmed. They were not. Nor was Microsoft capable of exerting monopoly power. Although Dr. Fisher had said competition with Windows was "a joke," Dr. Schmalensee disagreed. Microsoft could not raise prices at will, he said, because it confronted real competition—from Apple's Macintoshes, from the open-source Linux operating system, from the Palm Pilot, and from pirated copies of its own software. In fact, it was absurd to define PC operating systems as a separate market. Since non-PC devices also performed many of the same functions—word processing, e-mail, Internet access—they should be counted as well. The monopoly claim would then crumble, since Microsoft hardly dominated these devices. If Microsoft were truly a monopoly, he had asserted in his written deposition, it "would charge at least 16 times" more than it currently did for its operating system, or about eight hundred dollars per copy. Once again he repeated this assertion, relying on charts containing abstruse econometric formulas. And future competition, Dr. Schmalensee insisted, would be only more severe.

As Boies rose to cross-examine his first "hostile" witness, courtroom regulars leaned forward in anticipation. They were treated to a markedly different performance than what they'd gotten from the Microsoft team. Whereas the avuncular Warden and most of his pin-striped partners rarely asked one question where ten would do, Boies was ferociously focused, like a finely tuned athlete who blocked out everything but the contest. He had forgotten a handkerchief and approached the bench blowing his nose with a paper towel he had folded to fit into his back pocket. Pinched between his fingers was a single beige folder on which he had jotted the several key themes he wished to probe. Nearby rested a box with folders arranged alphabetically—AOL, foreclosure, predatory pricing, and so on—and in each folder were stuffed relevant e-mails and documents. Boies was guided in all of his cross-examinations by a simple philosophy. "There are only three things you ought do in a cross-examination," he told me. "Remember, it's not your witness. First, you want to confront the important points in the testimony. Second, if there's an opportunity, get some helpful admissions from him. And third, if there's an opportunity, attack the witness's credibility. You can have a cross [-examination] that misses point two or three, or even misses point two and three. You can't have a cross that misses point one."

Dr. Schmalensee, who has steel-gray hair and a thin mustache that makes him look like the actor Brian Donlevy, certainly presented Boies with an inviting target. Outside the courtroom, Schmalensee had a nuanced view of antitrust laws, believing that software, like manufacturing or any business, was not exempt from such laws. This was not the view Schmalensee was prepared to present, however. He entered court less as a disinterested scholar than as Microsoft's champion, a point on which Boies immediately pounced, asking Schmalensee whether it was accurate to refer to him as Microsoft's "house economic expert" and noting that he was paid eight hundred dollars per hour.

Boies then produced a January 5, 1996, e-mail from Gates in which he complained to his executives that computer manufacturers were displaying Netscape "in a FAR more prominently [sic] way" than Microsoft's browser. Could this, Boies asked, have been what led Microsoft to impose its contract restrictions on computer manufacturers? Was this not predatory? Schmalensee said he was ignorant of Microsoft's internal decision-making process.

Was it true that Microsoft held a monopoly over operating systems for Intel-based personal computers? The witness said that he did not consider this a "relevant" question.

Well, did he accept that in the short run at least there was no real alternative to Windows? Schmalensee reluctantly admitted that this was true. Since Schmalensee had declared in his written testimony that rival operating systems and such devices as the Palm Pilot posed "a significant" threat to Windows, Boies demanded to know whether the Palm Pilot was a "significant" threat at the moment. Schmalensee retreated. "As it stands, it is not a significant competitor. It is a germ of a potential competitor."

Boies asked him to square his October deposition, in which he said he was "not aware" of "viable competition" to Windows, with his testimony in court that it faced "significant" competition. If Boies could make Schmalensee appear to contradict himself and split hairs—as he seemed to do—his credibility would be tarnished and the legitimacy of his "facts" would be undermined. Schmalensee again hedged, saying the competition might come "in a year, in two years." Since he stated that competition constrained Microsoft's ability to raise prices, did he, as an economist, have quantitative proof of this? He did not. Boies also unearthed various things Schmalensee had written that seemed to contradict his testimony.

Judge Jackson helped keep the witness on the defensive by asking whether the viable operating-system competitors he invoked—Linux and Be—had made any money. "I would be stunned if they were making a lot of money," Schmalensee confessed.

Of course, Schmalensee was literally correct: other operating systems *might* become competitors, just as there might be a paradigm shift to another platform—perhaps a handheld wireless device—but so what?

Schmalensee left the witness stand pleased with his performance, as were Microsoft's lawyers, who believed he had posed a factual question the government couldn't answer: if Microsoft was truly a monopoly, why were its prices so relatively low? This proved, they said, that there were market-based price constraints. Thus: no monopoly, no predation. These were the facts that mattered. Boies, on the other hand, was confident he had eviscerated the credibility of the first Microsoft witness.

Boies was closer to the truth. Judge Jackson was impressed with the knowledge and verbal felicity of both Dr. Fisher and Dr. Schmalensee, but he thought Boies's cross-examination of Schmalensee was "a gem." Confronting him with "so many contradictory statements was, I'm sure, embarrassing to Schmalensee," Jackson later reflected. He blamed the lawyers: "The defense should have known that he had written these things that were contradictory. . . . Boies rendered him less convincing than Fisher was." Credibility was a matter beginning to weigh ever more heavily on Jackson's mind.

Fairly or not, credibility would be a problem for most of Microsoft's twelve witnesses, nine of whom were senior Microsoft executives. Most of them approached the witness stand belligerently, believing they would turn the case around for Microsoft. They would educate the judge. They would prove that David Boies was a computer illiterate. They would show they were smarter. They would take a bow.

Several Microsoft witnesses were effective. Unapologetically, Paul Maritz, 43, the black-bearded, Rhodesia-born group vice president for platforms and applications, the executive responsible for supervising the development of all versions of Windows, and the most senior Microsoft executive to testify, spoke of how static notions of monopolies couldn't apply to high-tech companies. Rapid innovation, he said, imperiled every company, none more than computer companies. Thus, the so-called applications barrier to entry was a myth. "In fact, most existing software products will be rendered obsolete in three years if not sooner."

He spoke of the "inflection points" which strike the industry suddenly and regularly. IBM was struck by one two decades before, when it continued to pour resources into large mainframe computers just as PCs were becoming more widely distributed and cheaper, opening the door to Compaq, Dell, and Gateway 2000. Microsoft had adapted to several subsequent inflection points, including the development of the mouse and the graphical user interface, and the rise of more powerful thirty-two-bit technology. But now, he continued, Microsoft was confronted by two new inflection points: the Internet and such information appliances as handheld devices and smart TVs. Unlike Bill Gates, Maritz acknowledged that Microsoft was concerned with Netscape's market share, was motivated to defeat Netscape, and was happy when Netscape's stock price fell.

But Maritz had his own credibility gap. He insisted, for instance, that the browser issue "was not an important part of the discussions" between Apple and Microsoft because the real core issue between them in negotiating the 1997 agreement was the billion-dollar patent dispute, not whether Apple aligned with them or Netscape. Boies retrieved a June 23, 1996, e-mail from Gates to Maritz and other senior executives describing a meeting Gates held with top Apple executives earlier that same week. At this meeting they discussed a Microsoft financial investment in Apple. In this eleven-paragraph outline of a possible modus vivendi, Gates did not focus on the patent dispute. The only time the word *patent* is used is near the end when Gates itemizes what each side would get from a truce and then, almost as an afterthought, says that both would get "patent cross license," which meant that they agreed not to sue each other over the outstanding patent issues and to share each other's patents. Boies then presented another e-mail describing the meeting, addressed to Gates, which similarly glossed over the patent issue. Judge Jackson interrupted to ask Maritz, Wasn't it true that the only mention of a patent dispute in this critical e-mail is in the next-to-last paragraph? Maritz was cornered.

In court, Maritz said Microsoft bundled the browser with Windows to bring "a key benefit to consumers." In his e-mails to colleagues two years earlier, however, he wrote that to defeat Netscape "we have to position the browser as 'going away' and do deeper integration on Windows." Maritz denied he had threatened to cut off Netscape's air supply. Boies then introduced a deposition in which Maritz conceded "it is possible" he had said just that.

Boies was eager to show that Microsoft had artificially bolted its browser to Windows, and on January 28, near the end of Maritz's fourth day on the stand, he bored in. The first version of Internet Explorer that came with Windows 95, Boies noted, was not integrated but was "a stand-alone browser application that ran on top of Windows 95. Correct?"

That's not a "test of integration," said Maritz, since other software Microsoft considered integrated was "distributed independently."

But the code was separate from Windows. It was, suggested Boies, clearly an application, not part of the operating system.

"It was a separate body of code that you could install for use with Windows 95," admitted Maritz. "But I'm not sure if I would say it's a stand-alone application per se." Since Microsoft's browser was born as a separate product, Boies left Judge Jackson to wonder why it didn't remain so. This was a natural lead-in, Boies hoped, to Microsoft's third witness.

Senior Vice President Dr. James Edward Allchin, 47, was the executive who, working for Maritz, supervised the development of Windows. A thin Southern gentleman with feathery-white hair and a doctorate in computer science, Allchin had been a fervent believer in open architecture when he was a young programmer, in computers that could easily converse. His Ph.D. thesis at the Georgia Institute of Technology posited an architecture for an experimental computing environment, called Clouds, that allowed computers to share resources, much as Sun's Jini would promise to do decades later. After Allchin joined Microsoft in the early nineties, he had a conversion, becoming a proponent of the Windows franchise and of using its proprietary architecture as leverage to build market share. Windows was the core asset and had to be defended at any cost, Allchin believed. There were those within Microsoft who challenged this Windows-centric view, arguing that Microsoft should become Internet-centric, should confront Java's "write once, run anywhere" software by creating a rival platform for Internet computing that would be open to all operating systems; this camp (as first reported in February 1999 by David Bank of *The Wall Street Journal*) was led by Senior Vice President Brad Silverberg.

A battle raged within Microsoft in 1996 and 1997, with Allchin leading the internal opposition to Silverberg and warning that Silverberg's argument was malignant. If adopted, it would, he said, eat away at Windows and play to Sun's strength, which was to shift the controlling software from the operating system to their own powerful servers. In a February 18, 1997, e-mail to Gates and Maritz, Allchin wrote that making Windows open ("cross-platform") would "dilute Windows. . . . I consider this cross-platform issue a disease within Microsoft." Allchin also disagreed with those who said Microsoft should not integrate its browser in with Windows. Instead, he said, Microsoft should use its Windows strength to shore up its browser weakness and to disadvantage the budding alliance between Netscape's browser and Sun's Java software. In the end, Bill Gates was forced to choose between the two approaches, and after a fierce debate he sided with Allchin.

Two years later, Allchin was in court to explain his position. Microsoft hoped he would also demonstrate how computing systems were rapidly changing and why it was a fallacy to think that a browser was not an organic part of an operating system, which must evolve and add new features, just as automakers have added air-conditioning, CD players, electric windows—and now navigational devices—to their basic packages to attract customers. Allchin conducted a videotaped demonstration to rebut the testimonies of Dr. Farber and Dr. Felten that a browser was a distinct product, and he demonstrated that Dr. Felten could not in fact remove the browser from Windows without making it nonfunctional. Consumers benefit, he said, because they pay less and get more; they have "fewer hassles because they do not have to install lots of individual features separately," and integrated features are easier to use. Developers benefit because "there is less software code for them to develop, test, localize, etc., which saves them money and time"; their products consume less of the PC's memory; and "it encourages greater consistency among the tools available to help them build applications."

Allchin's attractive wife, Catherine, a former employee at Microsoft's longtime public-relations agency, Waggener Edstrom, sat at the end of the first spectator row, hands folded, offering her husband moral support. He needed it. With this witness, as others, Boies demonstrated his standard courtroom technique. "During a cross-examination, David takes a friendly walk down the hall with you while he's quietly closing doors," observed Jeffrey Blattner, who sat on the bench behind Boies most court days and who served as Joel Klein's de facto chief of staff.

"They get to the end of the hall, and David turns on you, and there's no place to go. He's closed all the doors."

Allchin asserted that Microsoft intended to bundle its browser with Windows before the threat from Netscape surfaced. To prove they were a seamless duo, Microsoft played in court a videotape citing a long list of consumer benefits that flowed from integrating the two—that one could use links in the browser control panel to visit websites, that typing in the name of a website in the address window would immediately take the user there, that a user could drag a website to the desktop with a mouse, that a user could access the hard drive from the browser window, that a user could use the browser to alter and delete files from the hard drive, among others.

During his cross-examination of Allchin, Boies started closing doors. He rolled the tape again to show the first of these benefits—that clicking on links and typing in addresses would transport users to websites— then stopped it and asked, If the two products were separate, would consumers enjoy the same benefits?

Allchin paused, then conceded, "Yes, I believe that's correct."

Boies repeated this process a total of nineteen times, and each time Allchin was forced to offer a similar answer, involuntarily suggesting that Microsoft *had* artificially bolted the browser to Windows and thus violating antitrust strictures against illegal tying. Although Allchin devoutly repeated that Microsoft integrated the browser to better serve its customers, Boies produced a sheaf of contradictory evidence. One was a December 1996 e-mail from Allchin to Paul Maritz, which Boies considered one of the most incriminating pieces of evidence among the more than three million pages the government had collected. The e-mail suggests that this white-haired executive with the pretty wife and humble demeanor was as hard-core as Bill Gates. Ruminating about "concerns for our future," the very first of eight concerns that Allchin cited was how Internet Explorer was losing to Netscape Navigator. His solution—which Boies saw as proof that Microsoft was guilty of classic predatory behavior—was wickedly simple:

I don't understand how IE is going to win. . . . Let's [suppose] IE is as good as Navigator/Communicator. Who wins? The one with 80% market share. Maybe being free helps us, but once people are used to a product it is hard to change them. . . . My conclusion is that we must leverage Windows more. Treating IE as just an add-on to Windows . . . [loses] our biggest advantage—Windows market share. . . . We should think first about an integrated solution—that is our strength.

Boies moved on to discuss a Microsoft videotape purporting to show that Dr. Felten's program to remove Microsoft's browser from Windows 98 caused significant "performance degradation." While watching the videotape over the weekend, Felten and two associates noticed that when Microsoft claimed its browser was removed and the computer slowed to a crawl, the tiny text header on the screen still read "Microsoft Internet Explorer." Innocently, Boies opened a door by first getting Allchin to explain the experiment. When the Felten program was run, the header was removed, he told Boies. Suddenly, Boies slammed the door shut, stunning Allchin by showing him that the header still appeared in the upper part of the screen, meaning that the problems Microsoft enumerated were not caused by Felten's program. His voice rising, Boies wagged his finger at the witness and histrionically bellowed, "This video that you brought in here and vouched for and told the court how much you'd checked it, is a video that purports to show right here on the screen a performance degradation . . . and how it's due to the Felten program. And that's just wrong, right?" Sheepishly, Allchin conceded, "I do not think the Felten program had been run."

As David Boies continued slamming doors on him, Allchin began addressing him as "sir." The witness still had hours of testimony left, but Boies knew he had already won the psychological war. Boies had been insecure when he began this cross-examination, fearing he would be overmatched technically. Now, he felt in control, so much so that he overstated his own technical prowess. "I have this guy on the stand and he's Microsoft's chief technical guy," Boies later told me, "and he says if you take out the browser it will not be OK, and I say, 'Do you have HTLM built in?' He says, 'I don't know.' At that point you know that he knows that you know more about that stuff than he does. He knows that if he gets out of line, you're going to nail him. And once he knows that, he's going to tell the truth, which is what you want." Boies was so psyched for the rest of his questioning of Allchin that this creature of habit, who usually skips lunch during a trial, asked his wife, Mary, to bring him a bag of cinnamon-raisin bagels. He wolfed down seven while he studied documents in the witness room during the lunch break.

At the end of his second day of testimony, Allchin was humiliated and obviously furious at the video mistake. He left the courthouse, his arm shielding his face from cameras. The next day, he endured still another humiliation when Boies showed that another Microsoft videotape demonstration did not rely on a single PC, as had been implied, but, rather, spliced together footage of at least two different machines. Boies knew he had achieved a second, dramatic Perry Mason moment, still more evidence that Microsoft was contemptuous of this court and this trial. With Joel Klein and the entire Justice team beaming from the spectator seats, Boies abruptly announced that he was finished with the witness.

Stunned, Microsoft's lawyers hurriedly asked for a bench conference with Judge Jackson to request that he allow Allchin to prepare a new video overnight, which he would personally supervise and narrate.

The next day, Judge Jackson was distressed that the Microsoft witness didn't know if this demonstration involved two different machines. "How can I rely on it if you can't tell me whether it's the same machine?" he asked in open court. "It's very troubling, Mr. Allchin." Privately, Judge Jackson believed that Microsoft had made an innocent mistake.

The government got the headlines, but Allchin's testimony was not as bad as it seemed. As a matter of law, of the major claims made by Allchin in his 139-page deposition, Boies attacked relatively few. And the next day, in court, Allchin did finally show that Felten's program had wrongly asserted that it could decouple the browser from Windows; Felten had hidden the browser icon but could not entirely remove the browser, suggesting the two products were integrated.

Allchin had proved his point, but at what cost? He had shown some consumer and even developer benefits from integrating the browser, but that didn't answer the government's questions about Microsoft's intent. In judging Microsoft's intent, credibility mattered, and days like these helped to erode it.

Outside, Bill Neukom stood before the cameras and put a brave face on the experience, cautioning the press not to confuse theatrics with substance, not to miss that Boies had failed to challenge many of the facts in Allchin's written testimony. With his hands clasped behind his back, Neukom calmly tried to defuse the prosecutorial zeal of reporters.

He made light of the mishaps: "We make very good software. We did not make a good tape." It didn't matter what e-mails Boies produced in court insinuating Microsoft's various motives for bundling its browser in with Windows, he continued, what mattered was that the federal Court of Appeals had already sided with Microsoft, agreeing that if the browser was free and simple to use, then it benefited consumers. But, of course, Neukom was mischaracterizing the Court of Appeals decision, as we've seen, transforming a narrow procedural ruling into scripture. Neukom ignored another test applied in a courtroom: a judge or jury doesn't truly hear all the facts if a witness loses credibility. The next day, an avalanche of press headlines blared one unmistakable message: Arrogant, Misleading Microsoft.

Moreover, this embarrassment exposed the failure of Microsoft's legal team to subject the videotape to due diligence, as Boies had done. Prior to Allchin's appearance, Mary Boies recalled, her husband was so nervous that instead of coming home for the weekend, he decided to remain in Washington. Boies spent from Saturday through Monday morning in a room at Justice, parked in front of a PC with Felten and his associates, breaking only to sleep. "I watched the tape," he recalled. "I tried to replicate what was on the tape. If anyone on the other side had done that, they would have seen what I saw—if they had anyone as good as I had." He believed it was an honest Microsoft mistake but avoidable nevertheless. He blamed Bill Neukom's lack of courtroom experience: "If you haven't got a tough litigator in charge who looks at everything with skepticism—how many times has Neukom sat through trial? My theory is that John Warden is dying because he has to sit there and he doesn't have the authority to run the case. . . . If Warden were running this litigation, I don't think this would have happened."

Warden was not as kind to Boies. Privately, he groused that Boies's sensational approach to the videotape was "far more appropriate to Gerry Spence," a flamboyant defense attorney who enters a courtroom carrying his cowboy hat. Like Neukom, he insisted that facts are what matter.

Asked months later why his video was not vetted, Allchin told me, "Looking back, it's just a mistake." What did he learn from the mistake? "Do it yourself," he said. Asked what it felt like to be quizzed by Boies, Allchin said, "I can't say because that's emotional. I'm a computer scientist." So how did he react as a scientist? Allchin said he was stunned to be portrayed as a business shark: "The word *leveraging*—how would I have known that's such a loaded term?"

Yet leveraging was at the core of the government's case, and though Judge Jackson found Allchin credible in most respects and thought that Boies "to a certain extent" was guilty of pulling a melodramatic "stunt" by using the videotape to suggest something sinister, he didn't buy Allchin's definition of the word *leverage*. Jackson privately said of Allchin, "He euphemized so much that I finally said to him, 'What did you mean by the use of the word *leverage?*' He thought for a minute and said, 'Opportunity.'" Jackson laughed aloud at this. "Yeah, you could call it an 'opportunity' if you want!"

Even if Microsoft demonstrated real consumer benefits from combining a browser with its operating system, Boies knew that intent mattered. If the government could prove Microsoft intended to harm Netscape by giving away the browser for free, or by awarding gifts to some companies and coercing others, then, in the words of one Justice Department lawyer, "that's classic predatory behavior," in violation of section 2 of the Sherman Act.

Although Microsoft had promised that the trial would turn as their witnesses testified, their first several witnesses had not altered the case's momentum. Microsoft hoped that Michael T. Devlin, founder and CEO of Rational Software Corporation, would buttress Jim Allchin's testimony by showing how developers were building innovative software to take advantage of the browser technologies Microsoft now embedded in Windows. But it took Boies only a few moments to pounce, pummeling Devlin with questions that cast aspersions on the independence of his testimony and suggested Microsoft's enormous power. Wasn't it true, he asked, that Devlin's company was "dependent on its ability to support the Microsoft platform"? Wasn't it true that one of the quarterly SEC disclosure statements his company filed with the government said this? Wasn't it true that Microsoft licensed his product? Microsoft found that its technology arguments were drowned out by courtroom theatrics, and Devlin was off the stand in two hours.

Microsoft's fifth witness, Will Poole, who appeared on February 8, 1999, supervised the company's relationships with Internet-content providers (ICPs) such as Intuit. He brought to the stand the well-scrubbed look of an IBM salesman, with rimless round glasses, a white shirt, a simple blue-striped tie, and a navy suit. His hair was dark, thick, and neatly combed. He had good manners and prefaced his replies with "That's correct," and "Yes, sir." Microsoft intended for Poole to serve as the rebuttal witness to the testimony of Intuit's William Harris. He would show that Microsoft's contracts with ICPs were intended not to foreclose Netscape but to increase consumer awareness of its browser technologies.

Poole chose to verbally fence with Boies, which proved to be a mistake. He insisted that the simple explanation for each of Microsoft's actions was that it was trying to better serve its customers by offering them better technology than Netscape did. He tried to rephrase Boies's questions for clarity, saying he was not aware of a "specific" as opposed to a "general discussion" at Microsoft about ways to reduce Netscape's revenues. Poole was cornered, though: Microsoft had left a paper trail illustrating that one of its strategies was to preclude ICPs from paying money to Netscape, in return for placement on the Windows desktop. Boies attacked, documenting how Microsoft had, specifically, imposed this restriction on Intuit. Was there anything unusual about this contract? Boies asked. Poole hemmed and hawed and tried to avoid direct answers. "But please listen to his question," Judge Jackson admonished, shaking his head in evident frustration.

Boies did not indulge in clear-your-throat foreplay. With Poole, he simply homed in on contracts stipulating that if an ICP wished to be featured on Microsoft's desktop it was required to spurn Netscape. There was palpable titillation in court as reporters and spectators sensed that Boies had closed all the doors on the witness. Without hurriedly leafing through documents or reading scripted questions, and with his right hand placed firmly on his hip, flashing a message that he was in charge, Boies exposed Microsoft's predatory behavior document by incriminating document. He forced Poole to concede that Microsoft awarded preferable positions to companies that complied with its wishes. He forced Poole to confirm that Microsoft coerced Intuit to stop doing business with Netscape. He forced Poole to admit that Bill Gates insisted on this restriction. He forced Poole to concede that Microsoft's restrictive contracts were intended to boost its browser share. And although Poole mentioned other companies with restrictive contracts, Boies forced him to admit that he knew of no other company that had contracts as restrictive as Microsoft's. At one point, when Poole explained that the contracts were meant to create partnerships so that Microsoft's partners could build great content with Microsoft's technology, an audible groan went up in the press section. Microsoft attorney Richard Urowsky turned and glared, as if his worst fears about the animals in the rear of the courtroom had been realized. Boies punctured the witness's piety by producing on the screen a Poole document that described Microsoft's goal less loftily as to "drive towards our overall market share objectives."

Nevertheless, while the performance riveted spectators, Judge Jackson seemed to doze through significant parts of it, although he fought sleep by sipping water and chewing enormous quantities of ice. Jackson later explained to me that the combination of poor courtroom ventilation and "muddy," repetitive questioning sometimes made him drowsy. But, he quickly added, "I don't think I ever lost track of the proceedings."

In Poole's final day on the stand, Jackson had more reason to sleep. Boies performed more like a Microsoft attorney that afternoon, meandering as if lost. He didn't stick to a few facts, and when he did—concerning Microsoft's restrictive contracts and coercive behavior—he droned on and on. At one point, Jackson admonished him to speed up his questioning, a display of impatience he usually reserved for the other side's lawyers. Colleagues conceded that Boies was redundant and unfocused that afternoon. John Warden and other Microsoft lawyers remarked that Boies wandered because he didn't understand technology.

And Microsoft did make up some lost ground. One of Warden's colleagues at Sullivan & Cromwell, Richard Pepperman, read aloud the restrictive contracts of other high-tech companies—an AOL licensing agreement with Netscape, for example, that stipulated that AOL "will not accept" ads from Netscape competitors. However, the damage-control effort fell short; it didn't matter what AOL licensing agreements said, for AOL was not a monopoly. It didn't matter whether Microsoft succeeded in foreclosing the market for Netscape, Boies said on the courthouse steps that day, because the very act of trying was illegal. "We're not talking about Coke or Pepsi here. We're talking about a company with monopoly power."

Nevertheless, because Boies was less than stellar in questioning Poole, spectators wondered whether Microsoft might be ripe for a comeback. Perhaps Boies was paying for his insistence on personally conducting the cross-examination of eleven of the twelve Microsoft witnesses. In fairness, it was clear that he was distracted by painful back spasms, for he walked more slowly than usual, shuffling his feet like an old man. (This was the excuse Boies himself offered.)

Boies heard the murmurs, and the next witness, Cameron Myhrvold, would pay. When Poole got off the stand, Jeff Blattner leaned over the rail and whispered to me: "*Watch Boies go after Myhrvold.*" Boies's determination was clear from the moment he introduced himself to the witness that afternoon by declaring in his best don't-mess-with-the-sheriff tone, "My name is David Boies, and I represent the United States." Sporting a reddish goatee and a dark-olive suit, Myhrvold, the brother of Nathan Myhrvold, was a vice president who supervised the division that served as the liaison to Internet-service providers (ISPs). With Myhrvold, Microsoft hoped to demonstrate once again that the integration of the browser into Windows offered many benefits to consumers, including easier access to the Internet. And for ISPs, he would show that Microsoft's restrictive contracts were really joint marketing agreements that did not greatly crimp Netscape, since most companies with Microsoft contracts did distribute Netscape's browser.

Myhrvold approached the witness stand cockily, and once there quickly corrected some of Boies's questions, as if he were helping the lawyer better understand exactly what he meant to ask. Boies coyly set up his witness. "Most of my questions are not trick questions. Some are," he announced with a smile.

"Would you tell me which ones?" Myhrvold asked.

"If I'm going to ask a trick question, I'll raise my hand," said Boies, as Judge Jackson and Bill Neukom joined in the laughter. Boies then lobbed a softball: to distribute browsers, would Myhrvold agree that ISPs like AOL and computer manufacturers were the most important distribution vehicles? "I've certainly heard that," but it wasn't necessarily true, said the witness.

"Have you heard yourself say that?" asked Boies, provoking more laughter as he ostentatiously raised his hand. He asked the witness to look at page forty-three of his written deposition, on which Myhrvold had asserted that AOL and PC manufacturers were the crucial distributors of browsers. Myhrvold responded that although he said that then, he had since learned while preparing to testify that he was "actually wrong." He had since discovered that twenty-six million Netscape browsers had been downloaded in a recent eight-month period.

Boies pressed Myhrvold to concede that he was concerned with the market shares of Netscape and Microsoft among ISPs. The witness dismissed this as arrant nonsense. The company was concerned about market share, but he said he was concerned only with distribution share among ISPs, as opposed to usage share, as if there were a glaring difference. Boies then handed the witness a December 18, 1996, missive he had written to Brad Chase, in which he declared "ISP's drove browser market share."

"I would like to point out that this was a draft memo, and it was never sent," said the witness.

Boies handed him another e-mail "that purports to be from you" and that read, "I think we'd both agree the goal is market share." Myhrvold said this mail was sent, but he again offered qualifications. Impatiently, Boies asked if "you would agree that if you don't get distribution you're not going to get market share?" Yes, Myhrvold conceded.

To boost market share, you strove to get ISPs "to agree to limit their distribution of Netscape's product, correct?"

"No, sir—"

"Well, didn't you set quotas as to what the maximum amount of Netscape's browser the ISPs would be permitted to distribute?"

Only ten ISPs had such a "co-marketing program," said Myhrvold.

Wasn't one of the ten AOL, which provided online connections for about 40 percent of all online users?

Yes.

Didn't Microsoft's contracts stipulate, Boies asked, that 85 percent of the browsers shipped by these ISPs had to be Microsoft's Internet Explorer?

Not all of them had such a "goal," Myhrvold argued, before conceding that AOL did. Boies also got Myhrvold to concede that there were between forty and fifty million Americans hooked up to the Internet through ISPs, and though Microsoft had contracts with only ten ISPs, these contracts covered one half of all ISP subscribers. Between the fourth quarter of 1997 and the first quarter of 1998, said Boies, quoting from another Microsoft e-mail, the number of AOL subscribers "force-fed" Internet Explorer accounted for a fourfold increase in Microsoft's browser share among AOL users.

At another point, Boies induced Myhrvold to concede that Microsoft's contract also required that ISPs not offer a rival browser on the same webpage that offered Microsoft's. He displayed a Myhrvold chart showing that by March 1998 Microsoft's browser market share was rising rapidly, while Netscape's was plunging. Microsoft's restrictive contracts had exacted a toll. "Is it the case," Boies asked, "that what you were trying to do with the ISPs was to prevent the ISPs from presenting Internet [Explorer] and Netscape Navigator side by side and allowing the consumer to choose between them?"

Myhrvold had to acknowledge as much. "What we wanted to do, sir, was to encourage the distribution of Internet Explorer," he said. "Especially in the early days when we had no distribution of Internet Explorer through ISPs, when we had very, very small market share. . . . We were very concerned that if the user saw Netscape Navigator side by side with Internet Explorer, and Netscape having all of the mind share and usage share, we would lose all of those, or the majority of, those decisions. So we did specifically ask that ISPs distribute Internet Explorer by itself . . . so that we would not lose all of those side-by-side choices."

Boies thought he had extracted a damning admission from the witness, among the most damaging of the entire trial, and, so that neither the judge nor press would miss it, he repeated the question: "You were concerned that if you presented the consumer with a choice of the two browsers, side by side, they would . . . pick Netscape rather than yours, right?"

"Yes, that's right."

Boies believed Cameron Myhrvold was saying that only by rigging the contest could Microsoft win. On the face of it, Microsoft appeared guilty of restraint of trade and foreclosure, violations of the Sherman Act.

Witnessing painful exchanges like this, it was easy to wonder yet again what the impact on Microsoft's credibility might have been had the lawyers made a hard-core decision early on—before depositions were given—to acknowledge that they were concerned with market share and Netscape. They might have said: *What's wrong with that? That's the competitive marketplace at work. We were concerned that Netscape posed a threat to our Windows platform. We were agitated by the terrible things they said about us, about how they would slay the beast from Redmond. We were not about to act as IBM once did and become complacent. We're fighters. And by competing hard we produced a better browser for consumers.* If Myhrvold—and Gates before him—had done that, a good deal of Boies's cross-examination of Microsoft witnesses, particularly the extensive questions about market share, might have been neutered. It would not have lessened the damage done by Myhrvold's admission that they were afraid to offer consumers a choice of browsers, but it might have prevented a credibility gap from yawning as wide as the Grand Canyon. Instead, with the possible exception of Paul Maritz, the first six Microsoft witnesses were defensive and thus failed to provide a particularly auspicious beginning for their much-vaunted defense.

The jury that counted was Judge Jackson. As he listened to the parade of Microsoft witnesses, he later recalled, "so many of them were confronted by their own e-mails, and the e-mails were so inconsistent with the testimony they were giving that you have a tendency to discount the rationalization that you have been presented on the witness stand."

For the first time, Bill Neukom's nerves seemed frayed. After court adjourned on February 9, with Myhrvold scheduled to return the next day, I was off to the side on the courthouse steps, chatting with Jeffrey Blattner of the Justice Department. As I was taking notes, I noticed a pair of polished brown shoes attached to long legs suddenly materialize in front of us. They belonged to Neukom, his hands clasped in front of his double-breasted suit, his purple-polka-dot bow tie brighter than the tight smile on his face. He just stood there, listening. Blattner was stunned, because Neukom had studiously avoided speaking to him or catching his eye for months. Blattner stared hard, as if to say *What?*

Neukom just stared back. For a moment, they glared silently at each other—Blattner puzzled and Neukom determined to confront the official he believed was the choreographer, the great Satan, of the government's p.r. offensive. Although he can be affable, Blattner's dark sunglasses, thick mustache, and dark hair that fell to his collar no doubt reinforced Microsoft's sinister stereotype of him. Ever since Blattner joined Justice in March 1998, Microsoft believed he had orchestrated leaks to various reporters, particularly to those at *The Wall Street Journal*, a claim Blattner denies. Microsoft knew that Blattner, as chief counsel to Senator Edward Kennedy's staff on the Judiciary Committee, had played a pivotal role in the sometimes vicious battle to deny Robert Bork a seat on the Supreme Court. (Bork, ironically, was a paid consultant to Netscape and thus aligned with Blattner in this trial.) And once Joel Klein left the room in the May 1998 negotiations, Blattner was the Justice Department official Bill Neukom negotiated with directly. Bill Gates spits out the name *B-L-A-T-T-N-E-R* as if it is a curse. After staring at Blattner for a long, silent moment, Neukom declared, "This is a public space." He would not move, so we did.

This behavior was wildly out of character for Neukom. "Bill is preternaturally upbeat," observed Michael Lacovara. "I would have days where I thought I didn't do as well with a witness as I should have, and Bill's enthusiasm and confidence and good nature never flagged." When members of the team returned after the Christmas holidays, a gift and a personal note for each from Neukom was waiting. Mark Murray remembers receiving an expensive tie "nicer than any tie I ever owned." But as the trial wore on, it became clear that what friends describe as the fun-loving side of Bill Neukom had been subsumed. "The straitlaced side of his personality has taken over," observed his longtime friend Richard Emery, "and the romantic, adventuresome side has been suppressed with the passage of time."

Weeks later, when I asked Neukom about this encounter with Blattner, he said, unconvincingly, that he was not trying to make a statement. "I was interested in knowing what he was talking about," he said. "I may have misjudged his reaction. I didn't mean to make him feel uncomfortable."

Microsoft's witnesses got better—and worse. Brad Chase, the vice president who oversaw developer relations and Windows marketing, was among the most effective. He testified that AOL chose Microsoft's browser because it was technically superior; thus, despite what AOL's David Colburn had testified, Microsoft won on the merits. Moreover, he said, Microsoft's cross-promotional agreements with AOL and distributors did not foreclose Netscape from distributing its browser. Chase's demeanor was friendly, and from his unapologetically thinning hair to his baggy gray suit his appearance was as unpretentious as it was unprepossessing. Unlike many of the other witnesses, he did not avert his eyes when he saw government lawyers or the press but said hello. If he did not conclude his testimony in a few days, he would miss a holiday trip with his family, but he did not act put-upon. Nor did Chase ostentatiously deny the obvious. He conceded that if AOL subscribers wanted to choose Netscape, they had to download it from a website. AOL was not permitted to give Netscape equal billing on its site because AOL was getting certain benefits from Microsoft, so this was a fair exchange, he insisted. Sure, the handcuffs Microsoft placed in its contracts helped build its browser market share, but in return companies such as AOL and AT&T received real value. Sure, Microsoft tried to leverage its Windows power, but it had not choked off the distribution of Netscape.

Chase offered another reason AOL dumped Netscape, telling of his meetings with AOL executives and how they complained that Netscape was impossibly arrogant. He challenged one of the most potent assertions Boies had introduced into the trial record, a memo written by an AOL executive who described a January 18, 1996, meeting at which Bill Gates supposedly said, "How much do we need to pay you to screw Netscape?" Said Chase, "I was at the meeting, and Mr. Gates did not say that. We certainly were aggressive," but Gates never uttered those words. Chase offered a context for Microsoft's bluster, saying it was part of the company's culture "to take extreme positions sometimes to push ourselves."

Boies did on occasion throw Chase on the defensive. Chase asserted that it was "easy" to download Netscape from more than two hundred thousand websites, and that AOL, despite its contract with Microsoft, still supplied Netscape software to those who requested it and in a very limited way promoted Netscape as an alternative browser. Chase even brought with him a Microsoft videotape showing how easy it was to download Netscape and noted that James Barksdale testified that Netscape had forty million downloads in one nineteen-month period, and in July and August 1998 alone Netscape Navigator was downloaded 12.4 million times. In other words, Netscape's distribution channels remained open.

Boies picked these assertions apart. How long had it taken Microsoft to download Netscape's browser on AOL?

Ten minutes, said Chase.

How fast was the modem Microsoft had used?

It was ten megabits, the kind of speedy modem most corporations use, said Chase.

How long would it take to download on a 56K modem?

About twenty-five minutes, said Chase, and twice as long on the more common 28.8K modem.

But most AOL users are connected at home, and over 90 percent of home computers installed a year ago relied on 28.8K modems, right?

Right.

Boies also read to the witness a portion of the deposition of Microsoft program manager Joe Belfiore that said the downloading of Microsoft's browser "takes too long, is too hard." He later read from a Microsoft e-mail that said 60 percent of Web surfers had never downloaded any software. In short, Boies demonstrated that downloading was not a viable way to distribute browsers, certainly not when compared with having your browser as the default choice of AOL or already loaded on a new PC.

Nevertheless, over his three days as a witness Chase was able to demonstrate why Microsoft's browser was technically superior and offered features Netscape could not match. He also scored when Microsoft produced a strategic agreement between America Online and Sun showing that they planned to reinvigorate Netscape and challenge Microsoft's browser.

Chase's effective performance was generally not reflected in the press headlines. At the conclusion of his testimony, recalled a junior Sullivan & Cromwell attorney, "I had a reporter come up to me and say, 'What a boring day. I don't know what I'm going to write about.'"

"Why don't you write about what a good day it was for Microsoft?" asked the attorney.

Though Chase did not fare as badly as Allchin and others, the press did not treat his testimony as a plus for Microsoft. EXECUTIVE ACKNOWL-EDGES SEVERAL CONTRADICTIONS, read the headline in the February 17 USA Today. MICROSOFT UNDERSTATED NETSCAPE'S HANDICAP, declared The Washington Post that day. The Microsoft attorney had a simple if flawed explanation: "The press covered the case from the government's point of view. It was a way to sell newspapers, to get on the front page."

Among the least effective of Microsoft's witnesses was its eighth, John Rose, then a senior vice president and group general manager of the Enterprise Computing group at Compaq Computer, the world's largest PC manufacturer. Microsoft was particularly eager for a Compaq representative to testify; if Microsoft could demonstrate that it had not bullied manufacturers, then the government's accusation that they monopolized this crucial distribution channel would topple. In addition, a glaring weakness in the government's case, which Justice officials privately acknowledged, was that its lawyers had failed to recruit a PC manufacturer to testify against Microsoft.

Unfortunately for Microsoft, Rose looked like a cross between a squat, barrel-chested Jimmy Hoffa and a slick corporate operator. He wore a black suit and white, cuff-linked shirt, with short black hair combed straight back, accentuating a receding hairline. He shook the hands of reporters on the way in, as if accepting congratulations. When he got on the stand, he had a disconcerting habit of looking at the press section and grinning, and his curled-up eyebrows and glistening white teeth made him appear eerily like Jack Nicholson playing the Joker in *Batman.* Seated on the bench behind Boies, Joel Klein and Jeff Blattner also smiled, confident Boies would wipe the smirk off Rose's face.

Rose insisted that Compaq enjoyed a "frontline partnership" with Microsoft, but Boies quickly cast Rose as a puppy and Compaq as a company that jumped when Microsoft barked. Boies induced Rose to acknowledge that for PC makers there was no viable alternative to the Windows operating system. Then he set out to show that Compaq was terrified of offending Microsoft and thus losing both Windows and the unspecified (and confidential) price breaks it received on the copies of Windows it loaded on Compaq PCs. He introduced Compaq e-mail from May 1996 showing that they wanted to "feature the brand leader, Netscape." Then, according to other evidence Boies introduced, Microsoft warned Compaq that it would stop shipping Windows if Compaq chose Netscape's browser. Another internal Compaq e-mail dated November 12, 1996, cautioned: "Microsoft will be expecting an exclusive arrangement that would prevent us from putting Netscape on the desktop." Despite internal corporate opposition, Boies noted, Compaq surrendered to Microsoft's wishes and agreed to make Internet Explorer the default browser on all their PCs.

It got worse. On the afternoon of Rose's first day on the stand, Judge Jackson declared, "Mr. Rose has repudiated virtually two thirds of his testimony." Later, Judge Jackson wondered aloud, "Who speaks with authority" for Compaq? At another point, Jackson shook his large head and declared from the bench that several of Rose's responses concerning a contract "make no sense." Another document that made Rose squirm was dated January 1993 and spoke of Microsoft's "potential reactions" if Compaq decided to choose another software company to power its handheld devices. Speaking of Microsoft, the memo asked, "How retaliatory would they get?" The memo listed a dozen measures Microsoft might take to harm Compaq. Three months later, after signing a five-year licensing agreement with Microsoft at a price below that charged other PC makers, Compaq chose Microsoft software for its handheld devices.

Microsoft had four more witnesses to go, and arguably the most important would be Daniel Rosen, General Manager, New Technology at Microsoft and the senior executive who had worked with Netscape to explore a strategic relationship between the companies. Rosen appeared on February 22, 1999, and his mission was to show that Netscape's account of the famous June 21, 1995, summit meeting he had organized—the meeting that was at the core of the government's contention that Microsoft intended to divide markets and used its monopoly power to threaten to crush Netscape—was fictive. A stocky forty-nine-year-old mid-level executive with round, rimless eyeglasses and straight black hair, Rosen was disputatious from the moment he was sworn in. When Boies asked if Rosen had heard talk within Microsoft of "a browser battle," Rosen asked, "At what point in time, sir?" Then he asked Boies to define the context in which he had asked the question. And finally he asserted, "I'm not certain that I heard those specific words, no, sir."

Well, did Rosen ever hear, in the period between 1995 and 1997, Boies asked, that "Microsoft was seeking to gain browser market share?"

"No, sir . . . I don't know that I understand what *browser market share* particularly means."

Did you believe in the spring of 1995 "that Netscape was a competitive threat or a potential competitive threat to Microsoft?"

"Oh, no, Mr. Boies. I didn't believe that." Rosen said this was because Jim Barksdale and others at Netscape "were very clear that they did not see themselves as competitors to Microsoft. They wanted to structure a partnership with Microsoft."

Boies handed Rosen a copy of Paul Maritz's testimony, in which Rosen's superior agreed that by the spring of 1995 Microsoft considered Netscape a competitive threat. How did Rosen square his view with his boss's?

Rosen said he accepted the word of Netscape officials even though his own company had declared Netscape a competitive threat.

Boies later handed Rosen an e-mail he had composed on May 15, 1995, and that was marked "sent."

Rosen looked at it and said it was merely a "first draft," and had never been sent.

Boies showed the court that the missive was addressed to twelve Microsoft executives, including Maritz and Allchin, and had been sent at 12:48 A.M.

Rosen insisted that he had saved it at 12:48 A.M., not sent it.

Boies read from Rosen's e-mail: "The threat of another company (Netscape has been mentioned by many) to use their Internet World Wide Web browser as an evolution base could threaten a considerable portion of Microsoft's future revenue." Boies inquired: "Did you believe that, sir, at the time you wrote it?"

"No, sir," said Rosen, "I don't know why this is surprising. I had just joined the company a few months prior. I was trying to flesh out some ideas."

Boies said that he had joined the company in October 1994, a full seven months before drafting the e-mail. He continued to read from Rosen's own e-mail: "We should try to strike a close relationship with Netscape. In this relationship, our goal should be to wrest leadership of the client evolution from them."

Rosen squirmed but insisted that by *client* he was not referring to Netscape's browser, even though he had earlier defined a client to include a browser and even though most everyone in the courtroom believed he was saying his goal was to "wrest" the browser business from Netscape. Rosen went on to dig his hole even deeper, stating that he did not believe Netscape vied to be the browser for Windows 95 but would prefer to concentrate on other, slimmer businesses.

Boies produced Bill Gates's May 1995 "Internet Tidal Wave" memo that was circulated to Microsoft executives, and he noted that Gates had written, "A new competitor born on the Internet is Netscape." Was Rosen saying he disagreed with Bill Gates?

"Barksdale was telling me, and [James] Clark before him was telling me that that was not what they intended to do," he responded.

After the lunch break, Boies handed Rosen another e-mail he had written, this one on May 12, 1995, and addressed to Paul Maritz and other Microsoft executives. Rosen's first paragraph warns that the World Wide Web "has the potential to supercede [*sic*] Windows. . . . At all costs we must continue to lead the evolution of the desktop software." Did Rosen believe that when he wrote it?

"Yes, I did."

Boies continued to dissect Rosen's e-mail, reading from a Rosen rec-ommendation that Microsoft induce Netscape to partner with Microsoft: "I believe we should do this on the server side, but not the client." In other words, divide markets, ceding the server market to Netscape's browser and the consumer market to Microsoft's browser, just as Barks-dale had claimed. Boies produced another Gates e-mail, written May 31, 1995, which suggested a strategy in dealing with Netscape: "The con-cept is that for 24 months, Netscape agrees to do certain things in the client and we agree to help make their server business successful." Then Boies called Rosen's attention to an e-mail he wrote to Gates one hour later: "This is very much along the lines of the discussions I've already initiated with Jim Barksdale."

Boies had barely touched on the June 21, 1995, meeting and yet Rosen had already imploded. As Joseph Nocera wrote in the March 29, 1999, *Fortune,* the "truth" of what happened at that meeting "would ultimately come down to the question of who was more believable: Rosen or Netscape CEO James Barksdale. . . . And because courts demand rock-solid evidence for this kind of allegation, Rosen had the advantage. All he had to do was come away from the witness stand with his credibility moderately intact. . . . By the time Boies was finished with him, Rosen would wind up humiliated, his credibility in tatters."

Boies produced a memorandum Rosen wrote prior to the June 21 meeting in which he said Microsoft's first priority "was to establish Microsoft ownership of the Internet client platform for Windows 95."

"I was fairly new to Microsoft," Rosen said, "and the word *ownership* in Microsoft terms means that you are going to deliver on something you say you will—"

Startled, Judge Jackson, who takes pride in his own use of the English language, leaned over toward the witness and asked, "The word *owner-ship* means delivering on something that you promise . . . ?"

"Yes. That's correct."

When Rosen continued to insist that by *client* he did not mean *browser,* Boies felt confident he did not even have to question him about what occurred at the June 21 meeting. At 3:30 P.M., Boies abruptly announced, "I have no further questions." This kind of sudden tactical move was not atypical for Boies, for in court he seems certain of his every move. He has mental guideposts for how to deal with judges or juries or witnesses, guides that he enunciates as if reading from tablets chiseled into his brain, giving clients the comfortable feeling that their lawyer knows where he is going. Ask Boies, for example, what the dos and don'ts are for a lawyer in a courtroom, and he responds: "Don't put your credibility at risk by pushing real hard on an issue you're not right on. Instill fear in the witness that you know more than he does. Don't be unnecessarily mean to a witness. It will stimulate sympathy. Know when to fold your hand."

Surprised that Boies had so quickly folded his hand, Microsoft attorney Michael Lacovara asked if he could have the night to prepare his redirect examination of Rosen, which Judge Jackson granted.

It was Lacovara's mission the next morning to rescue Daniel Rosen, and as he rose to question his witness Judge Jackson smiled and commented, "Mr. Lacovara, it is always inspiring to watch young people embark on heroic endeavors." Embarrassed, Lacovara said, "Thank you, Your Honor."

Lacovara did succeed in partially rehabilitating the witness. Relying on Microsoft and Netscape documents, he demonstrated good technical reasons why Microsoft would want Netscape to embrace a common "client code" so the browser and operating system would mesh. He demonstrated that even though Netscape had announced its support for Sun's Java the previous month, Microsoft never discussed Java at the June 21 meeting and that, even if Netscape had agreed to all of Microsoft's requests, none would have blocked Netscape's use of Java. He demonstrated that long after the June 21 meeting Barksdale had said he was so shocked by, Netscape officials, including Barksdale, continued to solicit him and Microsoft.

But when Boies got his final crack at the witness, again he forced Rosen to make damaging admissions; and again he handed him e-mail he had written that contradicted what he was saying on the witness stand. Rosen, for example, said that before the June 21 meeting he had not yet gotten a look at Netscape's new Windows 95 browser and therefore did not know that it could pose a middleware threat to Microsoft. Boies handed him an e-mail Rosen wrote on May 11, 1995, asking a colleague, "Can I borrow the copy of the Netscape Win 95 new client they gave us?"

Rosen insisted it was just a test product and said he didn't get an actual copy of the browser until July.

"You don't remember that, do you, sir?" Boies asked. "You're just making that up right now."

"No, I remember it."

"You're sure it was May and not before May?"

"I am fairly certain."

Boies handed him an April 27, 1995, e-mail Rosen had written to a colleague: "Do you remember who took the Netscape Win 95 browser they gave us during our last meeting? I'd like to get a copy."

Rosen stared silently at the document, then meekly said, "I stand corrected." Boies then induced Rosen to concede that he attended an April meeting at which Netscape officials gave Microsoft their new browser. Boies was through with Rosen.

Microsoft had three more witnesses to call, and none—not Eric Engstrom, the general manager of MSN, who challenged Avadis Tevanian's assertion that Microsoft deliberately disabled Apple's QuickTime software and tried to show how Microsoft's multimedia technologies were a boon to consumers; not Senior Vice President Joachim Kempin, who tried to show that Microsoft's restrictive contracts with PC manufacturers were meant to ensure the integrity of Windows and thus protect consumers, not disadvantage competitors; not Senior Vice President Bob Muglia, who testified that Microsoft's version of Java improved rather than hindered it, leading to better products for consumers— seemed to sway Judge Thomas Penfield Jackson. Near the conclusion of Muglia's testimony on February 26, 1999, Jackson ordered him to stop talking. Muglia had strained to deny that Microsoft sabotaged Java; as the executive in charge of Microsoft's relations with Sun concerning Java, he asserted that Microsoft was only trying to aid consumers. Boies kept handing him Microsoft e-mails that contradicted what he now said, and Muglia kept denying their meaning. "I am hard-core about NOT supporting" the latest version of Java, read one May 1997 e-mail from Gates.

"I'm not certain exactly what Bill was referring to when he said *supported*. Let me give you an example of how he could have meant it," said Muglia.

Clearly irritated and ostentatiously shaking his head back and forth, Judge Jackson cried out, "Mr. Muglia, there is no question pending. I read it as saying he says he does not like the idea of supporting it. Let's not argue about it!"

"If I could clarify one more thing?" asked Muglia, and as Jackson nodded yes, Muglia launched into a defense of what he had said. Jackson's face reddened and with one hand held up like a traffic cop's, he bellowed, "No! No! Stop! There is no question pending!" Following Muglia's testimony, Jackson adjourned the trial for what he hoped would be just several weeks, after which each side would present its rebuttal witnesses.

The jury of one had not been impressed by the testimony of Microsoft's witnesses, or at least most of them. Asked months later to assay Daniel Rosen as a witness, Jackson responded in general terms: "Truth be told, a lot of Microsoft's witnesses were not credible. They were testifying in the teeth of e-mails that said something else. Or they were testifying in such a way that I had a distinct sense that they were offering spin. They didn't deny what the government witnesses said. They simply said, 'Oh, we didn't mean that.' And the spin that they put on it was that we were very cynical people. 'How could they assume that we would propose that they get out of the business of producing browsers. We were just proposing better synergies.' I simply had the sense that events as perceived by Barksdale were a lot more credible than events propounded by Rosen."

CHAPTER 12

Nerds in the Bunker

BEFORE THEY PRESENTED their witnesses, Microsoft was certain that they would incontrovertibly prove their facts. Afterward, the company's leadership was furiously mad—mad at Boies, whom they depicted as a demagogue; mad at Judge Jackson, convinced he would rule against them, though they were careful enough to not say this aloud; mad at the government; and mad at their enemies in Silicon Valley. Most of all, perhaps, they were mad at the media.

Their rage started at the top, with Bill Gates. And when Gates gets angry, a Microsoft insider who saw him regularly admitted, "he will lash out." Gates was incredulous that the press had settled on a David-versus-Goliath story line that lionized Boies. After Joseph Nocera penned a scathing account of Microsoft's first several witnesses in his biweekly *Fortune* diary, Jim Cullinan, a member of the Microsoft public-relations team, dispatched the following solecistic e-mail to him:

> To say I was upset and depressed by your last diary would be an understatement. The fact that you and the rest of the press are in love with Boies and overlook his mistakes and troubling change of story on the steps on a daily basis. Any effort to point of Boies' flaws makes you

guys protect him like a pride of lions. . . . We look at you guys because you all want Boies to get our witnesses and give him credit where none is due. You guys have no idea that a guy who knows nothing about this industry is reinterpreting our internal documents and changing the meanings to fit his story. It is ridiculous and all of our mistakes and errors in video production don't change the facts.

Microsoft felt more than picked on by the media. They thought reporters portrayed their video errors as a deliberate trick rather than as a comedy of errors. They groused about a sneering press, about the negative spin of too many accounts from the trial, about the hostile questions their people fielded on the courthouse steps each afternoon, about how the press swooned over David Boies. The government produced an e-mail snippet featuring a careless Microsoft statement and out popped sinister headlines. It didn't seem to matter whether Microsoft was actually a monopoly. The press acted shocked—shocked!—at their words, not just their actions, yet such bluster was commonplace in the industry and usually passed unremarked when voiced by others. Larry Ellison and Scott McNealy were outrageous big mouths, yet they seemed to amuse reporters, Microsoft fumed.

Microsoft thought reporters behaved like lemmings. A story appeared on the front page of *The Washington Post* on February 15 about the possible remedies the Justice Department and the states contemplated if Microsoft should lose, and suddenly nine cameras joined a battalion of scribes to quiz Neukom. Microsoft botched a video demonstration—which altered no facts and, arguably, was not the most substantive event of that day—and the media blew it up into a trial-transforming event. ABC News, which had not been in the courtroom for weeks, made frantic calls to courtroom reporters late that afternoon to determine if a decisive event had occurred; that night, Allchin's videotape incident was featured on its nightly newscast.

Few things rankled members of the Microsoft team more than the scene that transpired at the end of each court day as many reporters stood in the corridor and compared notes of what witnesses said, checked quotes for accuracy (the official trial transcripts were not available until early evening), and sometimes debated what the thrust of the story should be. "It's a rudderless pack," observed spokesman Mark Murray. "Twenty people who gather together to make sure that they're not going to be embarrassed the next day. What if nothing happened that day and they all have to write something?" Yes, nodded Bill Neukom, "The low-risk strategy is: don't get scooped. Go with the conventional wisdom about what is happening in court."

One heard from Microsoft the same complaints one hears from candidates in political races. They complain that the press covers them like theater critics, seizing on the most dramatic incidents of the day, not the most important, judging who performed best and worst, who's ahead. "I don't believe the press is trying to report each day's defense in terms of a legal standard," David Heiner observed. "They're reporting each day on any little moment or drama that occurred." A preoccupation with drama is, partly, a function of reporters and their editors getting a certain story line or narrative in mind and unconsciously sticking to it, as in Another Miserable Day in the Faltering Presidential Campaign of Bob Dole/George W. Bush/Al Gore/Bill Bradley; or, Bill Clinton's Nine Lives; or, Boies Scores Again. The narrative may change—as it did for Gore and Bush—but not easily. Partly, this is because form often dictates content. The form of daily journalism is this: offer a lead paragraph that sums up the drama of the event, reduce the story to a single headline and, hopefully, a single story line, identify the key actors and the setting, put it in a larger context, compress all this by filing time, and do it in two hundred (if for television) to maybe eight hundred words. Lacking the luxury of time or space, no matter how diligent, how professional—and many of the daily reporters covering the Microsoft trial were very knowledgeable and careful—the journalist is left little time to think and is reduced to being a reactive firefighter racing from his or her station when the alarm rings.

When the testimony of his twelve witnesses had nearly been exhausted in February 1999, Bill Neukom sat for a late dinner in a Georgetown restaurant, ordered a mellow bottle of red Burgundy, draped his tan sports coat over a chair, and said that he was certain that the government had not proved its claims and that Microsoft would prevail. Why, then, he was asked, was there such a disparity between what he saw and what the press reported?

"It's a combination of things. First, the technology at the heart of this case is so complex and changing so rapidly that even the top players in the industry can't predict for certain where it will go next. So it has been a challenge to put the government's accusations into a proper industry context for reporters. Second," he continued, a civil trial in federal court is not "spectator-friendly theater. It's not designed to be engaging to the gallery. It's pretty dry stuff, frankly. Third, the Sherman Act is a very short couple of paragraphs interpreted by federal courts, and it's much misunderstood. Some people want to believe that the Sherman Act is a sort of competitor-protection act," and it's not. The law "encourages rough-and-tumble competition so consumers get the best product at the lowest price. . . . Add to this deadline pressures. Our defense by its very nature was complicated and extremely dense with facts and economic analysis. We think the government's case has been short on facts but long on theater. The press has worked very hard . . . but given the deadline pressures it's no surprise that the theater often won out over the dry substance in the daily coverage."

Neukom was not alone in this critique. What the press often missed, observed George Washington University law professor William Kovacic, were the subtleties of the law. He thought Microsoft had a stronger legal case than was suggested by the press coverage, at least through the first twenty-four witnesses. Over the last hundred-plus years, the core concepts of the Sherman and Clayton acts have not changed, but the courts have interpreted the words differently. Today, the courts, he said, are more insistent on proof of consumer harm, more inclined to allow the marketplace rather than government to correct imbalances. "The press would have to be current on the law and on esoteric matters of legal doctrine that are ambiguous," said Kovacic. "Trying to capture the existing law is difficult." How, for example, does a court set a benchmark and then measure the innovation that has been lost due to Microsoft's alleged monopoly?

It was, inevitably, common for reporters to handicap the trial. The "software giant was on the ropes," ran a typical line, this one from *Business Week*'s May 24, 1999, issue. One press account, written by John R. Wilke, that Microsoft thought particularly influential and infuriating— entitled, AS MICROSOFT STRUGGLES WITH ANTITRUST CASE, TACTICAL ERRORS EMERGE—led the February 18 *Wall Street Journal*. It discussed weaknesses in Microsoft's legal defense, noting that Microsoft could have chosen to defend rather than deny its hardball tactics, to assert that consumers were helped by them; it could have acknowledged rather than denied that Windows currently enjoyed a monopoly, insisting this was transitory. "Instead, Microsoft refused to give an inch," Wilke wrote. Wilke also did something very smart in reporting on how Microsoft's defense team was "in disarray." He interviewed economists who were on a list the company gave the press of pro-Microsoft economists. The economists were uniformly and scathingly critical of the defense mounted by Neukom and his associates.

While some would say that the opinions of economists were less germane here than those of legal scholars—that the headline promised a legal assessment, which it did not deliver—Microsoft was in no mood to be philosophical. The company overreacted to the story. That morning, before Judge Jackson entered the courtroom, Mark Murray stationed himself in the press section and denounced the story as "riddled with inaccuracies." Executive Vice President and Chief Operating Officer Bob Herbold fired off a letter of complaint to the *Journal*. Microsoft p.r. deputy Greg Shaw arranged a dinner at the Four Seasons between a Microsoft group consisting of Neukom, his communications manager, Vivek Varma, John Warden, Murray, Shaw, and a *Journal* group of Wilke, his immediate editor and fellow reporter, Brian Gruley, and the *Journal*'s Washington bureau chief, Alan Murray. Wilke told friends beforehand that Microsoft was trying to take him to the woodshed. By most accounts, though, it was a convivial evening, with Microsoft peddling a memo they had written arguing that their legal case was stronger than it appeared in the media. There was good-natured kidding about the reasons Wilke arrived late for dinner and why, hours later, when the $1,300 bill appeared, he conveniently could not find a credit card that had not expired. (Alan Murray used his.) Nevertheless, there were moments at which the dinner "got heated," recalled a member of Microsoft's delegation. And, observed a *Wall Street Journal* reporter, it was typically heavy-handed for Microsoft to go directly to the boss: "The subtext for the dinner was: 'You guys are killing us.' "

Microsoft's memo and more aggressive salesmanship did make an impact at both *The Washington Post* and *The New York Times*, for within days each published prominent stories that, implicitly, alerted readers: *The daily accounts of Microsoft miscues you have read here should be viewed skeptically, since Microsoft stood on firmer legal ground than we led you to believe.* The *Times* story, written by Steve Lohr, appeared above the fold on page one and cautioned that courts are increasingly "reluctant to second-guess business decisions," particularly ones in which consumer harm is not clear-cut; further, much of the evidence against Microsoft

*Sony President Nobuyuki Idei:
a trained economist whose company
engages in what he calls "regional
wars" with Microsoft and who says of
Gates and Microsoft, "They want to
control us."*

*Steve Ballmer, CEO of Microsoft:
More Patton than Eisenhower, he is
an inspirational leader who can out-
shout Sam Donaldson and has
the heft of a linebacker.*

Judge Thomas Penfield Jackson:
an old-fashioned conservative who came to distrust Microsoft, not the government.

At a Washington press conference, the government team that joined in the successful
case against Microsoft: Janet Reno, Joel Klein, Richard Blumenthal, David Boies,
Philip Malone, and A. Douglas Melamed.

Apple CEO Steve Jobs and his research chief, Avi Tevanian:
Although Microsoft is a major investor in Apple, without a wink from Jobs it is not likely
that Tevanian would have testified against it.

David Boies: Judge Jackson described him as the best lawyer he's ever seen in a courtroom.

William Neukom, Microsoft General Counsel: Rain or shine, Neukom's sunny optimism never faded.

Neukom and John Warden: The "general manager" of Microsoft's legal team and his Sullivan and Cromwell "quarterback."

Bill Gates strikes a pious pose while testifying before Congress.

Steve Case, CEO of America Online, and Gerald Levin, CEO of Time Warner: new and old media hug.

An admirer of Gates, Liberty Media Chairman John Malone nevertheless says of him: "I don't think his emotional side is in sync with his intellectual side."

Steve Case and Bill Gates: By the time of the annual World Economic Forum in 2000, Case had supplanted Gates as the "rock star" in Davos.

*Richard Urowsky and Bill Neukom:
While Neukom referred to the brilliant
senior Sullivan and Cromwell partner as
the "architect" of Microsoft's legal strategy,
in court he muzzled him.*

*Linus Torvalds, creator of the Linux operating system:
In Washington, D.C., Microsoft was branded a
comfortable monopoly. In Redmond, Washington,
Microsoft executives fretted about
the threat posed by Linux.*

*Summoned to testify before the Senate
Judiciary Committee in 1998, Gates was
accompanied by two of Microsoft's foremost
enemies: Scott McNealy, the CEO of Sun
Microsystems, and James Barksdale,
CEO of Netscape.*

*Bill Gates in Davos:
For the two thousand
or so busy corporate,
government, and media
leaders who congregate
there, Davos is
one-stop shopping.*

Janet Reno and Joel Klein: The attorney general was his final boss, but Klein was the field marshal who ran the case and a man Microsoft came to distrust.

David Boies and Iowa Attorney General Tom Miller: The fellow plaintiffs are greeted by reporters outside the courthouse.

Judge Richard A. Posner: His awesome intellect brought the parties within inches of a settlement in March 2000, yet had he put them in the same room, perhaps that gap would have closed.

William Gates, Sr.:
He has the easy charm and diplomacy
his son often lacks, but his son learned
to be a warrior, at least in part, from pa
who transformed weekend games
into Olympic-style contests.

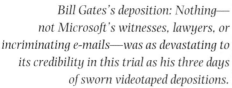

Bill Gates's deposition: Nothing—
not Microsoft's witnesses, lawyers, or
incriminating e-mails—was as devastating to
its credibility in this trial as his three days
of sworn videotaped depositions.

Bill and Melinda Gates:
She is Daisy Buchanan to his Jay Gatsby. Unlike Fitzgerald's lovers,
they are happily married to each other, and she has spurred him
to share his great wealth.

was hard to prove because it fell into the ambiguous he-said, she-said category. *The Washington Post* piece by Rajiv Chandrasekaran appeared the next day and was headlined, ISSUE OF CONSUMER HARM EMERGES AS KEY QUESTION IN MICROSOFT TRIAL. The government's chief economics witness, Franklin Fisher, the piece noted, had conceded in court there was no proof current consumers were harmed by Microsoft's actions, before he later retreated and said Microsoft's restrictive contracts deprived consumers of a full range of choices. Fisher and the government's notion of consumer harm was predicated on future Microsoft actions, the *Post* reported, and courts "have tended to take a skeptical view of claims of future harm." These legal truisms were often obscured by the daily play-by-play, dramaturgical coverage of the trial.

Microsoft, of course, bears a good measure of blame for shooting itself in the foot. At a March 1, 1999, executive-committee meeting, Jeff Raikes turned to Bill Neukom and told him that customers often asked about the trial. "What do I tell my customers?" he asked.

"You tell them," interrupted Bill Gates, "that no company involved in court cases wants to be judged by the press coverage of those cases." True enough, except that Microsoft's public-relations team had contributed to their miserable coverage. They might have more forcefully pushed to defend Microsoft's actions as typical business hardball. According to several accounts, which public-relations staffers deny, when members of the Microsoft team said they should be less pious, they were shouted down. "Americans don't want to hear of such tactics," one image maker reportedly replied. Microsoft's chief economic witness, Richard Schmalensee, confirms this debate, without pointing the finger at either the image crafters or the lawyers: "They were afraid to talk hardball. If you asked why they gave away free software, there's an obvious answer. It's in the e-mail: 'Netscape is trying to steal our business.'" Internally, Gates and Microsoft executives were alarmed by the Netscape threat, yet, adds Schmalensee, "when Gates and Microsoft executives testified they said, 'We didn't notice them.' I don't know why they took that line."

For a prominent, powerful company in the throes of a life-threatening lawsuit, Microsoft could be surprisingly inept in its dealings with reporters. Bill Gates or Steve Ballmer would decide not to talk to certain reporters perceived as critical (as opposed to avowed enemies), and the press office did not bang its head against the closed door. Some members of the press office were openly hostile: not returning calls or not supplying requested information. At the trial, beat reporters complained that members of Microsoft's p.r. team phoned them around 10 P.M. to check on the next day's story, and the next morning they'd often call them at home to protest. Reporters usually respect press representatives who level with them, telling them where a story was wrong. But reporters, like most humans, stop listening when yelled at or when their integrity is challenged or when the spokesperson acts *hurt*.

Reporters are also wary of the way Microsoft tries to shadow its own people. Nearly every Microsoft executive who sits for an interview, either in D.C. or on the Redmond campus, is accompanied by a colleague from public relations. "My shadow is joining us for dinner," a Microsoft official announced to me one evening. At face-to-face interviews with the lawyers over the course of the trial, Mark Murray or Vivek Varma or Jim Cullinan was always present, furiously scribbling down the questions and answers. At dozens of interviews on the Microsoft campus, a public-relations employee was always present, taking notes, sometimes interrupting to suggest that a question was out-of-bounds. The p.r. staff prepared dossiers on reporters: a multi-page memo was sent to Microsoft executives about to be interviewed, including the journalist's bio, his or her alleged biases, beliefs, and friendships, and questions the reporter had asked in prior interviews. Before one of my visits to Redmond, John Pinette, a former Catholic priest who was to be my pleasant but omnipresent shadow, e-mailed a three-page, single-spaced document, much like a raw FBI report, to people I was to interview. The memo asserted, for instance, that "David Boies and his wife are very close with Auletta." I had never met Mary Boies before Justice filed this case, and I knew Boies himself only superficially. Some excerpts from Pinette's memo:

Interview Objectives:
Our objectives in having you meet with him are to portray the company as still faithful to its fundamental vision—and working hard for customers. Either Lymann Bradbury or I will meet with you just prior to your interview to go over the kinds of questions that emerged from his first two days of interviews.

Microsoft is continuously working to reinvent itself:
Regardless of the DOJ's impact, the company's focus is on where the industry is going. . . .

Employees, at all levels of the company, are enthusiastic about the company and the technology they're involved in:
Ken wants to know if we are demoralized, and we want to show people who are excited about the contributions they're making. If they're paranoid about anything, it's not the trial, but the competitor's latest development that could make their product obsolete. This is the human side of Redmond. **Good people** (genuine, positive, forthright) with good motivations (wanting to make a contribution vs. greed or anti-competitiveness). . . .

Your approach to this interview:
. . . If he thinks you're just stating the party line, you will lose credibility in his eyes. Be sincere. It's okay to acknowledge that we can always do better as a company.

Inevitably, Microsoft's mania to control events stokes the fires of mistrust with the press. The Microsoft employee is aware of the shadow and is less likely to stray from the official line. No doubt this is the intent, but the unintended consequence is that reporters are more mistrustful of the information received. No matter how pleasant and unobtrusive the handlers strive to be, the reporter knows his or her questions can be shared with other Microsoft executives, robbing future interviews of their spontaneity. And while the presence of a shadow can be comforting to an official who is not accustomed to dealing with reporters, it can also belittle them, conveying a sense of Big-Brother-is-watching distrust. Reporters already believe Microsoft is too controlling, a sense reinforced at most Bill Gates press conferences, where someone from Microsoft usually serves as moderator, screening questions, directing the discussion to or away from certain topics. By trying to control or at least steer the dialogue, Microsoft inflicts two blows upon itself. First, it reinforces among reporters an impression that the negative things they're hearing in court about Microsoft might be true. Second, it reduces Microsoft's credibility because reporters come to believe that what they hear from Microsoft is staged, rehearsed. Thus, members of Microsoft's p.r. team often lose the authority salesmen need to succeed. At the end of one of several visits to the Microsoft campus, I asked John Pinette why he took such voluminous notes and what he did with them. He evasively said they provided a record of what each interviewee said, so that when the reporter's piece appeared in print Microsoft could rebut any inaccuracies. Months later, after I had seen Pinette's e-mail, I asked him: "Why are you folks so controlling?" He replied, "Indeed, it is a very aggressive approach to preparing people for interviews." I asked where he'd heard that I was "very close" to the Boieses. "I saw it in another document written by someone else in p.r.," he said.

Microsoft's press woes had many sources, but, as Shakespeare suggested, when looking for culprits it's not a bad idea to start with the lawyers. The lawyers, as Neukom would later concede (and David Heiner would not), should have vetted the videotapes played in court. From the moment government agencies started eyeing Microsoft in 1990, Bill Gates's father told friends, Neukom and the lawyers should have more strenuously vetted the company e-mail and cautioned employees to watch what they wrote. There was evidence suggesting that Paul Maritz had said Microsoft would "cut off Netscape's air supply"—on the witness stand, Maritz refused to flatly deny saying it when under oath, and there was a January 12, 1998, *New York Times* account of this remark that he never denied—and yet Microsoft insisted otherwise.

The lawyers might have interrupted Gates during his deposition to prevent him from appearing surly and sly. And when the government lost the bundling consent-decree case in the Court of Appeals in June 1998 and shifted the thrust of its approach to coercion, Microsoft's lawyers did not make a similar adjustment in their trial strategy. They left themselves exposed, especially since more often than not they portrayed Microsoft as saintly. Shaking his head in disbelief, Lawrence Lessig observed, "The core of a bullying case becomes a credibility case, which no court of appeals would touch." The lawyers' stubborn refusal to concede points—that Microsoft did have a de facto desktop monopoly and that Microsoft's APIs were not always open to competitors or to those it wished to punish—weakened their credibility. "They didn't want to say they believed in open standards because no one has completely clean hands on open standards. Everyone wants to keep some closed," said Dr. Schmalensee, who was considerably more candid off the stand than on.

Perhaps the most egregious mistake Microsoft's lawyers made was not to name Bill Gates as one of Microsoft's witnesses. Had they listed him, Boies would probably not have played Gates's video deposition before most witnesses spoke. And, if it dared, Microsoft could have later dropped Gates as a witness, substituting someone else, as they did when they dropped, say, Yusuf Mehdi, who was once listed as a witness. This might have offended Judge Jackson, who told me that under rule 32A2 he would have granted Justice permission to play the entire deposition in open court. But Jackson admitted, "I would suppose that had the entire deposition been played the significance of the incidents that Boies played would not have had the same impact." It is true that Microsoft did not know until October 9 that Judge Jackson would permit video depositions to be played in court. But the trial did not commence until October 19, and under court orders, Microsoft could have inserted Gates as a witness on the eve of the trial. And Gates did know before his deposition was taken at the end of August that the transcript would be used and that the deposition would be taped; after all, there was a camera in the conference room where he was deposed. "One of the most monumental mistakes we made was not understanding how Bill Gates's deposition could be used," admits a Microsoft strategist. "We never said, 'So it's videotaped. How will it be used?' We never focused on: 'How did he look? How did he act?' We did him a disservice. And, to a certain extent, he did himself a disservice."

The lawyers made another obvious mistake. They might have tried to better understand Judge Jackson. Any friend of his could have told them that Judge Jackson prides himself on being a straight-shooter and that his contemporary heroes were blunt men such as John McCain and Barry Goldwater. Unlike Microsoft's lawyers, David Boies would sometimes show up in court at 9:30 A.M. to watch Jackson for a half hour on those days Jackson fielded motions related to his many other cases. From this, Microsoft might have gleaned a better sense, as Boies did, of what Jackson expected from opposing counsel, of what types of arguments tended to persuade him, of how the credibility of a lawyer or defendant—not just the facts—moved him. A better reading of Jackson—and his opinions—might have made them less smugly confident that Jackson would feel constrained by the June 1998 Court of Appeals decision and would just serve as an amen chorus. It might have allowed them to understand that Judge Jackson was Everyman, a common American who shared an instinctive aversion to those who abuse power, make up their own rules, and obfuscate. When Boies spoke to Judge Jackson in the courtroom, he treated him as if he represented America; when Microsoft spoke to him, it was often as if he were an inconvenient obstacle on the way to the Court of Appeals.

Bill Neukom and the Microsoft lawyers did not focus as they might have on the public-relations trial because they fervently believed their mission was "to make a record." In this sense, they were legal nerds, who believed vindication would be found in their temple of pure facts. They believed there was no persuasive evidence of consumer harm, no evidence that Microsoft had foreclosed Netscape. Because the government didn't understand technology, they believed David Boies and his colleagues didn't comprehend their factual, technical explanations. Because only the facts mattered, Microsoft's defense team relied on no single lawyer, as the government did, but instead allowed seven different lawyers to question witnesses. Some of these lawyers had extraordinary talents. Urowsky is a brilliant student of antitrust law, though not a brilliant cross-examiner. Judge Jackson described Michael Lacovara this way: "He's brilliant. He's the Derek Jeter of their team." In his many conferences with the lawyers, Judge Jackson always thought John Warden was the team's decision maker. "In my chambers, Neukom said very little and Urowsky said nothing," Jackson observed. Told that Neukom, not Warden, was the decision maker, Jackson told me, "If Warden wasn't, that was probably the most serious mistake the defense team made."

When cross-examining the government witnesses, Bill Neukom's team often quibbled over small facts that didn't lead to a larger point that might, for instance, subvert a claim that Microsoft had harmed consumers. By contrast, Boies grilled all but one Microsoft witness and sounded like he was talking across the kitchen table; he rarely got tangled in a knot of details, choosing instead to target a handful of crucial facts. This might pose a problem for the government after the judge issued his verdict, for as he narrowed his focus Boies often left a good deal of each witness's written deposition unchallenged. Microsoft, on the other hand, often practiced cross-examination by checklist, diligently itemizing and questioning every one of the assertions government witnesses made in their sworn depositions. To the bitter end, Microsoft's lawyers professed that this tack was the correct one. John Warden contentedly noted late in the trial that Boies was not contesting many of the facts Microsoft had placed in the court record. "David is making a credibility play. Most facts are not in dispute. If you put a witness on who says the earth is flat and the fact is that it is round, what does it matter if you cast the credibility issue on one minor fact. The earth is still round."

Boies would agree that his case leaned mightily on credibility, for he was convinced that there are "important facts" and unimportant facts, and that credibility can matter more than facts. Facts are not inanimate objects. They are not like binary software code, like math or science. "Microsoft argues that technical expertise is key," Boies told me. "Bull. Credibility is." Take Cameron Myhrvold's testimony, for example. Boies asked: Was Myhrvold concerned with increasing Microsoft's browser share? Did Microsoft use its contracts with ISPs and ICPs to boost its own browser share? Had Myhrvold said yes to each question, he might have slowed Boies. Of course, the risk is that if the judge concluded Microsoft was a monopoly, those contracts might have been deemed to have crossed the antitrust line. But by denying such obvious "facts," Microsoft weakened its credibility and perhaps its ability to persuade Judge Jackson to accept other contested "facts." To cite another example, Microsoft played it safe when it chose not to call Michael L. Dertouzos, the director of MIT's Laboratory for Computer Science, as a witness. Dertouzos, as they knew, believed that Microsoft's decision to integrate a browser with Windows was consistent with the future direction of computing, which is to make it simpler for the user. Gates personally called Dertouzos to ask him to testify. But after his deposition, Microsoft was unnerved by his independence. He refused to accept payment, unlike other expert witnesses. And he insisted, as he told *The New York Times* in April 1999, that he wanted to testify in the European tradition "as a judge's witness rather than Microsoft's witness." He also conceded, "Historically and today, it is the case that browsers are treated as a separate application." That is to say, it is not a part of the operating system. Not wanting to hear this, and concerned more with control than credibility, Microsoft's lawyers yanked him from their list.

Jackson's colleague and friend Judge Thomas Hogan agreed that credibility was key. "I don't think you generally get the smoking gun in antitrust cases," he told me. "That's very rare. Most antitrust cases are a myriad of details." When he presided over government's antitrust action to block the proposed merger of Staples and Office Depot, Hogan recalls, "we had a lot of economic evidence, we had a lot of documentary evidence—although in that case, the econometric evidence that the government had . . . was not at all convincing to me. . . . I think the internal company documents were more convincing. That's why I stopped the merger." An antitrust case, Judge Hogan said, usually hinged on four or five key facts, not hundreds. While Microsoft shoveled facts at the judge, David Boies echoed Judge Hogan when he told me, "A case with a judge or a jury is won or lost on a handful of few key points. You want to identify them early, marshal your evidence, protect them, attack the key positions of your opponent, and not get bogged down in a lot of detail. Because, fundamentally, at the end of the day, this whole case is going to get boiled down to a thirty-five-page brief. At the appellate level, it's all going to come down to [that]." Finally, "it comes down to what every trial ultimately comes down to: who do you believe? . . . If you want to play the Microsoft game of saying 'We've got all the testimony,' the question is, Is it believable? Even more important, though, is the fact that they can win on two hundred and fifty issues but if they lose on ten, they've lost the case."

Boies thought he was attacking the facts that mattered; Microsoft thought he was ignoring critical facts and, in Neukom's words, attacking "on the margins," ignoring in his cross-examinations the bulk of the written depositions each Microsoft witness submitted in order to pursue selective facts. Each side thought the other was guilty of slighting facts. In an important way, the tactic each adopted reflected their overall strategy. By assaulting the credibility of the witnesses, Boies was trying to make it harder for the Court of Appeals—which generally defers to the lower-court judge to adjudicate credibility—to later overturn Judge Jackson. Because he was less confident of winning in Jackson's courtroom, Neukom emphasized such facts as Microsoft's need to meet with Netscape to agree on technical specifications and the absence of hard evidence of consumer harm, hoping to later show that the lower court had ignored critical facts.

There are legal scholars who agree with Neukom. Yale's George Priest, while praising Boies as "a great lawyer" and acknowledging that Microsoft's lawyers were made to appear "crazily unprepared," nevertheless thought the government had so far failed on several grounds. They had not made a convincing case that Microsoft's actions were an improper defense of its right to retain its intellectual property by improving Windows, a defense the higher court allowed in the *Kodak* case. They had not shown that the Court of Appeals was wrong, he believed, to rule that Microsoft's browser was an integrated product and was permissible under both the consent decree signed in 1994 and tying doctrine. They had not proved consumer harm. They had not proved that Microsoft's contracts had foreclosed Netscape.

By March 1, 1999, however, it was safe to say that the case was not going smoothly for Microsoft. And yet Microsoft's legal team maintained the same confident facade; it was hard to tell whether they truly believed their Panglossian pronouncements: the video mishaps were mostly the press's fault for sensationalizing them; Boies was winning if you're a theater critic; Dr. Schmalensee was an absolutely brilliant, unimpeachable witness; Microsoft won the browser war solely because it deployed superior technology; Microsoft is only concerned with customers; Microsoft will win. "I am more resolute than ever about the merits of our defense," Bill Neukom told me. "We have a terrific team of lawyers. The advice we've given to the client has been accurate and sound."

The danger for Microsoft is that this analysis may not be hard-core. If Microsoft's lawyers were lying to themselves because they were disconnected from reality and honestly thought they were winning when they were not, they were unlikely to seek a negotiated settlement before Jackson ruled, as they might if convinced they would lose and that their chances of winning on appeal were dubious. Was Bill Neukom so serene, I wondered, because he knew the facts were on his side? Or was he like Colonel Nicholson, the British POW commander portrayed by Alec Guinness in *The Bridge on the River Kwai*, the military martinet who was so insistent on following rules that he ordered his troops to follow Japanese rules and complete their railroad bridge. If they were misleading themselves, Microsoft's lawyers would sabotage their case, for they would not do what was necessary to enhance their chances of winning—perhaps throw a Hail Mary pass by calling Gates as a rebuttal witness; or calling an industry elder who is perceived as independent of Microsoft (Apple's Steve Jobs? Kleiner, Perkins, Caufield & Byers's venture capitalist John Doerr?) and is willing to argue that a government remedy is worse than the disease and that the speed of technological change is such that Microsoft will not monopolize the future. The other possibility was that Microsoft's lawyers were simply lying.

"We have the wrong lawyers," conceded a senior Microsoft executive, acknowledging he was in the minority at the company, but one that grew more vocal as the trial wore on. "These are antitrust lawyers. In most antitrust cases, there are no witnesses. It's all transcripts, briefs." This executive thought of Sullivan & Cromwell, as he did of Neukom, as Brahmins, unsuited for the rough-and-tumble of a public trial. The firm, founded in 1869, abhorred publicity or anything that smacked of self-aggrandizement. Its way was to do things quietly, just as it had been a century ago when it established holding companies and trusts for the Rockefellers, Harrimans, Carnegies, and Goulds. Its self-effacing culture was epitomized by its messengers, who famously wore plain brown coats bereft of the firm's name. Sullivan & Cromwell's success was envied by other lawyers. By 1988, the magazine *American Lawyer* estimated that in revenues per lawyer the firm led all but one other in America. But there was an underside to the firm, one that Microsoft dissidents had come to know. There was the time partner Steven Holley leaked court documents that he did not know were sealed when his firm was representing Bankers Trust, prompting a federal judge to complain and to enjoin *Business Week* from publishing the documents. There was the time the firm was chastened for intimidating witnesses and for violating disclosure rules. And then there was the firm's shocking unpreparedness for a public trial. "You'd expect that a firm like Sullivan & Cromwell would have some experience with a public trial like this," groused another Microsoft executive. Sullivan & Cromwell did have some experience with limelight trials—the soap-opera trial pitting the former maid/widow of J. Seward Johnson, son of the founder of Johnson & Johnson, against his children; or the Bankers Trust litigation versus Procter & Gamble; or the Eastman Kodak antitrust case handled by John Warden—but it is generally true that the firm's work tends more to behind-the-scenes labors and to filing appeals briefs rather than litigating in court. And isolation, as we've seen with Microsoft, breeds a certain hubris.

The first time Neukom was openly challenged by colleagues came on March 1, after he presented a generally rosy picture of how the trial was going to Gates and senior Microsoft executives. Colleagues were prepared to agree with Neukom that Microsoft would prevail legally, if not in this court then certainly on appeal. But a number of senior executives, including Greg Maffei, Nathan Myhrvold, and Dick Brass, went beyond just blaming the press or Boies's tricks for the public-relations failures. They questioned and challenged Neukom. Microsoft could do a better job, they said. They did not linger long over this subject, for Gates let it be known that he sided with Neukom.

But after the meeting, a senior Microsoft executive more freely expressed his disdain for Neukom's approach: "He likes to think of himself as a lawyer's lawyer. He's sensible. To his credit, up to now he's been successful at that. . . . He's as much a legal nerd as we're computer nerds." Indeed, a popular expression around Microsoft has always been *substance over style*, as if anything but facts, binary code, were beneath them.

Although this executive wrongly dismissed the effective factual case Boies had presented in court, he did pay unintended tribute to Boies, saying he wished Microsoft had hired a legal showman: "Normally, you wouldn't hire Gerry Spence or F. Lee Bailey for an antitrust case, but here we should have." Of course, one might describe David Boies differently, as a skilled storyteller, a male Scheherazade spinning stories that hold the rapt attention of a courtroom. In court, Boies often exhibited a mastery of detail, an ability to zoom in on key facts, a winning charm that allowed judges and juries to see him as a surrogate son. Even when Boies seemed to lose a point in court, he often won. When Intel's Steven McGeady was on the witness stand, with machine-gun precision Boies kept leading him through a small mountain of e-mails and asking rhetorical questions, prompting a Microsoft objection that Boies was leading the witness. Judge Jackson leaned over the bench and gently rebuked Boies for doing so.

Instantly, Boies responded: "Your Honor, it is. I withdraw it. I apologize."

Just rephrase the question, Judge Jackson said, smiling and obviously pleased with Boies's verbal dexterity and nondefensive posture. This was a taste of a Boies talent that draws less notice than his prodigious memory or storytelling skills. Some of the reasons for his success in a courtroom, observed his friend and partner Jonathan Schiller, were human qualities. He connects with juries or judges because he listens and anticipates what they want him to address. When Boies speaks in court, people don't say, "That's very clever," as if it was contrived. The key to his success, Schiller said, was "credibility."

Boies's record was not to be sniffed at. In the thirty-five years he had practiced law, he said, he has never had a trial victory reversed on appeal on cases he had started. The respected First Amendment attorney Floyd Abrams said of Boies, "In a very soft-spoken way he's able to lure people who testify for his opponent into utterly indefensible positions. Precisely because he doesn't scream at them, they feel more secure to state as fact matters that under cross-examination become highly dubious. The remarkable thing is that it happens over and over again."

By contrast, the Sullivan & Cromwell lawyers, said another Microsoft insider, "seem to be flat-footed," just a step slower than Boies and his Justice minions and lacking in experience or sensitivity to the public dimensions of such a trial. Microsoft's lawyers often meandered off into baffling digressions, like joke tellers who never get to the punch line. Asked why the press seemed not to hear the same version of Microsoft events he heard, Tod Nielsen conceded, "In hindsight, if I could replay the tape, what I would have done from a p.r. perspective is talk about only three things: innovation; foreclosure; and competition. Everything else is irrelevant, and I would throw it out. What has happened is that so much stuff was addressed that people lost the forest for the trees."

A senior executive voiced a view of Judge Jackson that was not uncommon at Microsoft: "He hates us." But while he thought they would probably lose the case in Jackson's courtroom, he remained certain—as did most senior executives—that they would win on appeal, and thus they united behind Neukom. Why they were so certain of victory on appeal was puzzling; at fact-based Microsoft, this optimism was an article of faith that few questioned. It seems to have been predicated, in large measure, on Microsoft's June 1998 victory in the Court of Appeals. Yet as we've seen, a careful reading of that three-judge ruling shows that Microsoft may have made more of this than they should. The higher court had been careful to state that it was only looking at the question of whether Microsoft had violated a 1994 consent decree "contract" when it integrated its browser into Windows. Judge Jackson had ruled in December 1997 that Microsoft was probably in violation of the consent decree; the Court of Appeals overruled him and warned Jackson and the lower courts about "second-guessing the claimed benefits of a particular design decision." To be sure, it was a victory for Microsoft and suggested that the higher court would be inclined to leave it to Microsoft to design its software. But the appeals court specifically cautioned that they had not reviewed evidence of whether Microsoft had violated the Sherman Antitrust Act. "The parties agree that the consent decree does not bar a challenge under the Sherman Act," two of the three judges wrote; the third, Judge Patricia Wald, dissented, in part, writing that if "more evidence" appeared to suggest to Judge Jackson that Microsoft had in fact illegally bolted the browser to Windows, she wanted him not to "be bound by the majority's conclusions" and thus be free to issue a preliminary injunction against it. This is hardly the money-in-the-bank decision gaseously portrayed by Bill Neukom.

Win or lose, mistakes had been made by Microsoft. It can be said that the fault lay at the feet of the client, not the lawyers or the public-relations apparatus. The client chose the lawyers and signed off on the legal and public strategy. The combative trial strategy adopted by Microsoft was embodied in Bill Gates's deposition. Instead of admitting that they played rough but in this business it was either kill or be killed, Microsoft chose to adopt the pose of a missionary rather than a merce-nary. When some advisers warned in December 1998 and January 1999 that this pose sapped their credibility both in the courtroom and among the press and opinion leaders, Bill Gates and Steve Ballmer turned for advice to their new pollster, Mark Penn, who had polled for President Clinton during his darkest hours of the impeachment ordeal. Penn returned with a comforting message for Gates: no need to panic. Clinton overcame, so can Microsoft. Fortified by Penn and his lawyers, Gates slammed the door on those who wanted to craft a more believable rationale for Microsoft's past behavior.

CHAPTER 13

Spring Break

BURDENED BY a backlog of cases and commitments, Judge Jackson recessed the trial on February 26, 1999. Among his 180 or so pending cases, Jackson had a criminal trial that could no longer be postponed. David Boies had a two- to three-week trial in Pennsylvania for another client; Bill Neukom had planned a fishing trip to Argentina; John Warden wanted to honor an annual tradition of renting a house in the Bahamas with his family, Richard Urowsky, and some other friends; and everyone else, press included, desperately craved a respite. The judge said he hoped the case could resume in five weeks; it did not resume for thirteen. A trial that Judge Jackson once hoped would consume only a few months had already consumed five. There were various reasons the trial had stalled, among them Jackson's schedule. He rarely held the trial on Fridays, since this was a day he devoted to his backlog of pending cases. The hours he did preside over the trial fell somewhat short of a full court day. Subtract the nearly two hours the court recessed for lunch and an additional forty minutes for a morning and an afternoon break and court days averaged about three and one half to four hours.

During the recess, pressures on Microsoft to settle intensified. Intel, on the eve of a March hearing in another case, suddenly reached an agreement with the Federal Trade Commission. The FTC had charged that Intel used its monopoly over microprocessor chips to bludgeon companies. By settling, Intel sidestepped both a long and embarrassing hearing and a formal government complaint that it was a corporate beast, thus avoiding the tag *monopolist* and building a potential firewall against private lawsuits. Although the charges against Intel were narrower than those lodged against Microsoft, they were alike in that each had a market share north of 80 percent and customers needed access to their architecture to design products that functioned in the marketplace. In each case, the government claimed the monopolist bullied its corporate customers and competitors to assure continued supremacy. And in each case the government asserted—despite the advent of the Internet as a more open distribution system and despite the vulnerability of Intel and Microsoft to swift technological change—that antitrust laws were as relevant to new as to old industries.

But unlike Microsoft, Intel kept a low profile from the start, treated the government respectfully, and did not deny the obvious: sure, it deprived computer manufacturers of technical information when there were business disputes. Intel skipped the piety and simply insisted that this was perfectly legal business hardball. They did, however, agree to amend some business practices, particularly the withholding of information on the architecture of its new chips from companies it was battling in court. While not explicitly conceding guilt, Intel, in effect, conceded that it had behaved wrongly, and they escaped largely unscathed.

Microsoft's lawyers insisted the Intel settlement didn't affect them because the core of their case was that bundling a browser with Windows served consumers. But the Justice Department believed the agreement ratcheted up the pressure to settle. Certainly, Judge Jackson began to apply pressure to both sides. In a status conference in his chambers on March 31, Jackson told the lawyers that when the trial resumed each side would be permitted three rebuttal witnesses, after which the court would recess for thirty days while Microsoft and the government prepared briefs defining what they believed to be the incontrovertible facts of the case. Then would come final oral arguments, followed by the judge's Findings of Fact ruling. This would be followed by another recess, during which each side would prepare a brief on how antitrust law should be applied to this case, followed by final oral arguments on the law, and then by a Conclusions of Law ruling.

By taking the unusual measure of splitting his fact findings from his law ruling, Jackson was now prolonging the trial in the hope of driving the two sides toward settlement. If, as seemed likely, the Findings of Fact went against Microsoft, they would have both the opportunity and the motive to come to the table before Jackson issued his Conclusions of Law. And, as Boies privately conceded, the government wanted to settle rather than drag this out; events were moving so swiftly in the industry as to affirm Microsoft's argument that competition was alive, and if Microsoft settled they could help craft an intelligent remedy. There may well have been another motive to split the facts from the law, whispered lawyers on opposite sides of the case: Judge Jackson was trying to box in the Court of Appeals. Guilty, Jackson later admitted to me, "The general rule of law is that the Court of Appeals is generally expected to defer to the trial judge as to matters of fact—unless the findings are clearly erroneous. . . . What I want to do is confront the Court of Appeals with an established factual record which is a fait accompli. And part of the inspiration for doing that is that I take mild offense at their reversal of my preliminary injunction in the consent-decree case, where they went ahead and made up about ninety percent of the facts on their own." Judge Jackson does not hide his contempt for the higher court, saying it is populated by "supercilious" judges lacking trial experience. "One of the most frustrating things for judges dealing with the Court of Appeals is the way they thrash through the thickets of legal scholarship. They embellish law with unnecessary, and in many cases, superficial scholarship."

In February, and again in late March, as Judge Jackson held closed-door meetings in his chambers and warned that both sides would be better served to settle rather than wait for a decree, other pressures converged on Microsoft. That winter, Justice officials began to whisper about a remedy task force they had formed and about how they were pondering solutions that ranged from structural—breaking up the company—to severe restraints on its business practices. The nineteen states that had joined in the lawsuit had their own, separate remedy task force. Meanwhile, in the winter and early spring of 1999, potentially seismic shifts occurred in the marketplace. The Internet had been available in 5.8 million U.S. households in 1994, would be in 45 million homes by 2000, and an estimated 60 million by 2003, reported Forrester Research. Just a minute ago—in 1994—a mere 15 million U.S. homes had a cell phone; by 2003, more than 60 million would. Everywhere, new competitive threats surfaced. The free-software movement that promoted the Linux operating system was attracting support from both friends and foes of Microsoft. Also, a new graphical user interface was devised to allow Linux users to point and click with their mouse rather than type esoteric commands; Microsoft could certainly appreciate the significance of this, given its history. Another boost to Linux came from Red Hat, a start-up that distributes and provides technical support for Linux, which received an infusion of cash from various established companies, including such Microsoft stalwarts as Compaq and Dell.

Companies that used to back down when Microsoft growled were suddenly less fearful. Intel, which once routinely retreated from software investments when Microsoft objected, invested one hundred million dollars in start-up software companies in May 1999. For years, Microsoft had resisted efforts by PC manufacturers to delete its browser icon from the opening screen, but this spring it relented and permitted Dell to delete the browser on PCs it sold to corporations. The Apple Macintosh, whose operating system had been ranked second to Windows with a mere 4 percent market share in the fall of 1998, had more than doubled its share by the next spring. Longtime Microsoft ally Matsushita Communication chose to invest in Symbian, a joint software start-up that is battling Windows CE to become the operating system for handheld wireless devices. Communications companies rushed to ally on different battlefields: America Online and Sun in the server market; America Online and Bertelsmann in Europe; News Corporation and Sony in Japan; AT&T and the Excite portal; *TV Guide* and Gemstar to produce online TV listings; MCI and WorldCom merged to forge not just a telephone powerhouse but a company that controlled a sizable portion of the Internet's plumbing; Time Warner and Roadrunner linked to provide instant Internet access. In a race that rewarded the swift, was Microsoft allowing the Justice Department and the states to slow its momentum?

But just as one sensed that Microsoft had become more timid, more tentative, it surprised with a bold thrust. When AT&T wanted a partner to help take over the nation's then fourth-largest cable company, MediaOne Group, Microsoft, as we've seen, agreed to put up five billion dollars. For this enormous stake in AT&T, Gates received potential broadband access to AT&T's partly owned @Home cable-modem service, as well as what he saw as a crucial commitment to employ Windows CE in at least 7.5 million cable boxes. Extending its quest to invade non-PC devices, in May Microsoft used six hundred million dollars to purchase just over 4 percent of Nextel Communications, a wireless-phone company, which pledged to steer its Web customers to Microsoft's MSN portal. Microsoft also acquired stakes in cable companies in England, investing three billion dollars to capture 30 percent of Telewest Communications and five hundred million to claim a chunk of NTL, that country's third-largest cable company. (Later, Microsoft gained one-third ownership of Cable and Wireless Communications's cable-TV business.) Microsoft also joined with media giant Bertelsmann in bidding for a major German cable franchise and announced various partnerships throughout the world.

Microsoft was also anything but tentative in altering the way it managed its more than thirty thousand employees and 183 products. That spring, Gates and Steve Ballmer announced that Microsoft would stay hungry by reinventing itself. The management of the company was radically reformed: restructured into eight divisions, all employees were said to be liberated to think Web, not Windows. No longer would they be a PC- and Windows-centric company fueled by Microsoft's traditional mission statement, "A computer on every desk and in every home." The new motto would be: "Empower people through great software, any place, any time, and on any device."

Despite these aggressive initiatives—and despite John Warden's cocky assurance that in regard to the trial, "I'd say we're on the other guy's twenty-yard line"—another, subtler shift took place at Microsoft during the recess. Microsoft began to act as if its back were to the goal line, as it moved away from long-held positions. Most significantly, perhaps, Microsoft had for many years opposed publishing the source code for Windows so that outside programmers could work on improving its software, as was the case with Linux. Microsoft said it was protecting its intellectual property; others said it was protecting its monopoly. In April 1999, however, Steve Ballmer said publicly that if PC customers wanted it, Microsoft would seriously consider opening the source code to the forthcoming Windows 2000. Among other things, this would mean that Microsoft would cede its power to punitively delay or deny code to other companies, as virtually the entire computer industry screamed that it had. "That could be significant—if they meant it," David Boies conceded during the trial break. "It might change the remedy." If Microsoft lost in court, the government might be less inclined to impose a "structural" remedy if Microsoft adopted this "behavioral" solution.

Another subtle shift was signaled by Microsoft's stance toward a negotiated settlement. Throughout the trial, a Microsoft insider admitted, Microsoft had thought that it would lose some and win some in Judge Jackson's courtroom and win everything on appeal. By splitting the Findings of Fact from the Conclusions of Law, however, Jackson threatened this core assumption; now more Microsoft executives feared that their chances of winning everything on appeal were more tenuous. A growing number were now prepared, the insider said, to cut the company's losses. "We've done it before, with the consent decree," he said. But they were still a minority.

In secret meetings at the Justice Department on February 24 and March 30, Bill Neukom submitted a draft memorandum that indicated slightly more flexibility. In it, Microsoft agreed to allow PC manufacturers to remove the Internet Explorer browser icon from the initial Windows screen and to permit a ballot screen so that customers could choose their own browsers. But they still insisted that Microsoft's browser could not be removed from Windows even if consumers chose Netscape, because it was truly integrated and to remove it would destabilize Windows. Justice was unsatisfied.

By June, Microsoft had submitted three different draft versions of a proposed settlement, and the government twice responded in writing that Microsoft had not gone nearly far enough. Joel Klein told Bill Neukom for the first time that the government favored a breakup of Microsoft, and Neukom said they would never entertain that idea. "We're running out of runway here," a Microsoft executive said. At least one government lawyer was encouraged that Microsoft's "settlement proposal is different than anything proposed before," but he seemed to be in the minority. I say *seemed to be* because both sides wanted to show Judge Jackson that they had heeded his admonition and were making an effort to settle. The prevailing private view at Microsoft, however, was that Justice wanted a pound of flesh, not a settlement. The prevailing private view at the Justice Department was that Microsoft's flexibility was not real. "They want to appear eager and willing," said Joel Klein on June 1. "But unless their proposals seriously address what the evidence shows, I don't see flexibility."

The hardest issue to address, the great chasm that was akin to "building a bridge across the Atlantic," sighed a Microsoft attorney, was the bundling issue. Klein feared that Microsoft would incorporate each new advance—speech or handwriting recognition, better graphics, some dazzling new application invented by an enterprising start-up—into Windows for free, thus using its dominance to persistently crush budding competitors. Gates and Microsoft, on the other hand, insisted they were offering consumers better choices because "integrated products," as they called them, were better, cheaper, and simpler to use; and in any case, Gates throbbed with genuine rage at the thought of software-design decisions being made by government fiat.

The government, however, had a different view of what separated the parties. Between the May 1998 filing of the lawsuit and the October 1998 start of the trial, the government had shifted its focus from bundling to Microsoft's coercive and anticompetitive acts, which in light of the Court of Appeals decision probably made for a stronger case. "This trial isn't about browser icons anymore," said a government attorney. "This is about whether Microsoft can continue to use their monopoly to crush competition." The broader charge made a settlement harder to attain, because the government was demanding that Microsoft alter its very culture, confess to vices that Bill Gates thought of as virtues.

Bill Neukom said he welcomed a separate Findings of Fact because it might "clear out the underbrush." The task facing Judge Jackson was prodigious. "There are places where the evidence is clear—what are the channels of distribution, for instance," Neukom told me. "But what happens when David Colburn says AOL did the browser deal with Microsoft because they wanted Windows, and Brad Chase says they did it because Microsoft's browser technology was superior? The judge has to decide on the basis of what's more plausible. That's where the finder of fact earns his keep." While respectful of the awesome task before Jackson, Neukom was certain that no matter how Jackson ruled on the facts, he believed the Court of Appeals could overrule him. "If the Court of Appeals thinks the decision is wrong on the facts, they can overrule."

Despite Neukom's philosophical stoicism, by late spring Microsoft seemed even less confident of judicial victory and thus even more flexible; Justice seemed more confident of their legal case, thus more intransigent. Each side did agree on at least one point: if settlement talks were to turn serious, it probably would not happen until late summer—just before, or just after, Judge Jackson issued his Findings of Fact.

In the meantime, everyone involved in this trial lapsed into guessing about which way Judge Jackson might be leaning. The government lawyers, mindful of Jackson's shock at Microsoft's video exhibits and his open disdain for the credibility of several witnesses, including Bill Gates, were so optimistic they were almost giddy. Publicly and privately, Neukom and Microsoft's lawyers never dropped their facade of optimism, although Microsoft insiders admitted they felt doomed. Nevertheless, even they held out the hope that Jackson might surprise them. They knew Jackson was a Reagan-appointed free-market conservative who instinctively veered from government regulation. This case posed a real dilemma for Jackson, guessed his former law partner Nick McConnell, for two values Jackson held dear—a free market and abiding by the rules—seemed to clash. "If he has a fundamental instinct," observed McConnell, "it's that people ought be allowed to compete unfiltered by government. On the other hand, Tom has a strong view of 'fairness.' If Microsoft violated the rules, he would be offended by that."

While Pen Jackson's former partners at Jackson & Campbell still socialized with him, they, too, were in the dark as to how he would rule. He did not discuss the specifics of the case or share his impressions of Bill Gates or Microsoft with them, only his excitement over the momentous matters that were before him. Jackson had once complained to former partner Elizabeth Medaglia that he didn't have any interesting cases. "Not now!" she said.

If Jackson was in high heaven, Microsoft was in a hell worse than it had imagined, and as the temperature rose, it struggled mightily to keep the trial's infernal vapors from poisoning the entire company at a make-or-break time in its history.

CHAPTER 14

Exile

D URING THE SPRING RECESS, I went to Microsoft to see Bill Gates. Among the forty-five buildings on the Microsoft campus, the one that houses Gates's office, in Building 8, is unusual: it has a waiting room, its floors are carpeted, and, compared with other offices, it is vast. At any other Fortune 500 company, it might house someone of the rank of, say, vice president for community relations. Gates's office has few personal flourishes: the desk is a slab of plain oak, and the only pictures on a wall are two framed covers from *The Economist* given to him by his sister Libby: they show a diagram of an Intel chip and a chart describing the bandwidth of various radio frequencies. His PC is a Toshiba laptop with a docking station and two oversized monitors (one screen is separated into four quadrants, which stream information from selected websites all day). A nubby gray upholstered couch rests on a beige industrial carpet in front of a square maple coffee table surrounded by four chrome-based, green-and-blue wool-covered Breuer-style chairs. The only ostensible personal touches are several family pictures on a credenza behind his desk and a single picture of a doe-faced Gates beside Paul Allen, encircled by the handful of employees who helped launch Microsoft. This familiar picture, with its innocent faces, speaks to a basic Microsoft contradiction. On the one hand, it captures the youthful zeal, the idealism of people who embraced software as a tool to change the world, to do incredibly *cool* things. Less apparent in those unlined faces is the competitive zeal that helped trigger a government lawsuit.

On this day in late May 1999, Gates wore a handsome, royal-blue open-necked dress shirt buttoned at the sleeves and embroidered with *WHG*, navy slacks, unpolished black loafers, and clear-framed oval eyeglasses. His skin was the color of an eggshell, a pallor born of having spent too many hours indoors. His hair was unwashed, the bangs chopped near the roots. The previous afternoon, Melinda Gates had given birth to their second child, a son, and Gates had spent part of the day at the hospital. On the day I saw him, Microsoft would announce the birth; yet even though I was not a stranger, Gates uttered not a word about this happy event. By contrast, in the first long interview I conducted with Scott McNealy of Sun, it took him about a minute to pull out a deck of pictures of his three young sons and his wife and narrate: that's my boy missing a tennis ball, that's another laughing so hard he's about to burst. With Gates, impersonal behavior is the norm. Visitors are often amazed that he fetches a soda for himself and neglects to offer one to them. Upon greeting me, Gates plopped onto one of the chairs, leaned forward and folded his arms across his thighs, and began rocking rapidly back and forth, slapping the carpet with the soles of his loafers, creating the impression that his body was a metronome.

Watching Gates, it was difficult not to compare him to that other towering business figure who ran afoul of the government, John D. Rockefeller. Both enjoyed a market share of more than 80 percent, made huge investments in R and D, were generous philanthropists, were messianic believers that their venture served the public weal, were magicians with financial numbers, were oblivious to creature comforts, although they did enjoy extravagant homes. (Rockefeller's Pocantico Hills estate stretched over three thousand acres, which had been landscaped by the firm of Frederick Law Olmsted, who had designed Central Park.) Each understood the underlying value of his business. Rockefeller knew that more money was to be made in processing oil than in drilling for it; Gates knew that more was to be made in creating software than in building hardware. Each endured a costly trial against the government that might have been averted had he been more flexible. And each proved to be a terrible witness; so recalcitrant was Rockefeller on the witness stand that one newspaper headline blared, ROCKEFELLER IMITATES A CLAM.

The differences between the two men were also vast, needless to say. Rockefeller was for much of his life scorned by the public, whereas polls suggest that Gates remains an icon for a majority of Americans. Rockefeller had ceded management of Standard Oil to underlings long before Teddy Roosevelt demonized him, and by the time government brought charges against his company he was spending more time on the golf links than in the office. Rockefeller was inscrutable, a figure drenched in mystery who rarely talked to reporters or appeared in public, unlike Gates. Rockefeller's Standard Oil dominated a scarce resource and the means of distributing it, whereas the kind of intellectual property that Gates owns is not scarce, and a distribution system like the Internet is not as susceptible to control, as were the railroads. Rockefeller was tightly controlled, rarely seen by most employees, and as parsimonious with his words as he was with a dollar for employees. Gates is more impetuous, more accessible to employees, and exceedingly generous with stock options. Rockefeller was cool, Gates is hot.

But both men, despite their wealth and power, felt scoundrelized. Although he has achieved near Olympian status with the public, Gates feels the press has been cruel, and sometimes he does not hide his sense of vulnerability. While the official line at Microsoft is that the trial in Washington, D.C., is like "white noise," shoved in the background so that the company can stay focused on business, this is a front. As Gates rocked back and forth in his chair during my visit, he was as agitated at what he thought of as the ludicrousness of the government's case as he had been a year before. "There is no monopoly," he told me. "If you have talented people doing the right thing, the shares—the position of the product—can be changed. . . . That's why we invest so much more in R and D every year. . . . Even with all the great people we have we face probably more intense competition now than ever before. Only in a courtroom can somebody say, 'Hey, Linux is a serious competitor,' and the press laughs in a way that the judge thinks, 'OK, that must be a false statement, that must be posturing.' Here, in my world, there is intense competition from Linux and many other products. The only sure winner in our game is the consumer, who's got the PC coming down in price, who's going to get more and more of that revolutionary improvement because there is such intense competition."

In discussing with Gates what he sees as a disjunction between the world of Washington and the business world he inhabits, I asked him if he felt another sort of disconnect. Did he sometimes feel, as a friend had said, like Joseph K., accused of crimes he did not comprehend? "I don't know Joseph K., sorry." On being told that Joseph K. was the main character and victim in Franz Kafka's *The Trial*, Gates said, "He sounds like my kind of guy!"

Turning to the charges presented against his company, Gates said, "Let's look at what actually happened. They went in saying that the consent decree banned us supporting the Internet, putting the browser capability into the operating system. They said, black and white, 'Hey, all you have to do is delete these files, and this pie here will be eliminated. So issue an order telling them to delete these files. It's that simple.' Well it wasn't." He continued, "Our guy goes in, testifies under oath, 'Hey, if you delete those files that thing doesn't boot right.'" Nevertheless, Judge Jackson, in December 1997, had ordered that the browser and operating system be untied. "Where did that all end up? The appeals court was very clear: the consent decree does not touch on this, what's gone on here, in any way." He cited as equally satisfying the appeals court's admonition that government should not attempt to design software products. Of course, the consent decree case did not probe Microsoft's behavior, as the antitrust trial did.

Yes, there have been discussions with Justice about a possible settlement, Gates said, but talking with them is frustrating. He explained, "We keep trying to get them to articulate: what features under this new law they're trying to create—what features are we allowed to add and what features are we not allowed to add. And we say . . . in any discussion we have with them, 'What is your principle here? How should we have known that you would think supporting the Internet is a bad thing?' And we say to ourselves, 'It's the most defensible feature that we've ever added in. It's more defensible than graphic interface, compressed file systems, printing, securities.' . . . Didn't we create the product that won all the reviews? Didn't we create the product that people didn't have to pay extra for? . . . Somebody who was paying attention, they would know to laugh!" In the real world, he continued, Netscape is bought for billions of dollars. Yet in a Washington courtroom the government cries that Netscape has been foreclosed and Microsoft has killed Netscape by offering a free browser. "What the heck logic is there behind this?"

The real world, of course, is a bit more complicated. A reason the Justice Department didn't laugh is that they believed Microsoft was a monopoly whose intent was to hurt Netscape. They didn't laugh because they believed Gates and his employees often behaved like thugs. Now, a year after he had failed to reach an out-of-court settlement that could have avoided this trial, did Gates regret having gone to court?

"I wish we could have settled. I wished that at the time. I wish that now. Look, I'm not in this thing to prove some principle. Thank goodness there are some principles and some laws in this country about how things are done. We've always wanted to settle this thing." The stumbling block, he said, was that he couldn't go back to the government for permission each time he wanted to add a new feature, just because a competitor like Netscape whined about it. "You have to have a business left when you settle," he said. At this moment, he saw no way out.

How did he evaluate the job that his legal team was doing? He rocked back and forth several times before answering, then talked about the six-year legal battle with Apple: "We went through a lot on that one," including bad press before their victory.

He hadn't answered the question, so I asked it again.

"Well, there's a lot of things about this that they don't control," he said. "They don't control the leaking of the government." Then he said, "I haven't been back there at all" and only "meet with the lawyers from time to time." Then he trailed off.

Again: "Do you think they've done a good job in the law?"

Again, there was a long pause before he replied, "Well, as far as this case goes they've certainly proved that Netscape was not foreclosed. And they've certainly proved that there are immense benefits to developers and users of our putting these Internet features as well as other features into the product. They've done a very good job establishing those things. And those are the issues at hand."

I asked what he admired about Bill Neukom. There was a pause of about ten seconds before he answered: "He's a very good lawyer himself, and he also brings in, both into his department and through outside relationships, people with a lot of expertise." He paused, thoughtfully, then continued: "I myself am not a lawyer."

Gates was unhappy about the broad brush applied to him and to his company, and he pressed me to cite one fact—one incident from Intuit, Intel, IBM, from "all this mud that's been slung"—that demonstrated bad behavior by Microsoft.

What about coercion, I asked—the charge that Microsoft muscled Intel to stay out of the software business?

"I don't know what *muscle* means," he said.

What if his daughter came to him some years hence and asked, Dad, how do you explain some of these e-mails and things like the threat to cut off Netscape's air supply?

Gates was composed, but he answered in a shrill voice. "A great lie! A great lie!" he cried out. "An unbelievable lie!" It was secondhand hearsay, he said. His voice rising, yet controlled, he went on, "Did anyone utter those words? Our e-mail, every piece of it has been searched. I wish we *had* found somebody who had said it. Then we could take him out, and we could hang the guy, then we'd say, 'OK, mea culpa. We found him—the guy who said, "I'll cut off your oxygen." ' First of all, there's no law against saying that. Second of all, I never heard anybody say it. Third of all—hey, if there's any company that you know damn well whether it was said or not, this is the company. Every piece of e-mail I have ever sent for the last ten years has been read and read, and if there is any way that people can misconstrue any statement that I've ever made it has been done. You look at any e-mail sent by me or received by me and tell me what is it you think is at all inappropriate?"

What about his offering a million-dollar "favor" to Intuit if it chose his browser over Netscape's?

"The fact that I was willing to put a million dollars into joint marketing, a million dollars into helping them do the engineering, just shows I was desirous of getting them to exploit our technology," he answered. "And what's wrong with that? This is the kind of thing that blows the mind! Yes, I was so anxious to have them show off" the new features of Internet Explorer that Netscape's browser did not have. "How can that be characterized as something inappropriate? I just don't understand it. If I hadn't offered that million dollars you'd have to say to me, 'Bill, are you doing your job?' " Besides, he lamented, it's all a moot point: "no such thing ever happened," since Intuit declined.

Push aside for a moment the legal questions, I said. What about the ethical dimensions of Microsoft's hardball tactics? How might he one day explain these to his daughter or son?

"There is nothing I want more than to find something to do a mea culpa on. The fact that we're so successful, people really do want to know that we're behaving responsibly, in terms of how we work with partners, how we work with customers, how we think about things in long-term ways, and I believe Microsoft has been exemplary in those things. Go ask the analysts how Microsoft behaves with them in terms of the integrity of the information. Go ask some of our customers. You take our relationship with Apple. This is a company where, during the time they sue us to try and put us out of business, who was developing more software for the Macintosh than anybody else? They're not letting us get the [Macintosh] OS information. They're discriminating against us. They're doing joint marketing with all of our competitors. Just mistreating us every single step of the way. We're always trying to figure out some way to help them, to work with them. The notion that somebody could misconstrue those negotiations with Apple! We did something incredibly valuable to them. We invested in the company where people had lost faith in Apple. We renewed our commitment to do all these new versions of software at a time when that was very important to them." What people misunderstand, he continued, is that Microsoft's belated discovery of the Internet was really what drove it to bundle the browser and to focus more on Netscape. "We were slow. We hadn't recognized the importance of it. And this trial, in a sense, comes out of that."

The government would phrase it differently. They would say that Gates is right that Microsoft only belatedly awakened to the Internet and that the trial flowed from this fact. But they would say Gates ignores how Microsoft did not just race to compete with Netscape but used its monopoly to suppress competition. To hear this surprises both Bill Gates and Microsoft executives. They don't see themselves the way they are portrayed in a courtroom three thousand miles away. By contrast to a monopolist who has the luxury of sitting back and behaving in a leisurely fashion, at Microsoft executives feel embattled. This sense of embattlement is deeply ingrained in the Microsoft culture.

James Allchin told me in the spring of 1999, "I feel like we're on the brink of disaster every day. If you're reading newspapers and watching what's happening—new devices, new operating systems, attacks that claim intellectual property means nothing—it's like a massive attack all the time." He worried about an attack from Sony and its "fixed game machines, because they're growing up," about cable boxes that could control all home electronics, about handheld personal digital assistants that can perform multiple tasks, about open-source software, about the "megaserver threat" posed by an AOL online operating system where "once you're in an AOL environment, you're in it holistically," about how the distinction between hardware and software companies blurs as Intel and Dell and IBM invest in software and AT&T is now a cable and an Internet-access as well as a telephone company.

Sam Jadallah, 34, who joined Microsoft in 1987 and was the vice president who oversaw the small-enterprise customer unit, like Allchin felt besieged: "My major competition is chaos." Most of the fifty-one million small- and medium-sized companies in the world that he sought to sell software to have neither planning departments nor the luxury of time to plan. They make snap decisions and are courted by an array of competitors, from IBM to Oracle to Novell. To appeal to these customers himself, Jadallah relied on 775,000 channel partners, usually small computer stores that service these companies. His job was to cajole, charm, and recruit others outside Microsoft to serve as middlemen, though they can, at any moment, take their services elsewhere. In Washington, Microsoft is portrayed as a Leviathan, but Jadallah described his business model this way: "It's not a control model. It's an empowerment model."

Success is fragile, insisted Ben Waldman, who oversaw relations with Apple Computer and had been working at Microsoft more than a decade. "When I started, Microsoft Word had a twenty percent market share. Lotus and WordPerfect dominated. They got complacent." So did IBM, DEC, Commodore, and Wang. Yusuf Mehdi, who directs marketing for Windows, said, "I don't think I've ever been more worried. Are we missing the boat? . . . The threat is obsolescence. How do we respond to people who say, 'My TV doesn't crash'? How do we respond to people who say, as Netscape does, 'Why do you need Windows? You can just use the Web.' We need to figure out how to make it in this new Internet world. I look around and see tens of companies that might have better ideas."

To unearth better ideas, Microsoft in 1999 spent an extraordinary three billion dollars on research and development. This represented about 17 percent of its revenues, a figure that dwarfs the 6 percent IBM spent, or the 10 percent of revenues expended by such companies as Intel and Sun. A sizable portion of this budget is earmarked for pure research—for recruiting and funding the best physicists and mathematicians and electrical engineers to undertake theoretical work that doesn't have a clear product payoff. In an era when such theoretical research is usually sacrificed as impractical and companies strive to cut costs and drive up their stock price, Microsoft is a rare oasis. It is also, needless to say, a place seeking to dominate the realm of new products: an electronic encyclopedia on Africa, *Encarta Africa;* browsers for wireless devices; WebTV, which brings e-mail and the Web to TV sets; WebMD, which shares health-care information online with doctors and consumers; software that might permit PCs to boot up instantly; laptop batteries that last for twelve hours; PCs that accept voice commands and translate handwriting into type; interactive toys and dolls and games; auto PCs that function as radios and CD players as well as navigation devices that offer voice instructions.

Rick Thompson, vice president of their hardware group, described his 225-employee division as "my own little sandbox." He tries to use software to devise ways to improve consumer devices from the telephone to the PC. He works on hardware designs—like a mouse or a portable personal digital assistant that becomes an electronic book—so that they are easier to grip and use. Most of their research efforts fail after they come to market. "It's a lot like the movie business. There are a lot of flops," he said. Among the development projects that Bill Gates was most excited about in 1999 was ClearType, which seeks to improve the resolution of typefaces on laptops and smaller screens as well as on PCs, so as to rival the resolution of print on paper. ClearType is the brainchild of Bill Hill, who was born in Scotland fifty years ago and joined Microsoft in 1995. Hill comes to work most days wearing Bermuda shorts, sporting a full beard and with his hair pulled back in a ponytail. Hill's mission was to increase the resolution on an LCD computer screen from 88 pixels per inch to 300 by using digital technology to make the pixels smaller and the image smoother. ClearType could spur advances in electronic books and in online reading. "Trying to portray type with a pixel is like trying to paint the *Mona Lisa* with a paint roller," said Hill. "We've changed the size of the paint roller."

Alvy Ray Smith is a Texan with a neat white beard who looks like Kenny Rogers. After a legendary career in computer graphics—first at Xerox PARC, where he wrote the first full-color graphics program in the seventies, then as cofounder of Pixar in 1986, then as a two-time winner of Academy Awards for computer graphics—Smith joined Microsoft six years ago as a Graphics Fellow to "do pretty much anything I want to," he told me. Smith felt he and his team were making incredible breakthroughs in computer graphics, learning how to rotate pixel objects and do 3-D graphics on a PC rather than on a monster three-hundred-thousand-dollar machine. Yet former associates and friends from Silicon Valley verbally flame the genial Smith when they see him at conferences. He struggles to explain: "This is the most innovative graphics program in history. And it comes from here. They won't listen. They think it's an evil, monopolistic empire. They think Microsoft is dominated by poor programmers. Paul Saffo looked at me and said, 'You've become one of them.'" To Smith, this is familiar: "When I was young, it was IBM we all hated."

Eventually, like the browser, many of these innovative products will probably be integrated for free into Windows. Alvy Smith's new graphics software—PhotoDraw 2000—will, he said, be part of the graphics package included in Microsoft Office 2000, a suite of programs for corporate users. ClearType was then expected to be included sometime in 2000 with an upgraded Windows and as software loaded into Microsoft Reader for their handheld pocket PC. Doug Heinrich, who is director of business development and is working on speech and handwriting recognition, said the plan was to include at least some of these innovative features in a version of Windows 2000. At Microsoft, what the government calls "bundling" is referred to as "integration," and not without reason. Integration lets programs running on Windows interact seamlessly, allowing users to switch back and forth with greater speed and ease than ever before. From the consumer's point of view, said Jeff Raikes, who is a member of the company's executive committee, "I look at the integration issue and I know we're right. If it had been banned seven years ago, we would not have integrated font management and graphic user interface. . . . I know we're doing the right thing for customers." The government's notion of an operating system as static is absurd, observed Craig Mundie, also a member of the executive committee. "I wrote an OS thirty years ago. If you had asked me to give a simple definition of what an operating system is, I would have told you it's at any given time the most recent collection of genuinely useful features that are broadly desirable by users and application developers." It used to be there was no printing support, no word processing, no fonts, no graphics. They were not deemed part of the operating system, he said, and now they are. Of course, this leads to a major disconnect between Microsoft and the Justice Department. Microsoft claims such additions serve consumers; the Justice Department claims they were intended to solidify Microsoft's monopoly. They probably do both. After all, Microsoft benefited consumers by reducing the price of browsers, and at the same time they undermined Netscape.

Microsoft executives see themselves as upright, public-spirited citizens, not the malevolent folks sketched in court. They also see Microsoft as benevolent. Barbara Dingfield, who became Microsoft's director of community affairs in 1994, said that by 1999 three quarters of all Microsoft employees made philanthropic gifts that were matched by the company, resulting in up to thirty million dollars in corporate giving to support homeless shelters, zoos, and efforts in twenty cities. Another seventy million to one hundred million dollars' worth of software was donated by Microsoft to schools and libraries. While Microsoft is "now in the top ten of American companies in philanthropy," she said, it is subdued about it.

While Gates's company has been quietly generous, Gates himself was at first reluctant to part with his money. Like his friend Warren Buffett, he said that philanthropy takes effort and time, which he didn't have. So aside from relatively small gifts for biotechnology and computer-science research and to his mother's favorite charity, the United Way, he was planning to wait until he was old and then would give most of his fortune away. In the last several years, Gates—unlike Buffett—has dramatically altered this stance and become the world's foremost philanthropist, having by January 2000 pledged $21.8 billion to the Bill and Melinda Gates Foundation, making it the world's wealthiest charitable foundation. Unlike many other philanthropists—such as John D. Rockefeller and Andrew Carnegie—Bill Gates is giving away large chunks of his fortune while he is still a young man, and his largesse already far exceeds theirs. In current 2000 dollars, reported Jean Strouse in *The New York Times Magazine*, Rockefeller's giving would have totaled six billion dollars and Carnegie's three billion. Both Buffett and Gates Senior attribute the change to Melinda, who has more time to devote to charity. "Melinda has spurred him," said Buffett. Cynics attribute these gifts to a Gates public-relations offensive designed to offset the black eye he has received from the trial. While press considerations may have been a factor in the timing of some gifts, that's a pretty steep price to pay for publicity. A slick public-relations ploy would have resulted in a superficial effort; it would not have earmarked the money as carefully—for cheap vaccines that so easily save lives, for library computers to help ease the digital divide between haves and have-nots, for minority college scholarships, for important medical and computer-science research—as have the Gateses. Even such critics as Steve Case and David Boies tip their hats to Gates's mature, generous giving.

And yet, how to square the many impressive and nice people one meets at Microsoft—gentlemen such as Jeff Raikes, Tod Nielsen, Sam Jadallah, or Greg Shaw, idealistic graphic programmers such as Alvy Smith, brilliant and ebullient personalities such as Nathan Myhrvold—with Microsoft's thuggish behavior? By trial's end, as all of Microsoft's rough tactics had been exhaustively aired, this disconnect yawned even wider.

Perhaps Microsoft's great strength, its zealotry, is also its great weakness. Those who treat their work as a cause often suffer from fogged judgment. History is replete with passionate idealists who did monstrous things in the name of noble ends. At Microsoft, executives and programmers speak of their work with genuine reverence, extolling the consumer benefits they bring, how they are pushing the envelope at the frontier of software. They can be as pious as mullahs or priests. When Ben Waldman is asked to describe the culture of Microsoft, he says with utter solemnity, "People are very passionate about creating great products. . . . We do things to help people solve problems." This righteousness fuels an upstart company, but in a successful company it can turn to arrogance. America Online's Steve Case observes, "They just believe they are right and everyone who expresses concern is wrong. I think they think they're still in the garage making software and don't fully appreciate the impact they're having in the world and the kinds of challenges they face and responsibilities they should shoulder. They're like the dog that's chasing the car, and they caught the car. Now what?" In many ways, Microsoft employees often behave like man-children, people with adult bodies who nevertheless have an innocent, childlike view that business competition is a video game, where competitors and those who don't wear the Microsoft white hat are zapped. On their enclosed Microsoft campus, far removed from competitors, staring at computer screens that show no blood, in a sense the work atmosphere may have become as unreal as a video game.

Of course, people are often contradictory. Truth, as novelist Christopher Morley once observed, "is a liquid, not a solid." The same Microsoft spokesman who one day tells me Gates was not upset in Davos, the next day says he was. A simple interpretation is that he was lying. A closer approximation of the truth might be that he wanted to believe Gates was not upset, so he came to believe it. The spinner had spun himself. Few people rise each morning determined to tell lies, to harm others. And even normal people can be schizophrenic. In his extraordinary biography of John D. Rockefeller, Sr., Ron Chernow explores the gap between what he called the man's "exemplary private life" and his "reprehensible business behavior." Rockefeller, he wrote, justified such behavior by becoming "self-righteous about his opponents," believing they were cheating him. Rockefeller honestly believed he served the public good. "To square his actions with his conscience," Chernow writes, Rockefeller insisted that Standard Oil was providing oil to light the homes of poor people. He knew Standard Oil honored contracts and paid bills promptly, so "to confirm his clean, sanctimonious image of himself, he reiterated these ideals with a kind of incantatory relish, and the more naysayers dwelled on his railroad dealings or secret subsidiaries, the more he affirmed his own compensating code of business honor. This was as much to preserve his own self-image as to persuade a skeptical public that he was honorable, for Rockefeller desperately needed to have a good opinion of himself." Chernow also shows that sometimes Rockefeller just plain lied. To many who watched his deposition in court, so did Bill Gates. When Gates refused to admit that he was concerned with Netscape's market share despite mountains of e-mail evidence to the contrary, he sounded like the husband found in bed with a woman not his wife who tries to gut it out by pretending she's not there.

It's not surprising that one could scour the Microsoft campus in vain for an employee who will admit that Gates was obfuscating; what is surprising is that one would be hard-pressed to find an employee who frankly admits that Microsoft is a for-profit company in the business of making money, not a beneficent foundation serving the public interest. Yusuf Mehdi talks of his work as if it were the frontier of medical science. "People refer to this as a college campus," he said, looking around as young workers in T-shirts and shorts bustled by. "There's the same feeling you have in college: 'I can do something great!'" How did he square these sentiments, I asked, with the sometimes John Gotti–like behavior described in court? "What I would say is that a lot of this legal stuff comes from competitors, not from end users. What the trial is is sensationalist bits and pieces. The trial was supposed to be about bundling. I'm not saying we're not aggressive. We get after it. But it's in the interest of doing what's best for customers."

Such sanctimony is common at Microsoft, from Bill Gates down. "What we aim to do is to make tools to make people's lives better," Gates once told a congressional hearing. There is a tendency at Microsoft to talk about consumers, not profits. No doubt, Microsoft could not recruit the best and brightest without conveying a belief that it is waging a holy war to better serve consumers, improve computing, do *cool* things. But it is weird that Microsoft executives rarely speak of fat profits or rich stock options, although executives in their twenties drive BMWs and those in their thirties establish private foundations and often retire, and Microsoft hogs as profit an extraordinary forty cents of each revenue dollar it collects. Jean-Louis Gassée, the CEO of Be, once likened Microsoft's behavior to that of believers in a religious order: "The Jesuits have this concept of holy effrontery—in defending their cause it's OK to use any means."

This "holy effrontery" is not unique to Microsoft, of course. Among those who've struck it rich in the digital economy, it is common to encounter this tendency to drape oneself in virtue—to extol the way your company is pushing the envelope, making life better for con-sumers—even as one gobbles up enormous profits and sets out to destroy challengers or waits for Microsoft, Cisco Systems, or some other elephant to pay a hefty premium to acquire your company. By 1999, it was difficult not to have your head turned by eye-popping accounts of the wealth amassed by our new billionaires—of Michael Saylor of MicroStrategy's $14.5 billion and Rob Glaser's $2 billion and Jeffrey Bezos of Amazon.com's $13 billion, and David Filo and Jerry Yang of Yahoo!'s $11 billion and Pierre Omidyar of eBay's $9 billion. Few of these new billionaires are ready to make Gordon Gekko–like pronounce-ments that greed is good. Because it is new wealth, people tend to be more self-conscious about it. No doubt, many are intent on doing good with their wealth. And, no doubt, talk of doing good and of pushing the technological frontier soothes many a conscience. Inevitably, however, the enormity of this new wealth creation can be subversive. Many Fortune 500 companies and major law firms developed trouble both retain-ing and recruiting talented people who now imagine that they, too, can strike it rich. Law and accounting firms, to cite another example, some-times accept dot-com stock in lieu of a fee, which invites abuses since the service firm's ability to give independent advice may be compromised by its interest in maximizing the value of its investment.

Microsoft shares this: it is part of an industry that behaves as if there will never be a morning after. Those who have joined the great Internet gold rush and have attached themselves to its stock-market bungee cord are believers, not pessimists. Ask them about nonexistent profits or why the number of visitors to their website is more important than their revenues or profits, and brace yourself to be attacked as a witch, a nonbeliever. Wonder aloud whether Gutenberg's printing press or Edison's electricity might have had a more profound impact on society than the Internet and risk being sneered at as an "old-media" fogey. Sometimes it is hard to separate spin from conviction. "The Internet, because it is a new industry making itself up as it goes along," writes Michael Wolff in his entertaining book, *Burn Rate: How I Survived the Gold Rush Years on the Internet,* "is particularly susceptible to the art of the spin. Those of us in the industry want the world to think the best of us. Optimism is our bank account; fantasy is our product; press releases are our good name."

Acutely aware of the warp-like speed of technological change and of how, in an instant, success turns to failure, new-economy CEOs from Gates to Case to Grove, as we've seen, preach paranoia. Each knows he leads a company that could quickly become extinct, as happened to portal-market leader Prodigy or to Wang or to Hayes, or that his company could slip almost overnight, as happened to Compaq in 1999. But preach paranoia, and inevitably employees may overreact and take radical measures because the company's very existence feels endangered. Couple the paranoia with youth, and you have a recipe for potentially extreme behavior. Young people have a tendency to take things personally, to become irate and righteous.

Is there another reason such bad behavior may be more prevalent in Silicon Valley than it is among mature industries? John Seely Brown, the chief scientist at Xerox and the director of Xerox PARC, its vaunted research center in Palo Alto, tells in an e-mail he wrote me of going as a young man to meet physicist George Pake, the founder of Xerox PARC:

One day I got a call from him to come up and discuss an issue about computer science. . . .

He said he was wondering why computer scientists were so incredibly arrogant. Yes, he realized we were a bright, brash group of researchers but why, oh why, were we so incredibly arrogant? Being somewhat arrogant myself, it took me only a nanosecond to respond. "Well, George, I think it's quite simple. In computer science being brilliant and clever is everything. But in physics, just being brilliant is not enough; in physics the most brilliant theories still have a chance of being just plain wrong; maybe the world doesn't work that way. In physics you have to explain the world and thus the world is the great equalizer and, as a consequence, brilliant theoreticians and physicists learn a certain humility and awe. In computer science, the world is not the arbitrator. If you're clever and logically coherent, then you carry the day. Brilliance reigns supreme and there is no final arbitrator and hence we grow up thinking we really are the masters of the virtual world."

Ah, how much simpler it is to be masters of the virtual world than the physical world. Humility need not apply.

Don't try to sell David Boies any mitigating explanation for Microsoft's behavior, because he isn't buying. How does he square the evidence with the idealism and fervor one encounters on the Microsoft campus? "If you've ever practiced criminal law you will recognize that when the accused is talking to the judge or the jury or even his own lawyer, the accused is often a model of sweetness and light. When people are challenged, they tend to be friendlier and nicer than when they were not observed." Boies thinks it is plausible that Microsoft executives honestly believe they are innocent and of honorable intent, but he cares more about their actions than their words. "There are people who get together in rooms and fix prices and really believe what they're doing is preserving the American farm. The people at most major corporations, and certainly at Microsoft, are intelligent and educated and articulate people, with the confidence and social skills that tend to cause success." But Boies doesn't believe you judge a person's public character by their words, their fervor, their talents, or how they treat pets. "I'm much more prone to reason from the character of the act to the character of the person."

CHAPTER 15

The Trial's Final Innings

I**N THE FINAL WEEKS** of the witness phase of this trial, starting on June 1, 1999, each side called its three rebuttal witnesses, like relief pitchers sent in late in a baseball game. Each side played it safe by recalling their lead economists, Dr. Fisher and Dr. Schmalensee. The puzzle was the other witnesses: how would each side decide to shore up their own weaknesses? Would they be cautious or bold? The government needed to better demonstrate consumer harm, and to do this they needed a PC manufacturer (OEM) to testify against Microsoft. "It's been very difficult to convince an OEM to appear in court without a hood," cracked Boies during the recess. Boies and Joel Klein labored over the spring to persuade an executive from either Gateway 2000 or IBM to testify. Microsoft had two glaring vulnerabilities: the discrepancy between its testimony and its deeds, and the one between the government's claim that Microsoft was a monopoly and Microsoft's claim that competitors circled everywhere. The great Microsoft mystery was whether they would dare call Bill Gates to the stand.

Neither side believed the outcome of the trial rested on their rebuttal witnesses. "It's very hard to materially affect the outcome once you get into rebuttal," Boies said. "Both sides have taken their best shots. There are very few cases—I never had one—where the rebuttal case materially impacted the outcome. This is not like a low-scoring flow game, like hockey or soccer, where a burst at the end can turn things around. A trial is more like baseball, where when you get to the bottom of the ninth inning it takes something extraordinary to change the outcome of a trial that is already very uneven."

Boies was speaking in late April, while headquartered in what he called a war room on the eleventh floor of the Solow building at 9 West Fifty-seventh Street in Manhattan. Sheldon Solow, his new real-estate client, hoped—as did other new clients, Howard Milstein, who was suing the estate of Jack Kent Cooke for blocking his purchase of the Washington Redskins, and comedian Garry Shandling, who was suing his former manager—to use Boies as a weapon to legally murder a foe. Clients were knocking on his firm's door. Another old friend, antitrust heavyweight Donald Flexner, had come aboard, making the young law firm Boies, Schiller & Flexner. It quickly swelled to nearly sixty lawyers and obtained a blue-chip client list, including Philip Morris, which it represented in three antitrust suits; America Online, a client of Flexner; CBS; the sultan of Brunei; 3Com; Northwest Airlines; Southwestern Bell; Unisys; Georgia-Pacific; and class-action groups in lawsuits against video-poker manufacturers, giant HMOs, as well as the Sotheby's and Christie's auction houses for alleged price-fixing. In addition, Boies often traveled to Alaska, where he represented the state against two oil giants, BP Amoco and Atlantic Richfield, and to Guatemala, where he was the pro bono counsel for an American woman attempting to reclaim her children from a wealthy Guatemalan who, she claimed, had kidnapped them. In Washington, D.C., a trial was pending for a class-action suit on behalf of giant corporations such as Kellogg's that purchase vitamins in bulk and were charging seven vitamin companies with price-fixing; he was also to be retained by fashion designer Calvin Klein when he sued his corporate parent, the Warnaco Group, charging that it had cheapened the value of his brand name, and by Napster, an online music service that was accused of allowing others to circumvent copyright laws and the major music companies by enabling the electronic distribution of music for free. (In arguing the case in federal district court, Boies would complain à la Bill Neukom that the plaintiffs were using snippets of Napster's e-mail to paint a distorting picture of the company.) By 1999, Boies's twin sons (Jonathan and Christopher) and a daughter (Caryl) had joined his firm, to his immense pleasure. Given his taxing workload, it no doubt improved chances of seeing their father.

On this warm April day, Boies lugged a laundry bag filled with striped shirts to his war room and seemed not to notice that the windows were shut and the air conditioner was silent. Joel Klein had finally succeeded in enticing IBM to allow a knowledgeable executive to testify in rebuttal, and Boies was almost smugly confident of victory. What would Boies do right now if he represented Microsoft? He would be bold, he said, contradicting what he had said a moment earlier about how difficult it was to "materially" impact a trial by the rebuttal stage. "Gates is the one witness they have who has the potential to be a witness with great potential to help, or hurt, their case. They have to explain all that has gone on before in order to win. That explanation can't come from lawyers or underlings. For Microsoft to win they have to explain away all the things Gates said and wrote. . . . I would call him." Joel Klein disagreed. Klein guessed that it would be a grievous mistake to call Gates because "his deposition locked him in" to positions Boies could exploit in the courtroom. On one thing Klein and Boies agreed, however: Microsoft's legal team didn't have the guts to call Gates.

Richard Schmalensee acknowledged the risk. "This is very emotional for him—this is his life's work. And Boies is very good at getting under his skin. There was a fear that Gates might blow up." Bill Neukom put it differently: since they didn't share Boies's belief that their back was to the wall, Microsoft's lawyers didn't expend time debating whether to call Gates, Neukom told me in mid-May. Neukom was convinced it would be pure theater, and he didn't even consider it. Had Neukom known what Judge Jackson was thinking, perhaps he would have reconsidered. "I think Boies's technique of starting with Bill Gates's deposition was a brilliant stroke," Jackson later told me. "Bill Gates was the personification of this company. To exhibit Gates on deposition, as he did, demonstrating such total lack of candor, really casts doubt on the veracity of all his subordinates who came in to testify. I kept waiting to see if Microsoft would bring Gates in as a rebuttal witness. Or woodshed the hell out of him. Or show other parts of his deposition that showed he was concerned with the implications of the questions asked of him. The questions I saw I thought showed nothing but disdain for the process: 'Who was this pest asking him embarrassing questions on how he managed his company?'" In fact, Gates wanted to testify, confided a Microsoft adviser. "The lawyers didn't think it was necessary."

In an office in Building 8, not far from Bill Gates's suite, the jazz of Dizzy Gillespie, Count Basie, and Marian McPartland can sometimes be heard. Their posters circle a large, black granite desk, as does Native American art and baseball memorabilia, including mementos from the San Francisco Giants, the team the office's occupant partly owns. In his office in May 1999, Bill Neukom looked different, for his bow tie was gone; he wore khakis and an open-necked white shirt with discreet red-checked boxes. But he remained as confident as ever. He was pleased that the only OEM the government could induce to testify was IBM, whose claims would be impaired because IBM software competed with Microsoft's and because IBM was not a large PC manufacturer, like Dell, Compaq, or Hewlett-Packard. Neukom adopted a cautious approach to rebuttal witnesses. His main rebuttal objective, he said, was "to expose their witnesses, particularly Fisher, as being uninformed about how the world works." To demonstrate the fluidity of the software business, he would call Gordon E. Eubanks, Jr., the chief executive of Oblix, a software company. For their third rebuttal witness, instead of choosing a prominent Microsoft foe with a loose tongue—say Scott McNealy of Sun or Larry Ellison of Oracle—or choosing a respected Silicon Valley figure to testify about how truly competitive the software business was, Microsoft chose to bring back a government witness, David M. Colburn, America Online's senior vice president of business affairs. Their aim, said Neukom, was to show that AOL, now linked with Netscape and Sun, was a formidable competitor. They would accomplish this by submitting internal documents from these companies revealing that their true aim was to hobble Microsoft.

When the trial resumed, each side still acted so confident of victory that when they secretly met in Joel Klein's office on June 2 to explore a negotiated settlement, talks went absolutely nowhere. Microsoft was more receptive to a settlement but not on the government's more stringent terms. Over the next three weeks of rebuttals, neither side altered the trial's narrative. In introducing Dr. Fisher, Boies tried to reframe the damaging admission Fisher made earlier in the trial that current consumers "up to this point" had not been harmed by Microsoft's monopoly. Fisher talked about how they were being harmed by "the applications barrier to entry." Because of Windows's dominance few software developers had an economic incentive to write new applications for anything other than Windows. Thus, consumers would never see innovations that would come from true competition. He also insisted that Microsoft would in the future be free to raise its prices at will and to use Windows to extend its monopoly into other devices.

Michael Lacovara hammered at Dr. Fisher. Rather than dwell on Fisher's claims that Microsoft was currently a monopolist, Lacovara dwelled on the future. He introduced documents revealing strategic discussions among America Online, Netscape, and Sun to supplant Windows with a Netscape browser that would, they said, "absorb more share of computing time" and ultimately become "the user's de facto environment." AOL could transform browser competition overnight, he noted, by replacing Microsoft with Netscape as its primary browser. He induced Fisher to admit that Microsoft's alleged monopoly could be subverted by the Internet. Even were Microsoft a monopoly today, to say it will be tomorrow is a statement of faith, not fact, just as it was a statement of faith for Dr. Fisher to assert that Microsoft did not yet charge monopoly prices because it first wanted to cement its monopoly and later would launch a sneak attack on consumers.

To divert attention and slow Lacovara's momentum, Boies asked Judge Jackson for a bench conference. As he and Lacovara and the judge conferred, Boies whispered a mild complaint about Lacovara's questioning of Fisher. Boies did this twice. When the two lawyers walked back to their places the first time, Lacovara murmured something and flashed a big smile, registering the impression that he was pleased. After the second bench conference, he did it again. "You did that twice. Why?" Boies quietly asked him.

"Because," Lacovara said, "I know what you're doing. You're trying to suggest to the judge and the press that I did something wrong with this witness, and I want them to understand it's not affecting me."

Boies looked at him, Lacovara remembered, and said, "You get it!" They both smiled. Lacovara knew Boies the gamesman was really saying "Nothing personal, Michael."

But by demonstrating how rapidly technology had transformed the PC and inevitably introduced competing platforms, Lacovara had driven home an important point. Implicitly, he was cautioning Judge Jackson: even if you find Microsoft guilty of infractions, beware of radical cures because the market provides its own swift remedies.

The government's second rebuttal witness, Garry Norris of IBM, offered far more damning evidence against Microsoft. Norris was responsible for negotiating IBM's Windows licensing agreements in the mid-nineties. Although IBM has four times the revenues of Microsoft (but roughly the same profits, nearly seven billion dollars), like all PC manufacturers it was a supplant for the operating system most consumers knew and relied upon. But there was a catch, Norris testified: Microsoft balked at IBM's plan to offer consumers a "dual boot" choice on each PC of either Windows or OS/2, IBM's own operating system. When IBM made it clear that it would continue to promote OS/2, said Norris, Microsoft punished them by charging more for each copy of Windows than Microsoft charged more pliant PC manufacturers. IBM went from paying nine dollars per copy for Windows 3.1 to seventy-five dollars for each Windows 95. In one year, the royalties IBM paid Microsoft rose from $40 million to $220 million. Cut back on promoting OS/2, a proposed Microsoft/IBM contract read, and IBM would enjoy an eight-dollar discount on each copy of Windows. IBM declined, missing out on up to forty-eight million extra dollars in 1995, reported Norris.

Tensions escalated. Microsoft executives, trying to play good cops, warned of "combative" people at Microsoft who wanted to go to war with IBM. They spoke of Gates as if he were God craving a sacrifice. When in 1995 IBM acquired Lotus, whose Lotus Notes offered its own APIs to software developers and thus posed a threat to Windows, especially since IBM could load its software products on new PCs, Microsoft protested. Norris told of being in the room when Bill Gates phoned his boss, Senior Vice President and Group Executive G. R. Thoman, and screamed profanities at him. In a July 24, 1995, memo recounting his telephone conversation with Gates, Thoman wrote, "Gates was irate because of the lack of respect he feels IBM has for Microsoft. He cited Lou Gerstner's quote in *Business Week* that Microsoft was a great marketing company, but not a great technology company, as an example. Gates, he said, accused IBM of conducting a "smear campaign." Microsoft executives dispatched e-mails and memos with further descriptions of how combustible Gates was. IBM had to placate Gates. Please make a peace offering, they pleaded.

IBM did strive to appease Microsoft. But when IBM refused to abandon its own infrequently used OS/2 software, Norris claimed, Microsoft began to cut off IBM's air supply. Norris's phone calls to Microsoft in the summer of 1995 were not returned. With Windows 95 to be shipped in August, IBM was desperate to sign a new licensing agreement so it could sell up-to-date PCs to the back-to-school market. There would be no licensing agreement, said Microsoft, until an independent audit was completed to determine whether IBM was selling more copies of its software than it was paying for. Although IBM offered to set aside ten million dollars to meet any shortfall, Microsoft declined to delink the audit from a new licensing agreement. Microsoft said it would settle the audit, Norris testified, if IBM agreed not to ship rival software. IBM refused. When they finally reached a licensing agreement in late August, IBM had been penalized, for the computer giant had been forced to sell its fall PCs without Windows 95, and it was late to deliver machines for the vital Christmas season. Nearly two years later, Microsoft again leaned on IBM, this time over a choice of browsers. Reading from handwritten notes he made in 1997, Norris read that his counterpart at Microsoft offered a discount on Windows—if IBM agreed to "no Netscape."

To Boies and Justice, IBM was a surrogate for consumers. Since consumers acquired their PCs and Windows from computer manufacturers, by proving IBM was harmed and denied a choice Boies would prove that consumers were as well. By proving that Microsoft charged more for Windows than it should have, Boies would show consumer harm.

Microsoft challenged the consumer-harm assertion. The antitrust laws were designed to protect consumers, not competitors such as Netscape or IBM, they said. To say that one day they would harm consumers was pure "speculation," not hard fact. What were facts, they said, were that browser-software prices had come down and the technical quality of the browsers had gone up. As for IBM's charges, Microsoft said the independent audit did reveal that IBM underreported sales of Microsoft software, and the company did agree to pay Microsoft an additional thirty-one million dollars. IBM, they demonstrated, did sign a Windows licensing agreement in 1995 that didn't stop it from shipping other software, just as they did in 1997 when they agreed to carry Microsoft's browser without promising to exclude Netscape. In fact, though Microsoft did not note in court that this was a policy change, Microsoft now placed no restrictions on what software OEMs could ship with Windows, nor on whether the PC manufacturer placed icons for other software on the Windows desktop. What Microsoft would not allow was for a PC maker to remove Microsoft's browser, because it was integrated into the operating system, or to modify Windows so as to interfere with it being a universal operating system that worked the same no matter what brand of PC or printer the user had. And the reason companies such as Compaq were charged lower prices for Windows 95, Microsoft said, was that Compaq had entered joint development and marketing agreements with Microsoft.

In the theater of the courtroom, Microsoft probably lost this exchange, yet the legal test on these matters is strenuous, and the evidence of coercion must be clear-cut. The usual test the courts apply is to determine whether the evidence is unequivocal, as a federal court ruled it was in 1984 when it rebuked American Airlines for attempting to enlist another airline in a scheme to jointly raise prices. In that case, the evidence was a tape recording of a conversation between the two CEOs. In this case, the evidence was murkier. Businesses, as Microsoft claimed, daily offer discounts and marketing-incentive agreements. Boies, however, thought he had produced the dead body, the proof of consumer harm, Microsoft said he lacked.

Judge Jackson was impressed with Norris. "He was not particularly happy to be there," Jackson said later, "and then the story he related about being systematically abused was very effective." Ominously for Microsoft, Jackson seemed to believe that the evidence that Microsoft had attempted to use its market power to harm IBM was uniquely unequivocal.

The third government rebuttal witness, Princeton computer scientist Edward W. Felten, was an odd choice. He had testified earlier that Microsoft's browser and operating system were not fully integrated and could be pulled apart and offered as separate products. Since so many Microsoft witnesses had testified that the two could not be separated, Felten worked up a new, improved version of his program that was intended to show that they could be. Steven L. Holley then did to Felten what Boies had earlier done to James Allchin: he revealed that Felten's demonstration did not do what he advertised. Holley went out and purchased a Toshiba laptop and placed it beside Felten on the witness stand, had him run his browser-removal program, then instructed him to access a "Windows Update" screen, and press the keys *Control* and *N*.

The browser reappeared, allowing Holley to declare triumphantly that Felten had failed, once again merely hiding the browser on the desktop, not removing it, strengthening Microsoft's claim that the browser and Windows were a single integrated product. On the courthouse steps after Felten's day of testimony, David Boies borrowed from the standard Microsoft defense playbook, lamely asserting, as Felten had on the stand, that the Toshiba laptop was loaded with other programs that might have corrupted the experiment.

In defending itself against the government rebuttal witnesses, Microsoft argued that the evidence presented was flimsy. In putting forth its own rebuttal witnesses, Microsoft sought to argue that even if the court thought it enjoyed monopoly power, this power was fleeting. Thus, even if Judge Jackson disapproved of its behavior, how could a conservative Republican judge impose a draconian sentence when the free market was about to pillory Microsoft?

To demonstrate that Bill Gates's perpetual paranoia was warranted—that Microsoft's foes were indeed conspiring against him—the team's first and, according to Microsoft, most important rebuttal witness was David Colburn of America Online. With Colburn on the witness stand, Microsoft did succeed in introducing various America Online, Netscape, and Sun documents demonstrating their joint desire to slay Microsoft. If enemies circled, Microsoft was saying, then the assertion that it was a monopoly crumbled. However, Microsoft stumbled because their lawyers failed to impeach Colburn's credibility or to demonstrate that he was a co-conspirator. This was partly because the cowboy-booted Colburn was more droll and less arrogant on the stand than he had been earlier, and partly because key strategic decisions were made above his pay grade. Colburn couldn't very well explain evidence Microsoft gleefully entered into the record when he had never before seen it. Microsoft fell short of its goals for this witness for a now familiar reason: flabby lawyering. No one seemed to sit down, vet the questions, and decide in a hardheaded way the narrative they hoped to present and the three or four key points they aimed to plaster onto Judge Jackson's—and the media's—brain. It was almost as if Microsoft had given up on this court and was squirreling away a bag of facts for an appeal.

John Warden, who conducted the examination of Colburn, offered a baffling chart containing numerous dates leading up to the November 1998 announcement that America Online was acquiring Netscape. He produced e-mail from CEO Steve Case in which Case wondered whether they should replace Microsoft's browser and e-mail from America Online president Robert Pittman in which he asserted that this would be a mistake. He produced AOL e-mail suggesting that prior to announcing a marriage with Netscape, AOL rushed to announce they were renewing Microsoft's browser so as not to undermine the government's claim that Microsoft was a monopolist. He produced e-mail from Case and from his public-relations advisers, as well as accounts of meetings on various unconnected topics. He produced memos from America Online executives he couldn't identify and memos he couldn't certify were sent because they were marked "draft." Watching Warden read his notes, an America Online lawyer in the courtroom whispered, "He signals his punches ten to fifteen minutes in advance." Each and every fact was treated equally, with little attempt made to tell a story or to elevate certain key facts. Warden's cross-examination by checklist induced stupor this first day. By 12:20 P.M., Judge Jackson, like more than one scribe, was asleep, his large head tilted down and resting on his robes. Warden, his eyes fixed on the lectern and his list of questions, hadn't noticed. A slip passed from a fellow Microsoft lawyer prompted Warden to look up and suddenly suggest, "Would this be a good time to break for lunch, Your Honor?" At the lunch break, a Microsoft attorney promised they would hammer Colburn in the afternoon session.

But after another hour of Warden asking Colburn about documents he was ignorant of, after the judge had admonished Warden for trying to introduce a document that had no names or dates and was, in Jackson's words, "just a free-floating document that doesn't prove anything," at about 3 P.M. Jackson summoned the lawyers to the bench and asked Warden to speed up his questions. "Let's get him off the stand today," Jackson admonished.

Warden replied that no witness was scheduled to appear the next day, and Jackson answered, "You don't have to kill time for me." Microsoft lawyers smiled deferentially, but they were shocked, since they had always expected to have Colburn on the stand for two days. They were even more shocked when Boies declined to cross-examine Colburn, satisfied that Microsoft had neutered its own witness.

"I don't understand then, or now, why they put him on the witness stand," Boies later told me. He still defended Warden, insisting that he would have performed superbly had he been able to escape Coach

Neukom's law-by-committee approach. Nonsense, snapped Michael Lacovara, who told me Neukom was "letting the trial lawyers try the case." Wherever the onus of blame resided, Boies observed that Microsoft's lawyers had failed: "What a lawyer is supposed to do is make good points and avoid damaging mistakes. Of these two, particularly for a defendant, the latter is more important than the former." Microsoft, he shrugged, did neither.

Nor did Microsoft score with its two remaining rebuttal witnesses. Software executive Gordon E. Eubanks, Jr., contended that the "PC-centric" world dominated by Microsoft was ending, replaced by a plethora of new platforms, particularly by programs that run on the Internet's browser platforms. Thus, the applications roadblock cited by Dr. Fisher and others was nonexistent. "The platform of choice for development is shifting" from Windows to Internet browsers, he said. This was bad news for Microsoft, except in this courtroom. The problem with this argument was that it was—like the government's assertion that Microsoft had retarded innovation—easier to assert than prove. Actually, Boies later told the press, "He made our point—the importance of the browser—and Microsoft's use of its monopoly power to protect its operating-system monopoly and to extend its monopoly into Internet software."

The final rebuttal witness, Dr. Richard Schmalensee, was questioned this time by Michael Lacovara rather than by Richard Urowsky. Lacovara is "better on his feet," and Urowsky is better at the kind of structured arguments one makes before a court of appeals, Schmalensee later explained. Left unsaid was that Neukom believed Urowsky was a red flag to Judge Jackson, since they had tangled in December 1997, and it was better to keep them apart. Off the witness stand, Schmalensee had a nuanced understanding of the gray areas of antitrust law and discussed how software companies were not exempt from antitrust laws and why regulators had to be ever vigilant. The weakest part of Microsoft's case, he told me, was its claim that Windows was not a monopoly. On the witness stand, Schmalensee came off as a $250,000 gun for hire, which is what he was paid, as his rebuttal testimony painted the issues in black and white. No, there was no consumer harm, he said. There was no Windows monopoly. There was competition among browsers. There was competition today. And there would be competition tomorrow in non-PC devices.

When Schmalensee had finished, on June 24, Judge Jackson brought his gavel down on a trial that had occupied 78 court days, 13,466 pages of trial transcript, 2,695 trial exhibits from three million documents collected, and 1,815 pages of written direct testimony. Jackson announced that he was directing each side to prepare by August 10 a brief specifying what they believed to be the incontrovertible facts of this case. After studying each other's briefs, by September 10 they were to submit their revised Findings of Fact briefs. Then, on September 21, the lawyers were to appear in his court to make their closing arguments, and at some undetermined date he would issue his Findings of Fact ruling. This would be followed, some months later, by his Conclusions of Law. He looked down from the bench and bequeathed a smile to the lawyers. "All right, gentlemen. It has been almost all pure pleasure up to this point. Let's keep it that way."

That evening, reporters invited both sides to the M & S Grill, the members of the press dividing the tab among themselves. This was not like the O. J. Simpson trial, during which opposing counsels often had to be kept apart. On Thursday nights at the end of each week the trial was in session, reporters had usually gathered upstairs at the District Chop House and Brewery on Seventh Street for drinks and hamburgers, and sometimes a game of pool, a Dutch-treat event attended by Boies and lawyers and press representatives for Justice, Microsoft, and the states, though never by Bill Neukom or Joel Klein. The lawyers also frequently chatted informally in the courthouse corridors or on the front steps.

On this particular evening near the end of the trial, there was an almost celebratory air. Lawyers drank and ate and swapped jokes and congratulations, triggering asides from Bill Neukom that they—and maybe the scribes—suffered from the Stockholm syndrome. Most of the lawyers were far from their homes and families. Phillip Malone, who heads Justice's San Francisco office, said that from October 1998 to mid-February 1999 he had been home only once; Bill Neukom and the Microsoft lawyers got home more often, but many of their weekends were spent in D.C. What happens in long cases, said Boies, "is that the only people you can talk to about the case is maybe your wife, if you're lucky, and the attorneys on the other side. . . . They know what you're going through, and you know what they're going through. It's like generals in a war." Added Boies, "I almost never had a case where I didn't like the other side. Part of it is liking people, part of it is good business."

Around the time the trial adjourned, Bill Gates was invited to appear before Congress's Joint Economic Committee to talk about the future of the Information Age. A year earlier, after testifying matter-of-factly before the Judiciary Committee while flanked by his adversaries, he had rushed from the hearing room. Not this day; Gates was no longer the same thumb-in-your-eye rebel who openly disdained Washington politics. With his hair neatly parted, he replied graciously to even the dimmest questions. "You've raised an interesting issue," he said repeatedly, and then he worked the room, bestowing friendly handshakes on senators. It was as if Gates now understood that Microsoft, like the software that had made him rich, needed an upgrade.

CHAPTER 16

The Trial Pauses,
the Planet Doesn't

T HE COMBATANTS did not gather in court again for three months, nor did they meet privately again to explore a settlement until November 18. Willfully, Gates and Microsoft strove to ignore the courtroom noise and the advisers who cautioned them to slow down, to avoid any hint of arrogance. For Bill Gates, government still wasn't the main menace; becoming a meek, enfeebled giant was the greater danger. So he hit the accelerator.

In July 1999, Microsoft announced that it was going to continue to bundle new software features into Windows. When a new consumer version of Windows, named Millennium, was introduced, new applications would be included: users would be able to scan, play, and store digital music files, a feature that would attack Rob Glaser's RealNetworks; another application would make it easier to scan and exchange photographs; another would connect multiple users in one home. In August, Microsoft announced that it would soon ship its long-awaited ClearType application in a software package it called Microsoft Reader; the company said it would be available for Windows-based PCs and laptops. To compete more rigorously with Priceline.com's hotel-reservation service, Microsoft announced in September that its Expedia travel site would incorporate the same reverse-auction system.

From late spring through the fall of 1999, Microsoft announced a raft of deals and alliances. In addition to its five-billion-dollar investment in AT&T, Microsoft, together with Hicks, Muse, Tate & Furst and other investment firms, put five hundred million dollars into Teligent, a company that uses advanced wireless technology to offer business customers voice, video, and data communications services and access to the Internet; by making this investment in Teligent, Microsoft was partnered with Nippon Telegraph and Telephone of Japan, the world's largest phone company. This partnership flowered as Microsoft then aligned with NTT's own DoCoMo, Japan's leading wireless carrier. In September, Steve Ballmer announced a joint venture to provide voice, video, data, and Internet transmission over a fiber-optic network linking Japan, China, Hong Kong, Taiwan, South Korea, Singapore, the Philippines, and Malaysia. In Brazil, Microsoft spent $126 million to purchase an 11 percent stake in that country's dominant cable-television company, Globo Cabo SA. In Europe, in addition to the three cable companies it part-owned in England, Microsoft bought a three-hundred-million-dollar stake in the continent's second-largest cable company, United Pan-Europe Communications, with cable access to twelve nations.

To gain a foothold in businesses where it was weak, Microsoft invested $1.3 billion of its stock to acquire the Visio Corporation, a leader in business-productivity software that allowed users to create diagrams, flow charts, and technical drawings. Coupled with its investment in WebTV, which is designed to bring the Internet to TV sets, Microsoft purchased 7.5 percent of Thomson Multimedia, whose corporate parent was the European manufacturer of RCA television sets; in a joint venture, they would create e-TVs, which would use Windows CE to produce interactive television. In addition, Thomson would sell Microsoft's WebTV boxes. To further improve its interactive and e-commerce efforts with television, Microsoft invested thirty million dollars in Wink Communications, a leader in developing interactive TV. To gain more direct exposure to consumers and to boost MSN in its flagging efforts to catch AOL, Microsoft invested one hundred million dollars in RadioShack.com and an unspecified amount to fix up seven thousand RadioShack stores so that each would feature a Microsoft "store," promoting such products as MSN Internet access, WebTV, and Windows CE handheld devices.

Despite the government lawsuit, between January 12, 1998, and November 11, 1999, Microsoft acquired or invested in a total of sixty-three companies, an average of more than one deal every twelve days. And this pace had accelerated throughout 1999, when Microsoft did a total of fifty-three deals, averaging one a week. While Microsoft dug into its pockets, its earnings continued to bulge, climbing faster than Wall Street analysts had projected, driving its stock price up and providing still more money to spend.

Scott McNealy carries in his briefcase a printout of these Microsoft investments he retrieved from Microsoft's investor-relations website. Over a turkey sandwich and potato chips in late 1999, he went down the list and expressed alarm. "Every one of those companies there is either a potential customer of mine, a supplier, or a platform partner that would write applications to my platform. Every one of them! Thomson. Hotmail. AT&T. Comcast. Rogers. Time Warner Roadrunner. These are not little customers. My worry is that they buy Microsoft products to keep their shareholder happy, not the best product to keep the customer happy. If Rockefeller had been allowed to buy twenty percent of the gas stations in the world, wouldn't that have been a problem for Shell?" Microsoft, he said, is "using its monopoly" in Windows and Office "to generate an immense amount of monopoly profits" and then employing that cash, plus "exclusionary contracts," plus "predatory and differentiable pricing policies, to leverage their products and technologies and services into other marketplaces—like servers, like appliances, like website services, whatever. . . . We launched Java initially to go after the set top–box market. Name one cable company that Microsoft doesn't have major equity influence on. They're pushing Windows CE, and the set-top box is one of the choke points. The next area we went after was wireless—Nokia, Motorola, all the rest of them. We just signed up NTT DoCoMo. We're going to put Java in about twenty-three million high-mode phones. Yet Microsoft just went out and did a huge joint venture with NTT DoCoMo. . . . We throw product and technology that we've invented to make things happen. They throw money at them."

In any resolution of the Microsoft case, McNealy wanted to ban Microsoft from investing its stockpile of profits in the intellectual property produced by others and from buying a stake in additional communications companies. Bill Joy, Chief Scientist for Sun Microsystems, invokes the rhetoric of those who impute only devious motives to

Microsoft's maneuvers: "You know what Machiavelli said about foreign lands: you either take it over, or you destroy it. That's Microsoft."

The software giant further enflamed the paranoia of enemies such as Joy and McNealy, who are convinced Microsoft is an untamed beast, by exponentially boosting their political giving. Microsoft's gifts to Republicans, which totaled just $60,000 in 1997, zoomed to $470,000 in 1998, reported *The New York Times*, and its lobbying budget nearly doubled to $3.7 million. By 1999, Microsoft's lobbying effort cost $4.7 million, and its political gifts to Republicans climbed to $866,548, with another $836,110 earmarked for supportive Democrats. A company that once proclaimed its political naïveté as a virtue now played the kind of political hardball long practiced by such corporations as Philip Morris or the telephone companies. Microsoft fielded an all-star team of consultants and lobbyists—including two former ranking officials of the Justice Department's antitrust division, plus an array of Democrats and Republicans—and was not shy about using strong-arm tactics.

Starting in the summer of 1999, Microsoft instructed its army of lobbyists to persuade Congress to slash nine million dollars from the Clinton administration's proposed antitrust-division budget. Even before Judge Jackson ruled whether Microsoft was guilty, Microsoft was trying to punish the agency it was fighting in court. At the same time, Microsoft surreptitiously funded nonprofit groups, *The New York Times* reported, that reached a supposedly independent recommendation that Congress should hack away at the Antitrust Division. "It's below the belt," Joel Klein told me. "We've sued American Airlines, General Electric, Archer Daniels Midland. They never did that. The proper forum is a courtroom. There was a time during the budget debate when I thought I'd have to furlough all my people for three weeks. If they're doing this in the light of day, what's going on in private?" Microsoft defended its actions as an attempt, in the words of Jack Krumholz, Director of Federal Government Affairs, "to call attention" to "inappropriate behavior by the government"—Justice leaked stories to the press, they said, and urged other nations to bring similar antitrust suits against Microsoft—and to inappropriate behavior by a handful of self-interested companies who induced the government "to start a taxpayer-funded lawsuit on behalf of Microsoft's business competitors." Microsoft also said it was simply exercising its constitutional right of free speech.

Again, Microsoft was being proactive, but at what cost? In the end, the budget effort fizzled, but it furthered blackened Gates's and Microsoft's reputations as bullies and brats, which begged this question: how could experienced Washington insiders have allowed Microsoft to make such a dumb political move? Or was this another puzzling incident—as was Bill Gates's awful deposition—that was, in David Boies's words, "client driven"? Was Gates somehow out of control? There are no black boxes to provide conclusive answers, as there often are in airplane crashes, but of this much Steve Case is certain: "Microsoft is so focused on protecting their businesses that they're not enough focused on the impact they have on other companies, other industries, and society at large." While it is true that all companies seek to use leverage, Case continued, "the bigger and more powerful you are the less leverage you should use. It requires enormous self-restraint. The notion that other companies do this misses the point. If you're the dominant player in, basically, an essential facility for PCs, which are increasingly becoming the nervous system of our society, and you control ninety-plus percent of them and how you build and integrate things into that will have a dramatic impact . . . it's a different thing. I don't believe Bill Gates's only job is to build shareholder value. Building a company and a culture that lives on even after he or others move on, making sure that you have a positive impact on society, that there's a legacy of not just what your stock price was but how it improves people's lives."

Case's piety might be more credible had he not sometimes done precisely what he accused Microsoft of doing. Despite AOL's criticism of Microsoft for trying to operate a closed system and subverting competitors, in July AOL took steps to protect its dominant Instant Messenger system. At the time, AOL was fielding more mail than the U.S. Postal Service—an estimated 780 million e-mails daily, about half of them instant messages. And worldwide, AOL's purchase of ICQ, an Israeli instant-messaging company for a more technically sophisticated customer, gave it more than seventy million users. AOL walled itself off from instant messages sent by Microsoft and Yahoo! customers who weren't AOL subscribers. Unlike e-mail, which waits in a recipient's mailbox until it is opened, instant messages immediately pop up on the user's screen. Microsoft and Yahoo! had tried to use software that tapped into the AOL servers that process and distribute the messages, thus permitting customers to communicate instantly with any of AOL's then eighteen million subscribers. When they did this, AOL responded by rewriting its software to once again block their messages. At that point, Yahoo! abandoned its efforts, but Microsoft persisted by rewriting its own software, to no avail. It was as if AOL were saying that callers who use AT&T could not talk to customers of WorldCom or Sprint. AOL complained, with a modicum of merit, that Microsoft and Yahoo! might open the system to hackers by asking customers to type in their user names and passwords and, in any case, were slyly trying to steal their customers. But even were there no security concerns, no doubt AOL, with a Microsoft-like 90 percent market share of instant messaging, would oppose the efforts of an industrywide consortium to devise a universal standard for instant messaging. AOL, like Microsoft, was protecting its dominant position and extolling open systems only when it didn't control them.

Given Microsoft's still anemic MSN, which had only two million customers, one expected Microsoft to use its deep pockets and dramatically underprice AOL by offering Internet access at a far cheaper rate than AOL's $21.95 per month. This might pose a real threat to AOL, since three quarters of its five billion dollars in 1999 revenues derived from its monthly subscription charge. But AOL had nothing to fear, for Microsoft raised its price. And with a base, by autumn, of nineteen million subscribers—soon to grow to twenty-four million—Steve Case enjoyed many advantages. "We have so many customers that we can beta-test and determine what people like," said Case. Of course, endless pretesting guarantees nothing, as any TV market researcher could attest. Nevertheless, those with access to a large pool of customers can in the long run make somewhat better guesses than can others.

And guessing is commonplace among companies that strive to divine what customers want. Case's deputy, Robert Pittman, said he worried about threats "that come out of left field. The broadcasting industry was concerned with cable. They worried about their piece of the pie. But for the first time the pie has shrunk and fewer people are watching TV. We're competing with people's leisure time. The competition is not MSN. The competition is time and what claims it." Nathan Myhrvold of Microsoft, by contrast, worried about AOL: "They want to be the next Microsoft. Their goal is for AOL to be the most important thing on your computer or any device. At the moment, the most important thing on the PC is Windows, for that's your ramp to everything else. That's what makes your hardware work, and that's your ramp to the Internet."

AOL and Microsoft had stakes in an even more momentous battle that heated up in 1999: high-speed, broadband cable access to customers. With its acquisition of John Malone's TCI, AT&T now owned the nation's second-largest cable company, and in what Malone characterized as "the scent gland" of the deal, the telephone giant became the largest shareholder in @Home, the cable-modem company. Because the cable wire is what is called a "fat pipe," once they invested to upgrade this cable then digital data and video can be transported over it at speeds variously estimated at from eleven to two hundred times faster than with a regular 56K telephone modem; there were no interminable waits to be connected to the Internet—it was like getting an instant dial tone, and video on the PC looked as it does on a TV, not like it was running in slow motion. Other cable companies were also investors in @Home or in Time Warner's cable-modem company, Roadrunner (as was Microsoft). At the same time, the Baby Bells rushed to perfect their own version of high-speed modems, using DSL (digital subscriber lines) technology, though they then trailed the cable modems and initially charged about eighty dollars per month rather than about forty. High-speed fiber-optic wires provided the highest speeds and were being pushed by a consortium of electric-utility companies but were expensive to install. Satellite and wireless modems were a tomorrow product; cable modems and DSL lines were today. By early December 1999, @Home reported that it had one million subscribers, nearly five times as many as it had had a year earlier.

If the buzz in, say, 1993 was that the killer app would be five hundred cable channels and interactive TV (not the interactive Internet), and in 1994 that Apple's handheld Newton would be the new, new thing, and in 1995 that the cable gatekeeper model was passé and that content was king, and in 1997 that high-definition TV would be a killer app, and in 1998 that Iridium satellites would provide wireless-phone service anywhere in the world, by 1999 cable broadband was the latest rage. Broadband Internet access was *projected* to rocket from 0.6 million American households in 1998 to 22 million in 2003, according to Forrester Research. Distribution was king, it was said. From December 1998 to December 1999, a total of $135 billion was spent on broadband acquisitions and investments, according to the industry newsletter *Broadband Daily*. Communications companies scrambled to invest, including Microsoft, America Online, telephone companies, cable companies, broadcast satellite companies, and Motorola. Case worried about Microsoft and AT&T, but he wasn't sure the world's largest media company, Time Warner, was a force to be reckoned with. He admired their assets but told me in the fall of 1999: "As relates to the Internet, they've been missing in action. They're also a company whose strength is their Achilles' heel. They run a remarkable decentralized company, where the head of each company operates as if he's running his own independent company. It has been a good model, but as the Internet drives convergence between the TV and PC, that model won't work as well when you need to move fast and coordinate to find synergies."

There was palpable fear that fall that the cable industry could become the Internet's gatekeeper. America Online and more than a few consumer-advocacy groups complained that AT&T and Time Warner would try to revive the cable model by creating a tollbooth to control Internet access, favoring their own content services and charging steep fees to fledging ISPs and ICPs. For consumers, the promise of "end to end" democratic access to the Internet would be blighted if they had to pay an expensive toll and were then routed to cable-programming choices, not their choices (as already AOL users were routed to AOL's choices). For AOL, the danger was that AT&T threatened to supplant them as the gateway to the Internet; the home page would be AT&T's, not AOL's, and thus more advertising dollars would flow to AT&T. Steve Case did not need big ears to hear cable executives, including Time Warner CEO Gerald Levin, clucking that their initial customers were abandoning AOL. George Bell, the president of Excite@Home, told me in September 1999 that when his cable-modem customers were offered broadband Internet access, 40 percent of them dropped AOL. Why pay $21.95 per month for AOL on top of the $40 for the cable modem when the cable modem offered most features found on AOL? Case feared AOL would be reduced to a superfluous middleman.

Joined by a broad coalition of consumer groups, America Online fought back, demanding first that the federal government require the same open access to the cable wire as is required of the local telephone wire. Then, when the federal government said it was too early to impose regulations on this nascent technology, America Online and consumer groups forged an organization, the openNET Coalition, to lobby local governments. They started in Portland, Oregon, urging regulators to step into the breach and demand that for a nominal fee the wire be open to all. "Do you want the Internet, which is this unbelievable case study for free-market competition, to be like the cable industry, where John Malone decided what kind of cable box you had?" asked Steve Case in October 1999. Case wanted government—he would prefer the federal government, he told me, but if need be he would take any government willing—"to step in as an arbitrator to broker some agreements as to openness. We're not asking for free access. Whatever deal AT&T cut with @Home we'll take." AT&T and Time Warner and the rest of the cable industry insisted that they wouldn't spend the billions required to upgrade the cable pipe unless they could be assured a fair return on their investment, which they said would never happen if ISPs such as AOL paid only a modest sum and were allowed to dominate.

The real question, insisted Steve Case, was whether AT&T thought of itself as a communications (transport) or a content company. No, the real question, insisted AT&T CEO Michael Armstrong, was not whether AT&T would share the opening screen with AOL (it would, as it does with local cable companies) but whether AT&T got a fair return for its huge investment. AT&T assured the government it was a content-neutral "facilitator" for consumers; it said it was merely a network company, whether a consumer wanted to make a phone call or connect to the Internet. "We are the connection broker for consumers," John Petrillo, Senior Vice President–Strategy for AT&T, told me in the fall of 1999. "That puts you in the position of not wanting to compete with your business customers who want to reach the same consumers." But AT&T *was* competing with AOL.

Both the AOL and AT&T approaches suffered from fuzziness, John Malone told me in November 1999, for neither addressed the real core question. Malone, who is AT&T's largest outside shareholder, said the key question was this: "Whose customer is it? If AT&T charges thirty"— or forty—"dollars per month, it's AT&T's customer." Permit AOL or another ISP to claim the customer, and "AT&T is just a dumb pipe," a wholesaler not a retailer. "If Steve Case can achieve that, his market cap will blow right by Bill Gates. What it does is turn AT&T into a common carrier. The fight is really a commercial fight over who owns the customer. Who's a wholesaler, and who's a retailer? That's a fight cable cannot afford to lose." What Malone wanted was for AOL to agree to be the primary portal site on AT&T's cable systems but not an ISP.

Another question asked in the summer and fall of 1999 was whether

America Online and AT&T could patch up their differences by forging a long-term business alliance. AT&T had been jolted when a once puny Mississippi-based telephone company, WorldCom, acquired MCI in 1998 and then announced in the fall of 1999 that it would merge with Sprint. Suddenly, the dominant long-distance company was confronted by a colossus that nearly matched it in long-distance business (which was on the decline) and, worse, exceeded it in wireless and Internet-backbone connections. AOL felt much more vulnerable to losing broadband access in October, after Sprint announced that it was joining the MCI/WorldCom fold and that the merged company would rely on building DSL and wireless broadband connections.* At the same time, the Baby Bells continued to consolidate and advance their own DSL ventures. America Online wrestled with whether it should make its own bid for Sprint, said Miles Gilburne, their chief strategist. But the more America Online talked, the more it realized that three broadband channels would compete: cable, the telephone wire, and wireless. With a powerful brand name and access to nineteen million customers, Gilburne told me in October, "We bring something to a telephone company. We provide a communications service. So our ability to sell a telephone-company service to our customers is huge." America Online could choose to ally with WorldCom, on the board of which Steve Case once served, or AT&T, or the Baby Bells. Or none, he said.

John Petrillo saw America Online's situation differently. He thought it had an "opportunity to be the premier interactive information/entertainment service in the U.S." The problem was that their "business model is predicated on having a proprietary, sealed system. . . . They sell the convenience of organized content services for the average consumer integrated with an Internet-access subscription service. What happens when they need to go to broadband?" Their business model is disrupted. Where AOL offers subscribers access to the Internet, cable companies such as AT&T and Time Warner sell something AOL can't offer: broadband access. And they sell it at cheaper monthly prices. If AOL switches emphasis and presents itself as a company that charges only for content, how do they compete with companies such as Yahoo!, to which access is free? There was a way for America Online to extricate itself from this

---

*Confronted by regulatory opposition, WorldCom was compelled in 2000 to withdraw from its proposed marriage to Sprint.

trap, he thought, and it could help extricate AT&T from its own dangerous dependence on a shrinking long-distance telephone business. If
America Online and AT&T partnered, he said, America Online could
cede its fast-growing long-distance Internet-telephone business to AT&T
and could agree to use the AT&T brand to connect its customers to the
Internet; in turn, AT&T would agree to use the AOL brand for content
and to provide AOL broadband access to the Internet.

The companies were left to ponder their next moves and to wonder
whether the speed-of-light changes meant that customers would
become competitors and competitors allies and that industries were
converging so rapidly that it was now meaningless to call AT&T a long-
distance telephone company or AOL an ISP or Microsoft a software and
IBM a hardware and Time Warner a content company. AT&T had
morphed into a cable-TV and an Internet-access and a local telephone
and a cellular and pager and portal and content company, as well as a
long-distance company. America Online was an ISP and a portal but
also a broadcast and a cyberspace real-estate baron and an e-commerce
and a content and a telephone company. IBM was an eighty-two-
billion-dollar hardware and software colossus, but its growth was pro-
pelled by services, including e-commerce, which accounted for $23.4
billion in sales and 17 percent of its profits at the end of 1998.
Microsoft was in software but also in cable and telephone and film animation and electronic publishing and access and e-commerce, and it
was competing with Sony in the game business. America Online was
Microsoft's foe, but not all the time. For example, AOL relied on its folder
on the Windows desktop to attract customers and on Microsoft's
browser to navigate the Internet. "It's a little like global politics. The
way the U.S. and China coexist," observed Steve Case. "You may not
agree on many things, but you've got to co-exist even if you fundamentally mistrust each other."

Even with a scorecard, it was confusing. Although Paul Allen had
claimed a seat at the cable-industry table when his Charter Communications spent massively to become one of the nation's five largest cable companies, in the fall of 1999 he expended another $1.65 billion to increase
his stake in a cable-industry nemesis, RCN. RCN does not accept, as do its
brethren, that cable companies should abide by a nineteenth-century
European balance-of-power model and divide spheres of influence
among various cable nation-states. RCN invaded these spheres and

aggressively added a second and usually more sophisticated cable option to many communities.

Paul Allen's maneuver complicated an already confusing scene, which became still more confusing when cable Goliath Viacom and broadcast Goliath CBS, which had long battled for audience, that fall announced a merger. AT&T, which in two years invested a staggering $120 billion in cable companies and billions more on upgrading cable wires for high-speed Internet access, nevertheless announced in September 1999 that in seventeen markets throughout the country where it does not own a cable wire it would invest in the rival DSL technology for business customers. AOL announced in November that it would help Blockbuster build a website, and toward this end took a 3 percent stake in Blockbuster.com. A week later, it came to light that AOL and other Internet-service companies, who customarily boast of how they have siphoned viewers from TV broadcasters, were intensely lobbying Congress to amend legislation so that they could carry the signals of local TV stations over the Internet. Sony, which traditionally sold itself as a hardware company that manufactures consumer electronics, had by late 1999 invested in TiVo, which produces digital devices that store TV programs on a hard drive instead of a videocassette; Sony could use this technology as a platform to promote its TV programs and films. And Sony's PlayStation 2, scheduled to go on sale in the United States in 2000, could, as already noted, with its powerful 128-bit chips anchor a Sony home network, controlling all other electronic devices in the home, as well as playing movies and music.

Those vying to become cyberbarons often liken their strategic moves to games. Sun's Scott McNealy compares what he does to the board game Risk. The aim of any company, he said, "is to accumulate the biggest pile of marbles" in order to attack and overwhelm competitors, as in the game. Steve Case compares the contest to a marathon rather than a sprint. John Petrillo of AT&T compares it to "three-dimensional chess, since it contemplates conscious moves you're making in anticipation of others and of changing market dynamics. This chess match has some degree of chance to it in that the rate of change is so fast one has to employ informed intuition to make moves at least part of the time." Nathan Myhrvold compares the contest to a game of stud poker—with five hundred cards to draw from, with no one knowing what hole card they'll get dealt, with a new round of betting on each card, and with no end in sight. To David Ronfeldt of the Rand Corporation, who wrote a paper on it, competing is like a stock-car race in which a car attains the greatest velocity when it moves in a pack with other cars and benefits from the aerodynamic pull, yet those who triumph not only cooperate but dare break from the pack and race ahead, even if it means betraying compatriots.

Whatever the metaphor of choice, if he or she is honest a would-be cyberbaron admits their calculus is predicated on guesswork. They are guessing, as inevitably they must, whether a cheap network computer that retrieves its software from the Internet is more viable than expensive PCs that contain their own powerful software and thus assure more user control; whether AT&T should own content or be in the transport business; whether AT&T can charge into local telephone service before the Baby Bells can charge into long distance; whether cable or telephone or fiber-optics or wireless modems will provide the best Web connections; whether Yahoo! can continue to thrive as a stand-alone portal site or must seek a merger partner; whether Amazon.com can successfully "extend its brand" from books to consumer goods; whether consumers will read enough portable e-books to make a business of it; whether technology that arms consumers with the power to block advertising will kill the force that subsidizes "free" Internet sites and broadcasting; whether a mass consumer market will watch TV on its PCs; whether the PC, like the TV, can be off the desk; whether the telephone or TV or Palm Pilot or cell phone will be popular devices for consumers to access the Internet; whether to bet on Intel chips or newer digital-signal processors (DSPs) to speed up wireless appliances; whether to bet on Microsoft or America Online or IBM. The value of "brands" is a comforting totem to many CEOs, but a sturdy brand did not spare Levi Strauss from terminating six thousand employees in North America and closing half its U.S. manufacturing plants in 1999. And "brands" can burst forth almost overnight, as happened with Amazon.com, eBay, and Yahoo!. Even those with a good track record guess wrong. In 1996, Bill Gates and Andrew Grove guessed, so far wrongly, that there would be a mass migration of consumers who would want to watch video on their PC screens. Everyone is guessing, because until consumers are offered real choices—simple-to-use Internet TV, high-definition TV at a price consumers can afford, a cheap network PC with high-speed Internet access—we can only guess what they will choose. The real game for would-be cyberbarons to play, said John Malone, is to hedge their bets by investing in many different companies and technologies and wait to see what works for consumers. "You keep the winners, and the losers you sell and take the tax deduction."

In the thick of this battle was Microsoft. In Washington, D.C., the news was that Microsoft held the new economy in a viselike grip, while in the state of Washington Steve Ballmer told analysts, "There is more competition today and stronger competition today than I think I've ever felt in my nineteen years at Microsoft."

The open-source software movement was continuing to gather strength. A principal distributor of free Linux software, Red Hat, which sold services and support to its users, floated an IPO in August 1999, and the price of its shares shot up on day one from fourteen dollars per share to fifty-two. By the end of the year, their shares jumped 1,944 percent from their opening price. The share price of another software start-up, VA Linux Systems, rocketed 698 percent on the day its stock went on sale, a record for an IPO debut. Microsoft's adversaries, as well as such allies as Dell, Compaq, and Hewlett-Packard, began making software and PCs compatible with Linux, no doubt believing Microsoft wouldn't dare retaliate during its antitrust trial. Microsoft's most important ally, Intel, which Microsoft had once persuaded so easily to abandon investments in rival software, in 1999 invested a total of $1.2 billion in 245 start-ups, many of them software companies.

Gates also saw Apple Computer's new iMac, introduced in 1998, boost Apple's share of the consumer market. And in late August, Steve Jobs announced that by 2000 the new Macs would feature a G4 microprocessor codeveloped by Apple, IBM, and Motorola that processes 128 bits of information per cycle (or hertz), in contrast to the 32 or 64 bits featured in most PCs.

In PC operating systems, Microsoft remained impregnable. After Apple with its now about 10 percent share of desktops, Microsoft's nearest OS competitors were Linux, OS/2, and Be, each with negligible market shares. Be, for instance, in the fall of 1999 ran on fewer than one hundred thousand PCs, compared with the roughly three hundred and sixty million powered by Windows worldwide. Nearly as many PCs would be sold worldwide as color TV sets, yet Gates knew that PC sales were flattening. While Microsoft reported that worldwide PC sales were

red-hot, jumping 17 percent in fiscal 1998 to eighty-four million personal computers sold and rising 14 percent in 1999, for 2000 it projected sales would grow by half that rate. That is still nothing to sneeze
at, but PC prices were dropping, and as they fell so did profit margins.
The PC was now a mature industry, and consumers were migrating to
other devices. And Gates worried as always about the middleware
threat.

Now, Gates saw America Online as his most imposing rival. Now that
it owned Netscape, he believed it would soon dump Microsoft's browser
and substitute its own. This was no minor matter, since by Microsoft's
reckoning AOL customers accounted for one third of Microsoft's
browser market share. Gates believed AOL had its guns aimed at a larger
target, at attacking Microsoft's operating systems for PCs and corporate
intranets and all other devices. Then, if AOL/Netscape/Sun could forge
an alternative operating system, AOL could replace Microsoft as the de
facto environment for each PC. Gates saw other threats, including powerful IBM, which was adopting Linux and bundling it on its servers and
PCs as an alternative operating system. Gates worried as well about
IBM's quiet but still powerful twelve-billion-dollar software business and
about how IBM was nurturing an array of small start-ups and assisting
major corporations, making them dependent on Big Blue rather than on
Microsoft.

Bill Gates worried as well about new platforms, new inflection points,
such as server rather than PC-based software. He worried that rival Sun
Microsystems had purchased a business-software company—StarOf-
fice—and begun to offer various applications—from word processing to
spreadsheets to e-mail—off the Internet. Although the software would
be free, Sun would make money because increased traffic would require
the use of powerful PC servers that are Sun's specialty. This move was
consistent with Sun's conviction that the PC of the future would be
cheap and would draw its software from "the sky," storing its data on
powerful servers; by contrast, Bill Gates argued that users would never
cede control to a network that might experience delays or busy signals
and would instead prefer to have more power under the hood.

Gates worried that Microsoft had repeatedly failed to achieve critical
mass with MSN, and he fretted that it would slip even farther behind its
two main rivals. He watched as AOL and Yahoo! announced alliances in
late 1999 with two of America's dominant retail-store chains, Wal-
Mart and Kmart, respectively. Each would promote the other's products

and brands, hopefully driving Wal-Mart or Kmart customers to shop online and AOL and Yahoo! users to shop at these retailers. Microsoft appeared to be collecting crumbs when, just days after these alliances were announced, it revealed that it would invest two hundred million dollars in the much smaller Best Buy.

Gates also worried about Windows CE, which had a mere 15 percent market share in the fall of 1999. Nor was Microsoft more successful in the cellular-phone market. Gates paid attention when the Palm Computing division of 3Com and Symbian, a consortium of the major wireless-phone makers, announced a joint venture: they would spurn Microsoft's Windows CE and instead combine the Palm and Symbian operating systems for wireless access to the Internet. Even Microsoft's longtime ally Intel announced it was manufacturing non-PC Internet appliances that ran on Linux. "Our relationship with Microsoft is very strong in the PC business," Claude Leglise, the general manager of Intel's home-products division, told *The Wall Street Journal*. "In the new market, we are agnostic."

Sensing that they were slipping, Gates and Ballmer began to preach a new religion with the fervor of converts. If the advent of the microprocessor was an inflection point and the Internet browser was another, they were now at another fundamental shift, what Paul Maritz called "the commoditization of communications through the Internet." Software was no longer proprietary; it was now a service, one that empowered individuals to customize websites and act as if they had a new sidekick, an intelligent robot that would pay bills, calculate taxes, access and communicate their schedules, assemble research, screen phone calls, order groceries or movie tickets, and dispatch digital pictures to family and friends.

Software made possible what Ballmer, in one of several 1999 speeches that were designed to raise his profile, referred to as "marketplace services. The Internet is not just a place for a manufacturer to talk to a customer, for a supplier to talk to a manufacturer, for a reseller to talk to a customer or a manufacturer. The Internet is a place where you can really bring together marketplaces where consumers and dealers and manufacturers and suppliers can all interact." Exhibit A in Ballmer's catalog—the "most profound thing that we're doing," he said in a September 20 presentation—was a joint venture launched by Microsoft and the Ford Motor Company to improve CarPoint. Started just over four years earlier by Microsoft, CarPoint matched consumers and car dealers, becoming the foremost car-sales site on the Internet, generating an estimated six hundred million dollars per month. The new CarPoint, Ballmer said, would allow the customer to talk directly to the manufacturer online, eliminating what Ballmer estimated would be 25 to 30 percent of the costs stemming from the "inefficiencies" of the supply chain by instead building made-to-order cars. Ford was the first car manufacturer to invest in this product-neutral site.

CarPoint was an example of how Microsoft would sell services as utility companies sell electricity. It would sell relationships. The software was seen as an enabler, a tool consumers would shape, not an immutable product handed down and controlled by Microsoft. It would be open, dependent on the collective Internet, not on a single box dominated by Windows. Microsoft began to speak of a "Personal Web" and an "Everyday Web," where services such as CarPoint were commonplace. A prime vehicle to achieve this connection, it hoped, would be MSN, through which consumers would connect to various services—from making travel arrangements to shopping for clothes to using bCentral, their consultant service for small businesses, to using the MSN search engine to locate whatever else they wanted on the Web. IBM might have been quicker to spot the service market and Sun to spot the server market, but Microsoft was determined to dethrone them.

But while Sun's Scott McNealy envisioned a post-PC world, Gates did not. In a keynote address at the COMDEX/Fall '99 gathering, he envisioned that "the PC will be a server, it will be the place that you store lots of information, it will be the place you create and edit documents." Gates believed the PC would remain central because it assured more control and reliability than did distant servers and dumb boxes, but he thought other devices would be used as well to access the Internet at any time and from any place. Gates sketched his vision of software as a service in a keynote address to the Consumer Electronics Show in Las Vegas. The Bill Gates house of today, he suggested, would be America's tomorrow:

> In your pocket, you'll have a screen phone, or a handheld game, or a personal information manager. Some of those will be purpose-built, and they'll only do that one thing. Others will be every one of those things, and some will have an add-on capability so, say, you could put a little camera module on and take your pocket PC and turn it into a great still or motion-picture camera. Because it's digital, because it's software driven, that kind of add-on flexibility will be characteristic of most of these new gadgets. We'll have big-screen devices because

they'll be in the den, the living room, we'll think of those like the TV, multiple people able to watch, able to play games together. . . . You'll be able to be notified that your kids upstairs are crying in their room or that somebody is at the door right there on that screen. Your buddy list that today you think of mostly as an online PC thing, you'll be able to see, if you've enabled it the right way, who is watching the same shows. If you want to chat with them by typing or talking as you're watching those shows. . . . The desktop screen, the screen you sit close to, whether it's the portable PC or a classic PC, that will be important if you're doing homework, doing work at home, anything that requires that kind of close screen creativity. . . . But even things like the washing machine, when it's done with a task, it will be able to send a notification across the AC power and show up on any of these different screens. Any of the speakers in the house will in the future have digital wireless connections, so any music you select you can take that little screen device, select what you want, know where you are, and that music will arrive.

So, the home itself will be almost like a computer system, and making it easy to know what's going on and easy to control, that is a great software problem, and one that many companies, including Microsoft, will be involved in.

What would bind these various devices together and make them work was software. Software to make TV set-top boxes interactive, to instantly retrieve movies or TV programs from *Citizen Kane* to *The Sopranos*, to download movies to PC hard drives, to surf the Internet on television sets, to download music and create a digital jukebox or a mix of favorite recording artists, to edit home videos or call up all the family photo albums, to tell refrigerators when supplies are low and to order more from the store, to control and seamlessly coordinate all the devices in the home and remotely set the thermostat on a country home, to play interactive games, to advance the portability first made possible by Gutenberg's printing press so that we can store five hundred books on a handheld e-book on which the screen is as clear and crisp as a printed page, to visit any of the world's libraries or archives without leaving home, to have one phone number follow us everywhere and to power wireless devices to access the Internet and buy and sell stocks, and to usher our cars to their destinations and to flash reminders of birthdays and anniversaries and appointments. It would be personal, controlled by each individual, becoming part of what Microsoft now referred to as "the programmable Web." Gates predicted that XML (eXtensible markup language), a relatively new computer language that tells various computer platforms how to interpret data and thus link and talk, would become the new "secret sauce" for communicating, superseding HTML, which merely told computers how to read a layout.

Gates didn't need a briefing on the dizzying velocity of change, of how change uprooted established businesses with tornadolike force. He knew that Napster, which was founded in May 1999 and facilitates the free downloading of music over the Internet, had collected twenty million customers in just one year. And its software did this not through giant libraries of central servers collecting and sending data to individual computers, which is the Web model, but through peer-to-peer computing, by allowing PC hard drives to send and receive music among themselves, thus bypassing not just the record companies but, potentially, any aspiring corporate gatekeeper. Gates remembered how Warren Buffett, whose Berkshire Hathaway owns the *World Book Encyclopedia* company, told him in the early nineties that bound encyclopedias would triumph over electronic versions because people wanted them on their shelves, because they liked the way they looked, the way they smelled. "We never could get the smell into our Internet version," Gates told attendees at the Consumer Electronics Show, "but still the digital encyclopedia outsells the printed encyclopedia ten to one." The same sudden shift was taking place in music, where he said 34 percent of college students—an advance guard of the revolution—were already downloading music off the Internet.

And if Gates still fervently believed in the PC model, he also saw a certain inevitability to the network model favored by Sun and others. As an instant Internet dial tone was offered consumers, and as handheld devices proliferated and would soon outnumber PCs, and as countless devices offered Internet access and an alternative to the PC, Microsoft's dominance would decline, though it can be only a guess when this would occur. It was time, again, to galvanize the troops, to recognize the enemy, to prepare for battle. In December 1999, Steve Ballmer announced another Microsoft reorganization to streamline the top management structure and to focus all of Microsoft's energies to "accelerate the company's vision for creating great products and services that can be accessed any time and from any device." Bill Gates's company still pushed the PC, but Gates knew that his nemesis Scott McNealy was not wrong in declaring, "The network is the computer," and he fretted that such a network was a dagger aimed at Microsoft's heart.

CHAPTER 17

Judge Jackson's "Facts"

F OR THE MOMENT, though, it was Judge Jackson's dagger that was Microsoft's gravest concern. The play was entering its final act. On August 10, 1999, Microsoft and the Justice Department and the states all filed briefs describing in excruciating detail the facts as each saw them. Microsoft's lawyers submitted a 397-page brief, a model of brevity next to Justice's 774-page tome. Each side hoped to influence Judge Jackson's Findings of Fact.

The nucleus of Microsoft's argument was that the government had failed to demonstrate either harm to consumers or to competition and that its claim that Microsoft was an impregnable monopoly was ludicrous given the new platform threats keeping Bill Gates awake nights. Microsoft gleefully reminded Jackson that the government's own chief economic witness, Dr. Franklin Fisher, when asked if Microsoft's conduct had harmed consumers, "candidly" replied, "On balance, I would think the answer was no, up to this point." Microsoft dismissed Fisher's other, more negative claims as pure speculation. What was real was that consumers got a free, technically superior browser. An applications barrier that kept software developers from working for other vendors was a paranoid fantasy. What was real, Microsoft insisted, was that at least

"12,000 firms are actively competing in the software industry" and that the browser war served the public because it spurred Internet usage. If Netscape were truly foreclosed, how did it distribute 160 million copies of its browser to consumers last year? Why was the Netscape browser used on about 40 percent of all PCs powered by Windows 98? Besides, in assuming that Microsoft was a monopoly, the government posited a ridiculously narrow definition of the marketplace, they asserted, excluding Apple's now roughly 10 percent market share, to say nothing of the new array of handheld devices and software downloaded from servers.

At its core, the government's brief rested on the assertion that Microsoft held a PC monopoly and would continue its choke-hold on account of the software applications barrier it enjoyed. Even if one believed that new platforms would gain market share, the government cited no less an authority than Bill Gates, who wrote a column in the May 31, 1999, issue of *Newsweek* asserting that for the foreseeable future the PC would continue to reign supreme. The government ran through its charges: that in order to maintain its monopoly, Microsoft was willing to sacrifice many millions to have a free browser. That it coerced companies to aid it in sabotaging Netscape and other middleware threats to its hegemony. That in hurting Netscape, Microsoft hurt consumers, because Microsoft chased away competition and therefore constricted consumer choices and also because Microsoft subverted Netscape's browser and Java by rejiggering its software code to assure that they did not run smoothly on Windows.

After a month of digesting the opposing drafts, the parties convened in court on September 21 for a final day of oral arguments. It was eleven months, almost to the day, since the trial had begun. Although the media was much more focused that day on Sammy Sosa's sixty-first home run of the season, which he had slugged over the weekend, the courtroom was packed. Assistant Attorney General Joel Klein was there with a score of Justice aides, as well as Tom Miller, the attorney general of Iowa, and the entire Microsoft legal and public-relations team, with the exception of Mark Murray, who was in southeast Asia on a long-planned holiday. Spouses of many of the lawyers were on hand. Everyone wondered whether, on this final day in court, Judge Jackson would reveal how he was leaning.

The most compelling presentation of the day was made by New York State's Stephen Houck. Houck had sat at the government table every day of the trial as the chief representative of the nineteen state attorneys general who were party to the lawsuit, but he had been heard from rarely. He had been essentially muzzled early in the trial when Judge Jackson ruled for the sake of speed that he would allow only one lawyer per witness for direct examinations, thus turning to Boies as the chief attorney. He would not permit a parallel trial in which the states would automatically conduct their own cross-examinations. Houck and the other attorneys general had been unhappy about this ruling, but Houck had cajoled the others into accepting this defeat without braying, and his humility and graceful team play made him a popular figure at the government table. His popularity climbed higher since colleagues knew that his stint as an assistant attorney general in New York was nearing its end, as his Republican boss had been defeated in the last election.

As Houck approached the small microphone at the lectern facing the judge, Jackson smiled and said, "Are you prepared to tell us how you spent your summer vacation?"

Houck chuckled—"I don't think you want to know," he said—then quickly became serious. He announced that, contrary to the claim that Information Age monopolies are fleeting, he would demonstrate how "durable" Microsoft's monopoly had been. He held up a chart showing that Microsoft had maintained a more than 90 percent market share on Intel-based PCs since 1991, that the number had remained in that range in recent years, and that it would continue to do so into the next century. And the reason it maintained this monopoly, Houck continued, was the applications barrier to entry. "There can be no doubt that Microsoft itself understood the crucial role applications have played to the success of Windows," he said, and went on to quote an e-mail from Microsoft's Brad Chase in which he warned that Netscape Navigator menaced Microsoft because it could attract its own applications. Chase wrote to colleagues, "You should worry about your browser share as much as Bill G because we will lose the Internet battle if we do not have a significant user installed base. The industry would simply ignore our standards. Few would write Window apps without the Windows user base." As for consumer harm, Houck said that Microsoft was able to price at whim, and as proof he said that although the price of an old product should go down as a new version is introduced, the price of Windows 95 actually climbed after Windows 98 appeared. Consumers are harmed when they are denied choice, Houck said, before turning to what he called "one of the most telling admissions of the entire trial"—Cameron Myhrvold's admission that Microsoft didn't want to allow ISPs a choice of browsers because it feared the majority of customers would choose Netscape.

At 10:15 A.M., Boies came to the lectern, his hair freshly cut, wearing his customary baggy blue suit, tie, striped shirt, and black sneakers. For the first time in the trial, he read from a rigid outline; his goal, he said later, was to walk through the key evidence "in as dispassionate a way as possible. Obviously, the judge looked at me as a partisan. But I wanted to perform, as much as possible, a law clerk's role." Boies dwelled on the details of the June 21, 1995, meeting between Netscape and Microsoft. This meeting peeks "into Microsoft's soul," said Boies, revealing its raw greed. Was their intent to produce better products for consumers, as Microsoft claimed, or to preserve a monopoly, as the government claimed? The true intent was to "stymie competition" by inducing Netscape to essentially abandon the browser market to Microsoft. The clues were abundant. They were found in Bill Gates's e-mails and in the e-mails from Daniel Rosen and Paul Maritz, each sketching Microsoft's scheme to commandeer Netscape's core business. There can be little question, said Boies, that Microsoft attempted to preserve its Windows monopoly and did this by bullying other companies, large and small. The real reason Microsoft eventually tied its browser to Windows, Boies reiterated, was to attack Netscape, not to improve Windows. He dwelled on Jim Allchin's e-mail and on his trial testimony. Boies recalled that after Allchin showed the court a tape of the nineteen great advantages of integrating the browser, Boies then took Allchin through each one, asking, "Could you get these same advantages" by separating the browser from Windows? In each instance, Allchin admitted the answer was yes.

After a brief lunch break, John Warden approached the lectern to read his remarks. Without citing Boies by name, he urged the court to ignore the trial's "melodrama" that sometimes "had the rapt attention of the gallery." The government had played a game of Let's Pretend and had "failed to present the evidence needed to support its claims," had failed to challenge "the central tenets" of the direct testimony of the twelve Microsoft witnesses. And "it is not just the facts that the government has disregarded. It has stubbornly disregarded the Court of Appeals decision on technological tying of the sort that's alleged here."

To disallow the tying, Warden continued, government had to prove there was no consumer benefit, and this the government had failed to do. If Microsoft was a monopoly, why did it spend so many billions each year on R and D? Why does each copy of Windows cost so little? Again, he cited the Court of Appeals decision that Microsoft's design choices should be respected as long as there is "a plausible claim" that this "brings some advantage," reminding Judge Jackson to beware: the senior court had already spoken on this crucial matter. He dismissed Microsoft's various restrictive contracts as essentially irrelevant. He dismissed the June 21 Netscape meeting as a nonevent because no agreement was ever reached and suggested that Marc Andreessen's notes describing it were "cooked" to lure the Justice Department into acting on Netscape's behalf.

The government's case, he suggested, melted like ice cream in the heat because Windows lacked "the traditional hallmarks of monopoly. There is no scarcity of the assets needed to develop operating systems: capital." Nor is there any "constraint on output," because intellectual property is not an expensively manufactured product but something that resides in an individual's brain. Nor was there a barrier to entry since the Internet offers free distribution. Thus, the very notion of monopoly was rendered obsolete by the Internet and by technology. As for the so-called applications barrier, Warden wondered, why does Sun "have a million people in its developer community . . . ? If ISVs write only for Windows, why did twenty thousand people show up at the last Java developers conference, which Sun says is the largest developers conference in the world?" Despite his refined attire and taste for upper-class British life, Warden attacked the government's claims not with a scalpel but with a cleaver, using the sort of colloquial put-downs—the charges didn't "amount to a hill of beans!"; government claims were "silly" and "pure baloney"—more commonly heard in a divorce court.

Court procedures allow the plaintiff's attorney the final word if he or she has any time remaining, and Boies had saved a half hour of his allotment for his rebuttal. He repeated the essentials of the government's case and parried Microsoft's thrusts. Consumers suffered, he said, because they were deprived of choice, were charged steeper prices, were denied innovations, and saw the performance of their PCs deliberately degraded when they chose to use Netscape's browser or Sun's Java. The claim that Microsoft's dominance was under assault from the marketplace and from new technologies, he said, was an assertion of faith, not fact. There is today no meaningful competition from handheld devices and other platforms, and therefore no proof that Microsoft's monopoly will wither. Microsoft, the government feared, would do with these new devices and the Internet what it had done with Windows: make sure that each new application would run smoothly only with a version of Windows. What Microsoft is really asking this court to do, he said, is to ignore its decade-old dominance, be patient, and trust that a competitor will emerge. Boies said that it was Microsoft that was playing the game of Let's Pretend: Let's pretend Microsoft's incriminating e-mails are just meaningless bluster. Let's pretend misleading depositions are about trying to avoid being tricked by Boies. Let's pretend Microsoft gave the browser away free because it wanted to serve consumers. Let's pretend every company does what Microsoft has done. Let's pretend meaningful competition has arrived.

Then, as if he was trying to meet the standard that strict conservative jurists such as Richard Posner, Chief Judge of the Seventh Circuit U.S. Court of Appeals in Chicago, have championed—that the laws are violated only if an economics test is applied and it can be shown that the offending company subverted competition and thus punished consumers—Boies looked at the conservative Republican judge two tiers above him and said, "What this case is about is a concerted series of steps that Microsoft took, and took with the expressed purpose and with the effect of stifling the emerging competition that Netscape and Java threatened." Believe the contemporaneous documents, he said, not what coached witnesses said in court.

Boies stepped away from the microphone. Judge Jackson gazed down at him, then at Warden. "Thank you, counsel. This case is submitted." In the five and one-half hours of closing arguments, Judge Jackson had asked not a single question.

On the courthouse steps, the parties gathered again, recorded by twelve television cameras, as a light rain fell. There were many introductions of spouses and hugs, as lawyers and reporters said good-bye to one another.

Despite the bonhomie, privately each combatant was implacable. The next day at lunch, Joel Klein likened Microsoft to an elephant accustomed to getting its way. He told a story about a man who offered to pay one million dollars to anyone who could get an elephant to jump on command without touching it. No one could. Finally, one man stepped forward and smacked the elephant across the head with a two-by-four. The elephant jumped. Because he touched the elephant, the contestant was disqualified. The next year, the same contest was held. Each contestant failed, until the man with the two-by-four came forward and whispered in the elephant's ear, and the elephant jumped. "How'd you do it?" the organizer asked.

"I just reminded the elephant that if he didn't jump I was going to whack him again!"

Klein had tried to reason with Microsoft, he said, but now his thinking had hardened. Now, he wanted to whack Microsoft with a two-by-four. "I'm inclined to think that the simple way to do this without the court having to administer Microsoft is to have a structural breakup," he said. He gauged the chances of reaching a settlement as being only 20 to 25 percent at the most. Klein recognized that the only way to get tough remedies was to win a total victory. Then, pressure would build on Microsoft to settle, though the government's appetite to settle would decline.

Bill Neukom and the Microsoft legal team also behaved as if they were dealing from strength. No matter how Judge Jackson ruled, they were privately confident they would win on appeal. Richard Urowsky assured them their legal claims were unassailable. On the day the rebuttals ended, Neukom told me over lunch, "I think we are making our record in every round."

I asked him if he saw a disconnect between his optimism and the pessimism of most non-Microsoft observers. He stiffened and fixed me with a stern stare. "It's my job to understand the strength of the government's case and the weaknesses of ours," he said. "I have to. There are times you have to tell your client to settle or change. I don't do any good for Bill or the company if I tell them what they want to hear. My job is to be an astute, impartial observer."

And what did he tell his client?

"The government case is weak and the law is very favorable to us."

Did Neukom really believe this? It was difficult to fathom how he could. Surely the government's charge that Microsoft held a monopoly over the PC and that it had abused this power was not "weak." Where Microsoft stood on firmer but still tenuous ground was with their claim that consumers were unharmed and that competition in other platforms was alive. Walking away from the courtroom, however, the crucial questions centered on Judge Jackson, and among them was this one: why had he asked not a single significant question that last day?

During the trial, it was not uncommon to hear lawyers, particularly Microsoft lawyers, grumble about Jackson's work habits or wonder about his intellectual bandwidth. Now, a government lawyer asked, Was Jackson silent because he has nothing to say or because he doesn't want to risk having his questions misinterpreted by the press? Jackson was secure enough to enjoy the speculation. He was silent, he later told me, because he worried that the media would dramatize his comments or questions as indicators of his hidden beliefs, and because he saw himself as a jury, and jurors were silent before reaching a verdict. Besides, Jackson knew how complicated the issues before him were. He had numerous judgment calls to make: what were the core "facts"? Did Microsoft bludgeon Compaq, as the government alleged and as Compaq and Microsoft denied? Did he believe Tevanian or Gates, Barksdale or Maritz? While it was undeniable that Microsoft worried that Netscape's browser threatened Windows's dominance and that it used its leverage to slow Netscape, the more critical legal questions were: did this result in foreclosure? And did it harm consumers? And while it was hard to dispute that Windows monopolized the PC, would Microsoft be able to extend this monopoly to emerging platforms? And, more philosophically, Were antitrust laws a relic in the Internet age? And how would Jackson resolve the inherent conflict between his conservative Republican free-market tenets and his belief in following rules and behaving responsibly, which the government said Microsoft had failed to do?

Seated in his sizable second-floor chambers the day after the closing arguments were made, Judge Jackson leaned back in his large desk chair, fiddled with an unlit pipe, and reflected on various aspects of the drama in his courtroom. The wire from his old-fashioned hearing aid was visible, the conference table to the left of his desk was piled with documents, including the 13,466 pages of trial transcripts, and the bookcase to his right was filled with legal reference books. The PC beside his modest wooden desk was silent, as always; above it was a picture of his home on the shore in St. Mary's County, Maryland, and another picture of a sailboat. Jackson did not talk about the legal aspects of the trial at this time, but he smiled as he discussed John Warden's closing argument, acknowledging that it was an attempt to remind him of the Court of

292 | WORLD WAR 3.0

Appeals decision. As a former litigator, Jackson accepted this as a shrewd nudge and spoke glowingly of the lawyers, singling out Warden, Lacovara, and Steven Holley as "superb" lawyers. He had little sense of Urowsky and Neukom. Jackson reserved his choice encomiums for Boies, who he said was the best lawyer to ever argue in his courtroom.

Told that Bill Gates was upset by the trial and more preoccupied with it than he publicly admitted, Jackson observed acidly, "It's a little late."

Jackson's intent was to issue his fact findings by November and his final legal decision, including any possible remedies, around the first of the year. From the summer through the fall, his conference table was piled with trial transcripts and the summaries his lead law clerk, David McIntosh, typed each day, describing what the witnesses said, plus the judge's own oversized green book that was two thirds filled by his neat jottings, plus the trial exhibits, depositions, and briefs. Normally, a district-court judge is allotted two clerks, but because of this trial Jackson received emergency funding for a third. Each day two of the three—McIntosh and Tim Ehrlich—burrowed into the material and distilled it.

Through the fall, Jackson read drafts from his clerks matching the salient facts against the major claims. The clerks were deputized to submit to him a first draft on each charge, and then Jackson, who enjoys writing, would sit in his office or in Maryland on the weekends and edit and amend drafts on a yellow legal pad. "Much of what I did, with the exception of some sections, was a rewrite of his [McIntosh's] material," said Jackson. "I'd take his draft and rewrite parts of it" and send it back with questions and requests for more research. As he did, one question hung in the air over the government and the world's foremost software company: whom did Judge Jackson believe?

On Friday, November 5, Justice and the states and Microsoft were alerted that Jackson's Findings of Fact would be issued that day, after the stock market closed. In Washington, D.C., the Justice Department sent Phil Malone to retrieve the opinion from the district courthouse. In the state of Washington, Bill Gates and Bill Neukom would wait for a minion from Sullivan & Cromwell's D.C. office to go collect the opinion on a floppy disk and e-mail it to Redmond. Ironically, since the file was formatted in

WordPerfect rather than Microsoft Word, there was a brief translation delay before the alleged monopolist could read the decision. Meanwhile, Malone was reading the 207-page decision as he headed down the stairs and out the building into an idling car that whisked him to Joel Klein's cavernous conference room, where Boies and Blattner and the rest of the team waited. Malone phoned from the car, recalled Blattner.

"How is it?" asked Klein.

"I'm not at the end, but on page sixteen it says, 'They're a monopolist!' "

Closed doors and the labyrinthine corridors of the Justice Department could not smother the cheers emanating from Klein's suite.

In Redmond, there was at first stunned silence. After reading a few pages, public-relations chief Mich Mathews and her deputy Greg Shaw looked up and chimed, "This is bad." Bill Gates had been at his family's Hood Canal cabin for his semiannual Think Week and had helicoptered back to his office in Building 8, where he conferred with Neukom and perused the decision. The ruling was the equivalent of a baseball no-hitter: one by one, on nearly every contested fact, Judge Jackson mowed down Microsoft's claims. He rejected the argument that the antitrust laws were from the Stone Age and no longer relevant. Jackson laid the foundation for his various conclusions by building from his central predicate, which was that Microsoft was a monopoly: "Viewed together, three main facts indicate that Microsoft enjoys monopoly power. First, Microsoft's share of the market for Intel-compatible PC operating systems is extremely large"—about 95 percent worldwide, and still "well above 80 percent" if Apple's Macintosh was included—"and stable. Second, Microsoft's dominant market share is protected by a high [applications] barrier to entry. Third, and largely as a result of that barrier, Microsoft's customers lack a commercially viable alternative to Windows." Nor was this PC monopoly about to erode, said Jackson, as he embraced the government's network-effects thesis. Not only would customers join a herd to buy Windows, he said, but this "self-reinforcing cycle" compels software developers to flock to Windows and to shun rivals. In the world of Judge Jackson, Windows's dominance over the PC was not about to end, no matter how much success Linux was currently enjoying.

Having established that Microsoft was a monopoly, Judge Jackson accepted David Boies's and the Justice Department's narrative, concluding that it used this monopoly power to suppress competition. One year after Netscape Navigator's startling 1994 debut, Microsoft, "with the encouragement and support of Gates," set out to marginalize it. Without using these words, Jackson found that Microsoft had sought to divide markets. Microsoft had proposed at the June 21, 1995, summit between the two companies that Netscape cease to develop its browser for Windows in return for a "special relationship" and the smaller territory of corporate servers and non-Windows PCs. Had Netscape accepted, Jackson wrote, it is "unclear" whether Netscape could "survive as an independent business." When Netscape rejected the noose, Jackson found, Microsoft hanged them anyway by withholding the APIs for Windows 95.

This was a relatively mild form of strangulation compared to what Microsoft next did; it bundled its own free browser in with Windows. While Microsoft might have eventually done this anyway, concluded Jackson, its "determination to preserve the applications barrier to entry . . . was the main force driving its decision to price the product at zero." Its intent was to gain share of browser usage, and so, he said, it coerced OEMs, ISPs, ICPs, and companies such as Apple to abandon the Netscape browser and promote Microsoft's version. And, Jackson noted, though Microsoft had waived contract restrictions on PC manufacturers in the spring of 1998, it was still unclear what the effects of those contracts would be (though Jackson left little doubt what he thought the effects would be). Jackson noted that for a period of about eight months, thirty-four ICPs were effectively prevented from distributing and promoting Netscape's browser; and for a year and a half, more than one hundred were required to promote Microsoft's browser. The judge rejected Microsoft's claim that the browser and Windows were seamless. They "are distinct" products, he said, and by combining them Microsoft cheated consumers of choice.

The judge rejected Jim Allchin's claim that when his December 1996 e-mail said Microsoft had "to come up with ways to leverage Windows," he really didn't mean to use Windows as a club to chase customers away from Netscape. Favoring the voluminous contemporaneous e-mails, as Boies had urged him to do, Jackson said that Microsoft's intent was to harm competition, to deny consumer choice, and to maintain its monopoly.

Microsoft's coercive tactics weren't limited to the browser, Jackson found. Unhappy that OEMs were reconfiguring the opening screen—in some cases inserting a second browser or removing Microsoft's Internet Explorer icon, in some cases removing Microsoft-chosen icons such as that for MSN, and in others adding third-party software or PC tutorials or promotions paid for by ISPs—Microsoft behaved as if it, not Compaq or Hewlett-Packard, owned the PCs. The "primary" reason the OEMs wanted to control the first screen, said Jackson, "was to make the experience of setting up and learning to use a new PC system easier and less confusing for users, especially novices. By doing so, the OEMs believed, they would increase the value of their systems and minimize both product returns and costly support calls." Secondary purposes were to differentiate their brand from competitors and generate more revenue from companies promoted on the Windows screen. Yet Microsoft threatened to deny Windows to any OEM that dared offer choices. Although Microsoft said it did this to preserve the integrity of Windows, Judge Jackson mocked this explanation, quoting from a January 6, 1996, e-mail Gates wrote to a deputy: "Winning Internet browser share is a very very important goal for us. Apparently a lot of OEMs are bundling non-Microsoft browsers and coming up with offerings together with Internet Service providers that get displayed on their machines in a FAR more prominent way than MSN or our Internet browser." Not acceptable, admonished Gates. In the spring of 1996, Microsoft imposed five new restrictions to block OEMs from either reconfiguring the opening screen or displaying third-party brands.

Judge Jackson rejected Microsoft's assertion that it did not muscle AOL to restrict its distribution of Netscape. He rejected Microsoft's assertion that it did not attempt to sabotage Java. He rejected Microsoft's assertion that its battle with Apple was really a patent dispute, not an effort to blackmail Apple to drop Netscape's browser. He rejected Microsoft's assertion that it had not bludgeoned Intel to drop its native-signal processing. He rejected Microsoft's assertion that its battle with IBM was really a simple accounting dispute. He rejected Microsoft's assertion that its cross-promotional agreements with ICPs such as Intuit were routine, not coercive. He rejected Microsoft's assertion that it did not intend to strangle RealNetworks's streaming media or to get it to use Windows-specific technology. And he rejected Microsoft's assertion that even if the court believed Windows exercised a dominant position over PCs today, by tomorrow the marketplace would impose its own correction. He wrote, "While some consumers may decide to make do with one or more information appliances in place of an Intel-compatible PC system, the number of these consumers will, for the foreseeable future, remain small. . . . One reason for this is the fact that no single type of information appliance, nor even all types in the aggregate, provides all of the features that most consumers have come to rely on in their PC systems and in the applications that run on them." Nor did he see any evidence that server-driven network computers posed any "imminent" threat.

Ostensibly, the Findings of Fact seemed to meet the demands of even strict economic constructionists. Jackson's interpretation of the facts fairly shouted his belief that Microsoft was guilty of causing consumer harm. While Jackson did commend the quality of Microsoft's integrated browser and how it "increased general familiarity with the Internet and reduced the cost to the public of gaining access to it," these virtues were not those Jackson chose to emphasize. Instead, he stressed how Microsoft's "actions have harmed consumers in ways that are immediate and easily discernible."

By denying computer makers a Windows version without a browser or preventing them from removing Microsoft's browser icon, "Microsoft forced OEMs to ignore consumer demand for a browserless version of Windows." By conspiring to deny OEMs the option of exclusively choosing Netscape's browser, Microsoft effectively denied consumers a proper browser choice. By setting Windows in such a way that Microsoft's browser would be activated even if the PC had been programmed to use Netscape's browser, "Microsoft created confusion and frustration for consumers, and increased technical support costs for business customers." By commingling a browser and operating system, Microsoft hogged more of each PC's memory, jeopardizing "the stability and security of the operating system" and increasing "the likelihood that a browser crash will cause the entire system to crash." By pressing Intel to curb its software-development efforts, Microsoft cut off potential innovations that would have benefited consumers. And the "actions that Microsoft took against [Netscape's] Navigator hobbled a form of innovation that had shown the potential to depress the applications barrier to entry," thus indirectly penalizing consumers. Finally, Judge Jackson held that Microsoft's monopoly imposed a somewhat inflated price on Windows. For those users of Windows 95 who wanted to upgrade to Windows 98, the judge quoted an internal Microsoft study that said the company could charge $49 but identified $89 as the revenue-maximizing price. "Microsoft," Judge Jackson concluded, "thus opted for the higher price." Jackson did not suggest this was an outrageously steep price for an operating system that provides ever more features, but he did caution that Microsoft enjoyed such an unassailable monopoly "that if it wished to exercise this power solely in terms of price, it could charge a price for Windows substantially above that which could be charged in a competitive market."

In the 412th and final paragraph of this decision, Judge Jackson painted a portrait of Microsoft totally at odds with the pious proclamations Gates offered in his deposition or that his lawyers recited in court. One could feel Jackson's heat, the sense that he was railing against an evil empire, in his thunderous closing:

> Most harmful of all is the message that Microsoft's actions have conveyed to every enterprise with the potential to innovate in the computer industry. Through its conduct toward Netscape, IBM, Compaq, Intel, and others, Microsoft has demonstrated that it will use its prodigious market power and immense profits to harm any firm that insists on pursuing initiatives that could intensify competition against one of Microsoft's core products. Microsoft's past success in hurting such companies and stifling innovation deters investment in technologies and businesses that exhibit the potential to threaten Microsoft. The ultimate result is that some innovations that would truly benefit consumers never occur for the sole reason that they do not coincide with Microsoft's self-interest.

What smacked either courtroom regulars or neophytes right between the eyes was that Jackson didn't believe most of Microsoft's witnesses. "He did not believe a word I said after 'Good morning, Your Honor'!" Dr. Richard Schmalensee admitted after the verdict. "It is hard to deny," conceded Michael Lacovara, "that in some basic sense he believed the government case and did not believe our case, either in particular events or in the broad ways the market works." Even Bill Neukom conceded, "You could interpret the Findings of Fact to say Judge Jackson was skeptical of the credibility of Microsoft's witnesses—but he did not enter a finding as to credibility." There was little reason the judge should have believed them, declared a Justice Department attorney. "As they say in New York, 'Don't piss on my head and tell me it's raining!'" Credibility mattered more than a recitation of hundreds of facts, Lacovara admitted, as did Boies's ability to sound "broad themes," to create a narrative, even though Lacovara continued to believe that Boies's narrative was simplistic and, by implication, that Jackson failed to grasp complicated technical arguments. It's revealing, for example, that Jackson accepted at face value America Online's claims after it purchased Netscape that it had no intention to dump Microsoft's browser or to revive the middleware threat to Microsoft, while he dismissed Microsoft's evidence to the contrary.

Jackson acknowledged that Boies was correct to emphasize credibility. "There used to be a legal maxim in jury instructions," he told me. "It's called *falsus in uno, falsus in omnibus*. It means that if a witness lies about one thing, you don't have to believe anything else he says."

Beyond credibility, two key facts swayed Jackson's thinking, he told me. First was the "realization that software code—in John Warden's words—'is infinitely malleable.' Which gives the lie to the assertion that the browser and the operating system are inextricably integrated" and suggests that Microsoft's intent was not to help consumers, as it claimed, but to hurt Netscape.* Second was the June 21, 1995, Netscape/Microsoft meeting, which also revealed Microsoft's intent. "It became clear to me exactly what was being proposed," Jackson said, "which was, in effect, get out of their way. This is our market."

Judge Jackson's Findings of Fact sometimes read like a government brief. To have sat in the courtroom throughout the trial or read the factual briefs submitted by both sides is to be reminded that people can witness the same event and honestly describe it in contradictory ways; that Jackson invariably sided with the government witnesses' accounts of events without describing why he rejected Microsoft's alternate accounts suggests the scorn he came to harbor toward Microsoft. For example, Jackson's contention that Microsoft caused consumer harm relies on the claim that Microsoft has benefited from an applications barrier to entry. But Yale's George L. Priest, who was later retained by Microsoft to write a brief analyzing Judge Jackson's rulings, argued in a *Wall Street Journal* op-ed piece that this claim is more theoretical than real, since consumers value Windows for serving as an operating system

---

*Warden's exact words were, "There is an infinite variety of ways in which instructions can be arranged."

that provides many applications, including a free Internet connection; and the existence of many viable operating systems would "reduce the efficiency and diminish the advantage of the network to the world's consumers." Priest was asserting that Microsoft's behavior was protected by previous "good monopoly" rulings. The government suggested that Microsoft's behavior was not sanctioned because these rulings were never intended as a license to use any means to eradicate competition.

Judge Jackson was contemptuous of Microsoft's claim that Windows is vulnerable to attack from non-PC competitors and stated as fact that it would be "several years"—he did not define whether this meant three or thirty—before other devices became truly ubiquitous. But the shipment of information appliances is expected to eclipse that of PCs by 2005. Microsoft's Windows CE had, at the time Jackson issued his Findings of Fact, just 12 percent of this market, and the market share of Palm Pilots was above 80 percent. If Judge Jackson was right, then the only way to curb the Microsoft monopoly was with a government-imposed remedy. But if he was wrong, then the marketplace was already imposing its own remedy. It is hard to avoid the conclusion that Jackson's views about the future were not so much deduced as asserted.

With Jackson's decisive ruling on the facts, Microsoft appeared to be buried. It had dug itself deeper into its hole, a hole started with its take-no-prisoners corporate culture, a hole that deepened when it refused to alter its behavior even though it had signed a 1994 consent decree to do so, a hole it then dug still deeper when it openly disdained Washington and government regulators or treated Judge Jackson as if he was a dim-witted Luddite when he ruled in December 1997 that Microsoft untie its browser from Windows 95, a hole it expanded when Gates did not reach a negotiated settlement with Justice in May 1998, and a hole it transformed into a cavern when a belligerent Gates was deposed.

On a Saturday morning several weeks later, I visited David Boies at his home in Armonk, in northern Westchester County, New York. Boies was ecstatic. Life was good, and not just because of Jackson's resounding verdict. On November 3, 1999, his new law firm had together with about fifty other law firms won a more than one-billion-dollar settlement from seven of the world's dominant drug manufacturers in a price-fixing case. Boies's firm had done about 35 percent of the legal work, and he expected his legal fee would total about forty million dollars and that Mary Boies's firm, which was also engaged, would pocket several millions more. A man who professed no interest in money, who wore the same clothes every day in court, and who was paid just over one hundred thousand dollars a year by the Justice Department, had joined the ranks of lawyers who had gotten rich from class-action lawsuits.

In truth, Boies is not as oblivious as he seems to the comforts wealth brings. His home is a spacious red-brick Georgian house on ten acres, with a veranda, a tennis court, a pool, acres of rolling land, and a commanding view of a valley and a tree-capped ridge that overlooks Greenwich, Connecticut. His enormous kitchen would please a professional chef. He has a handsome library (filled with history, biography, and legal-case histories but containing little fiction). His wine cellar, which is maintained at a perfect fifty-five degrees, by his count contains ten thousand bottles, and most of these are first growths—Château Lafite-Rothschild, Margaux, Latour, Haut-Brion, and Mouton Rothschild—from such great years as 1982, 1989, and 1990. He stores dozens of cases of champagne, but the most plentiful supply is of Dom Pérignon. Among the wines that are plentiful in this cellar, a 1982 case of any of these châteaus retails for about $8,000; a case of 1990 Dom Pérignon for just over $2,000; and some of their 1982 Bordeaux retailed for well over $1,000 per bottle. The Boieses have purchased hundreds of acres of farmland in northern California, where they hope one day to start a vineyard to produce cabernet sauvignon in the Bordeaux style.

Relaxing in his library in jeans, a frayed white turtleneck, and gray athletic socks, Boies reflected on Judge Jackson's findings. He guessed that Bill Gates's testimony had been decisive. "That deposition played a very important role in what happened at the trial. At the end of the day, when the findings are written, they can't be written without referring to the Gates deposition," he said. "That deposition did several things. First, it effectively knocked Gates out as a witness. . . . This deposition framed the trial. It made every Microsoft witness much more subject to a credibility test." Second, the deposition effectively "precluded Gates from testifying," because his lawyers knew their defense might be ravaged if Gates altered his earlier testimony and would certainly be ravaged if he did not. Third, the "Gates deposition effectively precluded Microsoft from coming up with a benign explanation for their behavior because Gates was the central decision maker, and Gates was unable to come up with the explanations." The nine Microsoft executives who testified were each compelled to adopt the same pious stance, the same singsong we-did-what-we-did-to-better-serve-consumers. "Finally, it allowed us to effectively frame the issues throughout the trial as 'Do you believe them or us?'"

This goes to the core of the credibility issue, Boies continued, looking out the library window at a ridge of leafless trees. Credibility is not just a question of whether Judge Jackson believed Jim Allchin or David Farber but whether he believed the documents or the testimony. A judge asks, "How much weight should I give the documents? And Microsoft says, 'The documents don't mean what they appear to say.' That's a credibility issue, too. The most important part of Gates's deposition was that it affected how much weight the court gave to the evidence versus what Microsoft testified now. If you have a company with enormous credibility you can sometimes convince the tryer of fact not to believe them." You can convince the judge that there is a broader context, that there were extenuating circumstances, that people were just writing in shorthand and therefore the e-mails didn't mean what they seemed to say.

The decision, Boies insisted, was not vulnerable to appeal. The Court of Appeals, he said, "can't retry it" because Jackson's court determines the facts and Jackson produced ample facts to buttress his conclusions. The rational conclusion, Boies said, is that Microsoft "has to settle. I don't know if they are going to be rational or not. If they were rational, we would settle this." What Boies didn't know, and what he said was the wild card in the coming months, was whether Bill Gates was the crazy uncle in the cellar that his lawyers couldn't reason with or whether he was as tough-minded about this business negotiation with the Justice Department as he was about, say, negotiating with IBM or America Online. "Sometimes a settlement passes because lawyers get in the way," Boies said, but this hadn't been true with Microsoft. He recalled the May 1998 negotiations on the eve of the lawsuit, in which Gates personally decided what Microsoft would concede and, Boies thought, personally pulled the plug on the discussions, sending the case to trial. What would Gates do now?

In the evening after Jackson's ruling on the facts, Bill Gates stepped to a microphone in Microsoft's Studio B, a large facility built to accommodate multimedia press briefings. Makeup added color to his cheeks. His hair was neatly parted, and he wore a three-button blue suit—which on him looked like a straitjacket—a striped red tie, and round, frameless eyeglasses. Gates neither looked nor sounded like a crazy uncle. Carefully reading a written statement, he said of the decision, "We respectfully disagree," and it was "just one step" in a long process. "The lawsuit," he said, "is fundamentally about one question: can a successful American company continue to improve its products for the benefits of consumers? That is precisely what Microsoft did by developing new versions of the Windows operating system with built-in support for the Internet." Gates pretended, as he always has, that the case was more an inconvenience than a distraction, for when asked by a reporter how he felt personally, he deflected the query by noting that he had just returned from his annual Think Week, during which he goes off by himself and reads and ponders the future, and he was "excited" about what lay ahead. He also pretended, as did Bill Neukom, that substantial sections of the decision vindicated Microsoft. "The court's findings do acknowledge that Microsoft's actions accelerated the development of the Internet, reduced the cost to consumers, and improved the quality of Web-browsing software," said Gates. Actually, while Judge Jackson did say the browser wars spurred the growth of the Internet and resulted in cheaper, technically superior browsers, he emphasized that Microsoft's actions hurt consumers, were coercively imposed, and, moreover, were intended to crush Netscape. Of the finding's 412 paragraphs, only one—number 408—mentioned consumer benefits; and lest this be misunderstood, Jackson reserved his harshest condemnation of Microsoft's behavior for the next four and final paragraphs.

Others' reactions to the verdict were mixed. Steve Case was pleased, needless to say, and openly rooted for the government to prevail. "You can't reward inappropriate, illegal behavior," he told me. "Microsoft went from being worth twenty-five billion to now being worth five hundred billion. And they got to keep it. That's one reason most people don't believe conduct remedies are sufficient." He believed he had a strong case to sue: "When Microsoft turned its death ray on Netscape it was more valuable than AOL. So if any company in the world was seriously damaged by Microsoft, it was Netscape."

While Case was happy, the decision prompted consternation within other corporations. Time Warner executives, who happened to be meeting the next morning, fretted that the ruling would strengthen the gov-

ernment's determination to aggressively referee the battles among corporate elephants, impeding Time Warner's own deals.

John Malone pondered the ruling's damage to Microsoft in the short
run, whether it was reversed on appeal or not. He said, "There are probably some deals Microsoft would like to do that they probably will feel
they better not try. There are some companies that would like to do
things with Microsoft but feel this might not be the right time to put
another issue in front of regulatory bodies. There will be a reduction in
transactions that get proposed on either side for a little while, while this
sorts itself out. They won't be as aggressive in the short run because
they'll be lectured by the lawyers to watch their p's and q's." Gates and
others will start to second-guess themselves. "My guess is that Bill will
probably be pretty miserable, feeling like he fucked up, and that's a new
experience for Bill. . . . It kind of reduces your enthusiasm to get up and
go to work. I think the biggest danger for Microsoft is that this thing
lingers for years and becomes a terrible distraction. A couple of people
that are in Microsoft that are excellent people, I know are thinking of
leaving because they're not having fun anymore. You're already rich, as
rich as you need to be. Bill's no fun anymore. He's preoccupied, he's
pretty bitchy. That can hurt a company because you tend to lose
that . . . fun, cocky, take-on-the-world quality that built Microsoft."

Malone spoke from experience. In the early nineties when the government and others began calling him a monopolist, when Senator Al Gore
demonized him as Darth Vader, and when his proposed deals were
microinspected by regulators, Malone lost his appetite for business: "The
whole idea that every morning you're rolling the dice on your reputation
and your personal wealth with forces that were pretty irrational, that
you couldn't predict, and . . . you were spending a lot of your time doing
things you really didn't like to do or necessarily were good at—like lobbying. . . . You couldn't be spontaneous. You didn't know for sure
whether the government was going to let you do x, y, or z." Malone was
rooting for Gates and Microsoft, but he nevertheless said of Gates, "He
screwed up by not settling." If the price of a settlement today was that
Microsoft consent to remove its browser from Windows, Malone said
he'd agree "in a heartbeat" because Microsoft can wrap its browser in a
separate box for free and "achieve the same ends."

In the days following the decision, it hardly sounded as if Gates and
company were ready to accede to what was once the government's prin-

cipal demand, nor to most others for that matter. Buoyed by another astonishingly strong economic performance, Microsoft had reason to allow pride rather than caution (or guilt) to dominate its thoughts. The company's performance in the 1999 fiscal year had shattered all previous milestones. It was Microsoft's twenty-fourth consecutive year of record results: revenues soared 29 percent to $19.75 billion, and net income jumped from $4.5 billion to $7.8 billion, with total expenses climbing only 11 percent. These numbers surely granted Microsoft executives a reason to feel defiant. The Windows segment of their business alone enjoyed a revenue spurt of 35 percent, to $8.5 billion. Microsoft's after-tax profit margin was 39 percent, which was taken by some as proof of monopoly profits and by others as proof of a remarkable company; Microsoft was unburdened by any long-term debt and had $17.2 billion of cash on hand. Despite Judge Jackson's opinion that its R-and-D budget was a weapon designed to perpetuate its monopoly, Microsoft decided to expand that budget by nearly 25 percent, to $3.8 billion. Nor were investors fleeing because of Microsoft's courtroom performance: its stock was to rise 68 percent in 1999, swelling the worth of the world's most valued corporation to $602 billion.

At its annual shareholders meeting on November 10, 1999, in Bellevue's Meydenbauer Center, a few miles from Microsoft's campus, Bill Gates sketched the company's strategy and expressed pride in all they had accomplished. Almost as an afterthought, he acknowledged the invisible gorilla the 2,500 shareholders on hand knew was lurking in the hall. "A lot of people have said to me that, as somebody who is quite pragmatic, and very interested in retaining one hundred percent of the focus of the company on building great software, why is it that you can't just settle this case? Well, throughout the case, we've welcomed any opportunity to resolve the case. That's very important to us, and we've put a lot of energy. . . . We're willing to go a long way to address the government's concerns, but if we can't get Internet support, we can't add any new features. If we can't define the user-interface experience of Windows so all Windows machines operate the same way, then the Windows brand becomes absolutely meaningless. No company should accept these kinds of limitations on their ability to innovate. And that's what's at the heart of this case."

Translation: the two central issues in any settlement talks—Microsoft's freedom to fold new features into Windows and its ability to design the opening desktop screen and continue to bar PC manufacturers from designing their own user interfaces—were off the table, despite Judge Jackson's findings.

Did Gates have any regrets about the way Microsoft and its lawyers had handled the case, a shareholder asked, particularly the way Microsoft had been "outmaneuvered by the government?" With Bill Neukom seated beside him on the dais, Gates said, "One of the most defensible things we've ever done" is to add a browser to Windows, and "we cannot back off on that." And while acknowledging that Microsoft could "have been smarter" concerning some of its company e-mail and its combative style, he treated these as meaningless sideshows. As for his lawyers and witnesses, Gates was unapologetic: "I'm quite proud of what's been done there."

Neukom was equally unrepentant. He told me he thought the District Court had erred in the Findings of Fact. "We believe, and intend to raise on appeal, the many instances in which the District Court found 'facts' which are not supported by the weight of the evidence. And in other instances, the court claimed to find 'facts' when there exists uncontroverted evidence to the contrary." Neukom cited as an example the amply documented evidence that Netscape shipped about 160 million copies of its browser in 1998, and yet "this uncontroverted evidence was ignored in the findings, and in still other instances the court did not enter a finding where Microsoft had introduced uncontroverted admissible evidence." Microsoft also planned to challenge other "facts" as based on inadmissible hearsay.

It wasn't clear whether Neukom's confidence—and Gates's pleasure at the job he had done—was real or feigned. Nor was it clear, as Justice officials claim, that the reason there had been no serious settlement talks since May 1998 was that Gates was holding out, hoping that the 2000 election would result in a more hands-off Republican administration, hoping that a more conservative appeals court would overturn Judge Jackson, hoping that the common front adopted by Justice and the states would fray, hoping that the passage of time would reveal that, contrary to Judge Jackson's "facts," the software industry was fiercely competitive.

Justice was equally recalcitrant. Joel Klein said publicly for the first time that a breakup of Microsoft was a viable option. The state attorneys general generally favored such a structural remedy, and after allowing Justice to argue their case in court they were restless to be heard. Ominously, they had their own remedy task force, and the two groups did not coordinate their efforts. The states began to speak of Microsoft, as they had spoken of tobacco, as a potential cash windfall, a new lottery that would gush billions to pay for state services. "If we're successful, we're entitled to civil penalties," said Iowa Attorney General Tom Miller. There was, obviously, some air between the position of Justice and the states. Unlike Justice, which was preoccupied with the law, most attorneys general serve as consumer champions, issuing press releases as well as filing lawsuits. Instead of speaking with one voice, as did the Justice Department, the states were represented by different elected officials, some Republican, some Democrat, some liberal, some conservative, all soon up for reelection. Although they had united in filing the lawsuit, perhaps the various government plaintiffs would divorce over remedies.

Judge Jackson's Findings of Fact were chum in the water for other potential litigators. Competitors, including AOL, lined up to say they would explore civil penalties against Microsoft. Also joining the lottery line were class-action attorneys who would represent consumers for a percentage of the verdict. They would cite as a fact Judge Jackson's observation, based on a relatively low-level staff report, that Microsoft might have charged an extra forty dollars for each copy of Windows and then assert that consumers were entitled to refunds. In such private lawsuits, victors can win triple damages. The U.S. lawsuit also helped provoke other governments to monitor Microsoft's practices. In Brussels, the European Commission announced that it was investigating at least two antitrust complaints lodged against Microsoft.

As positions hardened, Judge Jackson summoned the parties to his chambers on November 18 for what was announced as a routine twenty-minute session to discuss how to proceed. Jackson had decided to appoint a mediator to seek a negotiated settlement prior to the final Conclusions of Law ruling, which would come perhaps in the spring. Neither side was surprised; but they were floored when Jackson told them who it was. Instead of picking a professional mediator or a judge from his own court, Jackson announced that he had turned to a higher court. Richard Posner, the chief judge of the Seventh Circuit Court of Appeals in Illinois and perhaps the nation's most influential antitrust jurist, had agreed to serve, he said. "I think this is probably as propitious a time for any possible negotiated outcome as you could have," Jackson told them. He explained that the appointment was prompted, in part, "by what I think are somewhat disturbing reports in the press that the plaintiffs are proceeding on 'parallel tracks.'" He expressed the hope that Justice and the states would continue to act in "harmony." In any case, Jackson told his audience that Judge Posner was only a voluntary mediator; he had no power to arbitrate a settlement. Posner would have at least two months to see if he could coax the parties to an agreement, and if Posner failed, Jackson would not be apprised of the reasons for failure and would simply issue a decision and impose any potential remedy on his own.

Why had Jackson decided to appoint Posner? Jackson had first talked to Lawrence Lessig about Posner in December 1997, when he had appointed Lessig special master. Lessig had clerked for Posner, and Jackson was curious to know more about the man whose opinions were required reading for other judges. When it came time to choose a mediator, remembered Jackson, "I thought, 'Who can command the respect and attention of both of these behemoths, with egos to match?' I thought Posner was uniquely qualified because he is recognized as an authority on antitrust law and he is thought to be a judicial conservative." The latter was particularly "important in terms of Microsoft," he said. "But, also, you tell me who would be able to speak all the time to Joel Klein other than someone of Posner's stature." Before he called Posner, Jackson cleared the choice with Court of Appeals judge David B. Sentelle, one of three appellate judges who presides over the appointment of independent counsels and mediators. Judge Sentelle told Jackson it would be an unusual but worthy appointment. When Jackson phoned Posner on November 17, he recalls, the jurist "was immediately interested."

As Jackson had hoped, Microsoft was ecstatic about the appointment, hopeful that a kindred spirit might take a fresh approach and actually hear what they were saying; Justice and the states were more reserved, worried that Posner would be dismissive of their case, yet respectful of his intellect and fearful of offending him. Each side, once again, was reminded that Judge Jackson had a more supple mind than commonly assumed. Even critics now praised Jackson as a statesman who sublimated his own ego to advance a settlement. In *Slate* magazine, George Priest, who thought Jackson's Findings of Fact read as if he were a Justice Department stenographer, enthusiastically likened Posner's appointment to when Justice Learned Hand had been appointed more than fifty years before to head a special appeals-court panel to decide whether to break up Alcoa because it held too much concentrated power, even though it had acquired its monopoly fairly. Priest's analogy is not exact, for Judge Hand was selected for his task at random, and he did not perform as a mediator but as a decision maker. As Jackson had hemmed in Microsoft and the Court of Appeals by segregating the facts from the legal briefs, so now he had given the vanquished company an out by providing the ear of an esteemed jurist whom they revered. Perhaps Posner would tell Microsoft how arduous it would be to win on appeal and coax Bill Gates to listen and make a hardheaded decision to negotiate a settlement. Perhaps Judge Jackson could achieve the conservative solution he wanted: punish the miscreant yet do no violence to the free-enterprise system. But if the parties didn't settle, Judge Jackson, not Judge Posner, retained full power to rule as he saw fit.

David Boies was impressed by Jackson's "boldness and creativity." By November 1999, he was rooting for a negotiated settlement. In the game of poker they were playing, Boies believed the government held an unbeatable hand, yet he acknowledged that Microsoft held a few cards, too. "Microsoft can give us two things," he told me in early November. "One is much more immediate relief." By the time the appeals process was exhausted, two to four years could pass, allowing abuses to persist. "And Microsoft can enable us to tailor relief in the least intrusive, most competitive way. They can give us these two things that we cannot get no matter how complete a judicial win we get."

CHAPTER 18

The Mediator

JUDGE JACKSON chose the most unpredictable of jurists to orchestrate the mediation between parties that deeply mistrusted each other. He did not pick a practiced diplomat, a charmer, a man who had spent a lifetime searching for the middle ground. In Richard Posner, 61, Judge Jackson chose a man who did not recede. When he was young, Posner seemed destined to become a liberal icon. Born in New York City, he was raised a child of the left, studied English literature, and graduated summa cum laude from Yale and first in his class from Harvard Law School, where he was president of the *Law Review*. After clerking for liberal Supreme Court Justice William J. Brennan, Jr., he worked in the administration of Lyndon Johnson, where he was on the staff of the Federal Trade Commission, served as an assistant to Johnson's solicitor general, Thurgood Marshall, and then was general counsel to Johnson's Task Force on Communications Policy.

Whether the experience of working for these government regulatory bodies was the defining factor or not, sometime after joining the faculty of the Stanford Law School as an associate professor in 1968 and the University of Chicago as a full professor the next year, he became a champion of a free market. He became part of what Roger Parloff

described in *American Lawyer* as "the Chicago school of law and economics." In essence, Parloff explained, "followers of that school believe that a
key aim of legal rules and institutions is—or should be—the efficient allo-
cation of resources and the maximization of wealth." Posner viewed the
law through the prism of economics, which he thinks of as a science.
Since his 1981 appointment, at age forty-two, to the Seventh Circuit by
Ronald Reagan and his ascension to the chief judgeship in 1993, his
impact has been vast. "Posner is the first one you think of as having introduced economics into the law," observed antitrust lawyer Barry Hawk, a
partner at Skadden, Arps and a professor of antitrust law at Fordham Law
School. "When I started teaching in the sixties, economics and the law
didn't exist. It has become a big movement."

By 1999, Posner had written more than thirty books; not just his classic on antitrust law or works on economics and contract law but books on
AIDS, aging, sex regulations, political and moral theory, the impeachment of President Clinton, and literary criticism, not to mention 330
articles, mostly for scholarly journals but also book reviews for *The New
York Times Book Review* and *The New Republic*. He averaged seventy-seven
legal opinions a year—the typical appeals-court judge produces twenty-
eight—and by the time of his appointment as mediator had written more
than 1,700 opinions. Unlike Judge Jackson and many colleagues on the
bench, he drafts and completes his own opinions. Posner also still teaches
half-time at the University of Chicago's law school. He probably rivals
Oliver Wendell Holmes, Felix Frankfurter, and Louis Brandeis as the most
quoted legal scholar of the twentieth century. According to a 1994
analysis prepared by the Chicago Council of Lawyers, Posner's opinions
are cited by other circuit courts an average of 273 times each year, more
than four times the national average.

In light of Posner's benefactor, his theorems, and perhaps his rather
austere appearance, there is a tendency to brand him a conservative.
The label fits like an oversized suit. "He's an extraordinarily balanced
person," observed his friend and former law clerk, Harvard (now Stanford) Law professor Lawrence Lessig. "He was an English major who
studied economics and reads widely—he's the fastest reader I've ever
known. He's very skeptical of anyone who has a high theory. The thing
he hates the most is posing. He's very skeptical of people who use the law
to advance theories." He is, added Lessig, a conservative in that he wants
the courts to play "a minimalist" role, yet he disdains ideology.

Not everyone who has appeared before Judge Posner agrees with Lessig's assessment. He may not be a liberal, but he is a judicial activist, the mildly critical Chicago Council of Lawyers concluded in an assessment that appears on its website:

> Chief Judge Posner is a legal realist, who gives little weight to history and is famously derisive of original intent. He is candid about the fact that jurists, himself included, make choices that are not always dictated by precedent.... The tension between Chief Judge Posner's impulse to reach out and decide issues that are of interest to him and his inclination to construe procedural rules narrowly so as to limit access to the Court of Appeals creates an appearance of arbitrariness in his decisions. It contributes to the perception of many lawyers that the Seventh Circuit is unpredictable in the sense that lawyers cannot predict which issues will be decided in a case.

Posner can be withering from the bench when questioning or making observations about the lawyers who appear before him. Lessig has written of him, "There is something rare and extraordinary, if a bit ironic, about this uncalculating economist and public figure. But it reflects the deepest of Posner's beliefs: that the greatest sin of a scholar, and in turn a judge, is the sin of conformism. His is not a virtue our system rewards." The word *iconoclast* fits Posner better than does *conservative,* for while Posner has, like other conservatives, pronounced himself in favor of narrowing the scope of the antitrust laws and abolishing the Federal Trade Commission and eliminating prison terms for antitrust violators, he also supported the 1984 voluntary breakup of AT&T, for example. He has also advanced the libertarian position by being the only one of five Reagan appointees to dissent when his court voted to uphold state laws criminalizing "partial-birth" abortions; he favors decriminalizing marijuana use and has denounced the nation's drug laws as "savagely severe." He aroused the ire of the Catholic Church by ruling unconstitutional a fifty-year-old Illinois law that closed public schools on Good Friday. "The state has accorded special recognition to Christianity beyond anything that has been shown to be necessary to accommodate the religious needs of the Christian majority," he wrote.

And in a *New York Times Book Review* account of neoconservative paragon Gertrude Himmelfarb's *One Nation, Two Cultures,* Posner was mostly dismissive of her—and Robert Bork's—fulminations about America's moral rot, complaining that her probe lacked her usual intellectual rigor. In cool prose, Posner described how Himmelfarb, like other conservatives, often mushed together facts and "social phenomena that have different causes," and "the resulting stew is labeled a morally sick society." However, Posner observed, the pathologies of welfare dependency and crime "have been addressed effectively in recent years—for which, needless to say, Himmelfarb gives President Clinton no credit." The sexual liberation and divorce rate Himmelfarb decries is described by Posner as double-edged, for sex is safer, infant mortality has almost been eliminated, and a new service economy "in which little work requires masculine strength . . . was bound to free (or, if you prefer, eject) women from their traditional role, and by doing so bring about a profound change in sexual behavior and family structure. Unless we want to go the way of Iran, we shall not be able to return to the era of premarital chastity, low divorce, stay-at-home moms, pornography-free media and the closeting of homosexuals and adulterers."

Grasping for clues as to how Judge Posner might function as a mediator, Microsoft and government lawyers scrambled to consult his influential 1976 book, *Antitrust Law: An Economic Perspective,* now in its fifth printing. Microsoft found comfort here, for Posner asserted his belief in judicial restraint and wrote that "the only goal of antitrust law" should be to promote economic efficiency and thus competition; he also believed in good monopolies, if they lowered prices and promoted efficiency. Certainly, Microsoft believed that if it was a monopoly, it was a "good" one, because its dominant operating system promoted efficiency, providing a common software platform so that different computers could intercourse.

The government, on the other hand, pointed to those parts of Posner's text where he wrote that a good monopoly becomes bad if its "price reduction is below long-run marginal cost and made with intent to exclude." The government, unlike the Chicago Council of Lawyers, believed Posner often followed legal precedents even when he disagreed with them, and was heartened by those instances—such as his expressed support of the AT&T breakup and his 1986 ruling in *Hospital Corp. of America v. FTC* sustaining the FTC's rejection of a merger—in which he had sided with the government against corporate giants.

Perhaps a better text for clues to how Posner's mind works is a book that has nothing to do with antitrust law: *An Affair of State: The Investi-*

gation, Impeachment, and Trial of President Clinton, published in 1999. From it, we learn of Posner's drive to overcome emotion and of his eagerness to jump into vituperative cesspools of controversy and apply crisp, judicious logic. Explaining why he tackled the Clinton affair, Posner wrote that the first reason was that the intersections of law and morality "have long engaged my academic interest and attention. The second is its sheer multifaceted complexity—factual, legal, political, and moral—which cries out for the sort of synoptic, compendious treatment that I have attempted in several previous books. . . . The third feature that intrigues me is related to the second: the drama has so many 'angles,' and such an undercurrent of emotionality, that maintaining balance and perspective is an enormous challenge to one's powers of judicious reflection." What seems most to offend Posner is what he calls "the emotionality of the disagreement." He was offended by Special Prosecutor Kenneth Starr's use of salacious details about "Clinton's sexual proclivities" (because these were "a distraction" and damaging to the Office of the President) as he was by President Clinton's "pettifogging legalisms and diversionary arguments," which he thought were meant to sway public opinion, not uphold the law.

With the exception of when he dismisses Clinton as "a lying scofflaw of a President," throughout this lucid book Posner avoids sneering, carefully sifting evidence before issuing considered judgments. Clinton, he said, was clearly guilty of obstruction of justice, including perjury, but he did not believe these acts merited removal from office; although Starr's facts went largely unchallenged by the White House, the special prosecutor was guilty of zealotry and lack of judgment; many lawmakers were hypocrites, for Republicans such as Henry Hyde invoked morality but had fled from a moral stance when Republicans mired the country in the Iran-*contra* scandal, just as Democrats had condemned the lies of Oliver North and company but not those of Bill Clinton; he was appalled by the "hyperbole" invoked by "Clinton haters" such as William Bennett, Robert Bork, and the editorial page of *The Wall Street Journal,* as well as by the "academic 'loss of cool'" displayed by such liberals as Arthur Schlesinger, Jr., and Ronald Dworkin for publicly protesting Clinton's impeachment while neglecting "to mention that Clinton lied under oath and engaged in related acts of obstruction of justice."

One might ask, Should a sitting judge write such a highly opinionated book on a current legal matter? The question provoked a spat between Posner and Ronald Dworkin in the pages of *The New York Review of*

Books. Dworkin criticized Posner for holding forth publicly on a current legal matter whose participants, if not in this case then in others, might appear before the seventh circuit, provoking Posner to write a retort.*

Although Posner wrote a judicious book, one could claim it was injudicious of him to write it. At a minimum, Judge Posner flaunted Justice Frankfurter's dictum: "History teaches that the independence of the judiciary is threatened when the courts become embroiled in the passions of the day."

Posner's mission was, in words he used to dissect the Clinton impeachment imbroglio, to induce Microsoft and the government to shed "the emotionality" and come to a rational compromise. Toward this end, he sent an e-mail invitation to both sides to attend a private November 30 lunch at the Standard Club, half a block from the federal courthouse in Chicago. In attendance for Microsoft were Neukom, David Heiner, and three Sullivan & Cromwell partners, John Warden, Richard Urowsky, and Steven Holley. Representing the government were David Boies, Phil Malone, Jeff Blattner, and the attorneys general of Iowa, Connecticut, and Illinois. Posner strongly urged the parties to adopt one rule: no talking to the press about this or subsequent meetings. He said he had known John Warden and David Boies a long time, and he had no intention of trying to impose a settlement. Rather, he had read a good deal of the trial record and would, over time, share his insights about the case and the law. At this initial lunch, he said that he would keep their talks in strict confidence, and he urged both sides to do so as well. He would not intervene by telling either side they had a strong or a weak legal case, but he would try to deflate unrealistic expectations. He promised to devote himself almost full-time to the mediation process for the next two months, and he would ask each side to make detailed presentations concerning the facts, the economic and legal ramifications of its case, and the remedies it might consider. He hoped they could reach an agreement in principle by January 31, 2000.

David Boies came away thinking that Posner would create what Boies called "a Socratic dialogue. I think he will try and move the parties, but

*Dworkin's essay appeared in the March 9, 2000, *Review,* and Posner's letter in the April 27, 2000, issue.

he will more likely do it with questions than with declarative sentences. He'll do what a teacher does—'What about this? What would you do?'" Bill Neukom also likened the mediator's role to that of a teacher but one that was "very strict." This way the mediator would "help the parties be realistic, even pessimistic, about their prospects in the judicial process in order to motivate the parties to be very open, even generous, in the mediation process. It's common sense. If I'm going to be a mediator to bring peace to the Middle East, I will continue to remind the parties of the unattractive nature of the alternatives."

To assure a minimum of "emotionality," Judge Posner decreed that for at least the next month the parties would meet separately with him—the government each Monday and Microsoft each Tuesday. In January, Posner altered this approach to shuttle diplomacy and began to speak more regularly with Microsoft, but always by itself. In the meantime, Posner pummeled the participants with e-mail, posing questions, seeking clarifications. He began, in the words of a Microsoft negotiator, "growling at the other side, growling at us," cautioning Microsoft to be realistic about its prospects on appeal because Judge Jackson's Findings of Fact were so negative and the Court of Appeals might not take the time to find Microsoft's cherished "facts." There is "an inherent asymmetry to litigation," he told Microsoft's lawyers: the plaintiffs are always attacking, and the defendant is left to deny, avoid, or confess. Judge Posner cautioned the plaintiffs not to forget—despite the Findings of Fact—that the Court of Appeals had already ruled against them on the important tying issue and reminded them that higher courts generally supported tying one product to another where they found consumer benefit.

To each side, Posner sometimes wore his judicial robes, composing and sending to each a long analysis describing their legal vulnerabilities before a higher court. As a mediator, Posner allowed others to be added to each team, including: Charles F. (Rick) Rule, a Microsoft consultant who had held Jeff Blattner's job during the Reagan administration and who had once been a student of Judge Posner and, briefly, an employee of Lexecon, a company Posner ran before joining the judiciary; Joel Klein and Deputy Assistant Attorney General A. Douglas Melamed; and Dr. Richard Schmalensee for Microsoft and Dr. Franklin Fisher for the government. Posner also invited Paul Maritz to make a presentation in Chicago on December 15 on the integration of products such as a browser into operating systems; on Tuesday, January 11, 2000, Bill Gates spent the entire day with Posner, exploring a possible settlement but emphasizing that he would not accept a structural breakup of Microsoft. Impressed with his long, lucid analysis of Microsoft's legal vulnerabilities on appeal, Gates in January decided to share Posner's confidential brief with his board of directors, later retrieving each copy to minimize the chances of leaks. Joel Klein, who received his own tough brief from Posner, flew to Chicago eight times. Hopes were further raised on January 10, when Microsoft reversed course on the eve of another antitrust trial in Utah and suddenly agreed to a mediator's proposal to avoid a trial and settle for $275 million, without admitting guilt. The case had been brought by Caldera, a Salt Lake City software company that claimed, as Netscape had, that Microsoft had used illegal means to put them out of business. But the gap between the U.S. government and Microsoft was much wider—Klein was still pushing for a structural breakup—and consequently much more arduous to close.

CHAPTER 19

Disconnect: Washington, D.C., vs. Redmond, Washington

A REALITY GAP separated the government and Microsoft, and it was rooted in more than the law and the fact that each side believed its legal case was impregnable. In Washington, Microsoft was declared a stone-cold monopoly that would extend its hold over PC operating systems to all other electronic devices. Lobbying groups lent their voices to the chorus, including the Software and Information Industry Association, the country's largest such trade group, on whose twenty-three-member board Microsoft sat at the time. In a thirty-four-page amicus curiae brief filed in February 2000, the industry association lined up solidly in support of Judge Jackson's ruling.* The Microsoft monopoly, it said, had "a chokehold" over desktop operating systems and Web browsers and ruthlessly used its power "to harm competition and consumers." The notions that Microsoft possessed monopoly power and enjoyed an "applications barrier to entry are not fairly subject to debate within the industry." The proposition that Linux posed an immediate menace to Microsoft was ludicrous, the association said, because on the desktop "Linux is a niche player," with more appeal to

*Microsoft soon thereafter resigned from the association.

hobbyists than to consumers; ditto other devices to access the Internet, which are mere "complements, not substitutes for the PC." This brief painted a portrait of an "expanding" Microsoft monopoly, one that was threatened.

In Redmond, Microsoft executives wondered what planet Judge Jackson and the members of the association lived on. They felt vulnerable, not mighty. Since companies such as Napster could bypass the giant music companies, perhaps it would be possible to bypass the Windows gatekeeper as well. Wasn't the hub of computing moving from the desktop PC to giant Internet servers, and didn't Microsoft have only a measly 20 percent share of the server market? Soon handheld mobile devices would eclipse PCs in connecting to the Internet. Almost two and one-half times as many mobile phones were sold—275 million in 1999—as PCs, and Microsoft software animated few of these. Some of these cell phones already had connections to the Internet. And digital wireless devices were projected to be in the hands of a total of 1.3 billion consumers worldwide by 2003, according to the International Data Corporation. Over the next ten years, speculated Sun's Bill Joy, pocket devices would supplant the PC, be connected to a network, and would serve as an instant credit card, would make calls or reservations, send and accept e-mail, order prescription drugs, and become an all-around electronic assistant. Microsoft fretted about this wireless world and of how the center of gravity in computing was shifting to the Internet.

There were those who scoffed at this and agreed with Judge Jackson that Microsoft could extend its monopoly from the desktop to other devices. Steve Case and other Microsoft competitors were, not surprisingly, among them. "No question," Case told me. "We believe the world will converge, but it's not just going to be PCs and TVs and phones and stereos but how they're coupled together, and having a monopoly position in what is probably the central appliance and being able to leverage that to connect everything else together in a unified platform—clearly, they have leverage. Right now the markets are relatively separate. People think of the PC as one thing, they think of the TV as one thing, they think of the handheld device as one thing, they think of the cell phone as one thing. That's not the way they're going to think of it five years from now. And their ability to leverage a monopoly position in one to bridge together all of them is significant." What Microsoft is doing, and what they will continue to do, Case said, is tell customers that if they buy a device that uses Windows it "will be compatible" with the Windows desktop or the Windows server operating system. "So a lot of consumer electronics manufacturers are reluctant to do something else."

Microsoft, on the other hand, had some surprising allies who agreed they were indeed vulnerable—Lawrence Lessig for one. "I do think the competitive threat of Linux will undermine Microsoft's ability to control the APIs," he told me that winter. "In the long term, if the government doesn't prevail, I am quite confident that Microsoft will not hold the world." He thought the open-source movement would overcome the applications barrier to entry because "it is constituted as a neutral system. So developers know they won't get screwed. It's an operating system that's protective of competitive opportunities. . . . It's not just that Linux is free; it's a safe environment"—with no applications barrier, developers need not fear retaliation. "The threat of this is greater than Judge Jackson considered."

On the January 2000 morning that I next visited the Microsoft campus, the press was alive with reports that IBM had decided to adopt and invest in Linux as the operating system for its server hardware. With its deep pockets and marketing might, IBM was seeking to ensure that all companies used the same standard software language and, not incidentally, that they didn't use Microsoft's or Sun's. To the folks in Redmond, this was still another harbinger of potential doom.

On this particular Monday, however, the truly momentous story, an event Senior Vice President Bob Muglia likened to a nine on the Richter scale, was that America Online was going to deploy $165 billion of its "invasion currency"—its stock was selling at more than seventy dollars per share—to gobble up the world's largest media company, Time Warner.

This was nothing less than the biggest merger in history. A "new-media" company with just under five billion dollars of revenues would, because of its bloated stock valuation, acquire an "old-media" company with revenues of $27.3 billion. America Online had succeeded in becoming something Microsoft once aspired to be, a dominant content provider, with access to the most potent publisher of magazines (thirty-three titles selling one fifth of all magazine advertising); the second-largest cable-systems company, reaching 20 percent of all cable-wired homes; the Warner Bros. and New Line Cinema studios, with a domestic market share of nearly 20 percent and a factory that produced TV shows such as *E.R.* and *The Rosie O'Donnell Show*; Time Warner Music, which sells one of every six records (and they would bid to acquire the EMI Group, the world's third-largest music company and number-one music publisher); a burgeoning broadcast-television network (the WB network); three of the five dominant cable networks (CNN, HBO, and TNT); a book-publishing arm (Little, Brown; Warner Books, etc.); and the Book-of-the-Month Club. Time Warner also had a potentially important link to the nation's largest cable operator, AT&T; in acquiring the MediaOne Group, AT&T also purchased its 25 percent stake in Time Warner Entertainment, making it a principal shareholder in Time Warner's content businesses.

More worrisome to Microsoft, the combined company promised to become a gatekeeper over the distribution of all content. If America Online and AT&T were aligned, they would control nearly two thirds of all cable boxes. Between them, they already controlled high-speed cable access to the Internet, leaving them free to choose what services—such as MSN or Expedia—to feature or bury and to offer online, television, and telephone service. And although there were seven thousand Internet-service providers, 50 percent of all online users in America now relied on AOL to log on to the Internet. This merger was a nightmarish reminder that mighty Microsoft was anything but invincible.

While AOL's own market share did not approach Microsoft's, by early 2000 America Online and the family of services it owned, including CompuServe, functioned as the entry point to the Internet for more than twenty-five million Americans. And while its blistering pace of subscriber growth had slowed, the company hoped that with the addition of Time Warner's rich content it would be well on its way to becoming a one-stop service. "We don't want AOL to be a place people go through to get someplace else," Steve Case told reporters. "We want to be able to create an integrated consumer space. That's why, ultimately, the ownership of media brands will be important." If brands truly mattered in a domain where consumers were free to choose anything they wanted at any time, AOL Time Warner would be a colossus, poised to dominate the Internet and its bevy of connected appliances as surely as Microsoft dominated the PC. Microsoft might wish to sell itself as a software service for the Internet, but if AOL Time Warner was the service that ruled the tollbooth to the Internet, would other software—say, Netscape's—emerge?

Equally vexing to Microsoft, which had invested billions for its place at the cable table, America Online might threaten to subvert their plan there as well. Microsoft had long hoped to provide the operating system for powerful new cable boxes and had finally received a foot-in-the-door order from AT&T. But Microsoft had zero reason to believe America Online would welcome Microsoft to provide software for Time Warner's cable systems. The other reason for a seat at the cable table was to assure Microsoft broadband access to the Internet. Yet in a single swoop, AOL had gone from a supplicant, pleading to rent a wire, to the owner of a potent cable distribution system, Time Warner's Roadrunner. Would Microsoft, despite its own investment in Roadrunner, now become a supplicant to AOL?

To consumer groups, the AOL Time Warner announcement was cause for alarm. Four national organizations that bill themselves as protectors of the consumer—Consumers Union, the Consumer Federation of America, the Media Access Project, and the Center for Media Education—issued a joint complaint. Instead of a noisy, diverse Internet, open to a multitude of voices, including community and public-interest groups, the merger raised the specter of a corporate-dominated Internet that featured entertainment and crowded out serious news and open access for communities and for all those who either couldn't pay the toll or were business rivals. They prophesized an ad-drenched Internet on which, figuratively, sidewalks and the sides of buildings would be used to promote products. Consumer groups were concerned that the merged colossus would exert too much control over not just the cable wire to homes but the expanding direct-broadcast satellite-distribution system, since AOL had a $1.5 billion or 5 percent stake in Hughes Electronics, which owns DirectTV, America's market leader. To read the six-page, single-spaced AOL Time Warner press release is to notice that they paraded this merger as a promotional vehicle, as if all sister divisions would march in lockstep to "drive subscriber growth through cross-marketing with Time Warner's pre-eminent brands." Or, "We will use our combined infrastructure and cross-promotional strengths to enhance the growth and development of both America Online and Time Warner brands around the world." The new partners invoked the magic of synergy, predicting that after just one year of marriage the new couple would produce an extra billion dollars; by substituting house ads in all Time Warner venues, for instance, they expected to save part of the eight hundred million dollars AOL spent on advertising.

Ignored were the many nagging consumer questions, perhaps the foremost being, Would powerful toll keepers impede open Internet access and favor the elephants over the mice? If the original end-to-end architecture of the Internet was altered by the broadband toll keeper, might it mean that AOL Time Warner or AT&T and the local telephone companies—not the customers—would decide who got to travel on the Internet and to where, what road signs they saw, what rest stations and amusements were offered, and what ramps were available? The toll keepers, after all, were charging for access to the Internet, claiming that their highway could not accommodate everyone. The purest synergies would come if they could favor their own content. This was a rationale behind why companies such as Disney, Fox, Warner Bros., General Electric, and Viacom/Paramount owned television networks, for they ensured distribution for the shows produced in their own factories. Thus, when the six broadcast TV networks announced their lineups of new shows for the fall 2000 season, according to the May 19 *Inside.com*, the corporate parent owned all or part of 70 percent of these.

Similar laments, as Microsoft knew all too well, had been made by Steve Case when he was a mere renter and not an owner in this mighty distribution system. Before the merger proposal, Case had said he wanted the government to intervene to assure open access. After the merger was announced, Case reversed himself and said he believed the unregulated marketplace would protect the public interest. With the merger announcement, AOL and Time Warner also issued a press release vowing vaguely to assure "consumer choice." But they did not pledge to give competitors such as MSN—or Lycos, Excite, or Yahoo!—the same placement as AOL on the opening screen, the same price breaks, or the same ease of access to customers. And if John Malone, the largest single outside shareholder in the merged company (and in AT&T) had his way, access would not be equally open to all. The key issue, Malone told me, remained: who owned the customer? As he saw it, the ISPs would pay for their access to the cable wire, and the cable industry would bill consumers. And while he would open the wire to various portal sites, if AOL did not insist on billing cable customers for Internet access, he envisioned "AOL becoming the portal for the rest of the cable industry." The stakes were enormous, since high-speed cable access to the Internet was exploding. By the end of 2000, @Home, Roadrunner's chief competitor, expected three million subscribers, and by 2002 they expected ten million.

Uncertainty ruled. Microsoft was to have little reason to be comforted when, in late February, Case and Time Warner CEO Gerald Levin appeared before a congressional hearing and vowed not to favor their own products or discriminate about which ISPs could use their wires, nor would they block the direct access of competitors to customers. But, of course, the proof, as they say, is in the pudding. It wasn't clear how many ISPs could use their wire and whether heavy traffic would slow the high speeds. And other cable giants, including AT&T, had not spelled out similar open-access guarantees. Nor was it clear in January 2000—as it wouldn't be clear in January 2001—whether AOL or any entity could be a gatekeeper. Perhaps technology is moving as swiftly in high-speed Internet access as it is in handheld devices or new operating systems, and thus trepidation about AOL dominance may prove to be evanescent. Maybe the telephone companies' new DSL connections, which offer comparable speed and the promise of less interference during peak traffic periods, will catch up with cable modems. Maybe there will be breakthroughs in high-speed wireless modems. Maybe fiber-optic wires, which carry data converted into light waves (photons) before being translated into electrons and thus race faster to their destinations across many strands of glass fiber, will be the triumphant technology. Maybe more electric utilities will use their fat wire to enter the fray, as some already have. Should this competition bloom, then AOL Time Warner and AT&T will own—just as AT&T does with its long-distance wire—an expensive pipe that is soon to become a cheapened commodity. Then the balance of power would shift from the owner of the pipe to those who have a choice of pipes to rent. Again, only the passage of time will answer these questions.

Meanwhile, on the January 2000 morning that the AOL Time Warner marriage was announced, the reaction on the Microsoft campus was not relaxed or reflective. They did not react as if America Online had embraced a noncompetitive content strategy, with film and television and music and publishing offerings that did not collide with Microsoft's software-services strategy. Rather, it was as if a siren shrieked. Richard E. Belluzzo, the new group vice president for the consumer group, said he expected that the regular Business Leadership Team strategy session, which was chaired by Steve Ballmer and attended by Gates and about a dozen of the company's top executives, would alter its agenda this afternoon and dwell on this startling development. Another member of the team, Platform Strategy and Developer Group Vice President Paul Maritz, said, "It's obviously a very important deal. It's indicative of the way this whole industry is really still reacting to the deep implications of the synthesis of computing and communications." It was, he continued, an indication of "the changes in the alignment of the continents" that is occurring, "and no one knows what all the consequences are going to be."

In person, this bearded man with traces of a lilt from his native Rhodesia in his subdued voice is friendly, taking time to ask questions, acting unhurried, relaxed. In the courtroom, Maritz at first had acted put-upon. He had been curt when asked how he liked Washington, his e-mails had sometimes been brutal, and his testimony had been unabashedly unapologetic. Yet on this day, this decisive executive was no different from most communications executives when they are honest: he felt the fog of uncertainty come over him. "There are a number of pieces in motion, and I don't claim to understand all," he said. "We do see it affecting us. We have repeatedly said that we see the potential for AOL to metamorphize into a competitor to a number of Microsoft assets, including Windows. And this only reinforces that." He was anxious that AOL Time Warner might impede Microsoft's access to broadband cable pipes and perhaps to high-speed DSL telephone lines because of the deals AOL had made with three of the four Baby Bells. He was anxious that AOLTV could trounce Microsoft's plans to use its WebTV to fuse the TV and the PC. He was anxious about still another setback for MSN, whose growth crawled along while AOL membership climbed at a rate of one million new subscribers each month; he was anxious about AOL's plans to release Netscape's next browser version and when—not whether— they would dump Microsoft's browser; he was anxious about AOL's 1999 acquisition of MovieFone, the nation's leading telephone and online movie-listing and ticketing service; he worried about AOL's myriad software efforts and their alliance with Sun; he worried that AOL's e-commerce infrastructure and software might overshadow Microsoft's; he worried that AOL's instant-messaging service was supplanting the telephone and would soon blossom into a proprietary voice-message system for corporations as well as consumers, providing the kind of software services Microsoft dreamed of dominating.

The anxiety expressed by Paul Maritz was pervasive, as executives at other communications companies also asked, What does this merger do to my current business? What does it do to my stock price? Does it mean I must get bigger by merging with others? Does it mean I must buy another company before AOL Time Warner does? What does the market expect? Will the market continue to overvalue dot-com stocks, or will their "invasion currency" dwindle once old and new media link? Would AOL and AT&T make a deal whereby AOL, not Excite, becomes the pre-ferred portal site of the cable industry and @Home swallows Pathfinder to become the preferred ISP for AOL Time Warner (a scheme pushed by John Malone)? With half of all American households now invested in stocks, will the stock market punish a company for an acquisition that dilutes its cash or dividends in the short run but adds to the company's long-term value? George Bell, the president and CEO of Excite@Home, painfully remembers the time he had the chance to purchase the Israeli instant-messaging software company Mirabilis, but couldn't come up with the cash. "I was worried about dilution. I worried that Wall Street wouldn't accept it," he told me. So America Online bought Mirabilis and the "ICQ" service developed by the company now has seventy-three mil-lion worldwide instant-messaging users (plus sixty-five million users of Instant Messenger in the United States).

That particular week, speculation was rampant that Yahoo! might make a bid for Disney. A senior America Online executive said he heard that Mel Karmazin, the CEO of CBS and soon to be the COO of the com-bined CBS/Viacom, was out visiting Microsoft seeking to lure them into a partnership. Former Microsoft executive Patty Stonesifer had joined the CBS board six months earlier, it was noted. Would other content companies unite with Internet companies? Howard Stringer, the chair-man and CEO of the Sony Corporation of America, was in Hawaii attending a corporate retreat when news flashed of the AOL Time Warner alliance. "The frantic reaction to the AOL merger ruined my trip," he recounted. "Everyone is calling"—eager investment bankers and shareholders, insecure Sony executives, sniffing reporters—"to say, 'What is Sony going to do?'" By contrast, laughed Stringer, perhaps commenting on the difference between American and Japanese execu-tives, "Idei didn't think it was worth interrupting his golf game!"

Everything was happening so fast that it was disorienting. Anyone who looked at the shifting business landscape and didn't confess to being at least a little baffled was either insufferably arrogant or a fool. On this particular day, Bob Muglia even asked this heretical question: "In some ways, I wonder if it opens up an opportunity to work with AOL? If our focus is to build platforms and we know that the future of software is service based, that's very different from being a media company. . . . We went through a period where we thought we were a media company." Maybe a software and a media company would not bump into each other as everyone assumed.

Maybe elephants will fly. For a moment at least, Muglia was allowing his hopes to harness his fears. It is undoubtedly true that Microsoft and AOL will not battle on all fronts, and Microsoft could achieve a truce of sorts—as it did in 1996 when it made the hard-core decision to sacrifice its MSN baby by placing AOL in a folder on its Windows desktop in exchange for AOL's agreement to dump Netscape's browser. But abandoning MSN today was less likely since it is a central hub of Microsoft's software-as-service strategy. Each company hopes to create an online universe that users never want to leave because it provides their news, their schedules, their e-commerce, their e-mail, and their connections to individuals, data, other devices. Besides, the two companies appear destined to collide in PC software, in cable, in interactive TV, and in hand-held devices.

Not surprisingly, America Online executives went through the same thought process. Observed a senior strategist, "Some people in AOL said, 'I wonder if Microsoft will want to do more business with us?' We talked a lot about this the past few days. But," he added, "they will not be the first people we talk to." AOL has Microsoft in its crosshairs. A few days after the merger news burst into headlines, a senior executive chortled privately, "They should be more worried about us this week than last week." Indeed, after the announcement, Steve Case said that while many of their varied businesses would not clash, he expected a collision. "We, particularly with the Time Warner deal, are clearly focused more and more on the consumer experience—the music, the movie, the TV networks, the creative side of things, if you will," he said. "And they are more focused on the platform side of things, on enabling software. So to some degree, there should be some complementariness there. The reason there isn't, and likely won't be, is because we are wary of them."

If apprehension was the dominant emotion among senior Microsoft executives, bafflement that they were still being portrayed as a monopolist in Washington ranked a close second. "In my world," said Rick Belluzzo, who joined Microsoft in 1999 after two years as CEO of Silicon Graphics and twenty-three years at Hewlett-Packard, "if there's anything approaching a monopoly, it's not here." He didn't see it in handheld devices, or wireless phones, or games, or servers, or MSN, or streaming media, or WebTV. In Washington, D.C., the government said it was out-rageous for Microsoft to provide a free browser with Windows. In Wash-ington State, Tod Nielsen said it would have been nuts not to include a browser when every device is becoming Internet-centric. "Today, anyone who ships an operating system without a browser would be laughed at!" He noted that the newer Palm Pilots now included a browser, as did Apple's Mac.

While Judge Jackson envisioned a world where Microsoft would extend its Windows dominance over PCs to all other devices, Bob Muglia, whose responsibilities at Microsoft included not just Microsoft Office for businesses but the extension of the company's software to all wireless devices, scoffed at this. "When I wake up every day and think about what we need to do and how we're going to move forward, the thoughts in my head aren't, 'How can we extend our existing position?' It's, 'What are the things we need to do to be competitive into the future and to build the next set of products that people are going to want to use?' The reality is that if we just leave our existing products alone and don't innovate and don't change them, they will grow old very quickly and people will stop using them.

"Let me give you a classic example today," he continued. "I run the Office business," whose software applications for businesses bring in well over 30 percent of Microsoft's revenue and has a market share compa-rable to that of Windows. This business will change radically over the next few years. "If you look at where the world is moving, the delivery of and installation of packaged software is changing. People are utilizing the instantaneous communication that the Internet provides to move to a more service-oriented business model. It is going to be incredi-bly important for us to continue to evolve and change what we offer, to meet what people's expectations are." Already, products such as Intuit's personal-finance software are migrating from being reliant on desktop (Microsoft) software to being integrated on the Internet, where they might work on any operating system.

Muglia is no Cassandra. He has worked at Microsoft since 1988 and knows Microsoft has leverage. "Are there some things that customers may want that Microsoft is in a better position to deliver? We're a leading vendor of messaging technology to big corporations. Microsoft and Lotus are neck and neck. By most measurements, we have thirty-some-odd million people using our Exchange messaging software. Now that's an advantage. If I can get in a wireless space and say, 'Hey, thirty million people use Exchange inside the corporation,' and if I can use my phone to get at my Exchange mailbox, to look at my schedule, to have the phone read the e-mail off to me, there's some real potential benefit associated with that. And Microsoft can build upon the fact that we have these installed Exchange seats to help deliver services the customer may want."

In the end, however, Muglia insisted that such leverage was not crucial to success. Ease of use and quality—not marketing prowess or leverage from Windows or Office—opened the door to the promised land. "Service is the leverage point," insisted Rick Belluzzo. "If I have a handheld device and there are twenty million AOL customers, and my device doesn't work with them, I'm in trouble." Microsoft will continue to be successful, Belluzzo believes, if it succeeds in making software "more of the enabler than a product." A thin man who, unlike many of his fellow Microsoft executives, would not look uncomfortable in a suit, Belluzzo rises from his chair and heads for his whiteboard to draw a picture of a cloud. "Our basic view is that we will develop a set of services, a set of experiences that will become a central, indispensable part of people's lives, whether they're communications services, or e-commerce services, or educational services, or financial services—there's a full range of services that you can almost think of as a cloud." Like a cloud, these services will move over these islands (devices), transforming them into a linked network. "Where we really stand out in our view is about integration, about making these services work well together." The services seamlessly connect all the devices. Say your schedule, which is entered on a handheld device, calls for you to pick up your child in the afternoon at a day-care center, and you want to be reminded. Whether at work on your PC or in your car on a sales call or on your cell phone, a reminder can be flashed on any device. Individuals can sign up for Microsoft's Passport and enter billing and shipping information once; they can use Passport to authorize and authenticate credit-card transactions. Want to buy tickets to a football game? Consumers will use their handheld device to purchase the tickets online, then Passport will bill their credit card, and the network will place a reminder on their PC calendar and send an e-mail invitation to those invited to the game. Want to write on a tablet and have your notes transformed into type? No problem with

Microsoft's handwriting-recognition software. Every consumer device will connect—each using a version of Windows, of course. Similarly, in a joint venture with a sometime foe, IBM, Microsoft launched a company, Metronic.com, to allow heart patients to send instant data about their hearts to cardiac doctors over a secure Internet connection.

And with voice recognition, which Microsoft planned to integrate into Windows in the next decade, consumers will be able to replace keystrokes with voice commands. Ironically, as technology races forward it also sometimes moves backward, to the equivalent of the early candlestick telephone, which had no buttons and no numbers; callers just asked a community operator to connect them. "The telephone of the future is not going to be a telephone as we know it," predicts Jay Wilpon, Division Manager of Speech Processing Software and Technology at AT&T Labs. "It will be a TV, or the refrigerator. We'll get rid of the keyboard." Customers will just say, "Call Ben at work." Or the refrigerator will order milk and eggs when the supply gets low. Or any device will allow you to remotely change the temperature on your thermostat. Or the car computer chip can be asked for directions, and it will then guide you to your destination. Or suppose you're in Japan, said Wilpon, and you want to make a hotel reservation or get a plane ticket but don't speak Japanese. Easy. You talk into a device that is not connected to a person but to a server that recognizes speech and translates your speech into Japanese and back, making all the reservations. "What we want to do is put ourselves in the middle position of facilitating things for customers," said AT&T's Wilpon. Of course, that's what Microsoft hopes to do as well.

Which brings us back to Belluzzo's cloud. At the center of his cloud is MSN, which he believes has in the past lacked a consistent clarity of purpose. Instead of a proprietary connection to the Internet or a portal site, he envisions MSN as a service. Much as he knows AOL and Yahoo! envision themselves, he sees MSN as a collector of services and content, only he insists that Microsoft can find partners to supply the content and need not purchase a content company itself. As people now watch television, choosing to tune to a particular show, not a particular network, he believes that in the future consumers will shop for services, not particular software wrapped in a package. Microsoft is betting that software will become more, not less, important, in a world where consumers need intelligent agents to help sort through junk e-mail and a blizzard of channel and e-commerce and website choices. But to succeed, Microsoft must alter its culture and become more consumer oriented, a reason Microsoft allied with companies such as RadioShack and announced plans to jointly launch a Barnes and Noble eBook Superstore Online Bookseller using Microsoft Reader software. It is also a reason that—to better compete with IBM, Sun, and Oracle—Microsoft announced a joint billion-dollar effort with Andersen Consulting—called Avanade—to provide software and technical consulting to corporations wishing to establish e-commerce efforts.

While making these thrusts, Microsoft's core PC business remained strong. True, PC sales no longer explode, yet the PC market continues to expand. Jeff Raikes, who had Steve Ballmer's old job of overseeing worldwide marketing and sales, described the upside potential of PCs to me by pulling from a shelf a thick loose-leaf book prepared by Microsoft in July 1999. Of the 110 million PCs sold in that fiscal year, only 20 million were sold in Asia, and of that total half were in Japan. Microsoft derived two billion dollars in revenues from Asia, more than three quarters of it from Japan. Only 2.5 percent of its sales were in China, the world's most populous nation. The lesson? When the Internet catches on in the rest of the world, foreign sales should rocket. Already, Microsoft—like the Hollywood studios or the music companies—derives more than half its new revenues (about 55 percent, said Raikes) from business outside the United States.

It has been Steve Ballmer's mission since his elevation to the presidency of the company in 1998 to recast Microsoft as a consumer-oriented service company and to boost sales worldwide. Though quiet, the changes have been fairly dramatic. "Steve has a broader focus on the customer side than Bill has," observed Muglia, who reported directly to Ballmer. "That has had a broad and positive impact." Muglia went on to describe "the built-in tension between satisfying your customers' needs and innovating." If there were one hundred employees working on Microsoft Word, he explained, he could either assign half of them to "fixing bugs for existing customers" or assign them to "work on new features." Ballmer has "brought a broader balance" and shifted the emphasis more toward customer satisfaction, he said. Ballmer has also sharpened the focus of the company, narrowing those areas "outside our core expertise"—Muglia cited the sale of content businesses. "Bill is an incredible businessman, but Steve provides a little more focus."

Another change has been a broadening of Microsoft's management, setting up a regular series of weekly meetings and thus sharing more power. "It's not just Steve and Bill anymore," said Muglia. These moves have liberated Gates to spend more time pondering technology and Microsoft to spend more time climbing out of its insularity. The idea is to join the salesman and manager with the visionary.

This division of responsibility was formalized on January 13, 2000, when Gates conferred the CEO title on Ballmer, saying that he would remain as chairman and would assume the additional role of chief software architect. "I'm returning to what I love most—focusing on technologies for the future," Gates told the assembled press corps. "This was a personal decision, one I have discussed with Steve and our board of directors for some time. Although I've been able to spend more time on our technical strategy since naming Steve as president in July 1998, I felt that the opportunities for Microsoft were incredible, yet our structure wasn't optimal. . . . Steve's promotion will allow me to dedicate myself full-time to my passion: building great software and strategizing on the future and nurturing and collaborating with the core team helping Steve run the company." Kremlinologists wondered whether Gates was stepping aside as a public-relations ploy to win sympathy for Microsoft or as a prelude to a more flexible negotiating posture with the government. David Boies, for one, took Gates at his word. "I don't think it's related," he said. Gates's frequent business partner John Malone thought the move was related to the trial. Gates was relieved, Malone remembers, telling him, " 'Steve can sleep at night no matter what's happening. I can't.' "

The change in titles didn't change one obvious conclusion: many of Microsoft's wounds had been self-inflicted by the aggressive culture inspired by Gates and Ballmer. Steve Case, for one, envisioned little change. "Gates and Ballmer are far more alike than different," he said. "Steve is more outgoing and more of a salesman. But in terms of modifying the DNA of the company, Steve in some ways is more responsible for the DNA than is Bill." While most Microsoft executives would disagree with Case's diagnosis that their DNA was infected, some would agree that perhaps their competitive virtues became a corporate vice. Echoing something Steve Case had said months before, Senior Vice President Dick Brass, a former editor with the New York *Daily News* who had moved west a decade ago and struck it rich, a portly man with a walrus mustache and a voice every bit as loud as Steve Ballmer's, said, "Our company has to strike a balance now that we're a mature company in a mature industry. We have to be seen as a strong company, but not as zealots. We have to be good corporate citizens and work with others."

Steve Ballmer made a similar point in April when he told reporters something that Rob Glaser had once warned Bill Gates about: "We have spent the past twenty-five years thinking of ourselves as a small, aggressive company playing catch-up to large companies, even though at some point along the way we became a large company." But Ballmer insisted this was merely an image problem: "our passion for being the best has sometimes been misinterpreted." Microsoft was sometimes immature, he was suggesting, not brazen or brutal or unethical. Once again, the conclusion that perhaps Ballmer and Microsoft are afflicted by a disconnect from reality, unable to fully comprehend the consequences of their own behavior, was inescapable.

CHAPTER 20

Davos, Again

O NCE AGAIN, in late January 2000, Bill Gates attended the World Economic Forum in Davos. Once again, he addressed one hundred or so journalists at a Sunday lunch. Once again, he offered an impressive exegesis of Microsoft's future opportunities and pitfalls. Once again, he blew up at a reporter.

Before the luncheon, Microsoft public-relations aide John Pinette, sensitive to trial-related questions, stipulated to the forum staff that only non-American journalists should sit at Gates's table. The ten chairs at Gates's round table were tipped forward, and Pinette reserved a seat for himself across from Gates. He didn't want the editor of *Business Week*, Steve Shepard, there asking pesky questions; or *New York Times* and *Washington Post* columnists Thomas Friedman and Richard Cohen; or the Cox newspaper chain's Andrew Glass, who covered the Microsoft trial; or the editor in chief of *The Industry Standard*, Jonathan Weber. Instead, eight journalists who were thrilled to be invited had an in-depth conversation with Bill Gates centered on his philanthropic activities.

After the chicken entrée had been eaten, Gates rose and went to the microphone. He spoke about how excited he was by his new job, how good it was to shed management burdens and focus on developing great software, software to integrate a variety of devices, software that would provide incredible new services. Microsoft had bet the company several times in its brief history, he said. It bet first that the PC would supplant giant mainframe computers. It bet consumers would prefer the point-and-click graphical user interface of Windows over the typed commands of DOS. It "bet the company on the Windows NT" code base for corporate computing. He didn't mention that it also bet on integrating the browser with Windows, or that it bet the company in this antitrust lawsuit. And now Gates said it was betting the company again on integrated software-as-service. At Microsoft, he said, "we think everything is a software problem."

In the question period, I asked Gates to clarify Microsoft's future strategy by defining what he meant by *software*. If "everything is a software problem," might software include a Hollywood studio, a broadcast network, magazines, or a "content" company such as Disney?

"Some people when they say *software* they literally mean everything but the hardware," he answered. "And if you say it that way, it clearly includes movies and TV shows and everything under the sun. If your question is where do we see our focus, where do we see our core competence, we've been very consistent on this. We're getting a whole new round of questions on this—particularly because of the AOL/Time Warner merger—if that represents the direction a technology, online, procommunity-type company has to go? Do you have to have a movie studio?" If AOL owns most magazines and content, does it mean "the game is over because they have the ability to pull in exclusive content? It's a fascinating question, and one we've sat and talked about. We continue to do the thing that we're best at and define software in the more narrow, classic sense." He wasn't "rigid" about this, he said, only half acknowledging how deeply Microsoft had burrowed into such content investments as Expedia, MSNBC, Sidewalk (an online city guide), an animation investment with DreamWorks SKG, the online magazine *Slate*, Encarta, and games "that blur the boundaries" between software and content. "But we're not sitting around now saying, 'OK, what media companies should we buy?'"

In the future, Microsoft will partner with some companies and invest in others, as it did in cable, he said. "But we just don't see Microsoft owning one hundred percent, or fifty percent, or any huge sort of managing-type position in businesses that are primarily driven by pure content activities." There were enough software challenges ahead, leaving Microsoft in a position to stay "completely neutral" as to content and therefore not to have head-on collisions with companies like AOL Time Warner or Disney. Of course, there would still be collisions, but there might be more cooperation than conflict. Bill Gates fielded questions calmly, lucidly.

Then Thomas Friedman rose and asked Gates how he reconciled his assertion that he was on the side of consumers with the fact that Microsoft lobbied to reduce funding for the Justice Department's Antitrust Division, which is supposed to represent consumers.

Suddenly, Gates once again became a child, turning visibly irate. He glared a moment at Friedman, his eyes as concentrated as laser beams. Friedman was wrong, he insisted. "I think that's an outrageous characterization," he fumed. "It's untrue. The only thing that we've spoken out on in terms of funding is p.r. funding." Justice guidelines say the department should not "leak" stories to the media or urge foreign governments to attack U.S. companies. This the Antitrust Division has done, he said. But the only cuts in their budget sought by Microsoft were in public relations and to suggest otherwise was "outrageous," he said a second time. In fact, Gates was himself either being outrageous or uninformed, since Microsoft lobbied to cut nine million dollars of the division's proposed $114.3 million budget for fiscal 2000. The Antitrust Division said it has no budget for public relations; during the trial, its entire public-relations army consisted of an agreeable press officer, Gina Talamona, and her young assistant. Was Gates parroting the untruths of advisers, or was he telling untruths on his own?

The next morning, Gates was on the main stage of the Congress Centre auditorium along with Steve Case, Sumner M. Redstone, Chairman and Chief Executive of Viacom, Michael L. Dertouzos, Director of the MIT Laboratory for Computer Science, and the panel moderator, Nobuyuki Idei, President of Sony. Their topic: "Winning Strategies for the Internet Race." It was apparent that, unlike in prior years, Gates was no longer the magnet at this event: Steve Case was the new rock star of Davos. It was Case that Secretary of State Madeleine K. Albright asked to be seated next to at a dinner Saturday night, and Case that King Abdallah bin al Hussein of Jordan was seated beside Sunday night. In years past, no matter who else was onstage, the spotlight shone on Gates. This morning, Case fielded most of the questions; when Idei asked a general question of the panel, Case jumped in first, offering elongated answers to short questions, as if the audience expected this from him. Gates seemed to sink back into his beige leather armchair, hesitant to contribute. Gates looked markedly older than he had the year before. His face was marked by more wrinkles, and the skin under his eyes sagged.

Case spoke of his Time Warner deal and of how the combined companies would build "bridges" between appliances and of how the content of Time Warner would help "build some services that are really compelling." At that, MIT's Dertouzos tried to puncture the euphoria. "Everybody's hyperventilating about this deal," he declared, but content represented only 5 percent of all industrial work. Content would not propel the Internet; new technology that creates new businesses would. Hyperventilating himself, Dertouzos went on to say that the world has seen only three great revolutions: the American Revolution, the industrial revolution, and now the Internet revolution. So technology was now king.

No, said Redstone, reading from sheets of paper he held in front of his face. The merger of AOL and Time Warner was a reminder that "content is king," and that Hollywood, not a peninsula infested with engineers, would become the true Silicon Valley. "People do not watch technology. People watch what's on." Gates next spoke, and after graciously congratulating Case on "a very exciting" merger, he suggested that software was king. He saw software as the enabling tool linking content and technology and said Microsoft would stick to software, as it always has. At this point, it fell to Case to suggest there were many kingdoms, from "content" to "connectivity" to "context" (searching for material on the Web) to "community." It's "a big mistake" to argue whether content or technology or software—or distribution—is king. The only relevant question is, How do consumers look at it? And the answer, Case concluded, is that consumers look at it through many prisms at once. It was clear Case thought not a single idea but a single company—AOL Time Warner—would be king. And a reason for this was that Case believed, as did others who rushed to get bigger, that scale—the ability to outbid competitors for product or assets and employ leverage and achieve cost savings and synergies, spreading costs over many divisions—was king.

Afterward, I asked Case if he sensed a shift of focus away from Gates.

He acknowledged he was now "a little more" like a rock star and that the spotlight of celebrity now pursued him. "It goes with the territory," he said. He was also struck that Gates, with whom he's been on panels and attended conferences and had more than a few fractious negotiations, was "a little subdued. He seemed to be going out of his way to be more of a statesman." Not for one minute, however, did Case believe Gates when he said Microsoft would stick to software. It seems certain, Case later told me, that America Online and Microsoft would fight on opposite sides in World War 3.0. "It's highly likely that the destiny of our two companies is to duke it out for many years to come." Although Microsoft's software could be perceived as a complement rather than a threat to AOL's business, that's not how Case saw it. "We are wary of them. We don't see them as a software company. We see them as a to-the-death competitor. And they have determined, probably correctly, that if they want to be the most valuable company in the future they can't just be a software company. They need to be in communications, e-commerce services, content, and so forth." If Gates really meant not to be in the content business, said Case, "then he would have divested MSN and Expedia and all those businesses that are not software businesses." It is second nature for Case not to take Gates at his word.

This lack of trust was increasingly mentioned by other companies who contemplated partnering with Microsoft. Even John Malone, who probably has as many joint ventures with Microsoft as anyone, thought Microsoft's aggressive culture could disadvantage them in the future. "They want to win," he said. "They don't want their team to win. They're not team players by nature. They're ball hogs." Surely trust was now a missing ingredient in the relationship between Nobuyuki Idei and Gates. Idei is a trained economist who pushes his company to spend about the same on R and D ($3.7 billion) as does Microsoft ($3.8 billion), though the bulk of Sony's budget is spent on manufacturing development rather than research. Idei still saw Microsoft as "the biggest competitor of Sony." The two corporations were engaged, he said, in a series of "regional wars, not a world war." They battled in the game market, battled in designing software operating systems for cable boxes, battled in e-commerce, would battle when he launched a Sony-branded portal, as he had in Japan, to compete with MSN and others, and they would battle when the new Sony PlayStation became an inexpensive operating system for all home appliances. Idei had a private meeting in Davos with

Gates, as he did each year, but this year tensions flared. "He feels PlayStation is a real threat to them," Idei said. Microsoft aspired to provide the operating system for PlayStation, as well as for cable boxes or servers or PCs. Idei was unmoved.

Idei thought Gates had reason to be upset, unsure: "Microsoft is very uncertain about their future business model." In the two decades he had known Gates, Idei had never seen him so tentative. In halting English, this thin, taciturn man who wore a white silk shirt with a round collar buttoned at the top, said he thought Microsoft was slipping because their "business model is totally in danger." "Windows was designed for data," he said, and in the new broadband world music and television would be heard or seen "in real time," which he thought only powerful servers— not Windows—could accommodate. "Gates is an OS [operating system] dinosaur," he said, at a time when power is shifting. To get very large, companies required the right ideas, and Idei no longer thought Gates had these. "His mind-set is old," he said. He would no longer be able to license Windows as he once had. "Bill Gates is the IBM of today. . . . He wrote a book about the road ahead, but it is really the road back." Microsoft is losing good executives, he continued. Microsoft wants to build its service model around MSN, but when they head overseas AOL, Sony, and others have huge head starts. Microsoft wants to find partners, but human relationships are not its core strength. "Microsoft's soldiers try to behave like Bill Gates. They act more important than you," said Idei, making it clear that this further poisoned partnership prospects. This sense that Microsoft had slipped was echoed in the corridors at Davos. "Microsoft is increasingly becoming more and more like what IBM has become, a very important and successful company but one that is no longer at the center of the computing universe," observed Rob Glaser.

Yet Idei still saw Microsoft and America Online as the two principal future competitors with Sony. He hoped to reduce the battle to a one-on-one fight, which meant he might partner with either foe, though he wasn't sure he could trust Microsoft. However, even if Idei succeeded in eliminating a major enemy, he knew others would surface. Big companies will be assaulted by hordes of what he called "ants"—by free-software programmers using Linux, by copyright pirates, by newer, cheaper e-commerce websites, by makers of portable devices that access the Internet, by inventors of new technologies, by smaller, faster ISPs, by hundreds of local and state and federal government referees, and by the impact of free distribution, which might eventually allow anyone to make a movie or become a publisher. "A big company, like a dinosaur, will be eaten up by the ants," he said. Only the very large or the very small may survive, with those in between nibbled to death by the ants or crushed by the elephants. Uncertainty was a given, and there was no text or rule book to consult.

Idei was suggesting a central paradox of the Information Age: the emergence of both dinosaurs and ants—mice and elephants offer a more apt metaphor, since mice are nimbler than ants, and elephants are thought to fear them. The paradox is that, on the one hand, consolidation among old and new media companies marches forward and the elephants become larger, while at the same time appear thousands of mice— more channel and device and consumer choices, and unseen mice who sneak up on the elephants, as Napster snuck up on the giant record companies. How the tension between the elephants and the mice plays out, whether a company like Microsoft can continue to grow yet act as if it were small, and whether it can make peace with the even larger government elephant, is unclear. Nor is it clear that corporate elephants won't devise ways to best the mice, ways to control a new medium—the Internet—in which mice might otherwise thrive. Most of all, it is not clear what role the government will play in tracking the elephants. Will government serve as a referee, assuring that the elephants play by the rules, or as a spectator? Will government shape and define what now seems a rather quaint phrase, the public interest, or will government leave this task to the marketplace?

CHAPTER 21

So Much Effort, So Little Result

DISASTROUS as it might otherwise have been, the trial did bring Microsoft one small windfall: it converted Richard Posner into a Windows user. Posner had for many years been a Mac devotee, not because he was hostile to Microsoft but because he found the Apple machine and its software easier to use and less prone to crashing. For years, colleagues and staff members had urged him to switch to Windows, advancing the familiar network-effects argument: since most everyone used Windows, if he switched it would be easier to share files with fellow judges and academic collaborators. The argument carried more weight after Posner was appointed mediator, so he got himself a Sony laptop and switched to Windows.

On the eve of Bill Gates's departure for Davos, Judge Posner received a settlement proposal from the Justice Department. As he was to do with all government or Microsoft proposals, Posner translated it into his own language, tapping out on his new laptop Mediator's Draft Number 1 of a possible consent decree and e-mailed it to Microsoft. This draft was Posner's sketch of a possible settlement, and it came after he had invested almost two full months boning up on the court record and on technological issues and subjecting both sides to withering questions. He drafted this document and all others on his home PC, printed out a copy, edited it, and then e-mailed his official proposals to either Bill Neukom or Joel Klein, with copies to Tom Miller. Posner says that neither then nor later did he ever show a copy to anyone else, including his secretary and law clerks.*

The document shocked Gates and his colleagues, for it contained a proposal to split Microsoft into three companies: one responsible for the PC and server operating systems (Windows 98, 95, and NT), one focused on big corporate users (Windows 2000), and the third responsible for all other Microsoft businesses. Equally upsetting to Microsoft, it contained a Posner idea to solve the bolting or "integration" issue by creating an independent technical committee to approve or reject the integration of new features in Windows, based on whether they would benefit consumers.

While still in Davos, Gates conferred by telephone with Neukom. At a February 3 meeting, Microsoft responded with its own counterproposal. Microsoft said it would not even discuss a breakup of the company. Publicly and privately, Gates made it clear that splintering Microsoft was unacceptable because it would pulverize the team approach Microsoft needed to succeed. "What we want to do in the future requires integration"—not a shattered company—Gates had told the annual press luncheon in Davos. Microsoft also strenuously opposed the appointment of a technical committee, claiming it would become a bureaucratic nightmare. But Microsoft did offer to license to PC manufacturers the source code to exist-

---

*In reporting the mediation process, I interviewed representatives of the three parties to the negotiation and had access to crucial documents. Judge Posner and I had e-mail exchanges. I sent him a draft of this chapter and part of the earlier chapter relating to his appointment and initial meetings. His first e-mail to me began: "I have now read the two chapters you sent me. I would be grateful if, should you refer to my having read them and given you comments, you make clear that I have limited my comments to pointing out specific factual inaccuracies, so far as I can recall them. I have not consulted any notes or drafts that I made or obtained in the course of the mediation. Please make clear that I am not a source for your book and was not interviewed by you, but assisted only to the extent indicated above. . . . I don't want to comment on issues of characterization and interpretation and I have not gone back and checked the accuracy of your dates or of specific language from documents. . . . I hope you'll also make clear that the documents you quote or refer to did not come from me to you." In two extensive e-mail exchanges, Judge Posner confirmed the narrative contained in this chapter.

ing versions of Windows so they could choose to accept or reject new editions of Windows with added features; Microsoft also agreed to make Windows available for a published and fixed price, thus assuring that Microsoft would not favor certain vendors over others. Judge Posner was encouraged by this initial indication of Microsoft flexibility.

Over the next two weeks, a flurry of seven new drafts were circulated by Posner, mostly via e-mail. But by mid-February 2000, the mediation had stalled. Posner was talking to Joel Klein one-on-one now, in part because the state attorneys general said little in their meetings, and in part because Posner assumed the government spoke with one voice. Posner had separately presented to Microsoft and the government a memorandum explaining what he saw as their legal vulnerabilities and posited to each what he thought might be acceptable to the other. "He is now trying to stir the pot—'What about this? What about that?'" said a Microsoft negotiator. Privately, Microsoft officials were becoming somewhat paranoid, convinced that the government was acting out a charade because it believed it would win more in Judge Jackson's courtroom than it would from any compromise agreement. The government advanced a mirror complaint, insisting that it had put forth two ideas for a proposed settlement and Microsoft had yet to put anything on the table. Now, as always, neither side believed the other was open to a compromise. Meanwhile, Judge Posner prodded each side, keeping his own cards close to the vest.

The confusion each side sometimes felt was reflected by Bill Neukom, who said of Posner, "You keep asking yourself, Is he wearing his hat as a mediator, trying to motivate people to narrow their differences and come together, or is he speaking as the chief judge of the seventh circuit, who's an expert on antitrust law?" The confusion was heightened because each side felt conflicting pressures. Pushing Microsoft toward a settlement was the certitude that Judge Jackson would rule against them and the horror that such a ruling would unleash a plethora of lawsuits and raise the bar for an appeals court to overturn Jackson's judgment. They knew the trial was a major distraction to the company and a public-relations and a corporate black eye. Pushing in the opposite direction, however, was their fervent belief that Microsoft had done nothing wrong and their conviction that they would win on appeal. And then there was their political calculus: what if George W. Bush captured the presidency? Gone would be Joel Klein and David Boies, replaced by a Republican administration that might abandon this case, just as the new Reagan administration had exited the thirteen-year lawsuit against IBM. Besides, time could be Microsoft's ally, for almost daily it was revealed that technology might be moving faster than the law, proving the fragility of their so-called PC monopoly.

Propelling the government forward was an equal certitude: Microsoft had committed outrageous, even criminal, acts, and since Jackson was the adjudicator of facts, no appeals court was likely to overturn his ruling. The state attorneys general had a contingent of hawks who had always been fervently determined to punish Microsoft and who were less willing to settle, and, no matter who was elected president, without the concurrence of each state the lawsuit would not vanish. The states also posed a political public-relations problem for Joel Klein and the Justice Department, for Justice did not want to be accused of appeasement, of surrendering to a weak agreement the states disdained. This was the sword the states held over Joel Klein's head. But Justice and the states were more aligned than apart. Together, for two years, they had waged this righteous struggle, and now that the finish line was in sight they were determined to cross it.

Like Microsoft, however, the government also felt the tug of uncertainty pulling them toward a settlement. If Microsoft cooperated, they could impose a remedy immediately, and because Microsoft would help craft it, the remedy would be more likely to retard only Microsoft and not the vibrant high-tech industry as a whole. What if a Bush administration abandoned the lawsuit, eviscerating the legal monument they had built? Already there were signs that the Clinton/Gore administration might be getting cold feet. In a February interview with Wolf Blitzer on CNN.com, Clinton seemed to go out of his way to proclaim that while his Justice Department pursued Microsoft, he was neutral, a friend to all. Additionally, Klein was finding it difficult to induce his stealth corporate allies in Silicon Valley to speak out on behalf of rigorous remedies, a you-punish-them-but-keep-me-out-of-it hypocrisy first described by John Heilemann in *Wired*.

Then there was Judge Posner to contend with. Both sides furiously exchanged e-mails with Posner seeking to define and refine the various proposals, which Posner then ran through his own laptop before sending them back with questions. Although the proposals were always labeled "Mediator's Draft," neither side was ever sure whether they were reading a Posner proposal or one prepared directly by their adversary. Nor did either know what Posner said when he talked with Gates or Klein, if he even did talk with them. Each week, the parties would appear in Chicago on separate days and meet in a courthouse conference room, where Posner peppered them with questions and suggestions and then disappeared. Posner did not champion his economic interpretation of antitrust law. Rather, he described to me the approach he followed this way: "I would not transmit proposed decree provisions without editing to make sure not that they were 'good' in some ultimate antitrust sense, but that they were sufficiently clear to be judicially administrable and that (even if clear) they would not impose an undue administrative burden on the district court, which would have to administer the decree."

Both sides were often left to guess where they stood with Posner. "As the process wears on you get more and more of a picture of where he is," a government lawyer told me in February. "More and more he begins to let his own views filter in, and what we see is that Microsoft's stone-walling posture offends him." This was not, however, Microsoft's perception. They believed Judge Posner was not partisan. Yet within Microsoft there were varied interpretations of his stance. Some Microsoft officials believed that between a structural remedy that would split Microsoft and a behavioral remedy, Posner preferred a structural solution because it assured that no government bureaucrat would be perched over Microsoft's shoulder making software decisions. Yet it was Posner who proposed a technical committee to oversee some Microsoft software decisions. Still other Microsoft officials guessed that Posner was opposed to a more radical structural remedy. The conjecture extended to Judge Jackson's position. Microsoft's lawyers worried that Jackson favored a structural remedy, yet Jackson told me privately in February 2000: "Given my druthers, I'd much prefer a conduct remedy than I would a structural remedy." Jackson worried about "an excessively heavy" government role in policing a conduct remedy and wasn't sure "how I go about enforcing" it.

In hopes of pushing the negotiations along, Posner and Gates spoke on the telephone for two and one-half hours on February 24, with Gates seeking clarifications of various proposals contained in what was now Draft Number 9. Gates did not want another vaguely worded consent decree that either would impede innovation because the government was supervising software design or would end with the same collision they had over the 1994 decree. Posner said that after he heard back from Klein he would immediately compose Draft Number 10. At the end of their conversation, Gates expressed admiration for Posner and remarked to a senior colleague, "So much IQ on such a miserable topic." Privately, Gates and Posner were hopeful of a settlement.

The parties seesawed back and forth between optimism and pessimism. As the talks continued, it became clear that the bundling question was no longer the most contentious issue. Microsoft had won the browser wars; for the moment at least, Netscape posed no real threat. The government did still worry that Microsoft would bundle new applications—such as voice recognition—and so the issue was kept on the negotiating table. Microsoft still insisted it would never allow government "to specify what features they can add or must subtract from Windows," said a Microsoft strategist. Other issues faded as well. Microsoft's restrictive contracts were no longer a huge issue, since it had already abrogated most of these. Nor was selective pricing a bone of contention, since the dollar gap between what Microsoft charged "friendly" Compaq and "unfriendly" IBM for Windows wasn't vast, and Microsoft agreed to terminate differential pricing. The central point of contention became whether Microsoft would share more technical information. The Justice Department, which was canvassing Microsoft's enemies, had grown ever more concerned that Microsoft would keep non-Windows operating systems and non-Office software from interoperating smoothly with Windows.

In another phone conversation with Gates on February 28, this one running from 9:30 P.M. to well past midnight, Posner reportedly told Gates that they were only "five words apart" from a truce. But two days later, after state representatives protested to Posner that the proposed consent decree was "weak," Posner was gloomy. He was even gloomier on March 2, after receiving what a Microsoft official said were twelve new demands from Joel Klein. (Sources in Klein's office said these were merely clarifications and not new demands.) The parties now met biweekly, though still not in the same room, so guessing remained the norm. David Boies, who had been reasonably optimistic in December and January, was now morose, thinking there was only a 20 percent chance of a successful mediation. Boies guessed Posner didn't believe in conduct remedies, because ongoing government supervision was anathema to Posner.

For Boies, Posner was less of a mystery than Microsoft's legal strategy was. Although he admired the clarity of Microsoft's corporate strategic thinking, Boies was stumped by the conduct of its lawyers. "I don't know what their game plan is. The chance that Judge Jackson's findings don't become permanent, and the chance that the appellate court will reverse his findings, is unlikely. Microsoft has to have lawyers telling them that. A lawyer can tell them, 'You can win on this issue or that issue.' But I don't think a lawyer can tell them they can get the liability finding reversed." (In fact, that's exactly what Bill Neukom said he was telling Gates.) The only way Boies could make sense of Microsoft's legal strategy was to conclude they didn't have one and instead were driven into a corner either by Bill Gates's stubborn childishness or by his passionate conviction that he was right and the government was wrong. Or both. He couldn't imagine a lawyer would be so proud, so invested in a strategy that failed, that he would not be able to dissect the truth. Boies blamed Gates, believing he was pigheaded.

Or was he? Perhaps Gates and Microsoft wore good poker faces, since by early March the talks between Posner and the two sides heated up. Posner was talking directly to Bill Gates and separately to Joel Klein; he was not talking regularly to Tom Miller, who like his state colleagues was feeling left out. Posner merely sent copies to Miller of proposals he made to Klein. By March 2, Posner had circulated Draft Number 13. Among its familiar provisions, Microsoft could not retaliate against computer manufacturers that chose competing software; could not insist that computer manufacturers use its browser or other Microsoft middleware; could not discriminate as to the price of Windows; could not deny software developers access to the Windows code and to necessary technical information if they wrote applications for competing platforms. And, according to Microsoft, Posner told them that Joel Klein had added a new demand: Microsoft must disclose to competing software developers the Windows APIs invoked by Microsoft programs that run on servers, thus assuring that non-Microsoft software could connect to a Windows PC. Justice officials say they were merely seeking clarifications, because their great fear was that Microsoft would maintain its dominance by retarding the ability of non-Microsoft servers—servers being the vital, digitized, data-filled libraries that served corporate networks and the Internet—to hook onto PCs powered by Windows. If these servers could not link to Windows, or worked imperfectly, then the handheld devices that connected to them would experience difficulties as well. Exasperated, Posner told Microsoft it could consider this demand or offer a counterproposal if they wished, but he would not include this demand in his next draft. Instead, he insisted that unless Klein retreated somewhat and unless Gates accepted most of Klein's demands by noon on March 3, he would inform Judge Jackson that the mediation was ended.

Later in the day on March 2, Posner leaned a little harder on Microsoft, telling them that if they accepted Justice's new disclosure demand, Joel Klein and the Justice Department would sign the consent decree. Gates had been recalcitrant during the May 1998 negotiations and in his deposition and trial stance and at various times since the government began investigating Microsoft back in 1990, but he was not so now. He met with senior Microsoft officials and decided to surrender. According to Microsoft's account, a deflated Gates phoned Posner that night and told him that if the government would make a few small amendments he would hold his nose and sign the decree.

Posner called Klein, saying he expected Gates to sign Draft Number 14, and once he did Klein and the states would be granted eleven days to sign as well. On Friday afternoon, March 3, Gates affixed his signature. Senior government negotiators concede they were told this by Posner. Gates's signature "was a public-relations stunt," recalled a senior Justice Department official. "It was designed to get leaked. Joel can sign one of our proposals, too." But, of course, this fact never leaked. And Gates did sign what was essentially a Justice proposal. Judge Posner now gave the Justice Department and the states until Monday, March 13, to sign or abort the mediation.

After three and a half exhausting months—at one point David Heiner took an afternoon off to have his four wisdom teeth extracted and joked that it was a welcome relief—Gates and Posner thought they had a settlement. But over the next week, the state attorneys general let Posner know that Joel Klein did not speak for them and that they would respond separately. They told Posner that the states wanted tougher penalties, including guarantees that Microsoft would open relevant code to non-PC device makers. Posner was petitioned by a shifting cast of state attorneys general, including those of Iowa, Connecticut, New York, California, and Wisconsin. Some states pushed to stiffen the settlement terms. An emerging leader among the state hawks was California Attorney General Bill Lockyer, who recruited a former Netscape executive, Eric Hahn, for technical advice. Posner also heard from Illinois and Ohio, which favored more modest curbs on Microsoft's behavior. He wasn't sure what the majority of the states favored.

At the same time, Klein confronted another unanticipated source of pressure. He realized, probably for the first time, that Gates was ready to settle. So Klein thought more intently about loopholes in the draft agreement, about making sure Microsoft would be fenced in by it, about finding a formula that would satisfy both the states and Microsoft. While

Klein steered past these treacherous shoals, he confronted another reality: the Justice Department was defining and using technological terms it was struggling to comprehend. It did not have the ability Microsoft had to quickly digest technology. And in defining these terms, rampant mistrust would work against finding common definitions.

After many internal meetings and drafting sessions, and after consulting with technical experts at companies such as AOL and Sun, Klein asked Posner for further clarifications. At the end of the week, he sent to Posner language refining Justice's central demand. Their new language spelled out that Microsoft must disclose not only the APIs that competing software would need to connect to Windows from a server, but also the APIs used by Microsoft's own software applications for servers. Justice also extended their demands to include Microsoft's server APIs—thus guaranteeing that Microsoft could not withhold information in order to assure that only Microsoft-powered servers would work well with Windows.

Microsoft thought Justice was proposing to confiscate their intellectual property and make it communal property. Microsoft also believed that Joel Klein, outmatched technically, was showing the proposed settlement to its competitors, particularly Sun, AOL, IBM, Oracle, and Apple, who—again duping the government into waging war on their behalf—kept upping the stakes. Although Klein denies showing the actual drafts, he concedes, "We talked to various people at various times." The states compounded the disarray by further insisting that an agreement cover all handheld devices as well. Posner told the states that their proposals were unacceptable and pressed them to align with Justice. The irony was hard to miss. When the trial began, the government narrowly defined the PC as any desktop computer using an Intel processor, and now it defined it very broadly.

The government honestly thought it was trying to prevent Microsoft from doing what it had done in the past. The government had become convinced that it now understood Microsoft's scheme to extend its PC monopoly to other devices. Joel Klein and state officials were emboldened in their belief that "the evil empire" had a sinister master plan to extend its monopoly by an extraordinary Bill Gates e-mail they had unearthed. It was sent by Gates to his senior executives on July 11, 1999—just eight months earlier—after Gates returned from Allen & Company's annual Sun Valley conference. Gates was agitated and expressed alarm at how many non-Microsoft personal digital assistants

(PDAs) he had seen at the conference. And although his company had landed in court for using its Windows and Office monopolies to harm competitors, this did not deter Gates from proposing that Microsoft create technical roadblocks for non-Windows devices by leveraging the power of Windows. Although similar tactics had helped bring about a humiliating antitrust trial, Gates wrote:

> We really need to demonstrate to people like Nokia why our PDA will connect to Office in a better way than other PDAs even if that means changing how . . . we tie some of our audio and video advanced work to only run on our PDAs.

"What became clear in mediation was that they were not going to give this stuff up," said a senior Justice Department official. Justice also knew that Microsoft's Exchange, which offered an array of state-of-the-art Web-based applications, operated only on servers that used Windows NT or Windows 2000. So during the mediation, Joel Klein's office sought to tighten restrictions on Microsoft's ability to use Windows as a weapon. And the states sought to restrict Windows CE from getting the inside track on, say, the newest version of Microsoft Outlook, which permits users to synchronize the calendars and address books on their handheld devices with their PCs.

Though Justice and the states differed on some key points, each wanted Microsoft to reveal more of its source code and other technical information. As the industry and consumers moved toward network solutions where various devices talked not just to the PC but to powerful servers on or off the Internet, Justice reasoned, if non-Windows users couldn't effortlessly connect with Windows they would be compelled to switch to Windows products.

Judge Posner was discouraged, but he soldiered on. Once again, he leaned on Microsoft to bend. Posner phoned Judge Jackson on March 13 to ask for a little more time and told him that he was somewhat discouraged by the state demands, which he thought were extreme. After receiving Klein's response to Draft Number 15, on March 13 Posner incorporated many of these and the next day e-mailed a fourteen-page document: *Mediator's Draft No. 16 of Settlement Stipulation and Proposed Consent Decree.* These were some of the core terms of what Posner characterized to Microsoft as Justice's "final demands":

(1)   Government would wipe the slate clean, agreeing not to "oppose a motion by Microsoft to vacate the findings of fact" issued by Judge Jackson, which meant that these findings could not be used against Microsoft in subsequent lawsuits.

(2)   Microsoft would suspend its various contractual restrictions. For example, an OEM would no longer be denied Windows licenses if it "ships or promotes a competing platform software product"; nor would it be prevented from "displaying icons of a competing platform software product on the Windows desktop, provided only that the icons" did not mask Microsoft's icons; nor would it be prevented from designing "its own sign-up sequence" or from providing an option to remove the Microsoft browser icon from the Windows desktop and substituting another default browser, or from offering other non-Microsoft middleware.

(3)   Microsoft would not be allowed to play favorites through variable pricing and would agree to charge each PC maker "a uniform" price based on volume.

(4)   In its dealings with independent software vendors (ISVs), Microsoft would not deny them "timely access" to "technical information" and "communications interfaces" so that they could create Windows-based applications; nor would Microsoft condition the release of vital Windows technical information on an ISV agreeing to refrain from writing software for Microsoft competitors, providing that ISVs agree not to infringe on Microsoft's intellectual-property rights.

(5)   When Microsoft releases a new major operating system, it would not raise the license price for the previous Windows system for at least three years.

(6)   Microsoft would no longer have exclusive marketing-development agreements with OEMs; instead, the top twenty-five manufacturers who shipped Windows would share the same terms.

(7)   A technical committee would be formed within sixty days of the signing of a consent decree. It would be composed of three "technically qualified" members who have no financial ties to the government or Microsoft (one appointed by government, one by Microsoft, and the third by agreement between the two parties). This committee would be empowered to hire a staff. The main function of the committee would be to administer the consent decree, with particular emphasis on determining "whether the inclusion of one or more types of middleware in a major Windows operating system" was consistent with the decree. If inconsistent, Microsoft would be required to create a separate version

of that operating system (one without the integrated middle-ware) or one whose access to the new features was hidden. The government would have sixty days to register a complaint "following the submission to them by Microsoft of a release-candidate version of the new operating system," and Microsoft would have thirty days to respond, and the technical committee would then have thirty days to issue its decision.

(8) The consent-decree restrictions on Microsoft would expire after five years, except that the confidentiality of the technical committee's deliberations "shall remain in force in perpetuity."

(9) The Justice Department and one of the states would be empowered to enforce the consent decree. To secure compliance, government would be permitted, "upon reasonable notice given to Microsoft," to "inspect and copy" all Microsoft records and source code, to interview company officers and employees, and upon "written request and on reasonable notice," to require statements under oath.

By offering Windows according to a set price schedule and by regulating joint marketing agreements, Justice hoped to lessen Microsoft's ability to reward and punish with lower or higher prices. By making available to software developers more of Windows's secret code and interfaces, Justice hoped to end Microsoft's applications barrier. By sharing technical information about Windows in a timely fashion with any company that licensed the operating system, even a company such as IBM that had angered Microsoft, Justice hoped to end Microsoft's ability to reward allies and punish foes. By terminating exclusive contracts that imposed penalties on companies that did business with competitors or forced manufacturers to accept an additional Microsoft product as a condition for receiving Windows or by allowing PC makers to modify the opening Windows screen, Justice hoped to disarm Microsoft of a major coercive weapon. By placing limitations on Microsoft's ability to bundle new applications or middleware with Windows and by insisting that the company provide, when necessary, a debundled or masked version, Justice intended to grant consumers more choice.

Justice was making what Microsoft considered a fundamentally new demand. Convinced that it had figured out how to frustrate Microsoft's ability to leverage its Windows power into the post-PC world, Justice added a few words to its proposal to assure that any server "interoperating with Windows platform software" must have disclosed to it all "communication interfaces" and "technical information"—not just Microsoft's API codes. Thus, Microsoft's code for its "middleware" and "platform software," as well as its software installed on a server, must be disclosed.

Gates and Microsoft were surprisingly flexible, certainly when contrasted with their prior stance. The hard-core issues of yesterday disappeared, replaced by a desire to get this ordeal behind them. Gates, for example, relented and agreed to allow PC makers to uninstall Microsoft's browser. If he had made this concession in May 1998, a trial probably would have been averted. But Microsoft feared that Justice's new stipulations were either too broad or too vague. No longer was Justice just demanding open API codes. The effect of this broader definition, said Microsoft, would be to "open the source code to all its products." In addition, by insisting, for example, that "threats" be added to the lists of things Microsoft could not do in dealing with PC makers, Justice was also too ambiguous, for it left open the possibility that a government overseer might construe a simple Microsoft *no* as an ominous threat. The Justice Department believed Microsoft's objections were a smoke screen. Their most insistent demand became that Microsoft open its API codes, as well as other interfaces and codes.

At the same time, the list of state demands swelled, complicating matters. On March 14, a set of "tentative" consent-decree proposals was sent to Judge Posner from Tom Miller on behalf of six states—fewer than one third of those engaged in the lawsuit. Despite Judge Posner's earlier admonition, the states insisted the remedies were too timid to prevent Microsoft from repeating its predations. They wanted to include in any settlement an additional insistence that Microsoft reveal its codes for all non–Microsoft powered handheld devices. The states said the remedies didn't sufficiently punish Microsoft for breaking the antitrust laws. They attached new language to allow no room for Microsoft to wiggle out of another consent decree, imposed new strictures to ensure that it could not extend its dominance by, say, pushing Linux out of the market by assuring that Microsoft Office would work smoothly on the Linux operating system.

Judge Posner was upset. He had assumed that Joel Klein spoke for the states. Now he was certain this was not true. Equally troubling, not all of the states had spoken. The states said that Miller's letter represented the views of the executive committee of six or seven states, which just underscored Posner's anxiety. He vented his frustrations over the telephone, reports a Microsoft executive, saying that negotiating with the states was "like herding cats; they're hopeless." Posner does not deny he was upset with the states. "I suspect that they differed among themselves in their fierceness," he e-mailed me, "with the less fierce playing little role in the mediation (and litigation)." Posner told Miller he expected the states to go back to the drawing board and to make their proposals consonant with the Justice Department's. There were now three parties to the negotiations, and Posner knew they had reached an impasse.

An impatient Judge Jackson summoned the lawyers to his chambers on Tuesday, March 21, 2000. Judge Posner had deliberately kept Judge Jackson in the dark about what had transpired in the mediation process so as not to prejudice any later ruling Jackson might be compelled to make. But he did inform Judge Jackson of his concern that the states were disorganized and could sabotage the mediation. Jackson knew both sides needed a nudge. It was the first time the lawyers had been in the same room since their November 30 lunch with Posner. Jackson said he wasn't asking them to delineate the settlement proposals each side had made; he just wanted a status report. Dissatisfied with what they then told him, he warned that he was ready to issue his legal ruling and that it would find Microsoft guilty of at least one Sherman Act violation. Give us more time, both sides beseeched him, they were making progress. Jackson granted them another week.

Microsoft, which had decried government leaks throughout, spent part of the next week leaking stories about how flexible they were. The company would make "substantial" offers to achieve a settlement, Steve Ballmer said in an e-mail sent to company employees. "Judge Posner has created a wonderful environment in which to negotiate," said a Microsoft official. "My fear is that it will break down because of the recalcitrance of the states." But a Justice Department official, who acknowledged concerns that Justice and the states might be on different pages, nevertheless remained suspicious of Microsoft's intentions: "We're in an endgame, but it's not clear what the game is."

The perception gap was still vast. Both sides felt the other had misinterpreted the overly vague 1994 consent decree, and no one wanted history to repeat itself. If there was to be an agreement, government insisted that it be bulletproof, while Microsoft insisted that it be clear. And crucial matters remained unclear. What did revealing the API and other codes entail? Would Microsoft be free to bundle new features in Windows 2000, which is targeted at corporate networks?

In a nearly two-hour phone conversation with Posner on March 17, Gates said he was alarmed over the impact the new provisions would have on the integrity of Windows. Not long after the phone call ended,

Posner e-mailed Neukom and said that if Microsoft came up with a good answer to Justice's proposals as contained in Draft Number 16, one that allayed the government's fears concerning interoperability, then Posner was prepared to summon the parties to Chicago for face-to-face or shuttle negotiations starting Friday, March 24. Accept the basic terms contained in Draft Number 16 or else terminate the mediation, Posner e-mailed Microsoft. Sensing that Posner was siding with Justice against them, Microsoft became more paranoid. But Posner did not see his mission as the adjudication of the legal merits of the case, as Microsoft wished; his mission was to achieve an agreement. His one self-imposed constraint was that it be enforceable by the district court: in any statutory consent-decree hearing, he knew, he would be summoned to testify that the agreement served the public interest.

Seeking clarity, David Heiner tried to phone Phil Malone to wrestle with the definition of *interoperability,* but Malone said it would be inappropriate for them to talk except through Judge Posner. Microsoft believed Justice didn't understand all the technological implications of the language they were proposing and wanted to talk through the issues. Justice thought it understood the technology and Microsoft's intentions. What the government saw as a fence, Microsoft saw as a prison.

Microsoft scrambled to come up with a solution to the interoperability issue. James Allchin proposed to reengineer Windows so that all protocols supported in it would be "plug replaceable" through interfaces that were open. Any developer could then receive the same benefits a Microsoft developer would, since both Microsoft and non-Microsoft protocols would use the same "plugs" to connect with Windows. Joel Klein told Posner he was willing to meet with Microsoft—but only after Microsoft put in writing the changes it would make to Justice's last proposal.

Posner told Klein he was very concerned about the states falling into line. This helped provoke Klein to call a meeting on March 22 attended by half the state attorneys general, to get Justice and the states on the same page. Klein told Posner afterward that he thought they were.

Later that same day, Microsoft dispatched an eight-page, single-spaced proposal (which became the basis for Draft Number 17) to Posner with two ideas to break the logjam. First, as a substitute for the technical committee, they offered to give OEMs more access to Windows's code and said they would relax their restrictions so that manufacturers could use that code to modify Windows by hiding browser access and including a rival browser. After saying throughout the trial that browser access could not be easily concealed in Windows, Microsoft was now proposing to either publish the protocol or hide their browser. Second, Microsoft put forth Jim Allchin's "socket" plan to allow any competitive device or server to easily plug into Windows. Gates explained these proposals to Posner in a two-hour telephone conversation that night.

After Posner read the document, he and Gates again spoke on the phone on the evening of March 23, this time for four hours. According to Microsoft officials, Posner asked Gates to agree to return to Justice's proposed language on ten contested points in Draft Number 16. Gates reluctantly agreed. The intensity of these discussions was so great that through most of March Gates didn't dine at home a single night, he later told Steven Levy of *Newsweek*. As the weekend approached, Gates optimistically told his closest associates, "I think we're within a few words of having a settlement."

But Justice did not feel Microsoft went nearly far enough, and Posner told Microsoft he saw no point in a Chicago meeting until the two sides were closer. Still, Judge Posner was by March 26 optimistic enough to ask Judge Jackson to halt the clock. Jackson granted them another ten days. Posner laid out an aggressive schedule, in which he effectively cut the states out of the daily give-and-take but not out of the final decision-making process. The e-mail and telephone discussions would take place between Posner and Justice or Posner and Microsoft, and if they reached an accord the states would have a few days to ratify it. If Microsoft and Justice or Microsoft and the states achieved agreement within the week, Posner informed them, he would request an extra week to fine-tune it.

Although the attorneys general had been given a say, they were furious with both Posner and Klein. Observed one official close to the states, "Posner was more interested in dealing directly with Gates and Klein and didn't perceive that he had nineteen other parties to the lawsuit and didn't give as much time to the states as he should have. He got enamored with talking to Gates. And he's not a mediator by training and lacked basic mediation skills." One person who often attended the trial on behalf of the attorneys general observed of Joel Klein, "He likes to keep things close to the vest, and when you're dealing with other parties that becomes a problem. We never had a problem during the trial dealing with David Boies, but we did the higher up you got."

While the states let Posner and Klein know they might not go along with the compromise they were crafting, some preferring a breakup of Microsoft, others wanting stricter behavioral remedies, and all wanting to be treated as equals, nevertheless Bill Gates and Joel Klein now believed they had a shot at a settlement. Or so they say. While Judge Posner didn't hold judicial power, he did have political leverage; no one wanted to get blamed for a stalemate. "The mediation created some very strong dynamics because of the nature of the case and the stature of Judge Posner," observed Tom Miller. "None of the three sides wanted to be in a position where Judge Posner singled them out as saying no." That would amount to a political black eye. Moreover, it might offend the ultimate decision maker. "None of us wanted to be seen by Judge Jackson as frustrating a resolution," said Miller.

Posner spent the next few days wrapping his mind around Allchin's proposal and Justice's concerns that it was a trick. On the evening of March 29, Posner sent to Microsoft Justice's counterproposal, which became Draft Number 18. Both sides felt achingly close: Justice and Microsoft each expected Posner to summon them to Chicago.

Comparing Draft Number 17, which represented Microsoft's views, with Draft Number 18, a fourteen-page offer submitted by Justice and transmitted by Judge Posner six days later, reveals that in many respects, the ocean between Microsoft and Justice appeared nearly bridged. Despite differences in wording, they agreed:

- To vacate Judge Jackson's Findings of Fact so these could not be lodged against Microsoft in subsequent lawsuits;
- that Microsoft would neither hold back Windows from OEMs nor retaliate against OEMs that chose competing platforms;
- that Microsoft would not impose contracts on OEMs requiring them to license Microsoft middleware as a condition for receiving Windows;
- that Microsoft would cease offering better prices to some OEMs and would instead offer Windows under uniform terms;
- that Microsoft would allow OEMs more editorial control over the opening desktop screen;
- that when Microsoft came forth with its next Windows operating system, now code-named "Millennium," it would allow OEMs to remove access to its Internet Explorer;
- that Microsoft would terminate exclusive management-development agreements with OEMs;
- that Microsoft would not impose restrictions on ISVs limiting their ability to have their software compete with Microsoft's;

- that Microsoft would make available to ISVs necessary Windows APIs in timely fashion so that other software could hook on to Windows;
- that the new consent decree would last for five years;
- that in regard to enforcement, Microsoft and Justice agreed to drop the independent technical committee and substitute a Microsoft antitrust-compliance officer who would report directly to Microsoft's CEO. In addition, they agreed that to "secure compliance with this decree," representatives from Justice and the states would be empowered to inspect all Microsoft documents, interview its employees and officers, and require, if necessary, sworn testimony.

But a close comparison of the two documents reveals that the principal gap between the two sides revolved around technical definitions, with Justice pushing to guarantee what it called "interoperability," a word absent from the Microsoft document. Compare, for example, Microsoft's skimpy paragraph contained in Draft Number 17 with the more elaborate Justice proposal as outlined in Draft Number 18:

Mediator's Draft Number 17 (based on Microsoft's proposal):

Microsoft Corporation is enjoined from . . .

(8) refusing to publish, for use on Windows operating systems, the APIs that enable Microsoft middleware that is licensed for a positive price separately from Windows operating system releases or updates to run on those Windows operating systems, provided that nothing in this subparagraph shall be interpreted to require Microsoft to publish the source code of its operating systems, to maintain APIs, or to license parts of its operating systems.

Mediator's Draft Number 18 (based on Justice proposal):

Microsoft Corporation is enjoined from . . .

(8) failing to disclose (at the time such APIs, technical information, or communications interfaces are disclosed to Microsoft's own software developers) for use in interoperating with Windows operating systems and middleware distributed with such operating systems, the APIs, technical information and communications interfaces that Microsoft employs to enable—
   (a) Windows platform software to interoperate with Microsoft applications installed on the same personal computer, or

(b) Windows operating system software and middleware distributed with such operating system to interoperate with Microsoft middleware installed on the same personal computer if the middleware is

   (i) Internet Explorer, the Outlook Express e-mail client, Windows, Media Player, or the Java Virtual Machine, or their successors, or

   (ii) distributed separately from the operating system for installation on any Windows operating system; or

(c) a Windows operating system and middleware distributed with such operating system installed on one personal computer to interoperate with any of the following software installed on a different personal computer or on a server—

   (i) Microsoft applications,

   (ii) Microsoft middleware, or

   (iii) Microsoft client or server operating systems.

The differences between the two sides are reflected at the beginning of each draft, with each offering technical definitions of such terms as *personal computer* and *middleware*. Intent on handcuffing Microsoft, Justice's definitions are nearly twice as long as Microsoft's. Contrast their different definitions of *technical information:* the government's definition was eighty-two words, while Microsoft's was only twenty-eight words. The government's draft proposed that Microsoft provide the APIs and all other communications protocols and file formats and conventions and algorithms and registry settings that might be used to prevent interoperability. Microsoft's definition, on the other hand, stressed that only "competent" developers could be granted access to the code.

This chasm between the two versions was immense. Microsoft was concerned less with the issue of interoperability than it was with cloning, which is why in their proposal they stressed "publish[ing] for use on the Windows operating system" and "competent" developers. They did not want to risk giving away their entire source code to a pirate. Justice also asked that Microsoft not retire certain APIs and that it publish its file formats, demands Microsoft believed betrayed an ignorance of technology. APIs are dropped occasionally, as they were when PCs went from 16-bit to 32-bit and then to 64-bit architecture. File formats are changed regularly, and to lump together these and all "programmatic interfaces" and say they must be open and documented would hinder the company's ability to upgrade them. Microsoft feared they would be asked to keep technology it considered backward, and this would stall innovation. To Microsoft, Justice's version really said: you must give up all technical information and intellectual property in any software we deem to be a separate product. There is no definition of *separate*, and government reserved the right for anyone to challenge any feature added to Windows by claiming it is really a separate product. And any future changes in Windows must be approved by government. Thus, Bill Gates, as he had cried from day one, would not retain the freedom to innovate.

Justice, on the other hand, believed the core issues were opening up the system so that others could innovate and closing all loopholes. In its discussion of *middleware*, Justice included things that Microsoft views as being integral parts of the operating system: the Media Player, the Java Virtual Machine, the browser, and Outlook Express. Justice was intent on assuring that all non-Microsoft middleware could interoperate with Windows. They believed that if every new product could be defined as part of Windows, then Microsoft would have rigged the system.

Hidden in the technical jargon, however, were the same stubborn issues that had divided the parties throughout the litigation: what is Windows? Who gets to define it? What is the difference between "middleware" and part of the operating system? What is an integrated versus a separate product? Also, there remained a lack of trust. A reason Justice gave its proposed consent decree such specificity was that it didn't trust Microsoft. Why should government accept in good faith the assurances of a company that wouldn't even admit that it had been concerned with Netscape's market share?

Microsoft told Judge Posner they found government's technical proposals "extreme." Nevertheless, if Judge Posner could find a middle ground on the technical definitions, there was reason for Bill Gates and Justice to be optimistic. Posner pushed hard on Microsoft, hoping to nudge them closer to Justice's proposals. By early evening on Friday, March 31, the Justice Department and Posner had not received Microsoft's response to Draft Number 18, and Justice feared Microsoft would not budge from the remedy proposals it had agreed to in Draft Number 17. The state attorneys general then startled Posner by submitting on Friday their own set of what they called "preliminary demands," which astonished Posner because he had asked them to withdraw some of their earlier demands and they had not. The states were angry that they had been largely left out of the give-and-take, and they now registered opposition to parts of the Justice-approved Draft Number 18, weighing in with additional demands. According to both Justice and Microsoft officials, Judge Posner complained that the states' demands were completely unreasonable.

Judge Posner needed more time, but the clock had almost expired. He now knew that at this late hour he might have to negotiate with nineteen attorneys general, and he would have to choreograph what Klein could not: a single set of government proposals. And even if Posner could find common ground between the states and Justice, he still saw a divide yawning between the government and Microsoft. To the government, compelling Microsoft to open its code to developers was a way to hurdle the applications barrier to entry; to Microsoft, it amounted to theft of their intellectual property. The lack of trust between the parties was corrosive, making it difficult to settle the technical issues. Judge Posner didn't see a way out.

Posner made a decision even before Microsoft faxed to him early Friday evening its Draft Number 19, which attempted to respond to Posner's pleas for compromise. That evening, he telephoned Microsoft and Klein and announced that the mediation effort was over. He told Microsoft that he had not even studied their new draft, since the parties were so far apart on the technical issues. He told them that as a judge he had never invested as much time in any case as he had invested in this failed mediation. On Saturday, April 1, he notified Judge Jackson and the public that after four months of negotiations the gulf between the parties was too vast. Privately, Judge Posner complained loudly that the states acted like "assholes." Prior to the public announcement, Posner circulated to Justice and Microsoft a draft of the statement he would issue to the press, including a blistering denunciation of the attorneys general for their outrageous last-minute demands. Posner was persuaded—Joel Klein refuses to confirm or deny Microsoft's suspicion that he persuaded Posner—to remove this paragraph from the prepared statement. Posner is not sure he called the states "assholes," but he e-mailed me: "I can't swear that I didn't say this (though I don't think I ever speak 'loudly'), but it is very unlikely that I did. Not that I don't use such language, but although the mediation was informal I tried to maintain some minimum decorum, and I doubt that I would have used such a word to any of the people I dealt with in the mediation, and I am sure I would not have said it to someone not involved in the mediation—I have been very careful to avoid discussing the mediation publicly or privately (though in a sense I'm doing this in this email!)."

In his only prior public comment on the mediation effort, Posner's April 1 statement declared: "After more than four months, it is apparent that the disagreements among the parties concerning the likely course, outcome, and consequences of continued litigation, as well as the implications and ramifications of alternative terms of settlement, are too deep-seated to be bridged." He went on to say this would be his sole comment on the discussions and graciously thanked the Department of Justice, Microsoft, and Judge Jackson. He pointedly omitted thanking the states. "We certainly noticed we were left off," said Iowa Attorney General Miller.

So Bill Gates had reason to at least partly blame the states for the collapse. "Ultimately, it became impossible to settle because the Department of Justice and the states were not working together," he declared. While trying to muffle their differences, Justice and the states blamed Microsoft. The negotiations did not collapse because of state meddling, insisted a senior Justice Department official; they collapsed because Microsoft was "unwilling to forgo their ability to leverage" Windows into other markets.

Some of the lawyers on both sides wondered whether Posner made a mistake in keeping them apart throughout the mediation effort. With little personal contact, it was harder for Gates and Klein and their lieutenants to think of their adversaries as flesh-and-blood human beings, not demons. Each side was interpreting the proverbial shadows on the cave wall. Perhaps Posner's dry, intellectual approach to legal issues—like Bill Neukom's amassing of "facts"—ruled out the vital human factor, ignored how the mix of personality and issues can build, as well as erode, trust. On this point, too, Posner declined to comment.

Wherever the blame lay, one fact remained: it was indeed over. Front-page stories of the failed negotiations appeared in Sunday's newspapers. What the stories didn't capture was how eager Microsoft was to settle, so eager that Bill Gates had been willing to abandon endlessly touted principles to achieve an armistice. That much is clear. It also appears clear that the Justice Department was probably more ambivalent about a truce, partly because it could not deliver its state allies and worried they would be exposed politically if the states did not bless an agreement and pursued the lawsuit on their own. When Justice did set its mind to seeking a settlement, it could not focus on the technical terms of an agreement with the same organization and skill as could Microsoft. And the states were nineteen people without a single brain. Ironically, while Microsoft began this trial convinced, wrongly, that it was the victim of "politics," in the end it became a victim of both politics and its own mul-ish failure to settle earlier on much less onerous terms.

Bill Gates might have asked the same question German Chancellor Prince von Bülow once asked his successor after Germany was vanquished in World War I: "How did it all happen?"

"Ah," his successor replied, "if only we knew."

There would be no time to stew on what-ifs. On Monday, Judge Jackson informed the parties he would issue his legal ruling in the afternoon, after the stock exchange had closed. And at 5 P.M. sharp on April 3, Judge Jackson's Conclusions of Law were left in stacks at the district court-house for the parties and the press to retrieve.

To the surprise of no one, Judge Jackson found Microsoft guilty of vio-lating the nation's antitrust laws. Having concluded in his Findings of Fact that Microsoft was a monopoly, Jackson now found that Microsoft crossed the line from normal business hardball to "predacious" behavior. The "Court concludes," he wrote, "that Microsoft maintained its monop-oly power by anticompetitive means and attempted to monopolize the Web browser market, both in violation of [section] 2 of the Sherman Act." And in a direct assault on the Court of Appeals, Jackson wrote: "Microsoft also violated [section] 1 of the Sherman Act by unlawfully tying its Web browser to its operating system." When Microsoft recog-nized that Netscape's browser was middleware that could become "the Trojan horse" to overcome Microsoft's "applications barrier," he wrote, Microsoft intentionally orchestrated a campaign to defeat Netscape and all other middleware threats, mounting "a deliberate assault upon entre-preneurial efforts that, left to rise or fall on their own merits, could well have enabled the introduction of competition into the market for Intel-compatible PC operating systems." He found that Microsoft was a preda-tor, for it "paid vast sums of money, and renounced many millions more in lost revenue every year, in order to induce firms to take actions that would help enhance Internet Explorer's share of browser usage."

Jackson's judgment of Microsoft was even more damning than that of his law clerks, David McIntosh and Tim Ehrlich, who wrote the first draft. Jackson told me that one of the two sections that he completely wrote on his own was the finding that Microsoft had violated section 2, because the initial draft from his clerks asserted that Microsoft was not guilty of such a violation, as it had failed to eradicate competition in the browser marketplace. Jackson disagreed, believing, he told me, that "all we had to do was show an attempt" to monopolize and "a likelihood of success. The offer to divide markets with Netscape was an attempt to monopolize the market."

Judge Jackson did more than find Microsoft guilty. He also found the Court of Appeals guilty of misreading the tying law and of making "metaphysical assumptions" about the nature of products and markets when it ruled, in June 1998, that Microsoft benefited rather than harmed consumers when it integrated a browser in with Windows. This was the second section Jackson wrote on his own, telling his law clerks not to even offer up a draft because he wished to write it entirely from scratch. Jackson wrote that he did not believe the Court of Appeals decision bound him in this case. And if it did apply, he defiantly challenged the superior court's decision, asserting that Microsoft clearly violated the "restraint of trade" clause of section 1 of the Sherman Act when it exploited its "market power over one product to force unwilling buyers into acquiring another." Jackson, like Microsoft, treated the appeals-court decision as more sweeping than it was. With controlled disdain, he said the majority opinion of the higher court "evinces both an extraordinary degree of respect for changes" made "in the name of product 'improvement,' and a corresponding lack of confidence in the ability of the courts to distinguish between improvements in fact and improvements in name only, made for anticompetitive purposes. Read literally, the D.C. Circuit's opinion appears to immunize any product design . . . from antitrust scrutiny, irrespective of its effect upon competition, if the software developer can postulate any 'plausible claim' of advantage." In its rebuke of Judge Jackson, the Court of Appeals had accused him of placing his "thumb on the scale" and imposing excessive requirements on Microsoft by finding that it had violated the consent decree. With evident glee, Jackson invoked the same imagery, accusing Microsoft of placing "an oppressive thumb on the scale of competitive fortune." Jackson went on to invoke various Supreme Court decisions that seem to contradict the Court of Appeals's tying decision, describing these as "indisputably controlling."

Judge Jackson had found against Microsoft in every instance save one. While he had found that Microsoft attempted to monopolize in order to foreclose Netscape, he reversed one of his Findings of Fact and now concluded that Microsoft did *not* succeed in doing so because consumers could still acquire the Netscape browser. Thus, Microsoft was found not to have violated another part of section 1 of the Sherman Act, which prohibits "exclusive dealing." It was as if Microsoft, down 20 to 0 in the ninth inning, sent a batter to the plate who then smacked a solo home run.

This time, Microsoft did not pretend to have won more victories than the eye could see. Bill Gates simply said the company disagreed with Judge Jackson and would appeal.

Joel Klein, joined by Attorney General Janet Reno, the state attorneys general, and a turtlenecked David Boies, held a jubilant press conference. Klein had many reasons to be euphoric. In his four years at the helm of the Antitrust Division, he had succeeded in putting antitrust law back on the nation's agenda. They had stopped or modified about two hundred mergers, sent fifty-two executives to jail, collected whopping fines totaling two billion dollars. But no victory was sweeter than this one. And in going outside the department to recruit David Boies, he had been vindicated. Boies genuinely admired Klein and the intellect of the team he worked with at Justice, but on this day his thoughts turned to a man whose intellect was sometimes questioned: Thomas Penfield Jackson. Boies likened Jackson to Harry Truman and Ronald Reagan, two presidents who had been underestimated and had their intellects questioned yet surprised critics with their tenacious convictions and vigorous common sense.

The day Jackson's decision was released, Microsoft's stock price plunged $15.38 per share, falling to $90.88, an eighty-billion-dollar drop in market value; three weeks later, it fell further, to $66.62 per share. On April 3, the day of the decision, the NASDAQ consumer index, which is heavily weighted toward new-economy stocks, was jolted by its fifth worst day ever, and it continued to fall for days and months afterward.

Jackson couldn't believe Microsoft had allowed the case to spin out of control. Privately, as he made clear in a September 29, 2000, address to Washington, D.C., antitrust lawyers, he blamed "Microsoft's intransigence" for the failure of the parties to achieve a settlement before he had to rule. He had been deliberately and properly kept uninformed about the mediation effort and was unaware of Microsoft's eagerness to settle. But he was correct that Microsoft had permitted the case to spiral out of control. He wasn't sure whether to blame Microsoft's legal team, Bill Gates, or Steve Ballmer for being so damn confrontational and denying everything in court. "It might have helped," he later told me, had they been more honest. "It would have dispelled, to a large extent, any inference of malevolent motive. It would have disclosed that they were genuinely concerned that there might have been some merit to the allegations of improper conduct on their part. . . . It would have gone largely to the matter of motive. In one sense you have to give Microsoft credit for consistency. They have maintained, and continue to maintain, they have done nothing amiss." Judge Jackson blamed Bill Neukom for not warning his client to alter its behavior and for not settling before the markets were roiled and an unelected judge was forced to play God. "I don't think he's very smart," Jackson told me, disdainfully. "He's the general counsel of this company. He should have said, 'Look, you guys can't do this. Now is the time to be flexible.'"

Bill Neukom was more diplomatic but just as disdainful of Judge Jackson's legal reasoning. He remained unshaken in his belief that the law was Microsoft's shield. Days after Jackson's decision, in a conference room at Sullivan & Cromwell's midtown Manhattan offices, with Richard Urowsky by his side, he expressed unflinching optimism about winning on appeal in the face of Jackson's scathing ruling. "It's important to recognize that these Conclusions of Law very substantially narrow the issues remaining in this case," he told me. "The District Court did not think it worthwhile to address issues like 'monopoly leverage,' or 'essential facilities,' or 'predatory pricing,' or 'market division' per se. Those issues that you heard a lot about on the courthouse steps are all out of this case, permanently. The court only thought there were four issues worth addressing, despite the Findings of Fact. Of those four, the court dismissed 'exclusionary dealing' under section one of the Sherman Act. And that leaves just three causes of action. One was technological tying, where the District Court rejected the Court of Appeals decision that sided with Microsoft and concluded that the browser and Windows were separate products." This, of course, overstates what the appeals court said; as even Gates noted, the appeals court focused on whether Microsoft violated its 1994 consent decree, not Microsoft's intent or the evidence produced in a trial about its behavior. But, Neukom continued, the government "never proved there were two products. They've never even attempted to define IE—the alleged separate product—despite our many demands. And they've never proven a lack of plausible benefit that derives from the integrated design of the product." So he was "confident that on appeal the technological tying doctrine enunciated" by Judge Jackson would be reversed.

Second, he talked about "the attempt to monopolize" the browser market, noting that Judge Jackson relied on the American Airlines price-fixing case, in which there was a tape recording of the chairman of American Airlines proposing collusion to a fellow airline-company CEO. "That's the exception that proves the rule that courts are very, very, very reluctant to find activity or conversations that constitute an 'attempt to monopolize' a market. Nothing in this record comes within a country mile of that kind of conversation with its 'uniquely unequivocal' anti-competitive result. In fact, the findings themselves indicate that the record was ambiguous about what was said and what was accomplished in the course of that meeting" with Netscape in June 1995. And since Windows 95 featured the Netscape browser icon, he believed there was no basis for "an 'attempt to monopolize' case.

"The third area is 'monopoly maintenance,' under section two," Neukom continued. Judge Jackson cited Microsoft's "exclusionary deals" as the first example of his "monopoly maintenance" claim, even though, Neukom noted with a barely suppressed sneer, Jackson found these "not to be anticompetitive" under section 1. Second, Jackson asserted that Microsoft had sabotaged Java, but Neukom said this was "a weak reed" since it was based on flimsy evidence. Finally, the "thrust of the monopoly-maintenance conclusion is 'Microsoft's behavior taken as a whole,'" which Neukom said relied on the "monopoly broth theory" posited in *Continental Ore Co. v. Union Carbide & Carbon Corp.* In that Supreme Court case, the majority argued that if you can isolate instances in which the defendant's past behavior, in Neukom's words, "has some aspect of it which might appear to be anticompetitive—even though the act itself is not—you can aggregate those fractional, semi-anticompetitive acts and try to come up with a whole number, and somehow that constitutes anticompetitive conduct in support of 'maintaining a monopoly.' That law has—I think understandably because it is both irrational and untrustworthy in terms of giving business clear guidance on the rules of the game—has been criticized often since that 1962 opinion."

Neukom and Microsoft believed, further, that when the Court of Appeals or Supreme Court looked at the record, they would see that even if Microsoft was deemed to possess a monopoly, the record would show they had acquired a dominant position lawfully and that this lawful monopoly was not unlawfully maintained. It was Microsoft's private belief that a feature of the new economy was that monopolies would form quickly and lower rather than raise prices in a mad dash to please customers, then unleash new competition, because the rewards were so great in this winner-take-all competition, and then be supplanted by a new technology or competitor. Had Microsoft dared, it could have used the "increasing returns" argument advanced by the government as proof that they were serving consumers. But in court Neukom and Microsoft treated this argument as if it were radioactive, since they didn't want to concede they were a monopoly, even though a growing number of economists disagree with Adam Smith's laws of scarcity and believe such monopolies lower prices and lead to more innovation and competition because every entrepreneur and investor wants to snare the pot of gold, however briefly.

Had they been willing to associate with monopolies, Microsoft might have wished to quote from a speech Treasury Secretary Lawrence Summers delivered in San Francisco in the spring of 2000 entitled "The New Wealth of Nations." In it, Summers spoke of natural monopolies in the information economy, where "the only incentive to produce anything is the possession of temporary monopoly power—because without that power the price will be bid down to the marginal cost and the high initial fixed costs cannot be recouped. . . . So the constant pursuit of that monopoly power becomes the central driving thrust of the new economy. And the creative destruction that results from all that striving becomes the essential spur of economic growth."

The day after releasing his legal decision, Judge Jackson summoned the parties to his chambers and told them he planned to move fast, faster than they had anticipated. Jackson is impatient by nature, and he was particularly eager to get his ruling and eventual remedy before an appellate court. There would be a remedy phase, featuring briefs from each side, he told the parties, followed by a courtroom hearing on May 24. To hem in the nineteen states, Jackson announced that any separate remedy proposal they made had to reflect the will of a majority of them, foreclosing the possibility that a few recalcitrant states could impede the process. To hem in the Court of Appeals (and Microsoft), Jackson announced that he was inclined to invoke a little-used law known as the Antitrust Expediting Act to bypass the appeals court and go directly to the Supreme Court to speed the case along. If four of the nine justices agreed to hear the appeal, it would be so ordered.

So the battlefield would shift to the higher courts and, since this was an election year, to the political arena as well. Two days after a federal judge had ruled his company had broken the law, Bill Gates came to Washington. He was scheduled to attend a White House conference on the new economy and made a stop on Capitol Hill. Gates was not treated as a lawbreaker but hailed as a hero. President Clinton threw an arm around him at the White House. Lawmakers clamored for his autograph. Republican congressional leaders denounced the Justice Department. Senator Robert G. Torricelli of New Jersey, who chairs fundraising efforts for Senate Democrats, declared, "Only the United States would consider breaking up a company that has done this much economically to advance our national interest." Microsoft had again fortified its lobbying team with the addition of Ginny Terzano, a former Al Gore press secretary; James Houton, a former aide to Senate Minority Leader Tom Daschle; Tom Jurkovich, a two-time national field director of the Democratic Congressional Campaign Committee; and Craig Smith, a former White House political director and a campaign manager for Al Gore. And Microsoft had almost overnight become the sixth-biggest corporate donor of soft money in America, sprinkling more than three million dollars in contributions for the 2000 election, as well as money to other potential allies, including a fifty-thousand-dollar donation to the influential Congressional Black Caucus Foundation. On Capitol Hill, few voices were raised in praise of Judge Jackson and the Justice Department, suggesting another disconnect: between those who interpret the law in Washington and those who write it.

CHAPTER 22

Remedy,
and Appeal

I N THE WEEKS THAT FOLLOWED the ruling, the three principal actors in this drama—Judge Jackson, the government, and Microsoft—contemplated a remedy to fit the "crime." I visited Jackson one day in mid-April in his second-floor courthouse chambers, where he leaned back in a large leather swivel chair, his suit jacket off, his fingers fidgeting with a pipe he filled but never lit. He seemed relaxed enough, but he could contain his fury at Gates and Microsoft only with effort. I told him that Microsoft employees professed shock that he thought they had violated the law and behaved unethically. Did Jackson believe they were speaking the truth?

Jackson said he wasn't sure of the answer, nevertheless he was so agitated by what he called Microsoft's "obstinacy" that he carelessly compared their proclamations of innocence to those of four members of the Newton Street Crew convicted in a racketeering, drug dealing, and murder trial he had presided over five years before. There were brutal murders in that case, he recalled: three of the victims had their mouths sealed with duct tape before they were shot in the head with machine guns. The federal government brought racketeering charges against the defendants, and after a five-month trial the jury voted to convict. "On the day of the sentencing," Jackson remembered, "they maintained that they had done nothing wrong, that the whole case was a conspiracy by the white power structure to destroy them. I am now under no illusions that miscreants will realize that other parts of society view them that way." He conceded that at first Microsoft employees probably didn't think they were doing anything wrong, but "I think it should have dawned on them at a much earlier stage." Microsoft should have conceded mistakes and settled, he declared, as Intel did with the FTC in the spring of 1999.

As he waited for the Justice Department's and states' remedy briefs and Microsoft's rebuttal, Jackson was clear-eyed about a few of the vulnerabilities of the decision he had rendered. He acknowledged that his conclusion that Microsoft had harmed consumers was not airtight, at least by traditional measures. "There was insufficient evidence in the record to say Microsoft ever priced its operating system at the level that as a monopolist they could have," he conceded. But if Microsoft did not milk customers by charging steep prices, it was because they "sacrificed" price to create an "applications barrier to entry" that would "perpetuate" their monopoly. Many federal courts, he conceded, only adopt "the classic model" of monopoly power—pricing—and downplay the long-term model he was proposing.

Jackson also acknowledged that he was making a certain leap of faith in concluding that Microsoft will be able to extend its monopoly from the PC to other devices. "You can't deny that there are a lot of changes going on out there. It may be that I've underestimated the significance of Linux, which has seemed to grow in popularity since I closed this case. But at the moment I don't see it making significant advances on the desktop." What he did see was Microsoft making advances.

Still, as he thought about remedies, Judge Jackson fidgeted with his unlit pipe and said he was humbled. "One of the things I worry about is that I know far less about the economic impact of what I may do than I know about the rules of law. It's not clear what the best remedy is and what are likely to be the consequences of it. What is best is a far more amorphous concept than whether someone illegally tied one product to another." He fretted that government might become too intrusive, yet he wanted a government referee. Without benefit of Justice's recommendations and Microsoft's reply, he was inclined to favor behavior remedies over what he saw as more draconian structural remedies, though he wasn't sure.

Because of these uncertainties, even though Jackson was sometimes scathingly critical of the Court of Appeals and talked of circumventing it and taking the case directly to the Supreme Court, he was comforted that it hovered above him. "Strange as it may seem, there's a certain amount of comfort a district-court judge takes that his decision will be reviewed by an appellate tribunal. . . . I'm at that stage now. I want someone else to review this." The reason he pondered taking the case directly to the Supreme Court, he continued, was this: "What I really don't want is for Microsoft to have the advantage of a two-year delay and continue to do what they've been doing."

At bottom, Judge Jackson admitted that he just didn't trust Gates and company, and he wasn't concerned that he would be accused of harboring a prejudice against Microsoft for saying this. "My past experience with Microsoft, dating from the consent decree, was that I don't think that their proffer of some minimal conduct modification during the appellate proceedings could be trusted."

When Jackson picked up his copy of *The Washington Post* on April 19, 2000, he read of a visit Steve Ballmer had made to the paper the previous day. To a roomful of reporters and editors, Ballmer said, "I do not think we broke the law in any way, shape, or form. I feel deeply that we behaved in every instance with super integrity. I'm not saying we don't talk tough, that people don't get a little 'grrr' in their e-mail and all that." They simply had bad social graces, he insisted. Microsoft's problem was bad manners, not bad behavior.

Although Microsoft executives expressed pleasure with Ballmer's interview and with what a senior Microsoft executive that morning told me was Ballmer's belief "that we lost sight of things" and had to learn to be "a good partner," Judge Jackson was livid. "They don't act like grown-ups," he told me that same afternoon. He interpreted what Ballmer said this way: "We're a little rough around the edges, but you have to be tolerant!" Ballmer's interview proved to Jackson that "to this day they continue to deny they did anything wrong." A few days later, interviewed on the public-television program *Nightly Business Report,* Gates was even more emphatic than Ballmer: "It's important to understand that Microsoft is very clear that it has done absolutely nothing wrong."

"Their greatest vulnerability is themselves," Steve Case observed of Microsoft. "Their ability to recognize that they're not in Kansas anymore." Indeed, Ballmer's and Gates's comments enraged not just Judge Jackson but government lawyers, particularly the state attorneys general, who were then exploring what remedy to recommend to Judge Jackson. If Microsoft thought they did nothing wrong, then a conduct remedy where they were asked to alter behavior wouldn't work. "To see him say they did nothing wrong, that did bother us," said Iowa's Tom Miller of the Ballmer interview. "We talked about that. It looked like they missed the whole point. It fed our concern that they would try and do it again."

On April 28, 2000, the Justice Department and seventeen of the nineteen states submitted their remedy proposal. Ohio and Illinois dissented from the recommended cure but continued to support the lawsuit. In addition to many of the milder conduct remedies first suggested by Justice and the states in May 1998 and even most of the tougher conduct terms circulated by Judge Posner during the mediation process, the penalty had escalated. Now Justice and the states proposed to split Microsoft in two. Their reason was explicit: they did not trust Microsoft to carry out a conduct remedy that required its cooperation. The plan called for dividing Microsoft into two roughly equal ten-billion-dollar companies. One would be an operating-system company, handling all versions of Windows, and the second would be an applications company, containing the browser, Microsoft Office, Word, Excel (spreadsheet), MSN, and all Microsoft's content and Internet investments. Bill Gates and Steve Ballmer would each get to choose to work at one of the companies, and the Microsoft name would be affixed to just one. The three men who own more than 3 percent of the stock—Gates, Ballmer, and Paul Allen—would have to convert their Microsoft shares into just one company, while all other shareholders would have their shares converted to ownership in both companies. Although the Windows monopoly would not be structurally broken up, Justice hoped that since the two companies would have separate boards and interests, the applications company would come to compete with the Windows company.

Microsoft had secretly agreed to most of the conduct remedies proposed during the mediation process, though Justice and the states were not at liberty to disclose this, and Judge Jackson was unaware of this. To monitor these prohibitions, the directors of the two Microsofts would appoint a committee to select a chief compliance officer to work with the government to assure that these terms were to be imposed before the breakup was carried out. Three years after the breakup, these restrictions would be lifted.

Although the remedy was sweeping and its full consequences unknowable, Joel Klein said he was unburdened by doubts. Surrounded in his office by framed pictures of his hero, Justice Powell, and his boss, President Clinton, Klein said, "I don't have lots of doubts about the merits of this case or the power of this monopoly. I thought long and hard about remedies, and I firmly believe the one we chose was the right one."

Microsoft thought these remedies were preposterous. Bill Gates denounced the proposal as "radical," insisting that it "would hurt the company's ability to continue to innovate" because without relying on teams from different divisions "Microsoft could never have developed Windows," among other products. Bill Neukom told me: "Structural relief would be an extreme remedy in this case. The general rule of remedies in antitrust cases is that they should be the least intrusive possible. The intention is not to punish the defendant. The purpose is to enjoin the conduct the trial court has found violative of the Sherman Act. And on this record of evidence, and on these Conclusions of Law, there is no basis for anything as extreme as structural relief. In the one-hundred-and-ten-year history of the Sherman Act, there never has been a court-imposed divestiture or breakup of a unitary, organic operating company." By contrast with a horizontal trust such as Standard Oil or the more easily divided Baby Bell local and AT&T long-distance companies, a software company such as Microsoft was said to be not easily divisible since operations and applications people were often interchangeable. To Neukom, a breakup would be outrageously "punitive and regulatory." Microsoft said it would ask Judge Jackson to delay the remedy hearing to permit time to produce documents and take testimony.

Told that Justice believed a structural solution was better because a conduct remedy would require an intrusive government to oversee Microsoft on a daily basis, Neukom replied: "That's like saying to a patient, 'We can restrict the movement of one of your arms, or we can cut it off. It only takes one piece of surgery to cut your arm off. That's pretty intrusive for the rest of your life. But the good news is we won't constrain the movement of that missing limb!'"

Microsoft's legal team worked intently for almost two weeks, and on May 10 the company released its detailed response. In it, Microsoft requested that if Jackson decided in favor of the government proposal that the remedy process be extended at least six months, allowing them more time to inspect government documents and to summon witnesses, thus assuring that a remedy would not be imposed until 2001. Microsoft proposed its own conduct remedies, though these were less severe than those it had agreed to during the mediation process.

A senior Justice Department official savored the irony. He noted that had Microsoft accepted much more modest conduct remedies in May 1998, there would have been no trial. He further noted that Justice's original proposals were aimed more at opening the browser market than at curbing predacious behavior, a position that shifted dramatically—so much so, he said, that when he thinks back to government's May 1998 proposals he is embarrassed by how toothless they were. "We were prepared to accept a solution to the browser problem that may not have been adequate." Even had Microsoft settled, say, in the summer of 1999, before Judge Jackson issued his Findings of Fact, the terms would still seem modest compared to what government was now recommending.

As it readied for the final round in Judge Jackson's courtroom on May 24, 2000, Microsoft had hopes that, confronted with complicated remedy choices, the judge would elongate the process. They were to be disappointed. Jackson couldn't shake the memory of a former colleague, the late Harold H. Greene, who spent eleven months presiding over the AT&T antitrust trial and then many subsequent years micromanaging the execution of the settlement. So on this warm May day, when John Warden asked about the court's "consideration of a schedule for full proceedings as may be appropriate" to fully ventilate every possible remedy, Judge Jackson let him finish and then simply looked down at him and announced, "All right, I want to resolve any uncertainty on Mr. Warden's part at the outset, however. I intend to proceed to the merits of remedy today."

In private, Jackson likens himself to a nineteenth-century ship captain, a man forced to make decisions and stick with them. He had made his decision even before he had entered the courtroom. And for the rest of the day, except for one moment in the afternoon when his eyes closed and his tanned head fell to his chest, he was more assertive than he had been during closing arguments or prior to his Findings of Fact or his Conclusions of Law.

He dominated the proceedings with his questions, peppering Kevin O'Connor, an assistant attorney general in Wisconsin, who spoke for the states, and David Boies with queries: how would the two companies work together? Why not split off a third browser company, as recommended in what he called "an excellent brief" submitted by Microsoft's competitors from the Computer and Communications Industry Association and the Software and Information Industry Association? Would a special master be needed to enforce a remedy? Boies delineated for the court ten examples of Microsoft behavior Jackson had concluded were unlawful and about which, he asserted, Microsoft's proposed remedies were mute.

When John Warden stepped forward to offer his argument, Judge Jackson was comparatively quiet. He did not flog him with questions. He did not probe the limitations of Microsoft's proposed conduct remedies nor inquire as to why the government's structural remedies were "extreme" or might hurt consumers and retard innovation, as the company claimed. He did not ask how two Microsofts would separate a single division—Jeff Raikes's seventeen-thousand-employee sales, marketing, and services group—without inefficiencies; how they would divide the company's twenty-one-billion-dollar cash horde; or how to segregate research conducted for both Windows and Microsoft's various applications from Microsoft's R-and-D budget. Judge Jackson did not display the uncertainty as to proper remedies he had revealed privately. Nor did he display the kind of lively, curious intellect that, say, Judge Posner brought to the mediation process. In truth, Judge Jackson didn't seem excited about policy but about coming to a speedy end to this process, which infuriated Bill Neukom and the Microsoft legal team.

Whatever intellectual curiosity Judge Jackson may have lacked was overshadowed by the limitations of Microsoft's legal team. John Warden chose to address only two of the ten examples David Boies had offered of behavior that Judge Jackson had found predatory. Furthermore, Warden went on to lecture Judge Jackson on what his legal findings said, asserting that Jackson never found Microsoft guilty of using its power to maintain its monopoly. This prompted Judge Jackson to rebuke Warden like an errant student, telling him that he had, in fact, concluded that Microsoft had "extinguished" competition. Warden moved on to say that to impose "extreme" structural relief, courts require proof that competitors would have thrived had Microsoft not acted as it did. Jackson asked for specific Supreme Court citations to back up this thesis, and Warden finally admitted that although he could cite numerous related cases, "there is no case that directly addresses this point." Warden objected to the inclusion of Microsoft Office in the government's proposed remedy, since he said Office was not a point of contention during the trial, even though the judge had found that Microsoft had wielded Office as a club against Apple and had threatened IBM because its products competed with Office.

In the afternoon following Boies's rebuttal, Judge Jackson asked Warden if Steve Ballmer was quoted correctly in a software-association brief in which he was said to have declared, "40 percent of the functionality of the desktop version of Windows 2000 is useless without a Windows 2000 server." In other words, Microsoft products would only work well with Windows servers. Jackson was truly puzzled why Ballmer might make such an incriminating statement when such behavior was at the core of the government's case.

John Warden said he did not immediately know the answer, and Judge Jackson said he would allow him a five-minute recess to find it. When they returned, Warden asked his colleague Steven Holley to step forward to supply the answer, and Holley treated the question as irrelevant, emphasizing that the brief had been written by competitors, and went on to say that he could neither certify what Ballmer said nor what he meant, and, moreover, the question was irrelevant since Windows 2000 was not at issue in the trial. Holley left Jackson to smolder as he blithely moved on to detail why Microsoft thought the government was wrong to insist Microsoft could leverage its PC power into other devices. Finally, at just after 3 P.M., without having delineated for Judge Jackson why the company's own remedy proposals were adequate to redress the monopoly abuses Jackson had found and without offering guidance as to the remedy-hearing process it wished to recommend, Microsoft's John Warden looked up at Jackson and asked what further process he intended.

"I'm not contemplating any further process, Mr. Warden," said Jackson.

Steven Holley hustled to the microphone to submit a thirty-five-page brief containing a proposed procedure and a prospective witness list of sixteen—including Bill Gates and Steve Ballmer—and began outlining its contents. Judge Jackson interrupted to tell him he need not "go through the whole thing" since the document could speak for itself and the judge could read.

Holley continued, making another stab at promoting Microsoft's proposed remedy procedure, explaining that in "the brief time available" they had gathered valuable information, and more time would allow Microsoft to address such extreme measures as the dismemberment of a great company.

"In 'the brief time'?"

"That's correct, Your Honor," said Holley.

"This case has been pending for two years, Mr. Holley!" exclaimed an irritated Jackson.

Holley was, of course, correct that a remedy solution had been on the table for only a matter of weeks, not years, and such sweeping "solutions" might merit more than the submission of legal briefs. But Judge Jackson, as he once told me, is not a waiter: "I don't pretend to have an excess of patience." When Jackson said the case had "been pending for two years," he meant that Microsoft had had two years to settle it, which is what he had hoped for. Of Microsoft's claim that he short-circuited remedy hearings, Jackson later told me, "We did have a hearing on remedy. What I didn't want to do was take any testimony. . . . In essence, I felt that Microsoft was not surprised there would be no second trial on remedy, and their protestations of surprise were not genuine." He thought their hearing proposal "was a delaying tactic. The longer they staved off the conclusion of the case before me, the greater the likelihood they would be relieved of the obligation to do anything by political changes or by the passage of time. You know, judges have been known to die in office!"

Outside, a bright sun and fourteen cameras awaited the combatants. Boies, uncharacteristically, said the government had nothing further to say. Privately, the government team was jubilant. "The remedy hearing was the most important day of this trial, and they gave the judge no help," said a senior government lawyer. Bill Neukom and John Warden had plenty to say. "We have sought to have our day in court on the remedy phase," said Neukom. "The district court has decided not to grant that process. . . . We will be raising issues of procedure in our appeal as well as issues of fact and law." Privately, Microsoft chose to look past Judge Jackson to the appeals court, leaving a pleased but incredulous David Boies to shake his head and, once again, wonder what the hell

378 | WORLD WAR 3.0

Microsoft's lawyers were thinking. "When you're trying to persuade someone, it helps to try and understand what they want and need," Boies privately told me.

Though Microsoft had filed documents suggesting why Judge Jackson should go slowly, his remedy ruling was obviously prepared before these documents were filed. The only change Judge Jackson allowed was to delay his ruling by a week, making it appear as if he were digesting what was said. In truth, Jackson had heard enough. "There wasn't much more to learn," he said privately. "All the testimony to be taken would have been prognostications." In reading his June 7, 2000, remedy decision, once again his mistrust of Microsoft assaults the reader. He declared:

> The Court is convinced for several reasons that a final—and appeal-able—judgment should be entered quickly. It has also reluctantly come to the conclusion . . . that a structural remedy has become imperative. Microsoft as it is presently organized and led is unwilling to accept the notion that it broke the law or accede to an order amending its conduct. First, despite the Court's Findings of Fact and Conclusions of Law, Microsoft does not yet concede that any of its business practices violated the Sherman Act. Microsoft officials have recently been quoted publicly to the effect that the company has 'done nothing wrong.' . . . Second, there is credible evidence in the record to suggest that Microsoft, con-vinced of its innocence, continues to do business as it has in the past, and may yet do to other markets what it has already done in the PC operating system and browser markets. . . . Third, Microsoft has proved untrustworthy in the past. . . . Finally, the Court believes that extended proceedings on the form a remedy should take are unlikely to give any significantly greater assurance that it will be able to identify what might be generally regarded as an optimum remedy.

Judge Jackson went on to replicate almost the entire menu of struc-tural and conduct remedies supported by the Justice Department and seventeen states. Jackson said he did not craft his own proposals because he lacked the staff of economists and engineers available to Justice and the states—an intellectual modesty alien to, say, Judge Richard Posner, who struggled for four months to devise his own remedy. In a memorandum attached to his ruling, Judge Jackson wrote of the government plaintiffs: "These officials are by reasons of office obliged and expected to consider—and to act in—the public interest; Microsoft is not." In a brief *Washington Post* interview with James V. Grimaldi, Jackson defended what could be described as realism or intellectual sloth this way: "I don't claim any special expertise or special powers of judgment or discernment which entitle me to undertake to micromanage the industry." The only alterations Jackson made in the plan submitted by Justice and the states concerned timing and compliance. Assuming that the appeals courts upheld his rulings, including his remedies, Jackson ordered Microsoft to submit a plan not later than four months after the appeals process ended describing how it would split Microsoft in two. If an appeals court did not stay this order, in three months he would impose on Microsoft the various conduct remedies proposed by the government. In addition, Jackson refused to rely on CEO Steve Ballmer to appoint a compliance officer, as the government had proposed. Displaying his disdain for Ballmer, Jackson gave Microsoft directors ninety days to establish a compliance committee consisting of no less than three board members "who are not present or former employees of Microsoft," and empowering this committee—not the CEO of the company—to appoint a chief compliance officer to report to both the committee and the CEO.

Although they had the barrel of a gun stuck deep down its throat, Microsoft remained strangely upbeat. Bill Neukom told reporters he was confident Microsoft would win on appeal and said they would file the necessary papers within days. This is, Gates told reporters, "the first day of the rest of this case." Gates acted as if the entire trial was only about whether it was legal for Microsoft to include a browser in with Windows, insisting that "the higher court has already spoken on this issue." Gates and company persisted in pretending they were dealing from strength, not weakness. And they continued to behave as if they were being victimized not just by competitors who put the Justice Department up to this lawsuit, not just by government officials who didn't comprehend technology, but by a judge who had had it in for Microsoft since 1997, when he had ordered them to debundle the browser. "His open-mindedness was deeply affected by that previous case," Gates told the *Today* show's Katie Couric.

In mid-June, Microsoft dropped all pretense of politeness when it filed a motion for a stay with the U.S. Court of Appeals for the District of

Columbia that boldly attacked both Judge Jackson's conclusions and trial procedures. The judge, it said, made "an array of serious substantive and procedural errors that infected virtually every aspect of the proceedings." It accused him of "largely" suspending the application of federal rules of evidence by allowing "rank hearsay" to be submitted as fact. Even though Jackson had said early in the trial that he would carefully screen the findings to ensure that they corresponded to the complaint, Microsoft said, this was "an assurance the court would later ignore." They faulted his Findings of Fact: "Although 412 paragraphs long, the court's findings do not contain a single citation to the record, making it impossible to ascertain the purported basis for many findings and thereby compounding the many evidentiary errors at trial." They faulted many of his findings, insisting that many "consist of nothing more than sweeping, conclusory assertions," including his basic assertion that Microsoft "possesses monopoly power." The court's definition of the market was "too narrow," excluding the various competing platform technologies—Apple's Mac OS, middleware, handheld devices. They faulted his Conclusions of Law: "the court evinced a profound misunderstanding of the antitrust laws," noting that "the court did not find that Microsoft has the power unilaterally to raise prices in or exclude competition from the operating system business, the touchstone of monopoly power." They faulted the rushed remedy process he imposed, noting interviews he gave that suggested that he merely "rubber stamped" the governments' proposals. At the beginning of their brief, they cited press interviews Jackson had granted and that appeared after his remedy, faulting Jackson for talking to reporters about a pending case, a breathtaking departure from normal judicial etiquette. (At the Supreme Court, for example, talking to reporters about court business is akin to a national-security breach, and justices don't even deign to explain why they recuse themselves from particular cases.)

Finally, Microsoft faulted Judge Jackson for ignoring "the serious injury" Microsoft and the public would suffer if the proposed conduct remedies were not stayed by the higher court. They cited ten ways Microsoft would be harmed, including:

> The judgment will require Microsoft to disclose large amounts of proprietary information about its operating systems and other products to competitors. . . . The judgment will result in a direct and immediate

intrusion into Microsoft's product design decisions. . . . The judgment will result in the fragmentation of the Windows platform. . . . The judgment will require Microsoft to submit a 'proposed plan of divestiture' not later than four months after its entry. . . . Requiring Microsoft to submit such a plan will cause a huge diversion of effort by Microsoft's executives at a critical time when Microsoft is attempting to change its entire business and programming model to remain competitive in the Internet age.

Microsoft also cited various ways the public would be harmed, including:

The public will suffer serious and far-reaching harm if the Windows platform begins to fragment. Millions of computer users and thousands of software developers depend on the consistency and stability of the Windows platform. . . . The public will suffer irreparable harm if Microsoft cannot develop and release new products in a timely manner.

The first dose of judicial good news Microsoft was to receive came on the same June day it filed this appeal. The Court of Appeals immediately responded by announcing that the entire ten-member court, with three justices recusing themselves, would hear the case. They did this, said the court, in view of its "exceptional importance." No doubt, they also did it to prevent the Supreme Court from usurping their review authority and perhaps to caution Judge Jackson to slow down, to remind him that he was still answerable to them.

Jackson had overplayed his hand. For the first time since the trial began, he was roundly criticized for moving too fast and for denying Microsoft due process. It was common to hear complaints that Jackson's remedy was too severe, too intrusive, too unmindful of the law of unintended consequences, too dangerous to the nation's economic health. "Up until May 24, Jackson did a masterful job of managing this case—then he swerved off the road," observed William Kovacic, who had often been in the courtroom. "By foreshortening the remedy case he appeared to say, 'Nothing anyone can tell me will change my mind.' He made no apparent effort to link his remedy to his Conclusions of Law." By rushing, by not allowing Microsoft, say, three weeks for a remedy hearing, Kovacic said Judge Jackson failed to purchase "cheap insurance to avoid the appearance of shooting from the hip," which could prompt an appeals court to mistrust Jackson as "the filter" through which they view the case. Others chimed in that Jackson should not have granted brief interviews the day after his remedy decision to various newspapers, nor should he have talked to *The New York Times* several times during the trial. "I didn't talk to anyone about the merits of the case," Jackson told me in defense of his press conversations. In fact, however, as he acknowledged after I raised an eyebrow, he *had* talked to me about the merits of the case, but only for publication after he issued his decisions.

On June 19, the Court of Appeals announced a quick schedule to receive briefs and to speedily decide whether to stay Judge Jackson's conduct remedies. The appeals court was prepared to assert itself—unless, they said, Judge Jackson sent the case directly to the Supreme Court, in which instance the court said it would step aside and wait for the nation's highest court to render a decision.

The next day, Judge Jackson deftly invoked the 1974 Expediting Act and signed an order asking the Supreme Court to directly review his decision. Jackson also announced that he would stay the imposition of any conduct remedies until the appeals process had been exhausted. This was a shrewd move, for it deflated criticism of him. While this brought short-term pleasure to Microsoft, in the long term it weakened the company's claim that Jackson had behaved intemperately. A month later, Jackson's pipe was lit as he sat in his second-floor chambers and explained that he made this decision because he became convinced Microsoft was obfuscating the issue of their conduct by protesting so loudly about his procedures. "Microsoft's voluble appeal to the Court of Appeals made clear to me that they planned to obscure the merits of the case with pleas for sympathy. . . . I could easily see the Court of Appeals distracted by whether the remedy should be stayed, and [then] . . . they would not concentrate on the merits of the case."

In late July, Microsoft filed a jurisdictional statement with the Supreme Court, urging the Court not to take on the case directly because it would become enmeshed in a thicket of factual and technical arguments and because a case of this complexity required the Court of Appeals to help sift through the issues, including the "serious substantive procedural errors" made by Judge Jackson. Because of his alleged errors and because his comments to reporters raised questions about his "impartiality," Microsoft urged the Court at a minimum to send the case to another district-court judge. Certainly there was a precedent: in 1995, the Circuit

Court of Appeals had snatched the consent-decree case away from Judge
Sporkin and awarded it to Judge Jackson. The government filed its reply
with the Supreme Court in mid-August, arguing that the importance of
the case required a speedy finale to this opera. Again, Microsoft saw time
and the Court of Appeals as its ally, and the government saw each as an
adversary.

On September 26, 2000, the Supreme Court by a vote of eight to one
sided with Microsoft to slow down the appeals process. In a three-
sentence order, they agreed not to hear the case directly but instead to
return it to the Court of Appeals, suggesting that the issues involved
were so complicated as to require the filter of a lower court. The decision
pleased Microsoft and disappointed the plaintiffs, but it was merely a
procedural ruling, not a legal decision. Microsoft still had to surmount
the extensive evidence David Boies had entered into the public record
and the trial judge had affirmed. Perhaps by slowing the appeals process
the Supreme Court boosted the chances of a settlement. Perhaps a new
president would take another look at the case. Perhaps a breakup of
Microsoft was now less likely. The one certainty was that if the case was
neither settled nor dropped, the appeals process would likely exhaust the
better part of the next two years.

As he waited for a final resolution of the case and reflected on its
lessons, Judge Richard Posner did not question that century-old
antitrust laws were flexible enough to apply to the new economy. He was
silent as to whether he would have sided with Microsoft or the government. But the Microsoft case obviously haunted him, for in a speech he
delivered on September 14, 2000, to a Bar Association–sponsored conference in New York, Judge Posner argued that the political and judicial
system was not as "supple" as the law. He worried aloud about the divisive role played by the states, noting the "cluster-bomb effect" of
antitrust lawsuits, where the states jump on the antitrust bandwagon
and, ultimately, lengthen the lawsuit and "complicate [a] settlement."
He was troubled as well by the lack of resources that crippled the
Antitrust Division and the FTC, preventing these agencies from hiring "a
competent technical staff." No doubt, this thought crystallized as he
watched Justice fumble to define *interoperability* and saw that its technical people could not keep up with Microsoft's. And perhaps with Judge

Jackson's honest struggle to master XML and APIs in mind, Judge Posner cautioned that "the courts do not have adequate technical resources, and do not move fast enough, to cope effectively with a very complex business sector that changes very rapidly."

Judge Jackson emphasized different lessons. As he waited for a final resolution of this case, Judge Jackson harbored many worries. He worried that the higher courts could overrule him and subject him to a withering legal critique. He worried that maybe his remedy was wrong. And he wasn't comfortable that conservative friends castigated him for harming the free-enterprise system, as an old friend in Philadelphia and editorials in papers such as *The Wall Street Journal* had. But Jackson was certain they, not he, had abandoned conservative principles. "People talk about knee-jerk liberals," he said. "Well, there's a faction of the conservative movement in this country which is equally knee-jerk." They equate "commercial success" with conservative principles and suggest, as did his Philadelphia friend, that he had somehow "done a disservice" by treating Microsoft "like a common criminal." Not for one minute did Jackson buy this. On this issue, there was no gray. "They broke the law." Period.

Even if the higher courts did overrule Judge Jackson's remedy as too severe, as constitutional scholars think possible, it will be much more difficult to overturn his findings of liability—that Microsoft possessed a monopoly and abused this power. Perhaps an appeals court will affirm Microsoft's right to bundle or integrate a browser or other software with Windows. Perhaps a higher court will find less clear evidence of consumer harm or of foreclosure of competition, or will dismiss Judge Jackson's conclusion that Microsoft will be able to extend its Windows monopoly to other platforms. But even so, Microsoft will probably not escape Judge Jackson's liability ruling. Looking at the appeals process ahead, a Microsoft legal consultant who fervently believed Judge Jackson was wrong said of Neukom and the other lawyers: "If Microsoft's attorneys feel comfortable with the position they're in, it would be a big mistake. There is a tough row to hoe here." A senior Microsoft executive was equally gloomy. He knew that Microsoft was again betting the company, and he conceded, "It's a narrow crapshoot."

CHAPTER 23

Microsoft Loses Even if It Wins

I T HAD BECOME almost a chant around Microsoft: *We cannot get distracted by the trial. We cannot become cautious.* In many ways, they succeeded: Microsoft undertook a radical companywide restructuring during the course of the trial, shifting the company toward what it called "Next Generation Windows Services," aiming to promote a seamless Windows platform on any device connected to the Internet, integrating all services and applications. Of course, the services would work best for those who used Windows. At an all-day press event on June 22, 2000, at which Microsoft displayed its vision of a Microsoft.NET cloud that connected "islands" of devices to the same Internet platform, a reporter asked whether other platforms would enjoy the same rich experience as a Windows user. Gates admitted, "The richest experience would probably be the latest version of Windows.NET running on a fully configured PC." Microsoft could no more change its DNA than Gates could stop breathing. Mindful of the government Goliath looking over its shoulder, Steve Ballmer quickly interjected, "We want to be able to get richer clients as well that are non-Windows clients."

Microsoft believed that no matter how sophisticated Sun or IBM's hardware or how diverting AOL Time Warner's content or how fast

AT&T's broadband service, software would remain king. The smart bet now, Gates believed, was cross-platform software that could act as an intelligent personal agent. And no one, Bill Gates believed, did better software than Microsoft. Gates and Microsoft were making a second bet: that they could establish XML—eXtensible markup language—as the lingua franca of the Internet, an open standard that would be available to everyone, not just Windows users. XML would allow users to interpret and send data, putting data into fields that users could label, enabling, for example, consumers to use their cell phone or their PC to ask Microsoft.NET to assemble and sort their financial records from several banks and brokerage houses and credit-card companies or to compare the investment performance of various mutual funds or to allow an instant money transfer or the monthly payment of bills. First, XML had to be accepted as a standard language by other companies, including Microsoft's foes, but by late 2000 it was well on its way.

Microsoft did not let up. In the first half of 2000, the company previewed its Xbox, a new video-game console that could be linked to the PC or to the TV and aimed, when it debuts in 2001, at supplanting Sony's PlayStation 2. Microsoft pursued Rob Glaser's RealNetworks by integrating for free its Media Player software into Windows both for the desktop and for servers. Microsoft chased Palm and its more than 80 percent market share by introducing a new version of its Pocket PC software for hardware manufacturers such as Casio, now offering such enticing features as color, a Web browser, ClearType, and the ability to play music or video clips. Microsoft offered inducements for customers to sign up with MSN and its package of services, and for the first time in years it saw MSN's subscribers grow at a faster pace than AOL's—doubling in 2000—although by the fall of 2000 AOL had twenty-five million subscribers to MSN's mere three million.

Microsoft continued to make deals. It made a deal with Global Crossing and Japan's Softbank to wire Asia with undersea and underground fiber-optic cable; and a deal with the richest man in Mexico, Carlos Slim Helu of Telmex, to create a Spanish-language portal site in Latin America. And Microsoft continued its spending spree—spending more than two billion dollars on joint wireless ventures worldwide, billions on new wireless devices, and hundreds of millions on Web-hosting companies that deliver software online. Microsoft made big bets on cable here and abroad. In concert with John Malone's Liberty Media, Microsoft set out to construct a global cable empire. Microsoft owned an 8 percent stake in UPC, Europe's largest cable broadband company, whose reach stretched over twelve countries, including Israel; a $3 billion stake in England's Telewest and a $500 million stake in NTL, England's third-largest cable operation; a $40 million investment in Globo Cabo of Portugal; in addition to its American cable investments, Microsoft invested $400 million in Canada's cable giant, Rogers Communications; in Japan, it owns 24 percent of TITUS, that nation's foremost cable company; and it has cable broadband investments in Asia, Europe, Australia, and South America. Overall, by September 2000, Microsoft had made more than $11 billion in broadband investments worldwide, according to *Broadband Daily*, the industry's online newsletter. And during the first nine months of 2000, Microsoft invested in or acquired forty-two companies; at this rate, they will exceed the number of deals they made in 1999. Everywhere one looked on the new-media spider's web in mid-2000, Microsoft was positioned to pounce, with a $17.8 billion portfolio of equity investments in a variety of companies and $23.8 billion in ready cash and marketable securities to enter new ventures.

Politically, Microsoft became even more hard-core. It hedged its bets by adding still more lobbyists, including Bill Paxon, another former member of the Republican leadership team in Congress; it sweetened the contract it made in 1998 with consultant Ralph Reed, a key adviser to George W. Bush's presidential campaign and the former head of the Christian Coalition. Reed's new mission was to lobby Bush and his other advisers to oppose the Justice Department's lawsuit. (When *The New York Times* broke this story in April, Bush was embarrassed and Reed confessed he had made "an error," particularly since he said he hadn't told Bush he was wearing two hats.) Microsoft's D.C. lobbying staff went from zero in 1995 to fourteen, according to *Business Week;* and its unregulated soft-money gifts and targeted campaign contributions of $2.2 million from 1999 through the first quarter of 2000 propelled Microsoft to the number-three ranking among all corporations, trailing only Philip Morris and AT&T. (Microsoft was not the only high-tech company to wake up to the political goodwill that donations could purchase; Cisco Systems executives and their spouses, for example, made a total of $713,810 in campaign contributions by the spring of 2000, more than nine times the $74,570 they gave four years earlier.) Microsoft also contributed a total of two million dollars in 2000 to help underwrite the Republican and Democratic presidential conventions. These decisions had to be signed off on by Bill Neukom, to whom the government-affairs department reported. Speaking for Neukom, who did not wish to be quoted on this subject, Vivek Varma, his deputy, defended Microsoft by making an argument that paralleled Hillary Clinton's "vast right-wing conspiracy" claims: "It is no secret that many of Microsoft's competitors lobbied the DOJ to bring this litigation and . . . to lobby Capitol Hill and wage a combined public-relations attack against Microsoft. Our company will not allow our competitors to dominate the debate with their biased, anti-Microsoft rhetoric."

Nevertheless, the trial had exacted a heavy toll. Microsoft may be doomed to lose even if it ultimately wins in the courts, for this debilitating case may rob the company of the drive and the passion that have contributed to its extraordinary success, just as its antitrust lawsuit helped sap IBM of its passion. The more Microsoft doesn't change, the more intense the cries for them to change become. The contradiction was not lost on Senior Vice President Dick Brass: "The irony of this case is that the more we compete, the better for consumers. Yet the more we compete, the more we're attacked as ruthless. So you hurt the company if we're criticized, and you hurt the company if we don't compete."

Government is now in Microsoft's rearview mirror, tailing it everywhere, making it more uncertain. In the fall of 1998, a Clinton/Gore administration communications-policy strategist told me that government at all levels had already concluded that Microsoft had too much power, and thus Microsoft's future freedom to act would be thwarted. "Microsoft has already lost this issue, and that's the biggest loss they've suffered. This case was supposedly about the browser. That's already happened. That's history. What Microsoft did to WordPerfect was what it desires to do with Windows 2000. They want to use it to control the house, to leverage itself into other markets, to control the entire information age," extending its software dominance to the cable box and handheld consumer electronics devices and cellular phones and the Internet. Public exposure through a trial—"getting the information out," said Eric Schmidt of Novell—will force Microsoft to modify its behavior because the public has a better appreciation of the consequences if that behavior is not modified. And companies will become less fearful of challenging Microsoft. As Rob Glaser observed, "We've sort of reached glasnost at this point, regardless of the outcome of the trial. In the past, a lot of companies did things because of an aura of fear or an environment of intimidation, whether or not there was actual intimidation by Microsoft. That's forever changed."

Also tailing Microsoft are the more than three million documents the Justice Department collected for the trial. Those documents might be used against Microsoft in future lawsuits. There is a legal principle—known as collateral estoppel—which holds that once a court has issued a ruling, if that ruling is upheld on appeal, it establishes a presumption of innocence or guilt in future lawsuits. Once judged guilty, a lower burden of proof is required in subsequent trials. "A jury looking at a finding against Microsoft in an antitrust action," observed Boies, "is likely to demand a pretty substantial showing by Microsoft before they view that as rebutted. In this trial they started from a presumption of innocence and were not able to prevail. Now in these private cases they start from a presumption of guilt." It "shifts the burden of proof to Microsoft," observed Judge Jackson. Armed with a federal-court ruling, 129 lawsuits in twenty-six states and the District of Columbia were pending in October 2000, Microsoft acknowledged. And in each such lawsuit, victors are usually entitled to triple damages. Defending against lawsuits is not an incidental expense. A senior Microsoft official estimated that the legal cost to defend Microsoft in Judge Jackson's courtroom alone could reach one hundred million dollars, and this tab did not include executive time invested in the trial and in devising a possible settlement.* Bill Neukom said he was unfazed by the threat of additional lawsuits, since these lawsuits claim economic damage and Judge Jackson did not prove that Microsoft overcharged consumers. "They have a lot more they have to prove," said Neukom. That may be, but Neukom and Microsoft would rather have won in Jackson's courtroom and would rather not face the barrage of lawsuits and would rather not be exposed to the vagaries of the justice system.

But now that Jackson had ruled, unless Microsoft does the equivalent of taking two cards in hopes of pulling an inside straight in its appeal game of poker and is exonerated of all charges, Microsoft will be compelled to sign a consent decree, stationing the government over its shoulder, perhaps to wonder why ClearType or voice recognition, or Media

*The Washington Post reported in September 2000 that the Justice Department, since 1995, spent a total of $9.4 million to pursue the Microsoft lawsuit.

Player, is going to be bundled in with Windows. By alerting the courts and the public to what it sees as Microsoft's scheme to leverage its strength in Windows into servers and all other devices, the Justice Department has placed Microsoft on notice. Microsoft executives will constantly live in fear of subpoenas. And while they wait for a final ruling from the Supreme Court, which could take years, they may come to second-guess themselves, to be less combative.

John Malone described Gates in late 1999 as "depressed. He no longer looks forward to coming to the office." A reason Malone sold his cable company—aside from a desire to make a pile of money—was that he wanted to escape daily government scrutiny, which comes with any utilitylike company, whether it's in the telephone or cable or electricity or software business. And a reason he named his media holding company Liberty and hired only a single lawyer on a slim staff of thirty-nine, he told me, was to symbolize his independence. "It will become clear to Bill that he can't win," Malone predicted. "It's the Lilliputians. . . . This is about Bill Gates growing up and realizing that even for Bill Gates, government" is bigger. And although by April 2000 Malone said he thought Gates looked better for having shed his CEO burdens, and even after Malone registered his belief that the government case was wrong because there was competition and after he touted Liberty's various partnership deals with Microsoft around the world, he nevertheless concluded that Microsoft would never fully recover from this lawsuit.

"Now they're in the barrel," Malone explained. "There's going to be a pile of civil lawsuits. Now, if you're Bill and his guys, you're all the time on defense, all the time giving depositions. You're just harassed to death. Your stock is in a funk. It's not so much that the world thinks you're the bad guys; it's that the perception is that government regulators will hold up any deal," not just in the United States but around the world. Executives will say, " 'If I do a deal with Microsoft it will take me two years to get it through regulators.' . . . Whether they win or lose on appeal, this is a setback." In England, where Liberty Media has announced a partnership with Microsoft to forge England's foremost cable company, "Microsoft is having a hard time getting the deal past the Monopoly Commission."

The fifteen nations joined in the European Union have become aggressive about antitrust enforcement. Its executive arm, the European Commission, and its chief competition commissioner, Italian economist

Mario Monti, specifically rejected the notion that the new economy should operate by different monopoly rules than the old. By mid-2000, the European Commission had launched investigations of Microsoft's practices on five different fronts, including whether it threatened to monopolize cable television in England, its pricing of Windows in France, and its efforts to leverage the Windows PC to gain power over servers. Fearing Microsoft control of set-top boxes in England, the commission forced Microsoft to cede its voting rights in Telewest, assuring that Gates and Malone did not have majority control. In August 2000, the commission—spurred by a complaint lodged by Sun Microsystems and echoing Justice Department concerns—formally accused Microsoft of seeking to extend its monopoly from the desktop to the server markets. Microsoft was in conflict with governments elsewhere as well. In China, as another example, in the summer of 2000 the government declared that no foreign company should monopolize software and perhaps breach China's security. Henceforth, the government decreed, it would spurn Windows and instead back Linux as the operating system for China's computers.

Inevitably, CEOs may make the choice John Malone said Rupert Murdoch did in April 2000. "Rupert wanted Microsoft to be the technology supplier for his satellite platforms around the world," Malone, who is News Corporation's largest outside shareholder, said. "Yet in the end he decided he's better off with Nokia than Microsoft because Microsoft would bring controversy and introduce politics, and government would drag it along slowly, while Nokia is clean. It's very discouraging. If you're working at Microsoft you know you made the best bid, yet you lost it. It's extremely depressing to their enthusiasm."

In an era where convergence takes the form of partnering between companies, many companies as well as governments appear to be more wary of Microsoft. Despite the two companies' business relationship, a senior AT&T executive told me AT&T would never agree to make Microsoft the exclusive vendor for its eighteen million cable subscribers: "We're not going to create another MS-DOS. We don't want to see them in there offering communications services. That's our job and our revenue stream." If Microsoft agreed to offer just software for the set-top boxes, he predicted Microsoft would "get all" of AT&T's orders. However, by late September, frustrated with Microsoft's slow pace in providing interactive-television software for these boxes, AT&T began to consider replacing Microsoft with Liberate Technologies, Microsoft's chief inter-active-TV software rival. They granted Liberate a contract to test their system. And despite Microsoft's investment in United Pan-Europe Communications NV (UPC), the European cable operator was so distressed over Microsoft's late delivery of software for its digital cable boxes that it yanked Microsoft's Austrian contract and awarded it to Liberate.

Because of the lawsuit, observed a Justice Department official, "People push back in negotiations with Microsoft." And size makes it easier to push back. The fervent belief among business leaders that one must get big or die—a belief advanced at the time by AT&T's acquisitions, by the merger of Viacom and CBS, by AOL and Time Warner, by the merger of France's telephone, utilities, and cable company Vivendi with Seagram's, which owns the Universal Studios and Music Group—has produced communications colossi who do not behave as Microsoft supplicants.

With a boost from its so far successful effort to referee Microsoft's behavior, a more assertive U.S. government has also asked questions about the behavior of these corporate elephants. For example, for nearly two days in May 2000, the public was outraged that Time Warner had acted like a gatekeeper and blocked access to Disney-owned ABC in New York City, Los Angeles, and nine other cities. (Because they were engaged in a contract dispute, when the contract to carry ABC on its cable systems lapsed on May 1, Time Warner simply stopped carrying it.) Alarmed by this power over access to television and the broadband Internet wire, as well as the combined AOL Time Warner power to potentially use its wire to restrict content, the FCC held hearings on the merger in July 2000, and fellow elephants such as Disney and NBC sounded like Ralph Nader in denouncing this concentration of economic power. Similar questions were asked of AOL Time Warner by the European Commission, which in late 2000 blocked their acquisition of the EMI Group, fearful that the American giant would have a choke-hold over the music business.

Bill Gates is not blind to the trial's toll on his company. He told me before the verdict, "No matter what the outcome, the lawsuit is a bad thing. The costs to the company and the taxpayers have been huge. The last thing any company wants is to be sued by the government." Before Greg Maffei stepped down in late 1999 as the senior vice president and chief deal maker for Microsoft, he said, "There's not a deal we were stopped from doing. Maybe, subconsciously, we shied away from things."

What they now sought to avoid, he admitted, were deals the government could delay. Paul Maritz acknowledged, "In terms of deals we constantly have to think: will this pass regulatory muster?" Perhaps it is no accident that after investing in or acquiring a total of twenty-five companies in the first four months of 2000, since Judge Jackson's remedy verdict in early June this pace slowed dramatically, and Microsoft invested in just sixteen companies over the next four months.

Questions about Microsoft's legal travails flooded the press office. "Three quarters of what I'm asked is trial related," said Greg Shaw in January 2000. The trial, conceded Dick Brass, has "unfortunately been a distraction. . . . It's not stopping us from creating ClearType and e-books. On the other hand, I don't think a company can compete and prosper when there is an unending stream of vilification unleashed by the government and by the press." In the long run, he said, it might tarnish the Microsoft brand; in the short run, it depresses employees and emboldens competitors.

Microsoft loses in various other ways. They have suffered a serious brain drain. From 1999 through the autumn of 2000, for example, an army of top Microsoft executives left the company to pursue other interests, including Nathan Myhrvold, Cameron Myhrvold, Greg Maffei, Brad Silverberg, Sam Jadallah, Peter Neupert, Eric Engstrom, Thomas Reardon, John Ludwig, Rich Tong, Greg Shaw, Jon Roberts, Tod Nielsen, and Paul Maritz, among others. And as a legal cloud hovers above Microsoft and it becomes a less *cool* place to work, it becomes harder to recruit the best and brightest. And it becomes more expensive. An employee that might have been happy to receive fifty thousand share options, observed one former senior Microsoft executive, now wants two hundred thousand—a reason Steve Ballmer sweetened employee benefits and, in April, when the share price dropped to $66.83 and made the higher-priced shares granted executives in the prior year worthless, Ballmer offered seventy million new option shares to employees at that relatively low $66.83 purchase price. When Microsoft filed papers in May opposing a breakup, it warned that having this "Sword of Damocles" dangling over its head would prompt "irreplaceable employees" to flee.

As employees choose to go elsewhere, so Microsoft's adversaries and allies have been emboldened to operate outside its orbit, as Dell and Compaq and Gateway and Intel and Apple—and not just America Online or Sun or IBM—have embraced Linux software for parts of their business. Intel's Internet-access appliance, for example, relies not on Windows but on Linux. Longtime Microsoft allies, including Dell, Hewlett-Packard, and Compaq, in 2000 announced plans to sell powerful server computers that use Linux. Microsoft did not object when Dell removed the Internet Explorer browser icon from the desktop of Windows 98 in the PCs Dell markets to businesses, nor when Dell acquired a stake in Red Hat, a leading supplier of Linux. And as Internet access gravitated from the PC where Microsoft was dominant to other devices where it was not, Microsoft was put in a classic bind: this intensifying competition strengthened its court claims that it was not a monopoly, as it weakened its business and strengthened its rivals; but if Microsoft retaliated, as the court record suggested that it had in the past, it would buttress the government's case.

Although Jim Allchin remains, in his words, "super hard-core" in his belief that Microsoft is fighting to innovate and thus serve the public good, he acknowledged that "the negative p.r. we've endured [may] embolden competitors." Indeed, in June 2000 Rob Glaser and Apple's Steve Jobs announced that they would align their streaming-media efforts and would jointly attack the number-three streaming-media provider, Microsoft. Later that summer, AOL agreed to broadcast Real-Networks audio and video software to its members. At around the same time, America Online announced that it had purchased a stake in a voice-recognition company, hoping to go head-to-head against Microsoft in making software that obeys voice commands. And although Microsoft was a major investor in Japan's cellular-telephone giant, NTT DoCoMo, America Online boldly aced out Microsoft in the summer of 2000 and induced the Japanese company to ally with AOL rather than Microsoft's MSN. DoCoMo agreed to assume a 43 percent stake in AOL Japan and to run the enterprise, and together they would provide wireless Web access. As Microsoft's business model shifts from selling software in boxes to selling software as a series of services linked to the Internet, sharing and partnering become ever more vital, and Microsoft conceded in its May remedy proposal to Judge Jackson that potential "third parties may be unwilling to enter into routine business agreements with Microsoft while its continued corporate existence remains in doubt."

Evidence abounds that we live in a less Microsoft-centric world. The XML Microsoft is betting on will take off only if it is accepted as a common language by everyone, including Sun, America Online, and IBM.

And if it is accepted as the new standard language of the Internet, unlike Windows it will not be Microsoft's language. In the next couple of years, it is expected that those connecting to the Internet with wireless devices will exceed those connecting via their PCs. One sees Microsoft slippage when Case outdraws Gates in Davos; when such stalwart Microsoft allies as Dell, Compaq, and Intel in January 2000 invested fifty-seven million dollars in TurboLinux, a company pushing Linux worldwide; when four members of the original team that created the Apple Macintosh form a company called Eazel to improve Linux so it can compete head-to-head on the desktop with Windows; when PC sales slow and America Online and Gateway agree, as they did in April 2000, to accelerate the move to the post-PC era by producing low-cost Internet appliances that will use Linux; when Linux in 1999 snagged about 17 percent of the retail business for operating systems, according to PC Data, and when Windows's market share in early 2000 dropped to 82 percent, with Linux and Apple each claiming 9 percent; when Steve Ballmer takes pains to say that XML would assure that all devices, no matter their software, would run on Windows; when America Online strengthens AOLTV by investing two hundred million dollars in TiVo, building into its set-top boxes such features as storing, pausing, rewinding, and replaying; and although the browser wars now appear over—with Microsoft's browser market share surging to 86 percent and Netscape's plummeting to just under 14 percent, according to one research survey—America Online announced in the spring of 2000 the debut of the new Netscape 6 browser, which Steve Case insisted was superior to Microsoft's. Should AOL replace Microsoft's browser when their contract lapses in January 2001, Netscape's share of the browser market would jump to about 40 percent, Case knew.

In full-page newspaper ads in May, IBM hailed the free and open Linux operating system as "the fastest growing operating system in the world." As the Internet grows, Windows decreases in importance. Since the Internet is now based on communications standards that are open and not controlled by any software maker, the software applications that companies and others are embracing are designed as write-once/run-anywhere applications that hook onto middleware that sits atop various operating systems. Thus, the middleware that prompted Microsoft to attack Netscape has emerged triumphant. Observed Rob Glaser, "It really is a different world to have the ubiquitous platform be the network rather than the PC. We're transitioning from the PC to a network, and Yahoo! and AOL and RealNetworks and the MP3 player are all network-centric. In a network-based world, Microsoft's lock on computing becomes less. Because of this switch to the networked world of the Internet and because of the antitrust trial, we've seen that the aura of Microsoft as omnipotent has been shattered. This is no longer the Pax Microsoft era."

In his book *The Innovator's Dilemma* Clayton M. Christensen demonstrates how changing technology invariably tortures most market leaders, from DEC to IBM to Sears to Xerox to Control Data. The companies that originally fashioned the PC market—Apple, Commodore, IBM, and Tandy—have been eclipsed, just as have the early leaders in laptop PCs: Zenith, Sharp, and Kaypro. And it wasn't only new, "disruptive technologies" that account for corporate deaths (or near deaths). Christensen shows how even well-managed companies declined because their sizes became albatrosses or technology altered the playing field. Even though disk-drive companies such as Memorex and Control Data, or hydraulic-excavator companies such as Bucyrus-Erie, or companies such as Xerox and IBM were superbly managed, they all stumbled. They did what good companies were supposed to do—listened to their customers, aggressively invested in new technologies, studied market trends. The "dilemma" was that they became captives of their established customers, who wanted to stay with the technology they had, and it was perfectly logical for these established companies not to sacrifice fat-profit-margin businesses for newer, narrower-margin ventures. The mice, as Microsoft may find, enjoy certain advantages over the elephants, particularly with Internet traffic doubling every one hundred days. And even if the new paradigm isn't the Internet but peer-to-peer computing, in which the network is not connected by giant servers but by PCs forged into networks that download, say, free music from one PC to another or share hard-drive space and files, the mice will still be potent.

In addition, the stock market seems to have punished Microsoft. Although the value of Microsoft's stock doubled between October 1997, when Justice first sued the company for violating the consent decree, and April 2000, the stock did plunge 43 percent between January 1 and April 25, 2000. After the verdict, the stock and those of other high-tech and dot-com companies seemed to enter a free fall. Microsoft's legal woes are blamed for helping unsettle the market. By late October 2000, Microsoft's stock price was stuck at around $60 per share, having lost one half of its value in just nine months. If the stock continues to lag, it might intensify pressures on Gates to drop his appeal, assuming that Justice and the states would agree and would bar evidence gathered in this trial from being used in civil lawsuits. To insist on fighting the lawsuit all the way to the Supreme Court, it will be said, will harm Microsoft shareholders, setting up a clash between two of Gates's core beliefs: his conviction that Microsoft is right and his awareness of his fiduciary responsibility to shareholders. Once again, Bill Gates will be tested: will he strive to win the battle, even if it means losing the war? Will he be hard-core? He was hard-core in May 1998 when he could have had a relatively benign settlement.

For Microsoft, hindsight can lead only to regret. As time passed and government uncovered more Microsoft documents, government's remedy proposals could only harden, observed a senior Justice Department attorney. "As time goes on, we learn that there were lots of things we didn't know in the spring of 1998. The differential in knowledge for the defendant is always greatest at the beginning of a case. They should have taken advantage of that. Microsoft saved us from ourselves. If we had done the deal we offered them in May 1998, we might have wound up looking like the 1995 consent-decree folks. Why Microsoft didn't settle is a big mystery."

Judge Jackson thinks he might know why. Looking back on the case and puffing on a pipe in his chambers in mid-July 2000, Judge Jackson was only half kidding when he said: "If I were able to propose a remedy of [my own] devising I'd require Mr. Gates to write a book report." He'd ask Gates to review a recent biography of Napoleon. Why? "Because I think he has a Napoleonic concept of himself and his company. An arrogance which derives from power and unalloyed success, with no leavening hard experience, no reverses." Bill Gates, he implied, was not an adult.

Even if Bill Gates upgrades his haircuts and he and Steve Ballmer and Microsoft appear more grown-up, it is probably too late. Microsoft has been too consistently careless, offended too many with their brusque behavior, denied too much. As Nick Carraway, the narrator of Gates's favorite novel, says of Tom and Daisy Buchanan after Gatsby's death, "They were careless people, Tom and Daisy—they smashed up things and creatures and then retreated back into their money or their vast carelessness."

Glossary

applications (apps): Software that runs on top of an operating system. Examples include spreadsheets, graphics, tools such as spell checkers or a thesaurus, et cetera.

APIs (application programming interfaces): To work, software applications hook onto an operating system's APIs, which are blocks of code embedded in the software that allow applications to be attached and thus function. Because the operating system enables a PC's hardware and applications, it has a large number of APIs.

applications barrier to entry: The government asserted that Windows's 90 percent market share erected a barrier in two ways: (1) because Windows is so dominant, software developers are said to have scant financial incentive to write applications for other platforms; (2) to write these applications, software developers require access to Windows APIs and other code, which Microsoft can withhold. Innovation is the chief victim of such a barrier, claimed the government.

bandwidth: The amount of data that a communications system carries, which affects the speed (or brainpower) at which data, voice, or video is transferred. A "narrowband" telephone modem processing data in analog form may do so at up to 56 kilobits per second, while a faster ISDN (integrated services digital networks) modem transfers digital data at 128K. The next generation of "broadband"—cable, fiber-optic lines, dedicated telephone DSL (digital subscriber lines), or perhaps wireless connections—is (or is expected to) transfer digital data at speeds of up to 7,000 kilobits per second, thus allowing instant dial tone–like access to the Web as well as "full motion video": pictures would appear on a PC as they do on television.

broadband: A type of communications network that receives data, voice, or video at high speeds. Thus, it has high bandwidth.

browser: Software that allows users to more easily navigate and view websites on the Internet. The browser has APIs of its own which permit software to run on it. Netscape Communications introduced the first commercial browser in 1994.

default browser: The browser a computer will automatically activate, unless another is specifically selected.

bundling or tying: Promoting a weaker product by integrating it with a market leader, as Microsoft was said to have done when it challenged Netscape's browser by including a free browser (Internet Explorer) in Windows.

chips: Think motor. This tiny electronic device is composed of semiconductor material, such as silicon, on which an integrated circuit is embedded. Examples of chips include microprocessors and memory chips. The founders of Intel invented the silicon chip in the 1950s, and the chips now double in speed every eighteen months or so. Today, Intel is both the world's foremost chip maker and Microsoft's longtime business ally. The partnership between Windows and Intel is often referred to as the Wintel axis.

eXtensible markup language (XML): A next-generation successor language to HTML. Like HTML, XML can customize and display content on a webpage. It also indexes data, making it easier to retrieve and manipulate.

hypertext transfer protocol (HTTP): This protocol is the set of currency and rules that servers and browsers use to communicate. In order for computers to speak and send and receive information from websites, this protocol is essential.

hypertext markup language (HTML): The common language used to format documents that are viewed with a browser.

independent software vendors (ISVs): The developers that create application programs.

the Internet: A nonproprietary network of hundreds of millions of PCs in a worldwide electronic community, built upon architecture first developed by the Department of Defense. The data floating on the Internet is stored on servers and travels via "routers" that are housed in air-conditioned rooms and serve as the Internet's plumbing, transmitting digital packets of data.

Internet-content providers (ICPs): Organizations that offer a collection of webpages, as do financial-software companies such as Intuit.

Internet-service providers (ISPs): ISPs such as AOL provide connections to the Internet. For a monthly subscription fee, they can offer an array of "online services," although some ISPs provide Internet access but little content, and some charge nothing.

intranet: A proprietary network of PCs within a single institution or company that is usually tethered to a powerful server. Access to this network is closed to those outside the organization.

Java: A programming language created by Microsoft rival Sun Microsystems that permits programmers to write software that runs on any operating system or hardware. Comparable to Arabic numbers, which remain the same in every Western language, Java is meant to make software design easier.

Linux: A free operating system developed by Linus Torvalds, a Finnish programmer, who opened its source code and posted it on the Internet in 1991.

Microsoft Office: A collection of software applications such as Excel (for financial management), Word (word processing), and a variety of business applications. Microsoft Office has roughly the same 90 percent market share as does Windows.

middleware: Software that resides between other software and translates information between them, as a browser does. In order to function on a platform, middleware needs access to its APIs.

the middleware threat: Since middleware has its own APIs, it has the potential to become the equivalent of a standard electrical socket that any application can work on, which is why a browser was seen as a potential middleware threat to Windows.

OEMs (original equipment manufacturers): The PC manufacturers, such as Dell, Compaq, Gateway 2000, IBM, Hewlett-Packard, et cetera.

open-source software: Software whose source code is freely published, allowing other programmers to modify and improve it. Once viewed as a virtuous expression of openness, it has come to be seen as a practical response to networks such as the Internet, which democratize communications and allow others to chip in and improve computing.

operating system (OS): Think central nervous system. For a PC to be more than a dumb box, the OS software brings to life its various organs— recognizing the keyboard commands and transmitting and displaying them on a monitor, keeping track of files and directories, animating the mouse and printer and disk drive.

PC: Personal computer, which comes in desktop and portable laptop models.

peer-to-peer computing: The model under which software permits PCs to communicate directly to share files and other resources, as popularized by Napster and other services that download music. If PCs were connected directly, it might subvert the need for powerful, and expensive, servers.

personal digital assistants (PDAs): Handheld, wireless devices such as Palm Pilots that are used for personal functions such as storing telephone numbers, addresses, schedules, and, increasingly, using e-mail.

platform: Software with APIs onto which other software can attach and thus function. Microsoft's Windows is the dominant platform, but there are others, including Apple's Macintosh OS, the BeOS, IBM's OS/2, and Linux, not to mention browsers.

portal: Think AOL, Yahoo!, MSN, Excite. A portal is a website that offers an array of resources and services; for example, e-mail, online shopping malls, and search engines. A portal often serves as a user's "home port" on the Internet.

server: A powerful computer or device that is tied to a network and usually functions as a combination traffic cop and library, managing and storing the network's data.

The Sherman Antitrust Act of 1890: This vaguely worded legislation has two basic tenets. Section 1 declares it illegal for a company or a trust to conspire to restrain trade or commerce; section 2 declares it illegal for a monopoly to abuse its power by conspiring to control commerce.

universal resource locators (URLs): A Web address, accessed via HTTP.

Windows 98; Windows 95: Two versions of the Microsoft operating system that power about 90 percent of the world's PCs.

Windows CE: A scaled-down version of Windows for portable and consumer electronics devices.

Windows NT: Microsoft's operating system for corporate workstations or servers that are part of a network. Renamed Windows 2000 (Windows ME), it has been redesigned for more general use.

World Wide Web (www): Christened a decade ago by Tim Berners-Lee, who defined it as "a 'space' in which information could exist" and be shared as in a market economy, in which "anybody can trade with anybody, and they don't have to go to a market square to do it."

Acknowledgments

This book began as a magazine assignment for *The New Yorker*, for which I write Annals of Communication. Soon after the Justice Department and the states announced in May 1998 that they would sue Microsoft for violating the antitrust laws, I spoke with Tina Brown, then the editor, and suggested the trial might be a way to probe Bill Gates and the company that dominated the new economy. Tina agreed and, just as important, she granted me time to report, free from deadline pressures. Bless her.

I did not begin with an attitude, a belief that Microsoft was guilty or innocent. Because *The New Yorker* provides the rare journalistic luxury of time, from day one I assumed this was a long-term project and asked the protagonists to cooperate. I wanted to gather information for a behind-the-scenes account of the courtroom drama and to probe Gates and the Microsoft culture. I provided assurances that I wasn't chasing quick headlines and would not write anytime soon.

But to make a story come alive, to escape caricature, reporters require people to talk in ways they rarely do in press conferences or on a witness stand. This trial did yield an unusual richness of subpoenaed documents and sworn testimony. However, I could not have done my job without the cooperation of the cast of characters. In reporting this drama, I talked regularly with, among others, Assistant Attorney General Joel Klein, his brilliant courtroom captain, David Boies, and Klein's de facto chief of staff, Jeffrey Blattner, among other members of their legal team. Microsoft executives, from Bill Gates down, also cooperated. Microsoft Counsel William Neukom and his chief trial lawyer, John Warden, regularly made themselves available, as did other members of their defense team. Microsoft's public-relations team in Redmond and at the trial—Mich Mathews, Greg Shaw, Mark Murray, Vivek Varma, and John Pinette—opened doors and usually made my life easier.

A reason both sides cooperated was that I was not filing daily or weekly, and thus there was little immediate threat from me. I assured each that I really wanted to understand their position and would strive to be fair. Another reason they cooperated was because each worried the other side was talking, a fear I did my best to stoke. At first, the trial was expected to last just several months, and I assured the combatants my *New Yorker* account would not appear until later.

I had no idea how late. The witness phase of the trial did not conclude until the end of June 1999, and David Remnick, who had become the editor of *The New Yorker* eleven months earlier, indulged me. David allowed me to cover the battle inside and outside the courtroom for an entire year before I published a single word, and when I did he read the manuscript overnight and soon published more than twenty thousand words, the longest piece the magazine had run in decades. Elsewhere in this book a lawyer is described as the Derek Jeter of lawyers. Actually, Remnick is also like the versatile Yankee shortstop, a multidimensional man of dazzling talents.

I was fortunate as well to have my regular editor at the magazine, Jeff Frank, improve my words and help crystallize my thinking. Amy Tubke-Davidson tirelessly fact-checked the piece. A reason *The New Yorker* is so idyllic a place to work is that everyone from the editors to the fact-checkers to the copy readers cares as much about getting it right as does the reporter.

The magazine article did not please Bill Gates and more than a few Microsoft executives, who objected to my portrayal of them as sometimes unsocialized children. I was, by this time, well on my way toward a book, having signed a contract with Random House in the winter of 1999. I thought that the trial and Gates and Microsoft and its enemies was worth a book. I had written a book eight years earlier, *Three Blind Mice,* about an industry—broadcast television—convulsed by change. I thought it would be interesting to write about new media and its own incessant struggles to keep up. It would take me some months to overcome Microsoft's annoyance and rewin their cooperation; I never did regain Bill Gates's cooperation. However, in the end Microsoft generously extended itself. Thus, this tale is not told from the vantage point of a single party or point of view.

The ages and titles of the participants are as of the time they spoke. Most of the quotes in this book are based on interviews conducted by me, and there are relatively few quotes without names attached. I do not climb into people's heads. If I write that Gates was worried about this or Judge Jackson thought that, for example, it is either because they told me this or because documents or identified sources testify to this. I decided against including a separate section for notes because I saw no reason to list all the redundant citations of the various dates I interviewed various actors because the sources are cited in the text, and because most are easily searchable online. Nor do I offer e-mail and trial transcript citations, since all the trial exhibits are available (and searchable) on both the Justice Department and Microsoft websites. The trial transcript is available on the Microsoft site. In covering the trial, Joseph Nocera of *Fortune* and I asked our magazines to pay for a daily transcript from the court stenographer, and they generously complied. Many others gave generously of their time—John Malone, Steve Case, Nobuyuki Idei, William H. Gates, among others—and I thank them.

When the trial commenced in October 1998, I wrote Judge Jackson and told him I was covering it for *The New Yorker* and said I hoped one day to be able to talk with him. He invited me to drop by his office. We had a pleasant social visit but did not talk about the trial. I told him that I hoped that later on in the process I might be able to interview him. He was noncommittal. Eventually, Judge Jackson agreed to cooperate for the book. Other judges have on occasion talked with journalists about their work. As came out after he co-authored *The Brethren,* his book on the Supreme Court, Bob Woodward of *The Washington Post* persuaded Justice Brennan to cooperate. Woodward also talked to several other justices. But such interaction between reporter and judge is extremely rare. Judge Jackson granted me about ten hours of taped interviews. Though we met twice prior to the conclusion of the trial, once to say hello and once to discuss his significant prior cases, he did not talk about this case until a year after the trial commenced. Our first interview session was on September 22, 1999, and for four hours we talked on-the-record about his life and career as a trial lawyer and a judge. We next met for several hours on October 6, 1999, and began talking about the case. Our third session was on April 19, 2000, and our fourth and final session was on July 9, 2000. All of our sessions were taped and on the record, though unbeknownst to me the tape of our final one-hour interview malfunctioned, and I have had to rely on my notes. Since I always assume *something will go wrong* with the tape recorder, I take extensive notes anyway. I was pleasantly surprised that Judge Jackson cooperated. He told me that he knew this was a historically important trial, and he felt an obligation to comment for an account that would appear on bookshelves. I am most grateful to him.

By contrast, Judge Richard Posner, who served as mediator in seeking a settlement and who admonished both sides not to speak with reporters, was impossible to reach. He would not answer my e-mails or phone calls to his office during the mediation process or immediately after. I made one last attempt in August 2000, after I had pieced together a tick-tock account of the failed mediation effort, and after I had gathered key documents involved in the effort. I told a mutual friend that I had the crucial mediation documents and was now interested in assuring that my account was accurate, since each side was spinning me and Judge Posner was the closest thing to a neutral observer. Would he talk to me on a not-for-attribution basis? It was arranged that I would phone his chambers. I offered to e-mail part of chapter 18 describing his career and all of chapter 21 on the mediation. Would he correct any facts? That night Judge Posner e-mailed back:

> I have now read the two chapters you sent me. I would be grateful if, should you refer to my having read them and given you comments, you make clear that I have limited my comments to pointing out specific factual inaccuracies, so far as I can recall them. I have not consulted any notes or drafts that I made or obtained in the course of the mediation. Please make clear that I am not a source for your book and was not interviewed by you, but assisted only to the extent indicated above. . . . I don't want to comment on issues of characterization and interpretation and I have not gone back and checked the accuracy of your dates or of specific language from documents. . . . I hope you'll also make clear that the documents you quote or refer to did not come from me to you.

Judge Posner made nine specific factual corrections, ranging from the spelling of a name to saying that Justice did demand that Microsoft open the code to its Windows server software but never demanded that Microsoft be required to do anything to accommodate handheld devices; this position was advanced by the states. Thus, the essential factual account of the mediation effort contained in chapter 21 has been confirmed by Judge Posner. I am grateful to him. Nevertheless, it should be noted that chapter 21 has more blind quotes than any other chapter, and this is because the various parties who spoke with me wished to present their side but not to offend Judge Posner, and perhaps Judge Jackson.

Judge Posner checked the facts in one and a half chapters. Checking the facts throughout the book was a diligent future attorney, Adele Grignon, who kept her day job as a *New Yorker* fact-checker and slaved nights and weekends to complete this task. She was a gift. For ten hours per week over the course of a semester, I borrowed Columbia University graduate student Jennifer Uscher, who listened to tapes and searched for facts. She was great, as was Khrystine Muldowney, who also performed early research tasks.

Random House has published seven of my eight books, and for each of these books I have benefited from the editing brilliance of Jason Epstein. Jason's insights and wisdom were, as always, invaluable. The actual editing of this book was done by Scott Moyers. Scott didn't just read the manuscript and edit it; he read other Microsoft and new-economy books; he went back to the trial transcript and read that, too, prodding me with questions, even suggesting exchanges I might want to include. Scott became my backboard, my partner. If there were more Scott Moyerses there would be less reason for angst about the future of publishing. Ann Godoff, President and Publisher of Random House, has championed this book from day one. Sunshine Lucas, Scott's assistant, has let nothing fall between the cracks. Senior copy editor Timothy Mennel was as dogged as Scott, correcting some dumb mistakes, looking up old quotes on the Web, and even listing duplicated quotes or phrases hundreds of pages apart. Chip Kidd bestowed one of his typically brilliant jacket designs. Many others at Random House lent a shoulder to help this book—particularly the publicity team of Sally Marvin, Tom Perry, and Carol Schneider—and I thank them.

Readers will find some duplication in this book, for I am walking a line between the techie and the general reader. I will repeat, for instance, a definition of the so-called applications barrier to entry several times because for the uninitiated it bears repeating. My goal has been to write a book that is both sophisticated and comprehensible.

There are those who believe one must be a geek to write about Microsoft and the trial. This was certainly a prevalent notion at Microsoft, which believed it enjoyed an initial advantage in the courtroom because neither David Boies nor the trial judge, Thomas Penfield Jackson, even used a PC. They believed: once Microsoft explained the technology, the facts, they would swat away opponents and triumph. They were wrong, and a reason is that "facts" are not inanimate objects. Intent, interpretation, credibility matter, and these can be parsed by common sense. I use a PC and the Web, though I'm not a geek. I hope this book demonstrates that one need not be one to comprehend, for example, that Microsoft had market power and was using it to harm Netscape.

I am grateful to my agent, Esther Newberg, who watches my back and has been a friend for nearly thirty years. My wife, Amanda Urban, would be a brilliant editor if she changed careers, as her sharp eye improved this book. More important, she and our daughter, Kate, add zest and humor to the sometimes grim task of birthing a book.

Finally, to end on a dutiful note: while many lent their advice and assistance, ultimate responsibility for the words and facts in this book rests on my shoulders.

Bibliography

Andrews, Paul. *How the Web Was Won: The Inside Story of How Bill Gates and His Band of Internet Idealists Transformed a Software Empire.* Broadway Books, 1999.

Andrews, Paul, and Stephen Manes. *Gates: How Microsoft's Mogul Reinvented an Industry and Made Himself the Richest Man in America.* Simon and Schuster, 1994.

Berners-Lee, Tim. *Weaving the Web: The Original Design and Ultimate Destiny of the World Wide Web by Its Inventor.* HarperCollins, 1999.

Bollier, David. *The Networked Society: How Technologies Are Transforming Markets, Organizations, and Social Relationships.* The Aspen Institute, 1996.

———. *The Global Advance of Electronic Commerce: Reinventing Markets, Management, and National Sovereignty.* The Aspen Institute, 1998.

Boyd, Aaron. *Smart Money: The Story of Bill Gates.* Morgan Reynolds, 1995.

Brand, Stewart. *The Media Lab: Inventing the Future at MIT.* Viking Penguin, 1987.

Brinkley, Joel, and Steve Lohr. *U.S. v. Microsoft: The Inside Story of the Landmark Case.* McGraw-Hill, 2000.

Bronson, Po. *The First $20 Million Is Always the Hardest.* Random House, 1997.

———. *The Nudist on the Late Shift: And Other True Tales of Silicon Valley.* Random House, 1999.

Brown, John Seely, and Paul Duguid. *The Social Life of Information.* Harvard Business School Press, 2000.

Buderi, Robert. *Engines of Tomorrow: How the World's Best Companies Are Using Their Research Labs to Win the Future.* Simon and Schuster, 2000.

Carlton, Jim. *Apple: The Inside Story of Intrigue, Egomania, and Business Blunders.* Times Business, 1997.

Castells, Manuel. *The Rise of the Network Society. The Information Age: Economy, Society, and Culture,* vol. 1. Blackwell Publishers, 1996.

———. *The Power of Identity. The Information Age: Economy, Society, and Culture,* vol. 2. Blackwell Publishers, 1997.

———. *End of Millennium. The Information Age: Economy, Society, and Culture,* vol. 3. Blackwell Publishers, 1998.

Chandler, Alfred D., Jr. *The Visible Hand: The Managerial Revolution in American Business.* Belknap Press, 1997.

Chernow, Ron. *Titan: The Life of John D. Rockefeller, Sr.* Random House, 1998.

Christensen, Clayton M. *The Innovator's Dilemma: When New Technologies Cause Great Firms to Fail.* Harvard Business School Press, 1997.

Conot, Robert. *Thomas A. Edison: A Streak of Luck.* Da Capo Series in Science, 1979.

Cusumano, Michael A., and David B. Yoffie. *Competing on Internet Time: Lessons from Netscape and Its Battle with Microsoft.* Free Press, 1998.

Davis, Stan, and Christopher Meyer. *Blur: The Speed of Change in the Connected Economy.* Perseus Books, 1998.

Dertouzos, Michael. *What Will Be: How the New World of Information Will Change Our Lives.* HarperCollins, 1997.

Dyson, Esther. *Release 2.0: A Design for Living in the Digital Age.* Broadway Books, 1997.

Edstrom, Jennifer, and Marilyn Eller. *Barbarians Led by Bill Gates: Microsoft from the Inside.* Henry Holt, 1998.

Eisner, Michael (written with Tony Schwartz). *Work in Progress.* Random House, 1998.

Evans, Philip, and Thomas S. Wurster. *Blown to Bits: How the New Economics of Information Transforms Strategy.* Harvard Business School Press, 2000.

Ferguson, Charles H. *High Stakes, No Prisoners: A Winner's Tale of Greed and Glory in the Internet Wars.* Times Books, 1999.

Fitzgerald, F. Scott. *The Great Gatsby.* Scribner Paperback, 1925.

Garr, Doug. *IBM Redux: Lou Gerstner and the Business Turnaround of the Decade.* HarperCollins, 1999.

Gates, Bill. *The Road Ahead.* Viking Penguin, 1995.

———. *The Road Ahead* (revised). Penguin Books, 1996.

———. *Business @ the Speed of Thought: Using a Digital Nervous System.* Warner Books, 1999.

Gilder, George. *Life after Television: The Coming Transformation of Media and American Life.* W. W. Norton, 1992.

Gleick, James. *Genius: The Life and Science of Richard Feynman.* Vintage, 1993.

———. *Faster: The Acceleration of Just About Everything.* Pantheon, 1999.

Goodell, Jeff. *Sunnyvale: The Rise and Fall of a Silicon Valley Family.* Villard, 2000.

Grossman, Lawrence K. *The Electronic Republic: Reshaping Democracy in the Information Age.* Viking Penguin, 1995.

Grove, Andrew S. *Only the Paranoid Survive: How to Exploit the Crisis Points That Challenge Every Company and Career.* Doubleday, 1996.

Hagel, John, III, and Arthur G. Armstrong. *Net.Gain: Expanding Markets through Virtual Communities.* Harvard Business School Press, 1997.

Harr, Jonathan. *A Civil Action.* Random House, 1995.

Hillis, Daniel W. *The Pattern on the Stone: The Simple Ideas That Make Computers Work.* Weidenfeld and Nicolson, 1998.

Hiltzik, Michael. *The Internet as Paradigm.* Institute for Information Studies, 1997.

———. *Dealers of Lightning: Xerox PARC and the Dawn of the Computer Age.* HarperCollins, 1999.

Jackson, Tim. *Inside Intel: Andrew Grove and the Rise of the World's Most Powerful Chip Company.* Dutton, 1997.

Kaplan, David A. *The Silicon Boys: And Their Valley of Dreams.* William Morrow, 1999.

Keating, Stephen. *Cut Throat: High Stakes and Killer Moves on the Electronic Frontier.* Johnson Books, 1998.

Kelly, Kevin. *New Rules for the New Economy: Ten Radical Strategies for a Connected World.* Penguin Books, 1998.

Leadbeater, Charles. *The Weightless Society.* Texere, 2000.

Lessig, Lawrence. *Code and Other Laws of Cyberspace.* Basic Books, 1999.

Levy, Steven. *Insanely Great: The Life and Time of Macintosh, the Computer That Changed Everything.* Viking, 1994.

Lewis, Michael. *The New New Thing: A Silicon Valley Story.* W. W. Norton, 2000.

Liebowitz, Stan J., and Stephen E. Margolis. *Winners, Losers, and Microsoft: Competition and Antitrust in High Technology.* Independent Institute, 1999.

Lisagor, Nancy, and Frank Lipsius. *A Law unto Itself: The Untold Story of the Law Firm of Sullivan & Cromwell.* William Morrow, 1988.

Lowe, Janet. *Bill Gates Speaks: Insight from the World's Greatest Entrepreneur.* John Wiley and Sons, 1998.

Lundberg, Ferdinand. *The Rich and the Super-Rich: A Study in the Power of Money.* Lyle Stuart, 1968.

Margolick, David. *Undue Influence: The Epic Battle for the Johnson & Johnson Fortune.* William Morrow, 1993.

McChesney, Robert W. *Rich Media, Poor Democracy: Communication Politics in Dubious Times.* University of Illinois Press, 1999.

McKenzie, Richard B. *Trust on Trial: How the Microsoft Case Is Reframing the Rules of Competition.* Perseus Publishing, 2000.

McLuhan, Marshall. *The Gutenberg Galaxy: The Making of Typographic Man.* University of Toronto Press, 1962.

———. *Understanding Media: The Extensions of Man.* New American Library, 1964.

McLuhan, Marshall, and Bruce R. Powers. *The Global Village: Transformations in World Life and Media in the Twenty-first Century.* Oxford University Press, 1989.

Moore, James F. *The Death of Competition: Leadership Strategy in the Age of Business Ecosystems.* HarperCollins, 1996.

Morgan, Thomas D. *Modern Antitrust Law and Its Origins.* West Publishing, 1994.

Negroponte, Nicholas. *Being Digital.* Alfred A. Knopf, 1995.

Owen, Bruce M. *The Internet Challenge to Television.* Harvard University Press, 1999.

Pavlik, John V. *New Media and the Information Superhighway.* Allyn and Bacon, 1996.

Posner, Richard A. *Antitrust Law: An Economic Perspective.* University of Chicago Press, 1976.

———. *The Economics of Justice.* Harvard University Press, 1983.

———. *Overcoming Law.* Harvard University Press, 1996.

———. *Economic Analysis of Law.* Aspen Publishers, 1998.

———. *Law and Literature.* Harvard University Press, 1998.

———. *An Affair of State: The Investigation, Impeachment, and Trial of President Clinton.* Harvard University Press, 1999.

———. *Natural Monopoly and Its Regulation.* Cato Institute, 1999.

Postman, Neil. *Amusing Ourselves to Death: Public Discourse in the Age of Show Business.* Penguin Books, 1985.

———. *Technopoly: The Surrender of Culture to Technology.* Alfred A. Knopf, 1992.

————. *The Promise of Global Networks.* Institute for Information Studies, 1999.

Reid, T. R. *The Chip: How Two Americans Invented the Microchip and Launched a Revolution.* Simon and Schuster, 1984.

Rivlin, Gary. *The Plot to Get Bill Gates: An Investigation of the World's Richest Man . . . and the People Who Hate Him.* Times Business, 1999.

Rohm, Wendy Goldman. *The Microsoft File: The Secret Case Against Bill Gates.* Times Business, 1998.

Schement, Jorge Reina, and Terry Curtis. *Tendencies and Tensions of the Information Age: The Production and Distribution of Information in the United States.* Transaction Publishers, 1995.

Schiller, Herbert I. *Information Inequality: The Deepening Social Crisis in America.* Routledge, 1996.

Schwartz, Tony. *Media: The Second God.* Random House, 1981.

Seabrook, John. *Deeper: My Two-Year Odyssey in Cyberspace.* Simon and Schuster, 1997.

Seybold, Patricia B. *Customers.com: How to Create a Profitable Business Strategy for the Internet and Beyond.* Times Business, 1998.

Shapiro, Andrew L. *The Control Revolution: How the Internet Is Putting Individuals in Charge and Changing the World We Know.* Century Foundation, 1999.

Shenk, David. *The End of Patience: More Notes of Caution on the Information Revolution.* Indiana University Press, 1999.

Shimomura, Tsutomu, with John Markoff. *Takedown: The Pursuit and Capture of Kevin Mitnick, America's Most Wanted Computer Outlaw—by the Man Who Did It.* Hyperion, 1996.

Standage, Tom. *The Victorian Internet: The Remarkable Story of the Telegraph and the Nineteenth Century's On-line Pioneers.* Walker and Company, 1998.

Stoll, Clifford. *Silicon Snake Oil: Second Thoughts on the Information Highway.* Doubleday, 1995.

Stross, Randall E. *The Microsoft Way: The Real Story of How the Company Outsmarts Its Competition.* Addison-Wesley, 1996.

Swisher, Kara. *AOL.com: How Steve Case Beat Bill Gates, Nailed the Netheads, and Made Millions in the War for the Web.* Random House, 1998.

Tenner, Edward. *Why Things Bite Back: Technology and the Revenge of Unintended Consequences.* Alfred A. Knopf, 1996.

Toffler, Alvin. *The Third Wave.* William Morrow, 1980.

Wallace, James. *Overdrive: Bill Gates and the Race to Control Cyberspace.* John Wiley and Sons, 1997.

Wilson, Mike. *The Difference Between God and Larry Ellison: Inside Oracle Corporation.* William Morrow, 1997.

Wolff, Michael. *Burn Rate: How I Survived the Gold Rush Years on the Internet.* Simon and Schuster, 1998.

Woodward, Bob. *Shadow: Five Presidents and the Legacy of Watergate.* Simon and Schuster, 1999.

Woodward, Bob, and Scott Armstrong. *The Brethren: Inside the Supreme Court.* Simon and Schuster, 1979.

Wurman, Richard Saul. *Information Anxiety: What to Do When Information Doesn't Tell You What You Need to Know.* Bantam Books, 1989.

Index

ABOUT THE AUTHOR

KEN AULETTA has written "Annals of Communication" for *The New Yorker* since 1992. He is the author of seven previous books, including three national bestsellers. In ranking him as America's premier media critic, the *Columbia Journalism Review* concluded, "no other reporter has covered the new communications revolution as thoroughly as has Auletta."

He has written for various newspapers and magazines and appeared regularly as a television interviewer and analyst. He started writing for *The New Yorker* in 1977.

He grew up in Coney Island and now lives in New York City with his wife and daughter.

ABOUT THE TYPE

This book was set in Photina, a typeface designed by José Mendoza in 1971. It is a very elegant design with high legibility, and its close character fit has made it a popular choice for use in quality magazines and art gallery publications.